Spotlight on Literacy

Reading and language arts instruction that gets children ready and set to READ!

kinder garten

Print-rich

Skills-focused

Activity-based

McGraw Hill
McGraw.....
School Division

D1364933

Volume 2

	theme 5 Sing and Dance Away!	**theme 6** Paint It Up!	**theme 7** Eat It Up!	**theme 8** Build It Up!
Reading/Writing Listening/Speaking	▪ shares ideas about songs and dances ▪ participates in creating and presenting a song and dance show ▪ works well with others ▪ listens for a specific purpose ▪ responds to others in a variety of ways ▪ reads, writes, and draws pictures about song and dance ▪ retells stories ▪ writes in a journal ▪ participates in a variety of activities in response to literature ▪ develops and expresses personal interests and attitudes	▪ shares ideas about colors and shapes ▪ participates in creating and presenting an art gallery ▪ creates artworks ▪ uses a variety of art materials ▪ responds to others in a variety of ways ▪ reads, writes, and draws pictures about art ▪ retells stories ▪ writes in a journal ▪ participates in a variety of activities in response to literature ▪ develops and expresses personal interests and attitudes	▪ shares ideas about preparing food feast ▪ participates in creating and presenting a feast ▪ cooperates with others ▪ follows simple directions (e.g. recipes) ▪ appreciates and values diverse points of view ▪ reads, writes, and draws pictures about food ▪ retells stories ▪ writes in a journal ▪ participates in a variety of activities in response to literature ▪ becomes aware of cultural backgrounds, experiences, emotions, and ideas of self ▪ develops and expresses personal interests and attitudes	▪ shares ideas about building ▪ participates in creating and presenting a community model ▪ works together with others ▪ appreciates and values diverse points of view ▪ reads, writes, and draws pictures about building a community ▪ retells stories ▪ writes in a journal ▪ participates in a variety of activities in response to literature ▪ becomes aware of cultural backgrounds, experiences, emotions, and ideas of self ▪ develops and expresses personal interests and attitudes
Concepts of Print	▪ understands book concepts: cover, title, author, illustrator ▪ holds a book correctly and distinguishes between the front and back covers ▪ demonstrates awareness of directionality, letters, words, sentences, punctuation ▪ understands the relationship between print and speech	▪ understands book concepts: cover, title, author, illustrator ▪ demonstrates awareness of directionality, letters, words, sentences, punctuation	▪ understands book concepts: cover, title, author, illustrator ▪ demonstrates awareness of directionality, letters, words, sentences, punctuation ▪ uses parts of a book: index, table of contents	▪ understands book concepts: cover, title, author, illustrator ▪ demonstrates awareness of directionality, letters, words, sentences, punctuation
Phonics and Decoding	▪ discriminates the sound of letters: /h/ Hh, /m/ Mm ▪ identifies upper and lowercase letters: Hh, Mm ▪ recognizes sound/ letter relationships: /h/Hh, /m/Mm ▪ writes upper and lowercase letters: Hh, Mm ▪ identifies rhyming words	▪ discriminates the sound of letters: /s/ Ss, /b/ Bb ▪ identifies upper and lowercase letters: Ss, Bb ▪ recognizes sound/letter relationships: /s/Ss, /b/Bb ▪ writes upper and lowercase letters: Ss, Bb	▪ discriminates the sound of letters: /g/ Gg, /a/ Aa ▪ identifies upper and lowercase letters: Gg, Aa ▪ recognizes sound/symbol relationships: /g/Gg, /a/Aa ▪ writes upper and lowercase letters: Gg, Aa	▪ discriminates the sound of letters: /r/ Rr, /e/ Ee ▪ identifies upper and lowercase letters: Rr, Ee ▪ recognizes sound/letter relationships: /r/Rr, /e/Ee ▪ writes upper and lowercase letters: Rr, Ee
Theme Poem	▪ Singing-Time *by Rose Fyleman*	▪ Paints *by Ilo Orleans*	▪ Through the Teeth *a folk rhyme*	▪ Buildings by *Myra Cohn Livingston*
Theme Word	▪ Singer, Dancer	▪ Artist	▪ Cook	▪ Builder

Volume 1

	theme 1 Getting Together	theme 2 Sharing With Friends	theme 3 Speak Out!	theme 4 Listen for Sounds!
Reading/Writing Listening/Speaking	■ understands the concept of cooperation ■ shares ideas about helping ■ listens and responds to others ■ participates in listening, speaking and viewing activities in response to literature ■ appreciates and values other points of view ■ develops an awareness of the classroom as a community of learners ■ writes in a journal ■ retells stories ■ relates literature to personal experience	■ understands the concept of sharing ■ shares ideas about cooperative games and activities ■ participates in cooperative games and activities ■ makes friends during cooperative games ■ listens and responds to others ■ participates in listening, speaking and viewing activities in response to literature ■ appreciates and values other points of view ■ develops an awareness of the classroom as a community of learners ■ writes in a journal ■ relates literature to personal experience ■ retells the story	■ understands the concept of communication ■ participates in creating and presenting a classroom news show ■ demonstrates speaking skills ■ listens and responds ■ participates in listening, speaking and viewing activities in response to literature ■ appreciates and values other points of view ■ develops and expresses personal interests and attitudes ■ develops an awareness of the classroom as a community of learners ■ writes in a journal ■ retells a story ■ chooses to read and write for a variety of purposes ■ chooses to share writing ■ follows directions	■ shares ideas about sounds ■ participates in creating and presenting a sound celebration ■ demonstrates listening skills ■ listens for a specific purpose ■ responds to others in a variety of ways ■ appreciates sounds of language ■ reads, writes, and draws pictures about sounds ■ develops and expresses personal interests and attitudes ■ participates in a variety of activities in response to literature ■ writes in a journal ■ retells stories
Concepts of Print	■ understands book concepts: cover, title, author, illustrator ■ holds book correctly ■ turns pages correctly ■ demonstrates awareness of directionality, letters, words ■ understands the relationship between printed words and speech	■ understands book concepts: cover, title, author, illustrator ■ holds book correctly ■ turns pages correctly ■ demonstrates awareness of directionality, letters, words ■ understands the relationship between printed words and speech	■ understands book concepts: cover, title, author, illustrator ■ turns pages correctly ■ demonstrates awareness of directionality, letters, words, sentences, punctuation ■ understands the relationship between printed words and speech	■ understands book concepts: cover, title, author, illustrator ■ demonstrates awareness of directionality, letters, words, sentences, punctuation ■ understands the relationship between printed words and speech
Phonics and Decoding	■ recognizes letters of the alphabet ■ understands the connection between letters and sounds ■ recognizes his/her name in print ■ recognizes names of others in print	■ recognizes letters of the alphabet ■ understands the connection between letters and sounds ■ recognizes his/her name in print ■ recognizes names of others in print	■ recognizes letters of the alphabet ■ demonstrates an awareness of rhyme ■ participates in rhyming activities ■ understands the connection between letters and sounds	■ discriminates the sounds of letters: /k/ Cc, /p/ Pp ■ identifies upper and lowercase letters: Cc, Pp ■ recognizes sound/ letter relationships: /k/Cc, /p/Pp ■ writes upper and lowercase letters: Cc, Pp ■ recognizes rhyming words
Theme Poem	■ Together *by Paul Engle*	■ Making Friends *by Eloise Greenfield*	■ Good Morning *by Muriel Sipe*	■ Ears Hear *by Lucia and James L. Hymes, Jr.*
Theme Word	■ Helper	■ Friend	■ Speaker	■ Listener

Spotlight on Literacy Kindergarten
Print-rich, Activity-based, Skills-focused

Spotlight on Literacy Kindergarten is a print-rich, activity-based program that nurtures emergent literacy, phonics skills, and emergent writing. The program is organized into 16 theme units in 4 Teacher Planning Guides. Each unit includes 10 daily literacy sessions, an unparalleled collection of literature, and a wealth of opportunities for exploring sounds and print.

At McGraw-Hill, we believe that kindergartners should hear many types of literature—ABC books, traditional folk tales, classic children's books, award-winners, information books, poems, songs, rhymes, and counting books—so students internalize that print carries meaning while enjoying the stories.

In all, Kindergarten features 16 Literature Big Books and 48 Little Trade Books, plus 3 theme and alphabet Big Books.

Phonemic Awareness, Letters, Shapes, Sounds!

For every letter of the alphabet there is:

- A little trade book literature selection
- A song on the Sing a Sound Audiocassettes
- A nursery rhyme in the Big Book of Alphabet Rhymes and Chimes
- Activities for listening, repeating, and hands-on activities with letters and words.

For each of the 16 Theme Units— you'll find:

a Literature Big Book

3 Little Books

3 Spotlight: Early Readers

Stars of the future

The Comprehensive Theme Pack

The Comprehensive Theme Pack includes everything you
see here—total support for beginning reading instruction!

- ABC Cards

- 48 Little Books (3/theme)

- 48 Early Readers
  Spotlight Books (3/theme)

- 16 Literature Big Books
  (1/theme)

- Big Book of Songs

- Big Book of Poems

- Big Book of Alphabet
  Rhymes and Chimes

- Homewords

- Take-Home Books
  Blackline Masters

- A to EZ Handbook

- Read-Aloud Anthology

- Staff Development Guide

- Diagnostic Placement
  Evaluations

- Performance
  Assessment Handbook

- Lesson Planner

- Early Readers
  Teacher's Guide

- Alphabet Posters

- 4 Teacher Planning
  Guides (16 theme units)

- Practice Book

- Literature Activity
  Book

- Listening Library
  Audiocassettes
  (all literature from
  the 48 Little Books
  and all 19 Big Books)

Volume **4**

	theme 13 Find It Out!	**theme 14** Meet Ezra Jack Keats!	**theme 15** Thinking About Me!	**theme 16** Setting Out!
Reading/Writing Listening/Speaking	▪ shares ideas about museums ▪ collects and organizes information ▪ participates in creating and presenting a classroom museum ▪ participates in listening, speaking, and viewing activities ▪ reads, writes, and draws pictures about museum displays ▪ appreciates and values diverse points of views ▪ recognizes cultural attitudes and customs ▪ retells stories ▪ participates in a variety of activities in response to literature	▪ shares ideas about Ezra Jack Keats ▪ participates in creating and presenting an Ezra Jack Keats Corner ▪ reads, writes, and draws pictures about Ezra Jack Keats ▪ selects stories and books for personal interests ▪ appreciates the literary expression of our contemporary multicultural society and multicultural heritage ▪ recognizes cultural attitudes and customs in literary selections ▪ appreciates the artistic interpretation of literature through illustration, oral presentation, and other forms of expression ▪ retells stories ▪ participates in a variety of activities in response to literature	▪ shares ideas about him- or herself ▪ writes, draws, and presents an autobiography ▪ participates in listening, speaking, and viewing activities ▪ appreciates and values diverse points of view ▪ develops an awareness of the classroom as a community of learners that values cooperation, fair play, and respect for others and for oneself ▪ recognizes cultural attitudes and customs ▪ makes connections between one's personal life and literature ▪ retells stories ▪ participates in a variety of activities in response to literature	▪ shares ideas about explorations and journeys ▪ writes, draws, and creates works to present in a scrapbook ▪ appreciates and values diverse points of view ▪ recognizes cultural attitudes and customs ▪ makes connections between one's personal life and literature ▪ appreciates the artistic interpretation of literature through illustration, oral presentation, and other forms of expression ▪ retells stories ▪ participates in a variety of activities in response to literature
Concepts of Print	▪ understands book concepts: cover, title, author, illustrator ▪ demonstrates awareness of: directionality, letters, words, sentences, punctuation	▪ understands book concepts: cover, title, author, illustrator ▪ demonstrates awareness of directionality, letters, words, sentences, punctuation	▪ understands book concepts: cover, title, author, illustrator ▪ demonstrates awareness of directionality, letters, words, sentences, punctuation	▪ understands book concepts: cover, title, author, illustrator ▪ demonstrates awareness of directionality, letters, words, sentences, punctuation
Phonics and Decoding	▪ discriminates the sound of letters: /d/ Dd, /w/ Ww ▪ identifies upper and lowercase letters: Dd, Ww ▪ recognizes sound/letter relationships: /d/ Dd, /w/ Ww ▪ writes upper and lowercase letters: Dd, Ww	▪ discriminates the sound of letters: /j/ Jj, /l/ Ll ▪ identifies upper and lowercase letters: Jj, Ll ▪ recognizes sound/letter relationships: /j/ Jj, /l/ Ll ▪ writes upper and lowercase letters: Jj, Ll	▪ discriminates the sound of letters: /n/ Nn, /u/ Uu ▪ identifies upper and lowercase letters: Nn, Uu ▪ recognizes sound/letter relationships: /n/ Nn, /u/ Uu ▪ writes upper and lowercase letters: Nn, Uu	▪ recognizes sound/letter relationships: /v/ Vv, /o/ Oo ▪ identifies upper and lowercase letters: Vv, Oo ▪ discriminates the sound of letters: /v/ Vv, /o/ Oo ▪ writes upper and lowercase letters: Vv, Oo
Theme Poem	▪ Who? *by Lillian Moore*	▪ Picture People *by Myra Cohn Livingston*	▪ By Myself *by Eloise Greenfield*	▪ Come Out *by Karla Kuskin*
Theme Word	▪ Researcher	▪ Illustrator	▪ Child	▪ Explorer

Volume **3**

	theme 9 **Meet Pat Hutchins**	theme 10 **Share A Story!**	theme 11 **Act It Out!**	theme 12 **Wonder About It!**
Reading/Writing Listening/Speaking	▪ shares ideas about Pat Hutchins ▪ participates in creating and presenting a Pat Hutchins Corner ▪ cooperates with others ▪ appreciates and values diverse points of view ▪ reads, writes, and draws pictures about Pat Hutchins ▪ develops and expresses personal interests and attitudes ▪ becomes aware of cultural backgrounds, experiences, emotions, and ideas of self ▪ retells stories ▪ chooses to read and write for a variety of purposes ▪ participates in a variety of activities in response to literature	▪ shares ideas about stories and storytelling ▪ participates in creating a storytelling festival ▪ responds to others in a variety of ways ▪ reads, writes, and draws pictures about storytelling ▪ selects stories and books for personal interests ▪ appreciates the literary expression of our contemporary multicultural society and multicultural heritage ▪ recognizes cultural attitudes and customs in literary selections ▪ appreciates the artistic interpretation of literature through illustration, oral presentation, and other forms of expression ▪ shares writing ▪ participates in a variety of activities in response to literature	▪ shares ideas about dramatic performance ▪ participates in creating and presenting a dramatic performance ▪ works together with others ▪ reads, writes, and draws pictures about dramatization ▪ selects stories and books for personal interests ▪ appreciates the literary expression of our contemporary multicultural society and multicultural heritage ▪ recognizes cultural differences and customs in literary selections ▪ appreciates the artistic interpretation of literature through illustration, oral presentation, and other forms of expression ▪ retells stories ▪ participates in a variety of activities in response to literature	▪ shares ideas about the earth, sky, sun, clouds, and moon ▪ participates in creating and presenting a Works of Wonder display ▪ participates in listening, speaking, and viewing activities ▪ cooperates with others ▪ reads, writes, and draws pictures about natural phenomena ▪ appreciates and values diverse points of view ▪ develops an awareness of the classroom as a community of learners ▪ recognizes cultural attitudes and customs ▪ retells stories ▪ participates in a variety of activities in response to literature
Concepts of Print	▪ understands book concepts: cover, title, author, illustrator ▪ demonstrates awareness of directionality, letters, words, sentences, punctuation	▪ understands book concepts: cover, title, author, illustrator ▪ demonstrates awareness of directionality, letters, words, sentences, punctuation	▪ understands book concepts: cover, title, author, illustrator ▪ demonstrates awareness of directionality, letters, words, sentences, punctuation	▪ understands book concepts: cover, title, author, illustrator ▪ demonstrates awareness of directionality, letters, words, sentences, punctuation
Phonics and Decoding	▪ discriminates the sound of letters: /t/ Tt, /k/ Kk ▪ identifies upper and lowercase letters: Tt, Kk ▪ recognizes sound/letter relationships: /t/ Tt, /k/ Kk ▪ writes upper and lowercase letters: Tt, Kk	▪ discriminates the sound of letters: /f/ Ff, /y/ Yy ▪ identifies upper and lowercase letters: Ff, Yy ▪ recognizes sound/letter relationships: /f/ Ff, /y/ Yy ▪ writes upper and lowercase letters: Ff, Yy	▪ discriminates the sound of letters: /z/ Zz, /kw/ Qu, qu ▪ identifies upper and lowercase letters: Zz, Qq ▪ recognizes sound/letter relationships: /z/ Zz; /kw/ Qu, qu ▪ writes upper and lowercase letters: Zz, Qq	▪ discriminates the sound of letters: /i/ Ii, /ks/ Xx ▪ identifies upper and lowercase letters: Ii, Xx ▪ recognizes sound/letter relationships: /i/ Ii, /ks/ Xx ▪ writes upper and lowercase letters: Ii, Xx
Theme Poem	▪ Surprise *by Beverly McLoughland*	▪ Worlds I Know *by Myra Cohn Livingston*	▪ On Our Way *by Eve Merriam*	▪ I Arise, *an Eskimo song*
Theme Word	▪ Writer	▪ Storyteller	▪ Actor	▪ Thinker

phonics instruction

Spotlight on Phonics Kit

For additional opportunities in children's exploration of sounds and print, McGraw-Hill offers the Spotlight on Phonics Kit for Kindergarten including:

- Spotlight: Early Readers, Set of 48 Decodable Stories
- Take-Home Books Blackline Masters
- Alphabet Posters
- ABC Cards
- Word Building Kit
- Mini-Pocket Chart
- Sing a Sound Audiocassettes
- Word Mask
- Mother Goose Storytelling Puppet
- 'Tronic Phonics Introductory CD-ROM with 3 Storybooks

Also available separately

Literature Activity Book supplements each theme with activities including coloring, cut-outs, and much more. (A desk copy is provided in your Comprehensive Theme Pack.)

Practice Workbook supplements the comprehensive practice in the Teacher's Planning Guides with additional explicit skills practice. (A desk copy is provided in your Comprehensive Theme Pack.)

Rhyme and Chime Strips are illustrated strips for each nursery rhyme in the Big Book of Alphabet Rhymes and Chimes. The strips allow students to explore language patterns, concepts of print, and high-utility vocabulary.

Sing and Read Books and Audiocassettes contain familiar traditional songs and folktales to support each theme unit.

Songs and Stories Audiocassettes contain a Theme Song and 2-3 other songs or poems for each unit of the Kindergarten program plus recordings of the Read Aloud stories.

Meet Pat Hutchins

TRADE BOOK LITERATURE

EARLY READERS

OTHER RESOURCES

- Big Book of Songs:
  pp. 28–31
- Big Book of Poems:
  pp. 28–29
- Big Book of Alphabet
  Rhymes and Chimes:
  pp. 28–29, 18
- Read Aloud Anthology:
  pp. 72–75, 69–71

- Songs and Stories
  Audiocassettes
    Story Songs: Tape 3, Side 1
    Storytellings: Tape 3, Side 1
- Sing a Sound
  Audiocassettes: Tape 3,
  Side 5; Tape 2, Side 3
- Listening Library
  Audiocassettes:
  Tape 4, Side 8

THEME OBJECTIVES

READING/WRITING LISTENING/SPEAKING

- shares ideas about Pat Hutchins
- participates in creating and presenting a Pat Hutchins Corner
- cooperates with others
- appreciates and values diverse points of view
- reads, writes, and draws pictures about Pat Hutchins
- develops and expresses personal interests and attitudes
- becomes aware of cultural backgrounds, experiences, emotions, and ideas of self
- retells stories
- chooses to read and write for a variety of purposes
- participates in a variety of activities in response to literature

PHONICS AND DECODING

- discriminates the sound of letters: /t/ *Tt*, /k/ *Kk*
- identifies upper and lowercase letters: *Tt, Kk*
- recognizes sound/letter relationships: /t/ *Tt*, /k/ *Kk*
- writes upper and lowercase letters: *Tt, Kk*

CONCEPTS OF PRINT

- understands book concepts: cover, title, author, illustrator
- demonstrates awareness of directionality, letters, words, sentences, punctuation

Tell a Story/Sing a Song

AUTHORS

Elaine Mei Aoki

•

Virginia A. Arnold

•

James Flood

•

James V. Hoffman

•

Diane Lapp

•

Miriam Martinez

•

Annemarie Sullivan
Palincsar

•

Michael Priestley

•

Carl B. Smith

•

William H. Teale

•

Josefina Villamil
Tinajero

•

Arnold W. Webb

•

Karen D. Wood

 **Macmillan McGraw-Hill**

New York   Farmington

AUTHORS, CONSULTANTS

MULTICULTURAL AND EDUCATIONAL CONSULTANTS

Yvonne Beamer, Joyce Buckner, Alma Flor Ada, Helen Gillotte,
Cheryl Hudson, Narcita Medina, Lorraine Monroe, James R. Murphy,
Sylvia Peña, Joseph B. Rubin, Ramon Santiago, Cliff Trafzer,
Hai Tran, Esther Lee Yao

LITERATURE CONSULTANTS

Ashley Bryan, Joan I. Glazer, Paul Janeczko, Margaret H. Lippert

INTERNATIONAL CONSULTANTS

Edward B. Adams, Barbara Johnson, Raymond L. Marshall

MUSIC AND AUDIO CONSULTANTS

John Farrell, Marilyn C. Davidson, Vincent Lawrence,
Sarah Pirtle, Susan R. Snyder,
Rick and Deborah Witkowski

Macmillan/McGraw-Hill

A Division of The McGraw-Hill Companies

Macmillan/McGraw-Hill
1221 Avenue of the Americas
New York, New York 10020

Printed in the United States of America

ISBN 0-02-181368-X / K, U.9

2 3 4 5 6 7 8 9 BCM 02 01 00 99 98 97

Teacher's Planning Guide

Meet Pat Hutchins

Contents

Presenting MEET PAT HUTCHINS

Meet Pat Hutchins

A theme about the writer and artist Pat Hutchins!
Theme Word: WRITER
Theme Poem: "Surprise"
by Beverly McLoughland
Theme Song: "Read a Book"
by Marcy Marxer

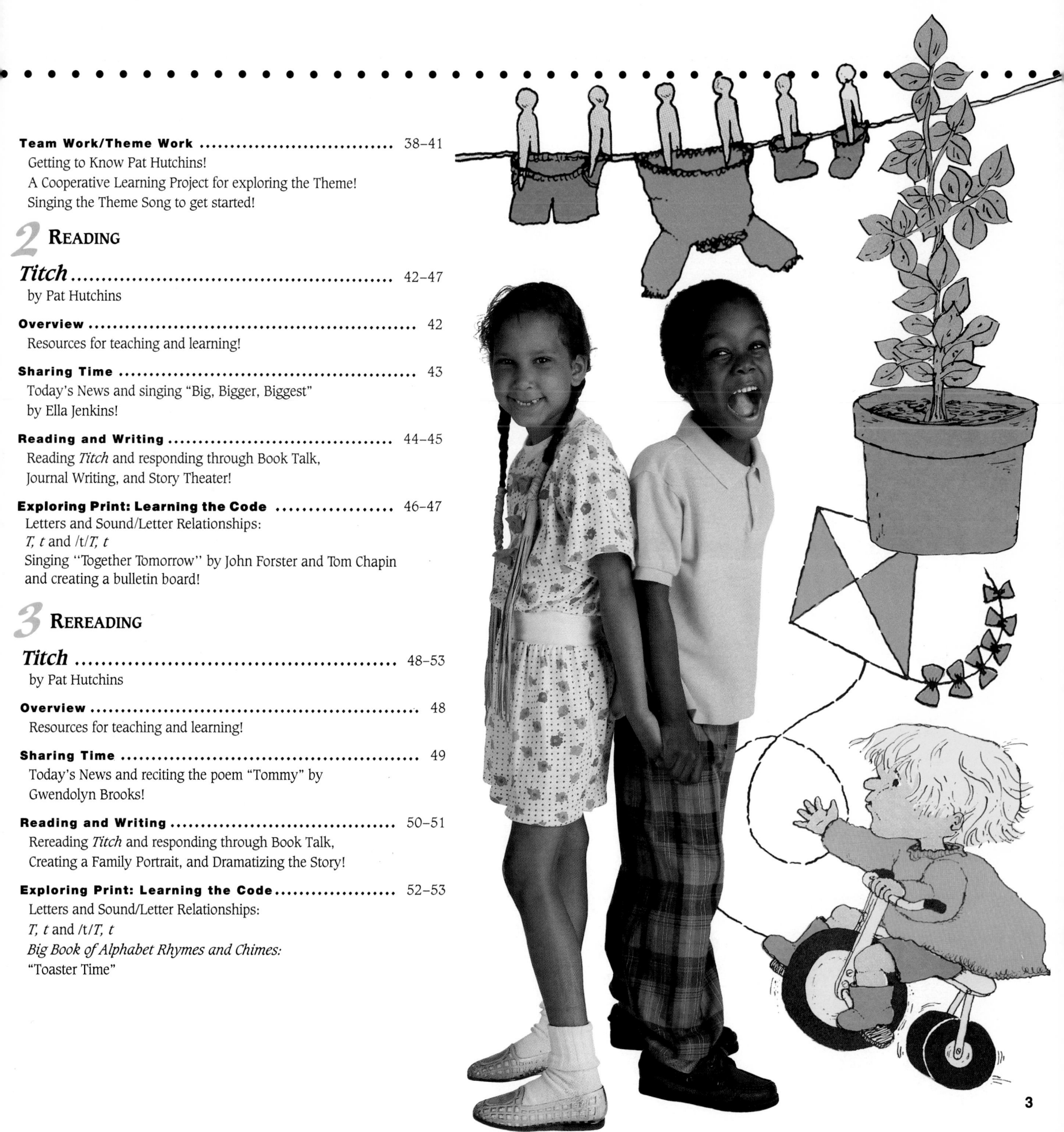

Contents

INTRODUCING TELL A STORY/SING A SONG

A New View of Kindergarten!

Welcome children to a print-rich, activity-based environment that nurtures emergent literacy!

19 BIG BOOKS!

48 TRADE BOOKS!

16 THEMES!

PROGRAM RESOURCES

Big Book of Songs
Theme Songs!

Big Book of Poems
Theme Poems!

The more we get together,
Together, together,
The more we get together,
The happier we'll be.

For your friends are my friends,
And my friends are your friends.
And the more we get together,
The happier we'll be.

Traditional

THE MORE WE GET TOGETHER

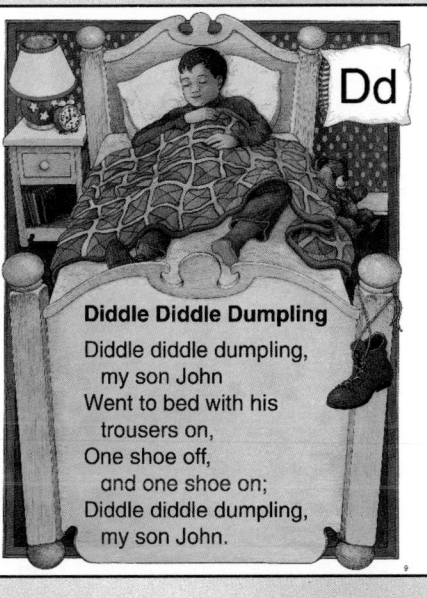

Cat's in the Cupboard

Great A, Little a,
Bouncing B!
The cat's in the cupboard
And can't see me.

Diddle Diddle Dumpling

Diddle diddle dumpling,
my son John
Went to bed with his
trousers on,
One shoe off,
and one shoe on;
Diddle diddle dumpling,
my son John.

Big Book of Alphabet Rhymes and Chimes
Verses for teaching the alphabet and concepts of print!
Plus the "Alphabet Song"!

Rhyme and Chime Strips
Each Rhyme and Chime
on illustrated strips to use in
pocket charts for
Hands On! Language
experiences!

Cat's in the Cupboard

Great A, Little a,

Bouncing B!

The cat's in the cupboard

And can't see me.

A a A a

B b B b

C C C c

Teacher's Read Aloud Anthology
32 Read Aloud selections
from cultures around
the world!

Plus —

STAFF DEVELOPMENT

A to EZ Handbook:
Staff Development Guide

Performance Assessment Handbook

Early Literacy Assessment

_I_ NTRODUCING TELL A STORY/SING A SONG

16 LITERATURE THEME PACKS

including 3 Trade Books (1 with a companion Big Book) and a Teacher's Planning Guide!

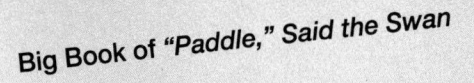

"Slither," said the snake in the cool morning air.

"Twitter," said the sparrows. "Trot," said the mare.

"Paddle," Said the Swan

Written and illus... Gloria Kam...

IN THE P... An Excursion in Four...

by ESTHER HAUT... Pictures by EZRA JACK...

Big Talk

By Miriam Schlein Pictures by Joan Auclair

Big Book of _"Paddle," Said the Swan_

Also Available—

LISTENING LIBRARY AUDIOCASSETTES for Big Books!

SONGS AND STORIES AUDIOCASSETTES with Theme Songs, sound effects, and storytellings!

SING A SOUND AUDIOCASSETTES with songs to encourage language play and to develop phonemic awareness!

TEACHER'S PLANNING GUIDE

SPEAK OUT!

MACMILLAN/MCGRAW-HILL

Teacher's Planning Guide for Speak Out!

Your resource for organizing activities—
• Sharing Time
• Reading and Writing
• Exploring Print
• Into the Learning Centers

NCILLARIES

Alphabet Posters
26 full-color posters!

ABC Cards
Textured letter forms
for tactile learning!

Sing & Read Books and Audiocassettes
16 little books, one for each theme song,
with audiocassettes of children singing
and then reading the selection!

Literature Activity Book with

- Activities for introducing
  each theme
- Tell-a-Tale Take-Home Books
- Responding to Literature pages
- Exploring Print activities
- Just for Fun pages, too!

Also Available—

HomeWords:
Newsletters and more
to send home each month!

Sights & Sounds:
Interactive software for children to use in their
exploration of the sounds of language
and the letters that represent them!

9

Tell a Story/Sing a Song

PROGRAM THEMES	TRADE BOOKS	READ ALOUDS
1 GETTING TOGETHER	**BIG BOOK: *Getting Together*** by George Ancona ***What Will Mommy Do When I'm at School?*** by Dolores Johnson ***I'm Busy, Too*** by Norma Simon, illustrated by Dora Leder	**The Great Big Enormous Turnip** a Russian tale by Alexei Tolstoi **The Rabbit and the Elephant** a folk tale from Ghana retold by Ruthilde Kronberg and Patricia C. McKissack
2 SHARING WITH FRIENDS	**BIG BOOK: *Frog in the Middle*** by Susanna Gretz ***Will I Have a Friend?*** by Miriam Cohen, illustrated by Lillian Hoban ***Friends*** by Helme Heine	**The Lion and the Mouse** a fable by Aesop **The Three Friends** a folk tale from India retold by Isabel Wyatt
3 SPEAK OUT!	**BIG BOOK: *"Paddle," Said the Swan*** by Gloria Kamen ***In the Park*** by Esther Hautzig, illustrated by Ezra Jack Keats ***Big Talk*** by Miriam Schlein, illustrated by Joan Auclair	**The Long One** a Masai tale from East Africa by Verna Aardema **The Boy Who Cried Wolf** a fable by Aesop retold by Anne Terry White
4 LISTEN FOR SOUNDS!	**BIG BOOK: *Rain Talk*** by Mary Serfozo, illustrated by Keiko Narahashi ***Country Crossing*** by Jim Aylesworth, illustrated by Ted Rand ***Apt. 3*** by Ezra Jack Keats	**The Bremen Town Musicians** a German folk tale retold by Anne Rockwell **The Race Between Toad and Donkey** a Jamaican folk tale edited by Roger D. Abrahams

THEME WORDS	THEME SONGS	THEME POEMS	EXPLORING PRINT LESSONS
LPER	**The More We Get Together** a traditional song	**Together** by Paul Engle	Games and activities related to children's names
END	**Be a Friend** a traditional song	**Making Friends** by Eloise Greenfield	Games and activities related to friends and their names, and days of the week
EAKER	**The Buenas Song** a Hispanic song by Aaron Schroeder and David Grover	**Good Morning** by Muriel Sipe	Rhyme Time: Games, songs, and activities for rhyming
TENER	**The Little Red Caboose** Bernice Johnson Reagon's version of the traditional song	**Ears Hear** by Lucia and James L. Hymes, Jr.	*Big Book of Alphabet Rhymes and Chimes:* **Cc** Cat's in the Cupboard **Pp** Pease Porridge Hot

Program Themes	Trade Books	Read Alouds
5 SING AND DANCE AWAY!	**BIG BOOK:** *Oh, A-Hunting We Will Go* by John Langstaff, illustrated by Nancy Winslow Parker *Max* by Rachel Isadora *The Little Band* by James Sage, illustrated by Keiko Narahashi	**The Twelve Dancing Princesses** a German fairy tale by the Brothers Grimm **The Clever Turtle** a Hispanic folk tale retold by Margaret H. Lippert
6 PAINT IT UP!	**BIG BOOK:** *Who Said Red?* by Mary Serfozo, illustrated by Keiko Narahashi *The little Bear Book* by Anthony Browne *circles, triangles and squares* by Tana Hoban	**The Black Cat** an American folk tale retold by Margaret H. Lippert **Ma Lien and the Magic Brush** a tale from China by Hisako Kimishima retold by Alvin Tresselt
7 EAT IT UP!	**BIG BOOK:** *Bread, Bread, Bread* by Ann Morris, photographs by Ken Heyman *Gregory, the Terrible Eater* by Mitchell Sharmat, illustrated by Jose Aruego and Ariane Dewey *What's on My Plate?* by Ruth Belov Gross, illustrated by Isadore Seltzer	**The Woman Who Flummoxed the Fairies** a Scottish folk tale retold by Sorche Nic Leodhas **Señor Billy Goat** a Hispanic folk tale retold by Pura Belpré
8 BUILD IT UP!	**BIG BOOK:** *Changes, Changes* by Pat Hutchins *I Read Signs* by Tana Hoban *Round Trip* by Ann Jonas	**The Three Little Pigs** an English fairy tale retold by Flora Annie Steel **Why the Moon Is in the Sky** an Ashanti folk tale from West Africa retold by Margaret H. Lippert

Theme Words	Theme Songs	Theme Poems	Exploring Print Lessons
NGER NCER	**You'll Sing a Song and I'll Sing a Song** by Ella Jenkins	**Singing-Time** by Rose Fyleman	*Big Book of Alphabet Rhymes and Chimes:* **Hh** Hippity Hop to Bed **Mm** Miss Mary Mack
TIST	**I Know the Colors in the Rainbow** by Ella Jenkins	**Paints** by Ilo Orleans	*Big Book of Alphabet Rhymes and Chimes:* **Ss** Sing a Song of Sixpence **Bb** Bounce High, Bounce Low
OK	**Short'ning Bread** a traditional Southern song	**Through the Teeth** a folk rhyme	*Big Book of Alphabet Rhymes and Chimes:* **Gg** Gobble, Gobble **Aa** Eat an Apple
ILDER	**Johnny Builds with One Hammer** a traditional song	**Buildings** by Myra Cohn Livingston	*Big Book of Alphabet Rhymes and Chimes:* **Rr** R Is for Ribbon **Ee** Engine, Engine, Number Nine

Tell a Story / Sing a Song

Program Themes	Trade Books	Read Alouds
9 MEET PAT HUTCHINS	**BIG BOOK: *Titch*** by Pat Hutchins ***Rosie's Walk*** by Pat Hutchins ***Good-Night, Owl!*** by Pat Hutchins	**It Could Always Be Worse** a Yiddish folk tale retold by Margot Zemach **Rainbow Crow** a Lenape tale retold by Nancy Van Laan
10 SHARE A STORY!	**BIG BOOK: *I Had a Cat*** by Mona Rabun Reeves, illustrated by Julie Downing ***Little Red Hen*** by Janina Domanska ***Nessa's Fish*** by Nancy Luenn, illustrated by Neil Waldman	**The Storytelling Stone** a Seneca tale retold by Joseph Bruchac **The Three Bears** an English folk tale retold by Margaret H. Lippert
11 ACT IT OUT!	**BIG BOOK: *Handtalk Zoo*** by George Ancona and Mary Beth ***Stone Soup*** by Marcia Brown ***I'm Going on a Dragon Hunt*** by Maurice Jones, illustrated by Charlotte Firmin	**The Three Billy Goats Gruff** a Norwegian folk tale retold by Margaret H. Lippert **The Terrible Tragadabas** a tale from Spanish New Mexico by Joe Hayes
12 WONDER ABOUT IT!	**BIG BOOK: *White Is the Moon*** by Valerie Greeley ***Half a Moon and One Whole Star*** by Crescent Dragonwagon, illustrated by Jerry Pinkney ***The Park Bench*** by Fumiko Takeshita, illustrated by Mamoru Suzuki	**The Spider Weaver** a folk tale from Japan retold by Florence Sakada **The One You Don't See Coming** a folk tale from Liberia retold by Harold Courlander and George Herzog

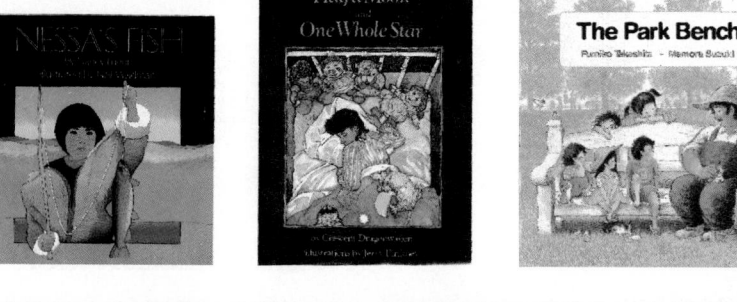

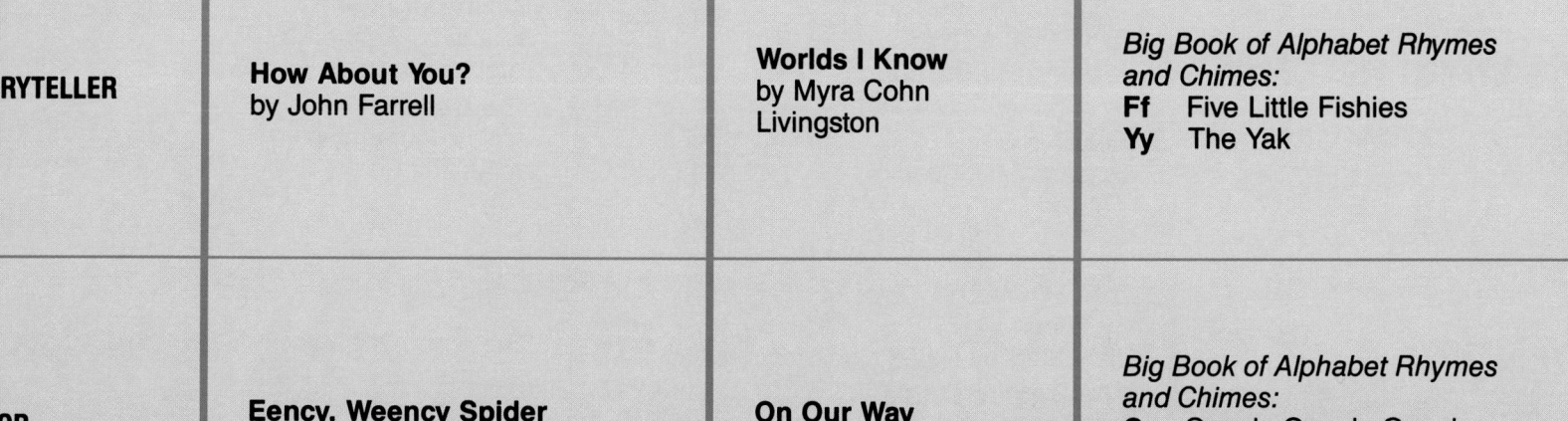

Theme Words	Theme Songs	Theme Poems	Exploring Print Lessons
RITER	**Read a Book** by Marcy Marxer	**Surprise** by Beverly McLoughland	*Big Book of Alphabet Rhymes and Chimes:* **Tt** Toaster Time **Kk** A Kettle's for the Kitchen
ORYTELLER	**How About You?** by John Farrell	**Worlds I Know** by Myra Cohn Livingston	*Big Book of Alphabet Rhymes and Chimes:* **Ff** Five Little Fishies **Yy** The Yak
TOR	**Eency, Weency Spider** a traditional song	**On Our Way** by Eve Merriam	*Big Book of Alphabet Rhymes and Chimes:* **Qq** Quack, Quack, Quack **Zz** Zippety! Zippety! Zim, zim, zim!
INKER	**Twinkle, Twinkle, Little Star** a traditional song	**I Arise** an Eskimo song	*Big Book of Alphabet Rhymes and Chimes:* **Ii** If All the World Was Apple Pie **Xx** What Words Begin with X?

Tell a Story/Sing a Song

Program Themes	Trade Books	Read Alouds
13 FIND IT OUT!	**BIG BOOK:** *What Do You See?* by Janina Domanska *Farm Animals* photographs by Philip Dowell and Michael Dunning *Changes* by Marjorie N. Allen and Shelley Rotner, photographs by Shelley Rotner	**Why Bears Have Short Tails** a Navajo legend from Arizona retold by Sandra Begay **The Plumage of the Owl/ El Plumaje del Mucaro** a Puerto Rican folk tale retold by Ricardo E. Alegría
14 MEET EZRA JACK KEATS	**BIG BOOK:** *Hi, Cat!* by Ezra Jack Keats *Kitten for a Day* by Ezra Jack Keats *Pet Show!* by Ezra Jack Keats	**Belling the Cat** a fable by Aesop retold by Joseph Jacobs **The Cat's Purr** a West Indian tale by Ashley Bryan
15 THINKING ABOUT ME	**BIG BOOK:** *All I Am* by Eileen Roe, illustrated by Helen Cogancherry *The Train to Lulu's* by Elizabeth Fitzgerald Howard, illustrated by Robert Casilla *Con Mi Hermano/With My Brother* by Eileen Roe, illustrated by Robert Casilla	**The Knee-High Man** an American black folk tale retold by Julius Lester **Anansi's Rescue from the River** a folk tale from West Africa retold by Harold Courlander
16 SETTING OUT!	**BIG BOOK:** *As the Crow Flies: A First Book of Maps* by Gail Hartman, illustrated by Harvey Stevenson *Look Out, Patrick!* by Paul Geraghty *Builder of the Moon* by Tim Wynne-Jones, illustrated by Ian Wallace	**Timimoto** a folk tale from Japan retold by Margaret H. Lippert **Jack and the Beanstalk** an English fairy tale retold by Virginia Haviland

THEME WORDS	THEME SONGS	THEME POEMS	EXPLORING PRINT LESSONS
SEARCHER	**Who Fed the Chickens?** by Ella Jenkins	**Who?** by Lilian Moore	*Big Book of Alphabet Rhymes and Chimes:* **Dd** Diddle Diddle Dumpling **Ww** Wee Willie Winkie
LUSTRATOR	**Library Song** by Michael Mark and Tom Chapin	**Picture People** by Myra Cohn Livingston	*Big Book of Alphabet Rhymes and Chimes:* **Ll** Lily's a Lady **Jj** Jack Be Nimble
ILD	**I Am a Person** by Sarah Pirtle	**By Myself** by Eloise Greenfield	*Big Book of Alphabet Rhymes and Chimes:* **Nn** Nicholas Ned **Uu** Umbrellas
PLORER	**The Bear Went Over the Mountain** a traditional song	**Come Out** by Karla Kuskin	*Big Book of Alphabet Rhymes and Chimes:* **Oo** Polly, Put the Kettle On **Vv** Very Nice

EMERGENT WRITING

MIRIAM MARTINEZ AND WILLIAM TEALE

The emergent literacy perspective is a powerful one because it lays the foundation for promoting children's literacy development through rich, exciting, and purposeful writing opportunities in the classroom.

1. **Drawing**

2. **Scribble**

Children's Writing Strategies

In their early explorations of the writing system, young children typically do not write in conventional ways. Careful observations of children's emergent writing have revealed a general, but rather complicated, developmental pathway. As children move along this pathway, they typically use some or all of the following strategies:

1. **Drawing**

2. **Scribbling**

3. **Randomly Chosen Letters:** The child uses letters, but there is not a relationship between the letters chosen and the sounds in the words that are written.

4. **Words Copied from Environmental Print**

5. **Developmental Spelling:** There is a relationship between the letters used and the sounds in the words that are written, but only one or two of the sounds heard in words are represented. This behavior later develops to the point at which children are able to use a letter to represent every (or almost every) sound in the words that are written.

6. **Transitional Spelling:** Features of conventional spelling, like silent letters or doubling of consonants, begin to appear.

7. **Conventional Spelling**

*R*ich, Purposeful Writing Experiences

∙∙∙∙∙∙∙∙∙∙∙∙∙∙∙∙∙∙∙∙∙∙∙∙∙∙∙∙∙∙

Young writers, like all writers, are most successful when they have interesting experiences to feed their writing. These include "hands on" activities, creative dramatics and art activities, content area experiences, explorations beyond the classroom, and opportunities to write about personal experiences beyond school.

Central to these efforts to ignite children's writing are rich literature experiences. One form that writing in response to literature takes is the journal. The journal is a place where children can record their thoughts, feelings, and reactions to a story they have just listened to or read.

Literature also nurtures children's own original story writing. Sometimes a storyline or story theme will serve as an invitation for the child to write about a similar experience. At other times, after reading a story with a distinctive predictable pattern, children may choose to use the same story pattern to organize their own writing.

andom Letters

REWRM
ERWDN
A EW R
A E W R

3.

Random Letters

YUVTOUSUCOt
CKOKOU
t OUOEUCI
OCUTCtCtC

2-6-85

3.

Emergent Writing

Children's Growth as Writers

Three dimensions signal growth in children's writing. First is evidence that the child is using increasingly more sophisticated writing strategies (drawing, scribbling, developmental spellings, and so on.). However, as we observe children's movement along this developmental pathway, it's important to remember that not every child uses all strategies, nor will a child necessarily, as he or she begins to use a more sophisticated strategy, leave less sophisticated ones behind. If anything, many children tend to expand their repertoire of strategies, using different ones for different tasks.

The second dimension of children's growth as writers is what they say. It is particularly important to look for evidence that children are learning to organize their writing better, to develop their ideas more fully, and to use features that are associated with written language rather than oral language (Once upon a time...).

However, a word of warning is in order. As children begin to use more sophisticated writing strategies (in particular, as they concentrate on developmental spellings), the content and organization of their stories and journal entries may appear to become less sophisticated for a period of time. Rather than being taken as a cause for alarm, this state of affairs should be viewed as more of a natural trade-off. When children do get more control over sound-symbol relationships, they will again be able to attend more closely to what it is they want to say and to whom they want to say it.

4.

Copying Environmental Print

Octobər 18

reM
ArT
MATH
BIOC

5.

Early Developmental Spelling

imT DPMREWR
RTDPR
PimD RCa
QRPRCQ
RPUQRPQRPROZO

rly Developmental Spelling

º W ᵼ C O p d B

Finally, it is important to remember that children's reading and writing development are integrally related, and this reading/writing connection must be taken into account in evaluating their growth as writers.

In particular, as a child reads what he or she has written, it is important to ask questions such as these:

- Does the child attend to the picture or the print in reading what she or he has written?

- Are the child's attempts to track the print successful?

- Does the child conventionally read what he or she has written?

- Does the child's intonation sound more like oral or written language?

As children move along the developmental pathway, their rereadings of their own writing become more print-based and sound increasingly like written language rather than oral language.

Full Developmental Spelling

I lik ron Bos Be kus tha
r Color fool

Andrew

Transitional Spelling

5-2-85

Andrew

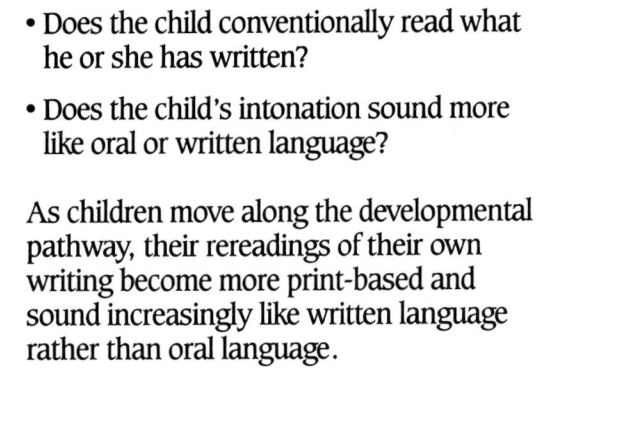

I lIke CooKes And Caks And I theK I Know To Mak theeM uoos flan Wet And egg

5.

6.

Students Acquiring English

Emergent Literacy in the Second Language

BY JOSEFINA VILLAMIL TINAJERO

The early childhood years are a remarkably active period for acquiring language and for learning about its written form. Classroom environments have a significant effect on children's language and literacy development. This is especially true for emergent readers and writers who are also acquiring English as a second language. The physical and social environment of the classroom, teacher beliefs and attitudes about language acquisition and emergent literacy, the types of activities planned, and the strategies and techniques used by teachers all affect the opportunities children have to emerge as readers and writers and to acquire a new language.

Supporting Kindergartners' Language Acquisition

It is our position that children *acquire* rather than *learn* a language in a natural progression of stages. As language is acquired, literacy in the new language develops. That is, current research suggests that the second language is acquired in the same manner as the first and that it is acquired most effectively in a highly interactive, total communication environment.

Children acquire language when they understand what people say to them or what is read. They acquire language by understanding messages and by responding to those messages in meaningful ways. Language must make sense to young children, and somehow it must be important for them to acquire it. Some of the best ways to encourage language development are to provide children with many opportunities to interact with other children, to encourage child's play, and to engage them in natural language activities. Songs, poems, stories, games, role-play, story theater, and dramatizations are especially effective because they allow students to hear natural English while providing a meaningful, motivating, and enjoyable context for learning.

Young SAEs need a favorable environment for language acquisition, an environment that is as natural and as language-rich as that within which they learned their first language. Kindergartners acquiring English, in particular, need many opportunities to hear and use English, to experiment with it, to take risks and try out their knowledge of the language. They need to be encouraged to express their ideas and feelings as they move along the pathway toward nativelike fluency.

When students offer responses, for example, their pronunciation may be poor and their grammatical construction may include elements from their first language. When this happens, teachers need to accept their responses, model the "correct" form in a tactful and unexaggerated way, and praise them for their contributions. Praising builds confidence and helps children feel valued as members of the class. They will also be much more motivated to "experiment" with the language and to take risks—that is, express their thoughts and ideas even if they are not yet fully fluent in the language.

Teachers can integrate the following techniques with activities planned for other children in the class.

Heterogeneous Grouping. One way to provide SAEs with opportunities to practice their English is to increase the frequency and variety of interactions among students. Pairing them with proficient English speakers for activities such as partner "reading" of Big Books and partner story retellings is one way

of increasing interaction. Grouping them with students of varying proficiencies for activities such as illustrating a new ending to a story or illustrating a character map is another. At other times, however, SAEs may be grouped together for activities such as listening to a story in their native language, working on a special project, or doing partner reading with other SAEs.

Cooperative Learning. Cooperative learning also increases the frequency and variety of second language practice through different types of interactions. It provides students with many opportunities to utilize newly acquired language and to "read and write" (scribbling and drawing are considered writing at this age) in English in a "safe" social situation where they don't feel threatened by error correction. Cooperative learning also provides students with opportunities to act as resources for each other and thus assume a more active role in learning.

When working with kindergartners acquiring English, it is also important to keep in mind that, as individuals, they are at different levels of English proficiency. Thus, when planning activities for them, teachers must be aware of the level of receptive and productive language they bring to the learning task. There may be some children who may not be ready to begin producing oral English. Some may be experiencing what is often referred to as the *"silent period" of language learning*. That is, second language learners go through a period of time during which they prefer to listen rather than to produce language. As with most second language learners, children's receptive

language skills develop earlier than their productive ones (Rice, 1989).
It is important, however, to keep in mind that language learning is taking place during this time (Evans, 1990). Children don't always need to respond in order to learn new language skills. They can benefit greatly from the opportunity to absorb the conversations of others (Rice, 1989).

$\mathcal{U}$sing Literature to Nurture Children's Language Development

The best language lessons are good books and interesting discussions in which children are absorbed in the meaning of what is said to them or what is read.

For SAEs, literature cultivates language, provides language models, and facilitates language acquisition. As children listen to rhymes, poems, and patterned/predictable stories in English, they learn new language patterns and idiomatic usages, which are assimilated as children apply them to express their own thoughts and ideas during meaningful, well-planned lessons. Children with limited vocabulary can latch on to the "new" language they have heard, suddenly discovering that their former limited vocabulary takes on new dimensions.

$\mathcal{S}$torytelling with SAEs

Because storytelling encourages physical, visual, and aural/oral participation of students, it is an excellent context for teaching language and concepts to SAEs.

Listening and speaking skills, for example, are enriched through the use of puppetry, tapes, dramatic presentations, and the teacher's systematic reading to children. Children will also enjoy retelling stories they have been told or sharing stories from their own cultures, stories they may have learned at home or in their neighborhoods. Children's own creativity and ingenuity can also be encouraged and supported by allowing children to create, tell, and retell their own stories.

Following are some suggestions to take full advantage of storytelling activities to enhance language development for SAEs.

Oral Previewing. This technique adjusts the teacher's language input to children's language proficiency and comprehension level during storytelling. For SAEs, oral previewing takes the form of paraphrasing or telling the story "in your own words," both to make the story as comprehensible as possible and to facilitate language development. When using this technique, follow these guidelines.

First, screen the story, taking into account the language and experiential knowledge of students. Select areas of difficulty such as idiomatic language and difficult vocabulary. Become familiar with the story so that the retelling is as natural as possible, and so that you can be cognizant of facial expressions that might indicate whether or not SAEs are understanding the story.

Then hold up a copy of the book as you lead the children orally through the story, establishing plot and setting. Use gestures, body language, and facial expressions to help convey ideas and

STUDENTS ACQUIRING ENGLISH

concepts. Use simple, well-formed sentences; limit sentence length and complexity while maintaining appropriate grammar and intonation.

Clarify the meaning of words, phrases, and idiomatic expressions using context clues, such as pointing to the illustrations or drawing simple pictures. Make frequent repetitions of key words and ideas. At times, incorporate role play to help children understand concepts and learn language through physical activity.

As you continue to go through the story, ask questions that require yes/no responses, a nod of the head, pointing to an illustration, or one- or two-word responses to check understanding. Also ask questions to relate the story situation to children's experiences. Remember that SAEs understand more than they can verbalize. As children respond using one or two words, repeat their utterances, use their words in an expanded comment. That is, use the *semantic expansion* technique, in which you as the teacher start with something the child said and elaborate to clarify or add to the response. Also, use structural expansion in which you as the teacher repeat an incorrect utterance correctly to model for the children. Finally, have children make predictions along the way to encourage language use and development of critical thinking skills. Remember to praise children for their contributions.

These types of teacher-child interactions with storybooks create a context for comprehending meaning, for making meaning. They help SAEs get past some of the difficult language so they can concentrate on the story line. Children also internalize new language related to the story they are about to hear.

The following storytelling variations help SAEs acquire language and make stories more comprehensible. Use them as often as possible. They are good for all children.

Puppetry. Puppets make stories come alive for children, and the actions associated with using them to tell or retell stories make language more comprehensible. Most important, however, SAEs are less reluctant to talk "when they take on other identities to perform. It is somehow less threatening to make a mistake as someone else; it becomes their mistake, not that of the student" (Evans, 1990).

Participation Stories. Certain stories invite children to participate actively as they respond to certain words that act as cues for actions like clapping or stamping their feet or shaking their heads. Before reading the story, the teacher introduces the cues. The children then act out the story as the teacher reads. These types of stories develop listening skills and facilitate language acquisition (Evans, 1990).

Pantomime. Through pantomime children use their whole bodies for making meaning as they participate in storytelling activities. Text becomes more comprehensible as characters come alive.

Story Retelling. Working with a partner, children retell stories to one another. Story retelling provides a great opportunity for children to use the language they have heard in the stories to express their own thoughts and ideas.

Tape Recordings. Tape recordings of stories are an excellent way to expose students to good literature that may be beyond their reading abilities but within their listening abilities. Children will also enjoy making their own recordings of

stories. These recordings also serve as good diagnostic tools.

Choral Reading. Choral readings of stories, with a mix of SAEs and proficient English speakers, give shy learners a safe way to practice formal speaking. Remember, the desire of SAEs to produce language varies greatly—allow them to join in when they're ready.

Shared Reading and SAEs

Another excellent way to provide SAEs with rich literature experiences is to conduct shared reading with books that contain repetitive language and/or predictable outcomes. The repetitive characteristics of the texts facilitate the natural acquisition of vocabulary, pronunciation, and language structures. Big Books are particularly effective for group study and for exposing children to print.

The repeated readings help children to read more efficiently, gain confidence, practice using their reading skills, and increase their sight vocabulary. And since the illustrations in the books are closely tied to the text, children get visual support for the rapid development of a wide range of vocabulary. The reading and rereading of stories also allow SAEs to hear and practice, in an informal setting, the rhythm and structure of English.

As children recite and participate in shared reading activities using rhymes, poems, songs, and pattern stories, they learn new language patterns. They internalize these patterns and then use them to express their own thoughts and ideas. Furthermore, through shared reading, children are exposed to the written and oral forms of language and are offered

numerous opportunities to develop listening, speaking, reading, and writing skills at the "teachable moment."

Shared reading activities also establish the kind of low-anxiety environment essential to language acquisition and provide SAEs at varying/lower levels of English proficiency with the opportunity to participate with the rest of the class. It is also a pleasurable experience that helps SAEs develop a positive attitude toward acquiring English and learning to read in a second language.

In selecting materials to use with SAEs, select those with texts containing features such as rhyme, rhythmic language, predictable or repetitive plots and language patterns, or illustrations that closely parallel the text. Screen materials carefully for overload of idiomatic language and situations that are culturally unfamiliar. Finally, select materials at the appropriate instructional level that foster students' appreciation of reading and develop positive attitudes toward learning to read in English.

Language Experience Activities

The language experience approach is particularly suitable for use with SAEs because the children's language proficiency, no matter how limited, is valued and used as a starting point for further development. And because SAEs' proficiency in English often varies significantly, language experience activities help build a common knowledge and language base for them. The approach also integrates children's ideas, interests, experiences, and natural language, using them to motivate students to read.

Through language experience, SAEs are also able to acquire the basic skills of reading and writing with familiar material—their own. Thus, the text is rich in comprehensible content that further develops children's language proficiency.

Establishing Partnerships with Parents

A primary way in which we can provide more supportive learning environments for all children is to involve their parents, working with them as colleagues, inviting them to participate as valuable resources of information and perspectives, and sharing with them ways in which parents enhance education at home.

Parents can assist teachers in creating more supportive and nurturing learning environments that offer the security needed for SAEs to participate in a culturally different setting. Parents can be invited to the classroom to tell stories from the oral tradition, to read stories, read or recite poetry, share "how to" information, and present topics that have inspired and informed their lives.

Parents often think that they cannot help their children at home if they do not speak English. Teachers need to make an effort to assure them that working with their children in their native language is of benefit because concepts learned in the native language will transfer to English.

The Challenge

Kindergarten is a critical point for students acquiring English. Beyond their needs for skills in academic growth, SAEs also have motivational and emotional needs that must be met. These needs are often magnified in importance where there are cultural and linguistic differences between the school and the home. They include children's need to feel a sense of identity, to belong, to be understood by and communicate with significant others, and to succeed in environments in which they are accepted and respected. Kindergarten teachers can make a difference in the lives of these children. By simply applying some of the basic principles discussed here, teachers can provide a nurturing and intellectually stimulating environment where students acquiring English can succeed and thrive.

References

Auerbach, E. (1989). Toward a social-contextual approach to family literacy. Harvard Educational Review, 59, No. 2, pp. 165–181.

Early, M. (1991). Using wordless picture books to promote second language learning. ELT Journal. Volume 45/3. July. pp. 245–250.

Evans, L. S. (1990). Storytelling and oral language development in ESL classrooms. TESOL Newsletter. October. pp. 3, 16, 18, 30.

Flood, J.; Lapp, D.; Tinajero, J.; and Nagel, G. Parents and teachers: Partners in developing literacy for multicultural students. (unpublished manuscript).

Nurss, J. R. and Hough, R. A. (1985). Story reading: Language arts for limited English speakers. TESOL Newsletter. Vol. 8, No. 1. pp. 1–2.

Rice, M. (1989). Children's language acquisition. American Psychologist. Volume 4. February. pp. 149–156.

*I*NTRODUCING MEET PAT HUTCHINS

Invite children to explore the life and work of Pat Hutchins through trade books, read aloud selections, poetry, and songs!

TRADE BOOKS

Titch
by Pat Hutchins
Titch's belongings are always smaller than those of his siblings, until his tiny seed turns out to be the biggest thing of all.
Available as a Big Book and little book, and included on the
LISTENING LIBRARY AUDIOCASSETTE

Good-Night, Owl!
by Pat Hutchins
Turnabout is fair play when, one night, an owl wakes up the neighbors who have kept him up all day.

Rosie's Walk
by Pat Hutchins
Rosie the hen takes a walk all around the farm and gets home in time for dinner, despite being pursued by a fox.

READ ALOUDS

TEACHER'S READ ALOUD ANTHOLOGY

Rainbow Crow
a Lenape tale retold by Nancy Van Laan
Rainbow Crow makes the journey to the Great Spirit to save all the animals from snow, and in the process is completely transformed.

It Could Always Be Worse
a Yiddish folk tale retold by Margot Zemach
A man seeks a rabbi's advice about how to improve conditions in his noisy and crowded hut, with surprising results.

BIG BOOK OF POEMS
Surprise
by Beverly McLoughland

BIG BOOK OF SONGS
Read a Book
by Marcy Marxer

Surprise

The biggest
Surprise
On the library shelf
Is when you suddenly
Find yourself
Inside a book—
(The hidden you)

You wonder how
The author knew.

Beverly McLoughland

READ A BOOK

If you want adventure,
You want to unwind,
Pick up a good story,
Get out of that old grind,
And read a book!
(Read, read! Read, read a book!)
Read a book!
(Read, read! Read, read a book!)

Also Available—

SING & READ BOOKS AND AUDIOCASSETTES
Read a Book

SONGS AND STORIES AUDIOCASSETTES
Story Songs—including the
Theme Song—and Storytellings

EXPLORING PRINT

**BIG BOOK OF ALPHABET RHYMES AND CHIMES
PLUS RHYME AND CHIME STRIPS**

- **Tt** Toaster Time

- **Kk** A Kettle's for the Kitchen

Toaster Time
Tick tick tick tick tick tick
Toast up a sandwich quick quick quick
Hamwich
Or jamwich
Lick lick lick!
Tick tick tick tick tick tick—stop!
POP!

Eve Merriam

Kk A kettle's for the kitchen,
A key is for the door,
A kitten is for playing with
And keeping on the floor.
Margaret and John Travers Moore

Also Available—

SING A SOUND AUDIOCASSETTES
Songs for language play and for
developing phonemic awareness!

THEME 9: MEET PAT HUTCHINS
Overview for Week 1

LITERATURE	SHARING TIME	READING AND WRITING
1 THEME POEM "Surprise"	**Today's News** and talking about books by Pat Hutchins p. 35	Reading the Theme Poem and Responding through **Poem Talk** and **Journal Writing** pp. 36-37
2 *TITCH*	**Today's News** and singing "Big, Bigger, Biggest" p. 43	Reading *Titch* and Responding through **Book Talk, Journal Writing,** and **Story Theater** pp. 44-45
3 *TITCH*	**Today's News** and reciting the poem "Tommy" p. 49	Rereading *Titch* and Responding through **Book Talk, Creating a Family Portrait,** and **Dramatizing the Story** pp. 50-51
4 READ ALOUD "Rainbow Crow"	**Today's News** and singing the song "Mama Crow" p. 55	Reading "Rainbow Crow" and Responding through **Book Talk, Thank-You Notes to Crow, Creating Picture Books,** and **Story Theater** pp. 56-57
5 *GOOD-NIGHT, OWL!*	**Today's News** and learning a Mother Goose rhyme about owls p. 61	Reading *Good-Night, Owl!* and Responding through **Book Talk, Journal Writing,** and **Story Theater** pp. 62-63

THEME WORD: WRITER

ch theme helps children see themselves from a different spective. This theme helps children see themselves as *ters.*

XPLORING PRINT

coding and Phonics
ters *T, t*
und/Letter Relationships /t/*T, t*
NG: "Together Tomorrow"
46-47

coding and Phonics
ters *T, t*
und/Letter Relationships /t/*T, t*
BOOK OF ALPHABET RHYMES AND CHIMES:
aster Time"
52-53

ncepts of Print
ectionality, Words
YME AND CHIME STRIPS:
aster Time"
58-59

coding and Phonics
ters *T, t*
und/Letter Relationships /t/*T, t*
ncepts of Print
ectionality, Words, Letters
YME AND CHIME STRIPS:
aster Time"
64-65

THEME GOALS AND OUTCOMES

The literature and activities in this theme were carefully selected and reviewed by the program authors and by the multicultural, literature, and educational consultants who worked together to develop the program goals and outcomes.

MULTICULTURAL PERSPECTIVES

Appreciate and value diverse points of view

Become aware of cultural backgrounds, experiences, emotions, and ideas of self and others through literature

Appreciate the literary expression of our contemporary multicultural society and multicultural heritage

Appreciate the universality of literary themes in many cultures and in many different times

Appreciate the significance of traditional literature within a culture

Recognize cultural attitudes and customs in literary selections

PERSONAL INTERESTS AND ATTITUDES

Develop an awareness of the classroom as a community of learners that values cooperation, fair play, and respect for others and for oneself

Select stories and books for personal interests

Develop personal reading and writing interests

Make connections between one's personal life and literature

Choose to read and write for a variety of purposes

Share, review, and recommend books to others

Participate in reading, writing, listening, and viewing activities

Appreciate the artistic interpretation of literature through film, illustration, photography, dance, oral presentations, and other forms of expression

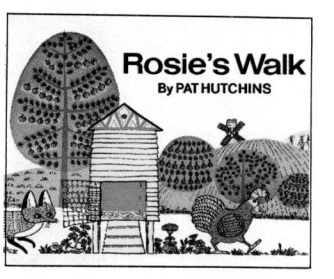

THEME 9: MEET PAT HUTCHINS
Overview for Week 2

LITERATURE	SHARING TIME	READING AND WRITING
6 GOOD-NIGHT, OWL!	**Today's News** and enjoying the poem "Night Creature" p. 67	Rereading *Good-Night, Owl!* and Responding through **Book Talk, Writing a Letter of Complaint,** and **Dramatizing!** pp. 68-69
7 ROSIE'S WALK	**Today's News** and playing "Follow the Leader" p. 73	Reading "Rosie's Walk" and Responding through **Book Talk, Journal Writing,** and **Story Theater** pp. 74-75
8 ROSIE'S WALK	**Today's News** and hearing the poem "Feather or Fur" p. 79	Rereading *Rosie's Walk* and Responding through **Book Talk, Writing About a Walk,** and **Creating Scene with Blocks** pp. 80-81
9 READ ALOUD "It Could Always Be Worse"	**Today's News** and talking about large families p. 85	Reading "It Could Always Be Worse" and Responding through **Book Talk, Extending the Story, Creating a Story Movie,** and **Dramatizing the Story** pp. 86-87
10 TITCH GOOD-NIGHT, OWL! ROSIE'S WALK	**Today's News** and saying the Theme Poem "Surprise" and singing the Theme Song "Read a Book" p. 91	Reviewing the theme trade books and Responding through **Book Talk** and **Journal Writing** pp. 92-93

INTEGRATING LANGUAGE ARTS AND OTHER CURRICULUM AREAS

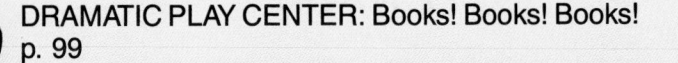

The books on these pages can be shared with children throughout the theme. The books can also be put into the Reading Center so children can read and enjoy them.

More Books by Pat Hutchins

■ CHANGES, CHANGES

(Aladdin, 1971). Cleverly conceived and executed, this wordless book has a simple story line. Two wooden dolls build a house from blocks. When the house catches fire, they rearrange the blocks to form a fire engine. The blocks are again manipulated to create a boat, a truck, and finally, a train engine that takes them to a distant land where they rebuild their block house.

■ DON'T FORGET THE BACON!

(Mulberry, 1975). In this charming circular story, a young boy is sent to market with an oral shopping list. He repeats the list over and over, but as he passes sights en route, the list changes. Amazingly, by the time he returns home, he has remembered what he was sent to purchase—except for the bacon!

■ THE DOORBELL RANG

(Mulberry, 1986). Two children are given a plate of twelve cookies to share as a snack. Each time the doorbell rings, another child arrives and the number of cookies allotted to each decreases. Finally, twelve children are seated around the kitchen table, each eagerly poised to devour his or her one cookie. Again the doorbell sounds. A dilemma. Should they answer the bell? All ends well, as Grandma enters with a fresh batch of cookies.

■ HAPPY BIRTHDAY, SAM

(Mulberry, 1978). Today is a special day for Sam; he is one year older. Sam is disappointed, however, to discover upon awakening that he is still too small to reach the light switch, the sink, or the clothes rod. A package arrives. It is a child-size chair—the perfect height to enable Sam to turn the knob to open the front door and greet Grandpa.

■ 1 HUNTER

(Mulberry, 1982). One unobservant hunter stalks through the jungle, oblivious to the two elephants, three giraffes, four ostriches (and so on), who are observing his progress. A delightful counting book filled with illustrations sure to tickle the funny bone.

■ THE SURPRISE PARTY

(Macmillan, 1969). Rabbit whispers to Owl, "I am having a party tomorrow. It's a surprise." As the secret gets passed from one friend to another, predictably, it changes. The next day, when Rabbit invites his friends to come with him to the surprise party, they each decline. Rabbit must shout out his invitation clearly before the misunderstanding is cleared up. This story lends itself to a discussion about communication.

■ TIDY TITCH

(Greenwillow, 1991). Noticing how tidy Titch's room is, Mother suggests that his older brother and sister clean their rooms, too. Titch volunteers to help by taking each discarded item to his own bedroom. As might be expected, Titch's previously tidy room becomes cluttered beyond recognition.

■ THE VERY WORST MONSTER

(Mulberry, 1985). Hazel Monster is jealous. Everyone in the family makes a fuss over baby Billy, calling him the very worst monster in the world. But Hazel finds a way to demonstrate her own talents and, finally, to accept Billy as well. Humorous illustrations of monster life add to the reader's enjoyment.

■ WHAT GAME SHALL WE PLAY?

(Greenwillow, 1990). "What game shall we play?" asks one animal of another. Before they know it, the animals are playing hide-and-seek as they search for each new friend along the way.

THE WIND BLEW

(Macmillan, 1974). Winner of the British Kate Greenaway Medal, this delightful tale, told in verse and captivatingly illustrated, describes the havoc created by a wind as it picks up, one by one, the townspeople's belongings and carries them, just beyond reach, to the edge of the sea.

WHERE'S THE BABY?

(Greenwillow, 1988). Billy conclusively demonstrates how truly monstrous a baby monster on the loose can be as, room by room, he wrecks the house. Each new escapade is warmly greeted by Grandma who has nothing but praise for his behavior. Alert readers will discover Billy peeking out from behind doors and furniture as the family rushes through the house searching for him.

YOU'LL SOON GROW INTO THEM, TITCH

(Mulberry, 1983). Titch is growing, growing out of his clothes. His older siblings offer hand-me-downs that are clearly too big. "You'll soon grow into them, Titch," they assure him. When it becomes obvious how ridiculous Titch looks, he receives a set of clothing of his own. Throughout the year, Mother's pregnancy has become more and more evident. Finally, on the day the baby arrives home from the hospital, it is Titch's turn to offer clothing and to utter the refrain he has heard for so long: "He'll soon grow into them."

MORE BOOKS ABOUT ANIMALS

ANIMALS OF THE NIGHT

by Merry Banks, illus. by Ronald Himler (Scribners, 1990). When sleepy children go to bed, the nocturnal animals come out of their hiding places to begin their "day." Within a simple text, Banks provides fascinating facts about many of these animals.

FIREFLIES!

by Julie Brinckloe (Macmillan, 1985). The summer evening is aglow with the light of fireflies flickering. The children run barefoot through the grass, capturing the insects in glass jars. One young boy carries his jar of "moonlight" home and places it next to his bed. Soon the light in the jar dims and the boy, in a generous act of kindness, releases the fireflies back into the night.

NIGHT OWLS

by Sharon Phillips Denslow, illus. by Jill Kastner (Bradbury, 1990). Aunt Charlene and William, two night owls, prepare a night picnic. They climb a tree and blow soap bubbles to decorate the night. Listening to the sounds and songs of the night creatures, they are assured that, indeed, something too wonderful to miss happens at night.

RAINBOW CROW: A LENAPE TALE

retold by Nancy Van Laan, illus. by Beatriz Vidal (Knopf, 1989). In this Native American tale, Rainbow Crow saves the animals from the snow and cold that have enveloped the earth. Alone, he seeks help from the Great Sky Spirit, and is given fire. As he journeys home, the fire scorches his multicolored feathers and the smoke turns his sweet voice into a crackle. For his bravery, Crow is rewarded with the gift of freedom.

CROW BOY

by Taro Yashima (Viking, 1983, originally published in 1955). Pat Hutchins and Crow Boy, the hero of this Caldecott Honor book, share a love of crows. Crow Boy learns to imitate the cry of crows on his lonely walks back and forth to the village school from his home on the far side of the mountain. This is a warm and sympathetic story of a young boy's struggle to attain self-assurance and the respect of others.

1

MEET PAT HUTCHINS

LITERATURE

Big Book of Poems: Surprise
  by Beverly McLoughland

Big Book of Songs: Read a Book
  by Marcy Marxer

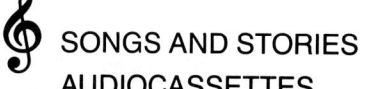 SONGS AND STORIES
AUDIOCASSETTES
STORY SONGS: Read a Book

 SING & READ BOOKS AND
AUDIOCASSETTES
Read a Book

Literature Activity Book: pp. 74–75
  Meet Pat Hutchins

STAFF DEVELOPMENT A to EZ Handbook

  • Emergent Literacy: p. 253

  • Journals: p. 264

Performance Assessment Handbook

HomeWords: Home-School Resources

OTHER RESOURCES

• CHART PAPER
• BIG BOOK STAND
• BIG BOOK POINTER
• TO MAKE JOURNALS:
   STAPLER
   UNLINED PAPER
   CONSTRUCTION
   PAPER

LITERACY SUPPORT:
BUILDING LANGUAGE AND CONCEPTS

For children acquiring English and/or needing more intensive support, you may wish to incorporate the following suggestions into the basic lesson plan.

Encourage children to begin seeing themselves as writers. Have children discuss their journals. Ask them to talk about one or two favorite entries. Then invite volunteers to share what they have written. Guide children to understand that they are all "writers."

SHARING TIME

TODAY'S NEWS

Gather children together and write and read Today's News. Point to each word as you read.

Today we will talk about a writer and artist named Pat Hutchins.

CREATING INTEREST AND BUILDING BACKGROUND

Because motivation matters!

Introduce the theme MEET PAT HUTCHINS by displaying a variety of picture books, including those for this theme. After displaying the letters *P* and *H,* challenge children to use their knowledge of those letters to find the books by Pat Hutchins. As children identify the books, list the book titles on a chart. Read the chart with children. As children discover other books by Pat Hutchins, add the book titles to the chart.

BOOKS BY PAT HUTCHINS

Titch

Good-Night, Owl!

Rosie's Walk

Encourage children who are familiar with any of the listed books to tell about them. Point to the word *writer* in Today's News and share that *writer* is the Theme Word. Tell children that the theme will focus on a famous writer and that they will have opportunities throughout the theme to be writers themselves!

READING AND WRITING

SHARING LITERATURE
"Surprise"

LISTEN TO THE SOUNDS OF POETRY   Invite children to listen as you read the Theme Poem "Surprise" by Beverly McLoughland.

Talk with children about what the lines "Find yourself/ Inside a book," might mean. Encourage children to think about their favorite books and the characters in these books. Do the characters do things that they like to do? Do they sometimes feel like the characters feel in these books? After discussing the poem, reread it.

SEE THE POEM IN PRINT   Display the Theme Poem "Surprise" on pages 28–29 in the *Big Book of Poems*. Explain that the poem children have been listening to and reciting is the poem they can see in the Big Book.

Read the poem again, tracking the print with the Big Book pointer or with your finger.

Surprise

The biggest
Surprise
On the library shelf
Is when you suddenly
Find yourself
Inside a book—
(The *hidden* you)

You wonder how
The author knew.

Beverly McLoughland

Big Book of Poems, pp. 28–29

RESPONDING TO LITERATURE

POEM TALK   Invite children to share their reactions to this poem. You may want to begin by discussing your reaction in order to provide a model for personal involvement with literature. The prompt below will help get the discussion started.

- *Sometimes a character in a book I am reading feels exactly the way I have felt. I think that's what the poet meant about finding the ''hidden you'' inside a book. Has this ever happened to you? Were you surprised?*

JOURNAL WRITING   Create theme journals for children by stapling approximately ten sheets of paper together, or have children bring in journals to use.

Invite children to personalize their journals by decorating the outside cover. Then encourage them to write about the poem ''Surprise'' and their reactions to it.

As children write, model writing in your own journal.

After writing, invite volunteers to share their reactions with the group.

TEAM WORK/THEME WORK THE PAT HUTCHINS CORNER

Introducing the Project: An Author Study
Tell children that all the books in this theme are written by one person, Pat Hutchins.

Let children know that as they work through the theme, they will create a special Pat Hutchins Corner. The Corner will include some of Pat Hutchins's books as well as projects that children will make about Pat Hutchins and her books.

Sing Out!
Generate excitement over the worlds that can be explored in books by having children sing the Theme Song "Read a Book" on pages 28–31 in the *Big Book of Songs.* Play the song on the STORY SONGS AUDIOCASSETTE a few times until children feel comfortable singing along. Then display the *Big Book of Songs.* Point to the words of the song with the Big Book pointer as children sing.

♪ SONGS AND STORIES AUDIOCASSETTES
STORY SONGS: Read a Book

READ A BOOK

If you want adventure,
You want to unwind,
Pick up a good story,
Get out of that old grind,
And read a book!
(Read, read! Read, read a book!)
Read a book!
(Read, read! Read, read a book!)

Big Book of Songs, pages 28–29

Planning

Encourage children to decide as a group on a location within the classroom for the Pat Hutchins Corner. Invite them to place the books for this theme in this area and to browse through them. You may want to take a trip to the library so that children can add more books by Pat Hutchins to the Corner.

Share with children the information on page 40 about Pat Hutchins. Or you may wish to discuss the information a little at a time as you work through the theme.

ABOUT PAT HUTCHINS

Pat Hutchins was born in 1942 in an army camp in Yorkshire, England. She lived there until she and her brother were found wandering across a rifle range during target practice. Then her mother decided it was time to move!

The Hutchins family's new home was in a quiet village surrounded by woods and fields. Pat and her six brothers and sisters often roamed the woods looking for animals and birds and brought home any that were sick or injured. One bird, a young crow who had fallen from his nest, became a special family pet and was named Sooty. Sooty became quite well known in the village, walking behind Pat or sitting on her head while she rode her brother's bike!

Besides the crow and the seven children, there were also a kitten who was terrified of the crow, five pigeons (until the kitten grew and climbed into the pigeons' loft!), several white mice, a hedgehog, and a dog. Pat says, "It was very cheerful and in spite of the overcrowding, everyone was welcome there."

When she was quite young, Pat enjoyed drawing pictures of the English countryside. Her interest in drawing increased at age seven, when an elderly couple offered her a bar of chocolate for each picture she drew! Often, to escape from the noise of the house, Pat and Sooty would set off across the fields, and while he rooted for grubs and worms, she would sketch. When she was sixteen years old, she began art school. After graduating from college, she went to London to work in an advertising agency.

Pat always dreamed of illustrating children's books, so when she moved to New York, she tried to find work as an illustrator. She showed her drawings to various publishing companies. The Macmillan Publishing Company liked her work. They asked her to try writing a story, a thing she thought she could never do, and *Rosie's Walk* was created!

Today Pat Hutchins lives in London with her husband and their two sons, Morgan and Sam. She is still writing and drawing, and recently published a new book, *Tidy Titch.* She says of her stories, "The basic idea is the most difficult part, to try to do something original. When I have an idea, I sit down and work out the best way of putting the idea across in book form; then I write the story and design the layout. It's very satisfying to know it's all your own work, from the original idea to the finished artwork."

INTO THE LEARNING CENTERS

You may wish to place the Sing & Read Book and its audiocassette for "Read a Book" in the Reading Center and invite children to listen to the tape as they read the book. See page 98.

2 MEET PAT HUTCHINS

LITERACY SUPPORT:

BUILDING LANGUAGE AND CONCEPTS

LITERATURE
Titch
    by Pat Hutchins

 **BiG BOOK**

LISTENING LIBRARY
AUDIOCASSETTES: Titch

SONGS AND STORIES
AUDIOCASSETTES
STORY SONGS:
Big, Bigger, Biggest

SING & READ BOOKS AND
AUDIOCASSETTES: Read a Book

EXPLORING PRINT

SING A SOUND AUDIOCASSETTES
Together Tomorrow

Learning the Code: T, t

Practice Book: p. 41

BRWL: Letterbook T(9)

STAFF DEVELOPMENT A to EZ Handbook
  • Big Books: p. 246
  • Shared Reading: p. 299

Performance Assessment Handbook

OTHER RESOURCES

• BIG BOOK POINTER
• BIG BOOK STAND
• WORD MASK
• JOURNALS

For children acquiring English and/or needing more intensive support, you may wish to incorporate the following suggestions into the basic lesson plan.

During the reading of *Titch,* use the illustrations to help children understand the difficult words in the text (*pinwheel, spade, wooden whistle*). Beginning on page 10, discuss what Titch's older brother and sister have. Then let children predict what Titch will have on the subsequent page. Help children understand that Titch always gets the smallest things.

Sharing Time

TODAY'S NEWS

Gather children together as you write and read Today's News. Point out the question mark at the end of the second sentence. Ask children to talk about how they have grown since they were babies.

All living things grow. How have you grown?

CREATING INTEREST AND BUILDING BACKGROUND

Because motivation matters!

To introduce children to some of the concepts that Pat Hutchins uses in *Titch,* sing the song "Big, Bigger, Biggest" together.

Big, Bigger, Biggest

I saw a **big** dog.
I saw a **bigger** dog.
I saw the **biggest** dog of all.

I saw a **tiny** bug.
I saw a **tinier** bug.
I saw the **tiniest** bug of all.

I saw a **small** bird.
I saw a **smaller** bird.
I saw the **smallest** bird of all.

I ate a **good** apple.
I ate a **better** apple.
I ate the **best** apple of all.

I saw a **nice** play.
I saw a **nicer** play.
I saw the **nicest** play of all.

I wore a **warm** sweater.
I wore a **warmer** sweater.
I wore the **warmest** sweater of all.

—Ella Jenkins

SONGS AND STORIES AUDIOCASSETTES
STORY SONGS: Big, Bigger, Biggest

READING AND WRITING

SHARING LITERATURE
Titch

BIG BOOK

LOOK IT OVER Display the Big Book of *Titch*. Explain that the Big Book lets everyone see the words and pictures in the book. Place a little book version of the Big Book in the Reading Center. Let children know that the little book version is there for them to look through. Hold up the cover of the Big Book of *Titch*, reading the title, pointing to it as you read. Invite a child to point to the boy Titch and to find the word *Titch*. Ask children if they know who the author and illustrator must be! Read together the title of the book and the author's name.

Invite children to predict what the story might be about by examining and talking about the items pictured on the cover. Open the book to display the front and back covers. Children may enjoy discovering how the images on the front and back covers are related.

SHARE THE STORY Invite children to describe and compare sizes of the slippers on the page before the title page. Then talk about the clothing hanging on the line on the title page.

Read the dedication together and invite children to guess who Darren is. To whom might the mittens belong?

As you read, point to each word or letter.

About the Author/Illustrator

Pat Hutchins called this book *Titch*. Later she wrote two other books about the character Titch: *You'll Soon Grow into Them, Titch* and *Tidy Titch*. He has become quite a famous character!

His sister Mary
was a bit bigger.

And his brother Pete
was a lot bigger.

8

9

RESPONDING TO LITERATURE

BOOK TALK   Invite children to share their wonderings and comments about the story. Model your own response to the story by sharing your ideas.

- *You know what I thought about when I read* Titch? *I remember being the youngest in my family and always wanting to do what the big kids did! It was hard waiting to grow up!*

- *Did you like the ending? I didn't know how Pat Hutchins was going to end this story! The ending made me feel happy!*

JOURNAL WRITING   Invite children to write about their favorite parts of the story in their journals. Model journal writing in your own journal as children write and draw. Then invite them to share what they have written with each other.

STORY THEATER   Invite children to add sound effects and actions as you reread the story. Encourage them to vary the loudness of the sounds and the intensity of the actions according to the size of the objects mentioned.

TEAM WORK/THEME WORK
Do any of the children want to make their responses to *Titch* a part of the Pat Hutchins Corner? Invite volunteers to tape record what they've written in their journals and place the tape in the Corner for others to hear. See pages 38–41 and 94–95.

INTO THE LEARNING CENTERS
Today might be a good day to direct children to the Reading Center where they can write the title *Titch* on a leaf of green construction paper and add it to the book tree. See page 98.

Today would also be a good day to have children visit the Art Center to make handprints. See page 103.

Laura chose to write first and then illustrate her writing. She is moving into developmental spelling. Laura read her message like this: "The little boy was sad because his brothers and sisters had bigger toys."

45

EXPLORING PRINT LEARNING THE CODE

In the Exploring Print lessons for this theme, children will learn about the letters T, t and K, k and the sounds they represent. Take advantage of opportunities to point out these letters and the sounds they represent as you share Today's News, as you talk with children about their writing, and as you reread the theme-related trade books.

DECODING AND PHONICS

LETTERS: *T, t*
SOUND/LETTER RELATIONSHIPS: /t/T, t

Developing Phonemic Awareness
Remind children that they just heard a story about Titch, a little boy who is very close to his brother and sister. Here is a song that the three children might sing at the end of the day.

Sing or play on the SING A SOUND AUDIOCASSETTE "Together Tomorrow," and encourage children to join in. Sing the song again and have children stand up when they hear the phrase *together tomorrow*. Point out that *together* and *tomorrow* begin with the same sound. Say these words again, accenting the beginning sound.

Together Tomorrow

I don't like to say good-bye.
I don't want today to end.
But we will be happy together tomorrow,
Together tomorrow again.

Together tomorrow,
Together tomorrow, my friend.
Tonight when I'm sleeping, I'll dream of us being
Together tomorrow again.

—John Forster and Tom Chapin

SING A SOUND AUDIOCASSETTES
Together Tomorrow

Developing Print Awareness
Write the song title and the last line of "Together Tomorrow" on the chalkboard or on chart paper. Encourage children to say the title and last line with you and to follow as you point to each word.

Together Tomorrow

Together tomorrow again.

Use a word mask to frame a capital and lowercase *t* in the word *Together* and *tomorrow*.

- *Let's look at some t's together. Here is a capital, or uppercase, T in the word Together. What other word can you find in the title that begins with capital T?*

- *Here is a lowercase t in the word tomorrow.*

- *The letter t stands for the sound you hear at the beginning of the words together and tomorrow. Say together with me.*

Encourage children to come forward to point to and trace over with their fingers uppercase and lowercase *t*'s in the title and last line.

You might want to create a "Together" bulletin board using construction paper to show a scene of things that people can do together. Encourage children to draw and label pictures of other items whose names begin with the sound /t/. Add these to the scene.

3
MEET PAT HUTCHINS

TITCH
by PAT HUTCHINS

LITERATURE
Titch
by Pat Hutchins

LISTENING LIBRARY
AUDIOCASSETTES
Titch

SING & READ BOOKS AND
AUDIOCASSETTES
Read a Book

EXPLORING PRINT
*Big Book of Alphabet Rhymes
and Chimes:*
Toaster Time

Alphabet Poster for Tt

ABC cards

Literature Activity Book: p. 76
Learning the Code: T, t

Practice Book: p. 42

BRWL: Letterbook T(9)

 **STAFF DEVELOPMENT** A to EZ Handbook
• Masking: p. 273
• Retelling: p. 295

Performance Assessment Handbook

OTHER RESOURCES

• CHART PAPER
• BIG BOOK POINTER
• BIG BOOK STAND
• MARKERS
• WORD MASK
• INDEX CARDS

SHARING TIME

TODAY'S NEWS

As children gather around to watch you write and hear you read the message, invite them to repeat the questions and discuss them with a partner. Point out the question marks, which show that you are curious about something and that you are asking questions.

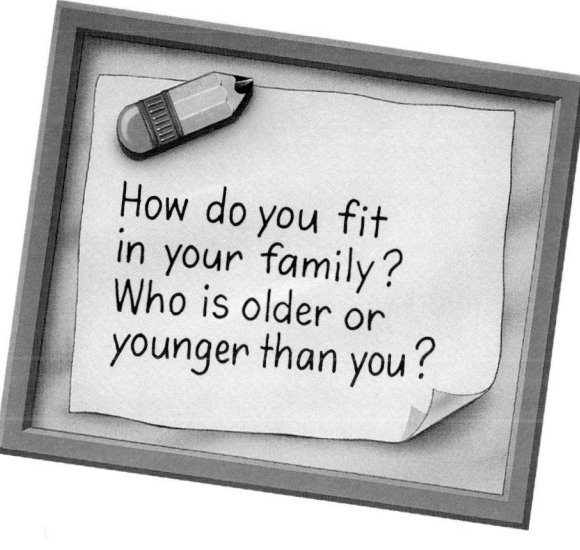

How do you fit in your family? Who is older or younger than you?

Make a chart of children's responses to the questions. Include yourself on the chart and save it for future use.

Oldest	Middle	Youngest	Only Child
José	Marta	Susan	Jon
Ana	Philip	Alex	Alice

CREATING INTEREST AND BUILDING BACKGROUND

Because motivation matters!

Share the poem "Tommy" with children and ask if they are reminded of the ending of *Titch*. Ask whether Titch may have felt the same way as Tommy.

Write the poem on chart paper and invite pairs of children to practice reciting it together, with one child saying the first verse and the other child saying the second verse. Display the chart in the Reading or Writing Center.

Tommy

I put a seed into the ground
And said, "I'll watch it grow."
I watered it and cared for it
As well as I could know.

One day I walked in my back yard,
And oh, what did I see!
My seed had popped itself right out,
Without consulting me.

—Gwendolyn Brooks

READING AND WRITING

SHARING LITERATURE
Titch

BIG BOOK

REREAD THE STORY Invite children to listen again to *Titch.* On this rereading, invite children who have said they are the oldest or are only children to chime in with Pete, children who are in the middle to chime in with Mary, and children who are the youngest to chime in with Titch.

PRINT AWARENESS

Repetition
Count the number of times the word *big* occurs in the story. Invite volunteers to point to it as you reread the story. Make a chart with children to help them notice the repetitive pattern in the story. Invite children to draw pictures of each item described in the book.

Biggest   Bigger   Little

Pete had a great big bike.

10

Mary had a big bike.

11

RESPONDING TO LITERATURE

BOOK TALK Invite children to look carefully at the simple illustrations and use of white space in *Titch*.

- *I found myself watching Titch. His face changed as the story moved along. Let's see if we can imagine what he might be saying in each picture!*

- *Did you like the sound of Pat Hutchins's words as she described what each child had? I especially liked the way she described the kites flying over trees and houses and then when she wrote about Titch's pinwheel, she didn't use many words. That made me realize that Titch must have felt just the way her illustrations looked!*

CREATING A FAMILY PORTRAIT Invite children to draw pictures of their family members. Encourage them to make themselves the size they really are in relation to family members. Label the drawings with everybody's names and positions in the family (oldest, middle, youngest).

DRAMATIZING THE STORY Divide the class into sets of three. One child in each group can play the role of Pete, one can play the role of Mary, and one can play the role of Titch. Give the groups of three some time to practice retelling the story. Then invite volunteer groups to act out the story for the rest of the class, using their invented dialog.

TEAM WORK/THEME WORK
Invite children to place their family portraits in the Pat Hutchins Corner. See pages 38–41 and 94–95.

INTO THE LEARNING CENTERS
Today would be a good day to have children visit the Math Center where they can explore the concepts of *big, bigger, little,* and *tiny* by measuring things in the classroom. See page 102.

Exploring Print   LEARNING THE CODE

DECODING AND PHONICS

LETTERS: *T, t*
SOUND/LETTER RELATIONSHIPS: */t/T, t*

Developing Phonemic Awareness
Remind children that they are learning about the sounds of language and the letters that stand for those

sounds. Ask children to listen as you read "Toaster Time" on page 28 in the *Big Book of Alphabet Rhymes and Chimes*. As you come to words that begin with *t*, slightly emphasize the initial sound. Repeat the rhyme a few times, encouraging children to chime in.

- *Listen to the sound you hear at the beginning of* toaster *and* time. *What other words do we know that begin with the same sound?*

Toaster Time

Tick tick tick tick tick tick tick
Toast up a sandwich quick quick quick
Hamwich
Or jamwich
Lick lick lick!
Tick tick tick tick tick tick—stop!
    POP!

Eve Merriam

Big Book of Alphabet Rhymes and Chimes,
pages 28–29

turtle

Developing Print Awareness

Display "Toaster Time" on pages 28–29 of the *Big Book of Alphabet Rhymes and Chimes* and say the rhyme with children. Use the Big Book pointer or a word mask to point out or frame words that begin with uppercase or lowercase *t*.

Reread the rhyme and encourage children to act out the "POP!" of the toast as it comes out of the toaster.

Then display the Alphabet Poster and ABC cards for Tt, or write the letters on the chalkboard or on cards of your own.

Have children compare the *t*'s on the Big Book page with the letters on the poster and cards. Encourage children to talk about the turtle pictured on the poster.

Point out to children that many different words begin with *t* or *T*. Talk about any children's names that do.

■ **Literature Activity Book:** page 76

Invite pairs of children to go on a Word Hunt around the room to find words on charts, signs, and in books that begin with the same sound and letter as *together* and *tomorrow*. Have them copy the words on cards and then share and display them on the bulletin board.

INTO THE LEARNING CENTERS
Encourage children to visit the Hands On! Language Center to use the resources there for more activities with sounds and letters. See page 100.

53

4 MEET PAT HUTCHINS

LITERATURE

Read Aloud Anthology
   "Rainbow Crow"
   a Lenape tale
   retold by Nancy Van Laan

SONGS AND STORIES
AUDIOCASSETTES
STORY SONGS: Mama Crow

SONGS AND STORIES
AUDIOCASSETTES
STORYTELLINGS: Rainbow Crow

 SING & READ BOOKS AND
AUDIOCASSETTES
Read a Book

EXPLORING PRINT

*Big Book of Alphabet Rhymes
and Chimes:*
   Toaster Time

Rhyme and Chime Strips:
   Toaster Time

Learning the Code: T, t

BRWL: Letterbook T(9)

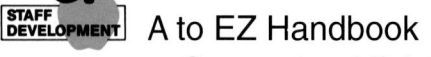

STAFF DEVELOPMENT   A to EZ Handbook
   • Concepts of Print: p. 248
   • Music and Movement: p. 274

Performance Assessment Handbook

OTHER RESOURCES
• WORLD MAP OR GLOBE
• CHART PAPER
• MARKERS
• MUSICAL INSTRUMENTS SUCH AS BELLS OR TRIANGLES
• BIG BOOK POINTER
• BIG BOOK STAND
• WORD MASK
• POCKET CHART AND STAND

SHARING TIME

TODAY'S NEWS

Write Today's News and then read it to children, pointing to each word as you read.

People everywhere tell stories.
Today we will hear one about a crow.

CREATING INTEREST AND BUILDING BACKGROUND

Because motivation matters!

Relate this story to Pat Hutchins's life by reminding children that when Hutchins was growing up, she and her six brothers and sisters often roamed the woods looking for animals and birds and brought home any that were sick or injured. One bird, a young crow who had fallen from his nest, became a special family pet and was named Sooty.

Tell children that today's story is about a crow like Sooty. Explain that many years ago, people all over the world made up "why" tales to explain why things in nature are the way they are. Prepare children for "Rainbow Crow" by generating a list of "why" questions about crows.

"Why" Questions	
Why can crows fly?	Mara
Why do crows have wings?	John
Why are crows black?	Vijay

To generate anticipation for the story, sing "Mama Crow." Play the song on the STORY SONGS AUDIOCASSETTE a few times until children feel comfortable singing along.

Mama Crow

Chorus
Mama, mama crow, fly up to the mountain.
Mama, mama crow, fly up so high.
Mama, mama crow, fly up to the mountain.
What do you see as you pass by?

I see 12 deer running down the mountain,
11 buffalo running so free,
10 camp fires with people stirring food pots,
9 ears of corn just a-waiting for me.

Chorus

I see 8 streams a-rolling down the mountain,
7 little fishes just a-swimming so free,
6 sparks of lightning on the mountain,
5 rain clouds just a-waiting for me.

Chorus

I see 4 stars rising up the mountain,
3 little crows a-waiting in their nest,
2 hoot owls saying night is coming,
1 moon telling me it's time to rest.

Chorus

What do you see as you pass by?

—Sarah Pirtle

♪ SONGS AND STORIES AUDIOCASSETTES
STORY SONGS: Mama Crow

READING AND WRITING

SHARING LITERATURE
"Rainbow Crow"

SHARE THE STORY   You may choose to play the STORYTELLINGS AUDIOCASSETTE instead of reading or telling the story yourself. Afterward, invite children to describe their favorite parts of the story and tell why they liked them. Then reread these parts to the class.

■ **Read Aloud Anthology:** pages 72–75

About the Story

Developing Multicultural Awareness

Share with children that this story was first told to the author Nancy Van Laan by Bill "Whippoorwill" Thompson, a Lenape elder. The Lenape Indians, who are also known as the Lenni Lenape or the Delaware, originally lived in what is now New Jersey and eastern Pennsylvania. Invite children to find these states on a map or globe.

♪ SONGS AND STORIES AUDIOCASSETTES
STORYTELLINGS: Rainbow Crow

RESPONDING TO LITERATURE

BOOK TALK   Invite children to share their reactions to the story. You may wish to prompt the discussion with these questions.

- *I was surprised that Great Sky Spirit could not stop the snow. Did that surprise you? What else in the story did you wonder about?*

- *Do you think this story tells the real reason why crows are black? Why do you think so? Did the story answer any other questions you have about crows?*

THANK-YOU NOTES TO CROW   Invite children to write notes to Crow, thanking him for his actions. They may wish to write the notes as the animals that Crow saved, or as themselves, thanking Crow for bringing to earth the "grandfather of all fires." Encourage volunteers to share their work with the group.

CREATING PICTURE BOOKS   Invite children to work in small groups to illustrate various events in the story. Talk with them about the important events:

1. Rainbow Crow tells other animals he will talk to Sky Spirit.
2. Sky Spirit gives Rainbow Crow fire.
3. Rainbow Crow melts snow with fire, which turns his feathers black.
4. Rainbow Crow observes the tiny rainbows in his feathers and feels content.

Children in each group should decide who will illustrate each event. When the illustrations are complete, they can put them in the proper sequence. When completed, staple each group's book along the spine. Encourage children to retell the story using the books.

STORY THEATER   As you reread the story, encourage children to act it out. Groups of children may make the sounds of the animals, move their hands to portray the falling snow, or move their bodies to show the flight of Rainbow Crow and the animals dancing. Children may also use classroom musical instruments, such as bells or triangles, to create the songs of Rainbow Crow and the other animals.

EXPLORING PRINT   DEVELOPING CONCEPTS OF PRINT

Using the Rhyme and Chime Strips gives children a Hands On! Language experience that allows them to explore important concepts of print.

CONCEPTS OF PRINT
Directionality, Words

Developing Print Awareness
Display pages 28–29 in the *Big Book of Alphabet Rhymes and Chimes* and encourage children to recite the rhyme with you as you use the Big Book pointer to point to each word.

Use a word mask to frame the words in the title. Point out the space between the two words. Explain that spaces help readers see where one word ends and another begins.

Use strips and word cards cut from the Rhyme and Chime Strips for "Toaster Time" to build the rhyme in the pocket chart. Recite the rhyme as you build it in the pocket chart and encourage children to recite it with you.

Toaster Time

Tick tick tick tick tick tick tick
Toast up a sandwich quick quick quick
Hamwich
Or jamwich
Lick lick lick!
Tick tick tick tick tick tick—stop!
    POP!

Eve Merriam

Big Book of Alphabet Rhymes and Chimes,
pages 28–29

Tick	tick	tick	tick	tick	tick	tick

Toast up a sandwich	quick	quick	quick

Hamwich

Or jamwich

Lick	lick	lick!

Tick	tick	tick	tick	tick	tick–	stop!

POP!

Use the picture cards to have children match the pictures of bread in the toaster, a ham sandwich, a jam sandwich, and toast popping as you and the children recite the appropriate phrase.

Encourage children to pick out word cards with words that end the same way or rhyme:

tick   quick   lick

Ask children what they notice about these words.

As you replace the word cards in the pocket chart, invite children to recite the rhyme with you again.

INTO THE LEARNING CENTERS

Allow children to use the *Big Book of Alphabet Rhymes and Chimes*, the Rhyme and Chime Strips, and the word cards to build the rhyme "Toaster Time" in the pocket chart in the Hands On! Language Center. See page 100.

Toaster Time

Tick tick tick tick tick tick tick
Toast up a sandwich quick quick quick
Hamwich
Or jamwich
Lick lick lick!
Tick tick tick tick tick tick–stop!
POP!

Eve Merriam

5 MEET PAT HUTCHINS

LITERATURE
Good-Night, Owl!
by Pat Hutchins

SING & READ BOOKS AND
AUDIOCASSETTES
Read a Book

EXPLORING PRINT
Alphabet Poster for Tt

Rhyme and Chime Strips:
Toaster Time

Learning the Code: T, t

BRWL: Letterbook T(9)

STAFF DEVELOPMENT A to EZ Handbook
- Nursery Rhymes: p. 276
- Pocket Chart: p. 285

Performance Assessment Handbook

GOOD-NIGHT, OWL!

PAT HUTCHINS

OTHER RESOURCES
- CHART PAPER
- POCKET CHART AND STAND
- JOURNALS

LITERACY SUPPORT:
Building Language and Concepts

For children acquiring English and/or needing more intensive support, you may wish to incorporate the following suggestions into the basic lesson plan.

Before reading the selection, build background about owls. Show children a picture of an owl and discuss their physical attributes, where they live, what they eat, and when they sleep.

Also, before reading the selection, encourage children to brainstorm a list of animals that make trees their homes: squirrels, monkeys, and birds.

SHARING TIME

TODAY'S NEWS

As children gather around for you to write and read Today's News, place them in pairs to discuss the message.

Think about the sounds you might hear if you were in the forest.

CREATING INTEREST AND BUILDING BACKGROUND

Because motivation matters!

To prepare children for a book about owls and their habits, talk about what children already know about owls. Then share the following owl poem with the group. You may wish to write it on chart paper to display to the class.

Of all the gay birds that e'er I did see,
The owl is the fairest by far to me:
For all the day long she sits in a tree,
And when the night comes away flies she.

—Mother Goose

Owl Poem

Of all the gay birds that e'er I did see,
The owl is the fairest by far to me:
For all the day long she sits in a tree,
And when the night comes away flies she.

Mother Goose

READING AND WRITING

SHARING LITERATURE
Good-Night, Owl!

LOOK IT OVER   Hold up the cover of *Good-Night, Owl!*, reading the words of the title and tracking them with your finger as you read. Invite a child to point to the author/illustrator's name, Pat Hutchins.

Talk with children about what they notice on the cover. Encourage speculation about what the title means. *Who is saying "good-night" to Owl?*

Show children the title pages and point out how the words are formed with sticks of wood from trees. Children may enjoy matching the animals on the cover with the animals on these pages. Help them identify the cuckoo, squirrel, crows, starlings, doves, robin, jays, woodpecker, and sparrows.

About the Author/Illustrator

Pat Hutchins says her ideas for *Good-Night, Owl!* came from the realization that a tree is the home of hundreds of birds, insects, and animals. Hutchins, who has a passion for wildlife, especially birds, was delighted to paint so many different kinds of wildlife for one story.

SHARE THE STORY   As you read, track the words with your finger. Make the sounds of the various animals as you read.

The woodpecker pecked,
rat-a-tat! rat-a-tat!
and Owl tried to sleep.

13

12

RESPONDING TO LITERATURE

BOOK TALK   Invite children to share their personal reactions to the story. Share your own reactions, too. The following prompts may broaden the discussion.

- *I've never known exactly how owls sound. I always thought they made more of a hooting sound than a screech. Now Pat Hutchins makes me wonder! Have you ever heard owls at night?*

- *Were you surprised by the ending? What did you expect?*

- *I loved the sounds of the animals! They made me realize that words can help you know what sounds creatures really make.*

JOURNAL WRITING   Invite children to draw or write in their journals about their favorite parts of the book. You may wish to write about *your* favorite part of the book. Share your writing with children and encourage children to do the same.

STORY THEATER   Invite children to dramatize *Good-Night, Owl!* Begin with Owl sitting quietly with eyes closed as you or another narrator says, "Owl tried to sleep." Then have children represent each of the animals in the book that sit near Owl, making the sounds indicated in the story. After each new animal joins the group, repeat "And Owl tried to sleep." Encourage the child playing the part of Owl to use facial expressions to indicate Owl's feelings about the noises.

After the last animal has arrived, invite all the animals to repeat their sounds, one after the other, with no narration. Then, all the animals fall asleep, to be awakened at the end by Owl's loud screech!

This drawing was very important in Frederick's response. He is at the stage of early developmental spelling. Frederick read his message like this: "This is when the owl woke all the animals up."

TEAM WORK/THEME WORK
Today might be a good day to take the children to the library in order to find other books by Pat Hutchins. Afterwards, have children place the library books in the Pat Hutchins Corner. Set aside time to read the new books to the class. See pages 38–41 and 94–95.

INTO THE LEARNING CENTERS
Invite children to visit the Science Center to make a chart of animals and the sounds that they make. See page 105.

EXPLORING PRINT

LEARNING THE CODE
DEVELOPING CONCEPTS OF PRINT

HANDS ON LANGUAGE

DECODING AND PHONICS

LETTERS: *T, t*
SOUND/LETTER RELATIONSHIPS: /t/*T, t*

CONCEPTS OF PRINT
Directionality, Words, Letters

Developing Phonemic Awareness
Remind children that they have been learning about the sound heard at the beginning of words like *Titch, tricycle, trumpet, trees, tried, to, twit-twit, tiny, tip, tail, toaster,* and *time* (words found in *Titch; Good-Night, Owl;* "Rainbow Crow"; as well as "Toaster Time"). Ask children to suggest other words that have the same beginning sound.

Developing Print Awareness
Display the Alphabet Poster for Tt and point to the word *turtle.* Frame the letter *t* in the word. Remind children that the letter *t* stands for the sound heard at the beginning of the word *turtle.*

Use the word cards from the Rhyme and Chime Strips for "Toaster Time" to build the rhyme as shown below.

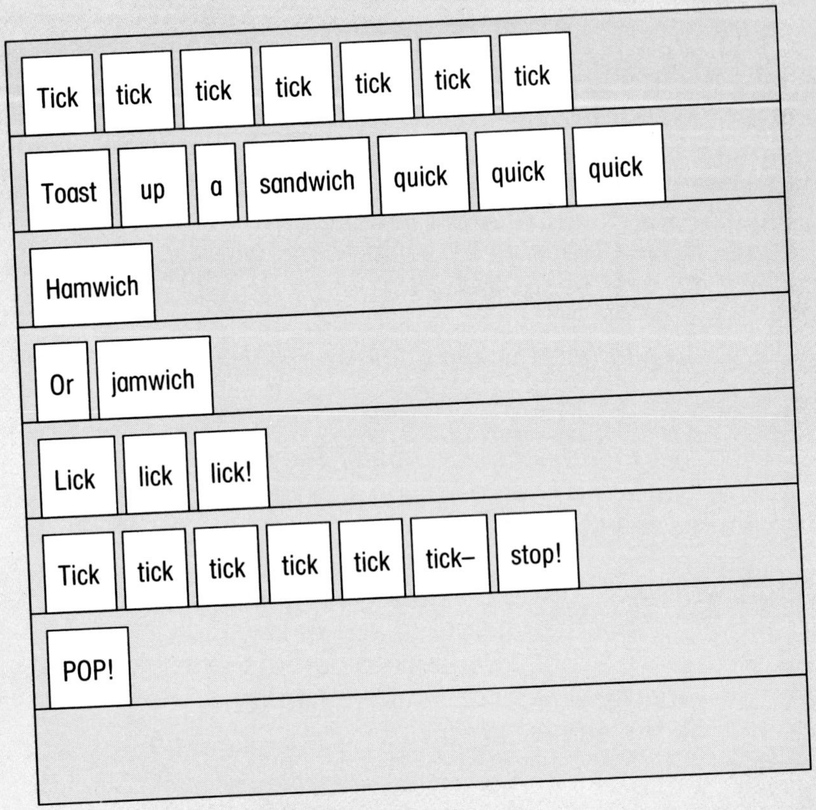

Tick tick tick tick tick tick tick
Toast up a sandwich quick quick quick
Hamwich
Or jamwich
Lick lick lick!
Tick tick tick tick tick tick– stop!
POP!

Encourage children to say the rhyme with you as you point to each word with the Big Book pointer. Have children clap each time they hear a word with the same beginning sound as *turtle*.

Ask children to recite the rhyme and clap again. This time remove any word card for which children did not clap.

Tick	tick	tick	tick	tick	tick	tick
Toast						

Tick	tick	tick	tick	tick	tick–

Frame the first letter in each word left in the pocket chart and have children name it as *t*. Emphasize that the letter *t* stands for the sound heard at the beginning of the words *toaster* and *time*. Use letter cards for *T* and *t* from the Rhyme and Chime Strips and match them to the words that begin with those letters.

Review all the charts and other print resources in the classroom to find words that begin with the same sound and letter as *toaster*.

INTO THE LEARNING CENTERS
Using letter stamps, sponge letters, and magnetic letters in the Hands On! Language Center is a motivating way for children to experiment with print. See page 100.

6

MEET PAT HUTCHINS

LITERATURE
Good-Night, Owl!
   by Pat Hutchins

 SING & READ BOOKS AND
AUDIOCASSETTES
Read a Book

EXPLORING PRINT
SING A SOUND AUDIOCASSETTES
Kookaburra

Learning the Code: K, k

Practice Book: p. 43

BRWL: Letterbook K–Q(21)

STAFF DEVELOPMENT A to EZ Handbook
   • Dramatization: p. 252
   • Phonemic Awareness: p. 281

Performance Assessment Handbook

OTHER RESOURCES
• CHART PAPER
• MARKERS
• CONSTRUCTION PAPER
   FOR COSTUMES SUCH
   AS MASKS, BEAKS,
   AND WINGS

Sharing Time

TODAY'S NEWS

As you write and read Today's News, ask children to draw either a sun or a moon on slips of paper. Collect their responses and then tally them. Share the results with the class.

Are you a day person ☼ or a night person ☾?

CREATING INTEREST AND BUILDING BACKGROUND

Because motivation matters!

Talk about animals that are awake at night, such as raccoons, skunks, and owls, and people who do their jobs at night, such as truckers, hospital attendants, and police officers.

To invite children to explore the habits of nocturnal animals, share the following poem. You may wish to write it on the chalkboard or on chart paper so you can continue to share it throughout the week.

Night Creature

I like
the quiet breathing
of the night,

the tree talk
the wind-swish
the star light.

Day is
glare-y
loud
scary.
Day bustles.

Night rustles.
I like
night.

—Lilian Moore

READING AND WRITING

SHARING LITERATURE
Good-Night, Owl!

REREAD THE STORY   Invite children to listen again to *Good-Night, Owl!* On this rereading, invite children to chime in as you read "and Owl tried to sleep."

PRINT AWARENESS

Sound Words
Make a list of the animals in *Good-Night, Owl!* and their sounds.

Repeat the sounds made by the animals. Explain that Pat Hutchins wanted readers to know exactly how the noises sounded so she wrote them that way.

The robin peeped,
pip pip,
and Owl tried to sleep.

20

21

68

PHONEMIC AWARENESS

Initial Sounds: /t/t
Display page 4 of *Good Night, Owl!* and ask children where owl is trying to sleep. Emphasize the initial sound /t/ as you repeat the word *tree*. Then read page 5, asking children to listen for any words that begin with the same sound as the word *tree*. Next, display pages 14 and 15, again asking children to identify any words that begin with the same sound as *tree*.

RESPONDING TO LITERATURE

BOOK TALK　　Invite children to share their reactions to Owl's preference for sleeping during the day and to talk about the very specific setting of the story. You may want to use some of the prompts below to get the discussion started.

- *What could Owl and the other animals have done to make everybody happy? I thought maybe Owl would move to another tree, but perhaps he wanted to be with the other animals. What do you think?*

- *What parts of Pat Hutchins's story were interesting to you?*

WRITING A LETTER OF COMPLAINT　Invite children to pretend to be Owl and write letters complaining that they never get any sleep during the day. Encourage them to think of solutions to Owl's problem. You may wish to share a letter from a newspaper written to complain about a specific problem. As children write, write your own letter to the animals. Invite children to share their letters when they are finished.

DRAMATIZING　　Write the names of the characters (28, including 10 bees) on slips of paper and invite children to choose a piece of paper that will tell them their part in a play version of *Good-Night, Owl!* Simple costumes such as masks or beaks can be made out of paper, or for more elaborate costumes, wings or capes can be decorated with paper feathers.

TEAM WORK/THEME WORK
Invite volunteers to place their letters from Owl in the Pat Hutchins Corner. Set aside time to write a group letter to Pat Hutchins on chart paper and display this letter along with those from Owl. See pages 38–41 and 94–95.

INTO THE LEARNING CENTERS
You may wish to take this opportunity to have children visit the Science Center where they can draw pictures of and write about animals that sleep during the day and are awake during the night. See page 105.

EXPLORING PRINT LEARNING THE CODE

In the Exploring Print lessons for this theme, children will learn about T, t and K, k and the sounds they represent. Take advantage of opportunities to point out these letters and the sounds they represent as you share Today's News, as you talk with children about their writing, and as you reread the theme-related trade books.

DECODING AND PHONICS

LETTERS: *K, k*
SOUND/LETTER RELATIONSHIPS: /k/K, k

Developing Phonemic Awareness
Remind children that in *Good-Night, Owl!* Owl screeched and woke everyone up. Here is a song about another type of bird that has a cry that sounds like someone laughing loudly. Sing or play "Kookaburra" and encourage children to join in.

> **Kookaburra**
>
> Kookaburra sits in the old gum tree,
> Merry, merry king of the bush is he,
> Laugh, kookaburra, laugh, kookaburra,
> Gay your life must be.

♪ SING A SOUND AUDIOCASSETTES
Kookaburra

Developing Print Awareness
Write the song title and first and second lines of "Kookaburra" on the chalkboard or on chart paper. Encourage children to say the title and first two lines with you and to follow as you point to each word.

> Kookaburra
>
> Kookaburra sits in the old gum tree,
> Merry, merry king of the bush is he,

Use a word mask to frame a capital *K* in the word *Kookaburra* and the lowercase *k* in the word *king*.

- *Let's look at some k's together. Here is a capital, or uppercase, K in the word Kookaburra in the title. What word in the first line begins with a capital K?*

- *Here is a lowercase k in the word* king.

- *The letter k stands for the sound you hear at the beginning of the word Kookaburra. Say Kookaburra with me.*

king kangaroo

katydid and kite

koala in a kayak

kookaburra with a kaleidoscope

Encourage children to come foward to point to and trace over with their fingers the uppercase and lowercase *k*'s in the title and first and second lines.

You might want to create a Word Wall for the letter *k*, like the one shown at left.

Encourage children to add "k" animal words to the Word Wall.

7

MEET PAT HUTCHINS

BUILDING LANGUAGE AND CONCEPTS

LITERATURE
Rosie's Walk
  by Pat Hutchins

SING & READ BOOKS AND
AUDIOCASSETTES
Read a Book

EXPLORING PRINT
Big Book of Alphabet Rhymes and Chimes:
  A Kettle's for the Kitchen

Alphabet Poster for Kk

ABC cards

Literature Activity Book: p. 77
Learning the Code: K, k
Practice Book: p. 44

BRWL: Letterbook K–Q(21)

STAFF DEVELOPMENT A to EZ Handbook
  • Invented Spelling: p. 260
  • Language Experience Writing: p. 268

Performance Assessment Handbook

OTHER RESOURCES

• STORY PROPS SUCH AS TABLE, BLUE PAPER, TWIGS, CHAIRS, AND DESKS
• BIG BOOK POINTER
• BIG BOOK STAND
• INDEX CARDS
• JOURNALS

For children acquiring English and/or needing more intensive support, you may wish to incorporate the following suggestions into the basic lesson plan.

Before reading the selection, familiarize children with "farm-related" vocabulary. Use pictures found on the title page to review words such as *pond, haystack, mill, beehives, chicken coop, tractor, barn,* and *wheat fields.* Depending on the level of English proficiency, have children point to something and identify it or have them say what you are pointing to.

Sharing Time

TODAY'S NEWS

As children gather around while you write and read Today's News, explain to children that they will be playing a game of "Follow the Leader" before they read the story.

> Let's take a walk.
> Then let's read about another walker.

CREATING INTEREST AND BUILDING BACKGROUND

Because motivation matters!

To prepare children for the setting of *Rosie's Walk,* talk with them about what they know about farms. Share information about the tools farmers use such as rakes, pitchforks, and wagons. Invite children who have visited farms to describe them.

Talk about the relationship between hens and foxes. Ask children if they know any stories or songs about these two animals. *How well do you think hens and foxes get along?*

Children will be learning about directional concepts as they read *Rosie's Walk.* To prepare children for following directions, play a game of "Follow the Leader" in which the leader leads the group over and under objects and obstacles.

73

READING AND WRITING

SHARING LITERATURE
Rosie's Walk

LOOK IT OVER   Hold up the cover of *Rosie's Walk*, reading the words of the title and tracking them with your finger as you read. Invite a child to point to the author/illustrator's name, Pat Hutchins.

Talk with children about what they notice on the cover. Encourage children to predict who Rosie is and what the fox is doing. Open the book to display both front and back covers simultaneously so children can become acquainted with the setting of the story.

SHARE THE STORY   As you read, take time to show the amusing illustrations and to let children discover how Rosie unknowingly leads the fox on a chase through the barnyard.

You may want to reread the book immediately so children will be able to understand what is happening to Rosie and to the fox.

About the Author/Illustrator

Pat Hutchins said about her writing, "I like to build my stories up, so the reader can understand what is happening and, in some cases, anticipate what is likely to happen on the next page." At appropriate times during the reading of *Rosie's Walk*, ask children if they can predict what is going to happen on the next page.

RESPONDING TO LITERATURE

BOOK TALK   Invite children to share their reactions to the story. Talk with children about your response the first time you read about Rosie.

- *I loved reading about Rosie the Hen! I was so afraid she would get caught! Do you think she even knew the fox was following her?*

- *What do you think was the funniest scene in the book? I laughed when the flour fell on top of the fox—I had to go back and see how that happened!*

JOURNAL WRITING   Invite children to draw and write about the funniest part of the story. As they write, you may wish to write in your own journal about the part of the story that you found most amusing.

STORY THEATER   Children may enjoy walking along with Rosie as you reread the story. Recreate the farm scene from the story. You may wish to use props, such as a table for the henhouse, a Big Book pointer for the rake, a large sheet of blue paper or fabric for the pond, a pile of twigs for the haystack, a shelf with a bag filled with paper for the mill, a group of chairs for the fence, and a group of desks or chairs for the beehives.

INTO THE LEARNING CENTERS
Today would be a good day to invite children to the Social Studies Center to create the story scene for *Rosie's Walk.* See page 104.

Chad isolated a specific incident in *Rosie's Walk* and focused on it. He was fascinated by the pulley. His writing is a good example of developmental spelling. Chad read his message like this: "I liked when the flour spilled on the fox."

HANDS ON LANGUAGE

DECODING AND PHONICS

LETTERS: *K, k*
SOUND/LETTER RELATIONSHIPS: /k/*K, k*

Developing Phonemic Awareness

Ask children to listen as you read "A Kettle's for the Kitchen" on page 18 in the *Big Book of Alphabet Rhymes and Chimes.* As you come to words that begin with *k,* slightly emphasize the initial sound. Repeat the rhyme a few times, encouraging children to chime in.

Talk with children about the sound they hear at the beginning of the words *kettle, key,* and *kitten.* Invite children to name other words that begin with the same sound.

Developing Print Awareness

Display "A Kettle's for the Kitchen" on page 18 of the *Big Book of Alphabet Rhymes and Chimes* and say the rhyme with children. Use the Big Book pointer to point out words that begin with *k.*

Kk

A kettle's for the kitchen,
A key is for the door,
A kitten is for playing with
And keeping on the floor.

Margaret and John Travers Moore

Big Book of Alphabet Rhymes and Chimes,
page 18

■ **Literature Activity Book:** page 77

Then display the Alphabet Poster and ABC cards for Kk, or write the letters on the chalkboard and on cards of your own.

Have children compare the *k*'s on the Big Book page with the letters on the poster and card. Encourage children to talk about the kangaroo pictured on the poster.

Point out to children that many different words begin with *k* or *K*. Talk about any children's names that do.

Invite pairs of children to go on a Word Hunt around the room to find words on charts, signs, and in books that begin with the same sound and letter as *kangaroo* and *kettle*. Have them copy the words on cards and then share and display them on the bulletin board.

Kk

kangaroo

8
MEET PAT HUTCHINS

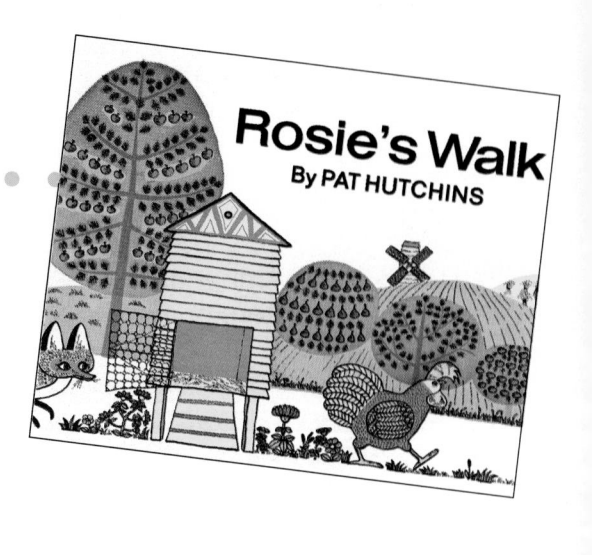

Rosie's Walk
By PAT HUTCHINS

LITERATURE
Rosie's Walk
   by Pat Hutchins

SING & READ BOOKS AND
AUDIOCASSETTES
Read a Book

Literature Activity Book: p. 78
   Just for Fun!

EXPLORING PRINT
*Big Book of Alphabet Rhymes
and Chimes:*
   A Kettle's for the Kitchen

Rhyme and Chime Strips:
   A Kettle's for the Kitchen

Learning the Code: K, k

BRWL: Letterbook K–Q(21)

STAFF
DEVELOPMENT   A to EZ Handbook
   • Dramatic Play: p. 250
   • Hands On! p. 258

Performance Assessment Handbook

OTHER RESOURCES

• CHART PAPER
• BIG BOOK POINTER
• BIG BOOK STAND
• BLOCKS
• POCKET CHART AND
  STAND

Sharing Time

TODAY'S NEWS

Gather children together and write and read Today's News, pointing to each word as you read. Ask children to remember some of the places that Rosie went on her walk and where the fox was as Rosie walked.

Let's take another walk with Rosie, the hen.

CREATING INTEREST AND BUILDING BACKGROUND

Because motivation matters!

To help children focus on the ways in which hens and foxes are different, read the following poem aloud.

Feather or Fur

When you watch for
Feather or fur
Feather or fur
Do not stir
Do not stir.

Feather or fur
Come crawling
Creeping
Some come peeping
Some by night
And some by day.
Most come gently
All come softly
Do not scare
A friend away.

When you watch for
Feather or fur
Feather or fur
Do not stir
Do not stir.

—John Becker

After they listen to the poem, children may enjoy creating finger paintings of a hen or a fox. Scraping paint off with straightened paper clips will produce feather patterns and moving cotton balls in a circular pattern on wet paint will simulate the texture of fur. You may wish to copy the poem onto chart paper to display in the Reading or Writing Center.

READING AND WRITING

SHARING LITERATURE
Rosie's Walk

REREAD THE STORY   As you reread the story, encourage children to imagine that they are the fox and to describe how he feels as he fails to catch Rosie time after time.

PRINT AWARENESS
....

Directionality
Invite a child to track the print from left to right on each page as you read. Children will soon discover that there are some pages with no words.

RESPONDING TO LITERATURE

BOOK TALK   Invite children to take a close look at the story setting and to discuss where Rosie went on her walk.

- *Let's walk through the story and list all of the places that Rosie went. Where did Rosie start from? Where did she end up?*

- *What finally happened to the fox? Do you think the fox will ever come back to Rosie's farmyard. Why or why not?*

WRITING ABOUT A WALK Take the class on a walk around the school, inside or outside the building, and ask children to note how they are moving. Then ask them to write about their walk in small groups, using direction words. For example, a language experience chart might look like this:

Our Class Walk	
Where We Went	**What Happened There**
Across the hall	Visited other Kindergarten class
Around the cafeteria	Smelled lunch cooking
Up the stairs to library	Looked at books

CREATING A SCENE WITH BLOCKS Invite small groups of children to recreate Rosie's walk with blocks. The title page of the book provides a good view of the setting and can serve as a model.

TEAM WORK/THEME WORK
Invite children to place the Class Walk chart in the Pat Hutchins Corner. You may wish to have children build the block scenes in the Pat Hutchins Corner, so that they can become a part of the display. See pages 38–41 and 94–95.

INTO THE LEARNING CENTERS
Today would be a good day to direct children to the Dramatic Play Center where they can create a bookstore featuring books by Pat Hutchins. See page 99.

Using the Rhyme and Chime Strips gives children a Hands On! Language experience that allows them to explore important concepts of print.

CONCEPTS OF PRINT
Directionality, Words

A kettle's for the kitchen,
A key is for the door,
A kitten is for playing with
And keeping on the floor.

Margaret and John Travers Moore

Big Book of Alphabet Rhymes and Chimes, page 18

Developing Print Awareness
Display page 18 of the *Big Book of Alphabet Rhymes and Chimes* and encourage children to recite the rhyme with you as you point to each word.

Explain that there are many different words in the rhyme. Each word has a space in front of it and at the end of it.

Use the word cards cut from the Rhyme and Chime Strips for ''A Kettle's for the Kitchen'' to build the rhyme in the pocket chart as shown. Recite the rhyme as you build it in the pocket chart and encourage children to recite it with you.

A	kettle's	for	the	kitchen,
A	key	is	for	the	door,
A	kitten	is	for	playing	with
And	keeping	on	the	floor.

Then use the picture cards to have children match the pictures of the kettle, kitchen, key, door, kitten, and kitten on the floor to the appropriate word or phrase.

Display the word cards for *kitchen* and *key*. Ask children what they notice about these two words. Which word has more letters? Which word is longer?

As you replace all word cards in the pocket chart, invite children to recite the rhyme with you again.

INTO THE LEARNING CENTERS
Allow children to use the *Big Book of Alphabet Rhymes and Chimes*, the Rhyme and Chime Strips, and the word and picture cards to build the rhyme "A Kettle's for the Kitchen" in the pocket chart in the Hands On! Language Center. See page 100.

83

9
MEET PAT HUTCHINS

LITERATURE
Read Aloud Anthology
  "It Could Always Be Worse"
  a Yiddish folk tale
  retold by Margot Zemach

 SING & READ BOOKS AND
AUDIOCASSETTES
Read a Book

Literature Activity Book: pp. 79–80
  Tell a Tale

EXPLORING PRINT
Alphabet Poster for Kk

Rhyme and Chime Strips:
  A Kettle's for the Kitchen

Learning the Code: K, k

BRWL: Letterbook K–Q(21)

STAFF DEVELOPMENT A to EZ Handbook
  • Environmental Print: p. 255
  • Zone of Proximal Development: p. 303

Performance Assessment Handbook

OTHER RESOURCES

- CHART PAPER
- LONG PIECES OF PAPER
- PAPER TOWEL TUBES
- STORY PROPS SUCH AS
  KERCHIEFS AND CAPS
- POCKET CHART AND
  STAND

Sharing Time

TODAY'S NEWS

Ask for a volunteer to point to the exclamation mark in Today's News and discuss with the class what it means. Then ask children to think about what it might be like to live with a large family.

Today we'll hear a story about a big, crowded, noisy family!

CREATING INTEREST AND BUILDING BACKGROUND

Because motivation matters!

Relate the next story, "It Could Always Be Worse," to Pat Hutchins's life by reminding children that she came from a family of nine people and that her family always had many animals around. (See page 40.) Tell children that today's story is about another family of nine who has several animals. Encourage children to talk about what it might be like to live in such a large family and record their responses on a chart.

LIFE IN A LARGE FAMILY

It's noisy.

It's fun because you have someone to play with.

There's someone to help you do chores.

Older children take care of younger children.

You're never lonely.

Read the chart to children when it is finished, pointing to each word as you read.

READING AND WRITING

"It Could Always Be Worse"

SHARE THE STORY   You can make your reading or telling of this story funnier by deliberately reading the man's dialog in an increasingly agitated voice and reading the Rabbi's dialog in an extremely calm voice.

About the Story

Developing Multicultural Awareness

Share with the children information about the story.

- *The story takes place in a shtetl. These were small, isolated Jewish villages or towns in Eastern Europe. The Jews lived in shtetls because they were not allowed to live with non-Jews.*

- *Because they were restricted from certain occupations and prohibited from owning land, the people in the shtetls were usually quite poor.*

- *There was no government in the shtetl. The Rabbi—the religious leader of the community—was usually the person people turned to for advice.*

■ **Read Aloud Anthology:** pages 69–71

RESPONDING TO LITERATURE

BOOK TALK Invite children to talk about their reactions to the story. If you wish, use the following questions to help get the conversation started.

- *I think the Rabbi was very smart, don't you? How did he help the man solve his problem?*

- *Why do you think this story is called "It Could Always Be Worse"? Do you agree that things could always be worse? Do you think the man in the story would agree?*

EXTENDING THE STORY Children may enjoy extending the story by writing or drawing an additional episode in which another animal is brought into the house. The extensions might be displayed on a bulletin board entitled "It Could *Even* Be Worse!"

CREATE A STORY MOVIE Have children work with partners to make a story movie. They may illustrate the story on long pieces of paper, including opening and closing credits. Tape the beginning and end of the paper onto paper towel tubes. Children can then "broadcast" the movie by unrolling the scroll and retelling the story.

DRAMATIZE THE STORY Children may act out the story using simple costumes such as kerchiefs and caps for the people and masks, tails, or beaks for the animals. Recreating the setting, including a house for the Rabbi and a roped-off area for the hut, will help simulate the progressively cramped atmosphere. Since the noise was an important aspect of the man's problem, encourage children playing animals to chime in with appropriate sounds!

DECODING AND PHONICS

LETTERS: *K, k*
SOUND/LETTER RELATIONSHIPS: /k/K, k

CONCEPTS OF PRINT
Directionality, Words, Letters

Developing Phonemic Awareness
Remind children that they have been learning about the sound heard at the beginning of words like *kite, kettle, key,* and *kitten* (words from *Titch* and "A Kettle's for the Kitchen" on page 18 in the *Big Book of Alphabet Rhymes and Chimes*). Ask children to suggest other words that have the same beginning sound.

Developing Print Awareness
Display the Alphabet Poster for Kk and point to the word *kangaroo*. Frame the letter *k* in the word. Remind children that the letter *k* stands for the sound heard at the beginning of the word *kangaroo*.

Use the word cards from the Rhyme and Chime Strips for "A Kettle's for the Kitchen" to build the rhyme in the pocket chart.

A	kettle's	for	the	kitchen,
A	key	is	for	the	door,
A	kitten	is	for	playing	with
And	keeping	on	the	floor.

Encourage children to say the rhyme with you as you point to each word with the Big Book pointer. Have the children clap each time they hear a word that begins with the same sound as *kangaroo*.

Ask children to recite the rhyme and clap again. This time remove any card for which the children did not clap.

	kettle's		kitchen,
	key	
	kitten	
	keeping	

88

A Kettle's for the Kitchen

A kettle's for the kitchen,

A key is for the door,

A kitten is for playing with

And keeping on the floor.

Frame the first letter in each word left in the chart and have children identify it as a *k*. Emphasize that the letter *k* stands for the sound heard at the beginning of the words *kettle* and *kitchen*. Use letter cards for *K* and *k* from the Rhyme and Chime Strips and match them to the words that begin with those letters.

Review all the charts and other print resources in the classroom to find words that begin with the same sound and letter as *kangaroo*.

INTO THE LEARNING CENTERS
Using letter stamps, sponge letters, and magnetic letters in the Hands On! Language Center is a motivating way for children to experiment with print. See page 100.

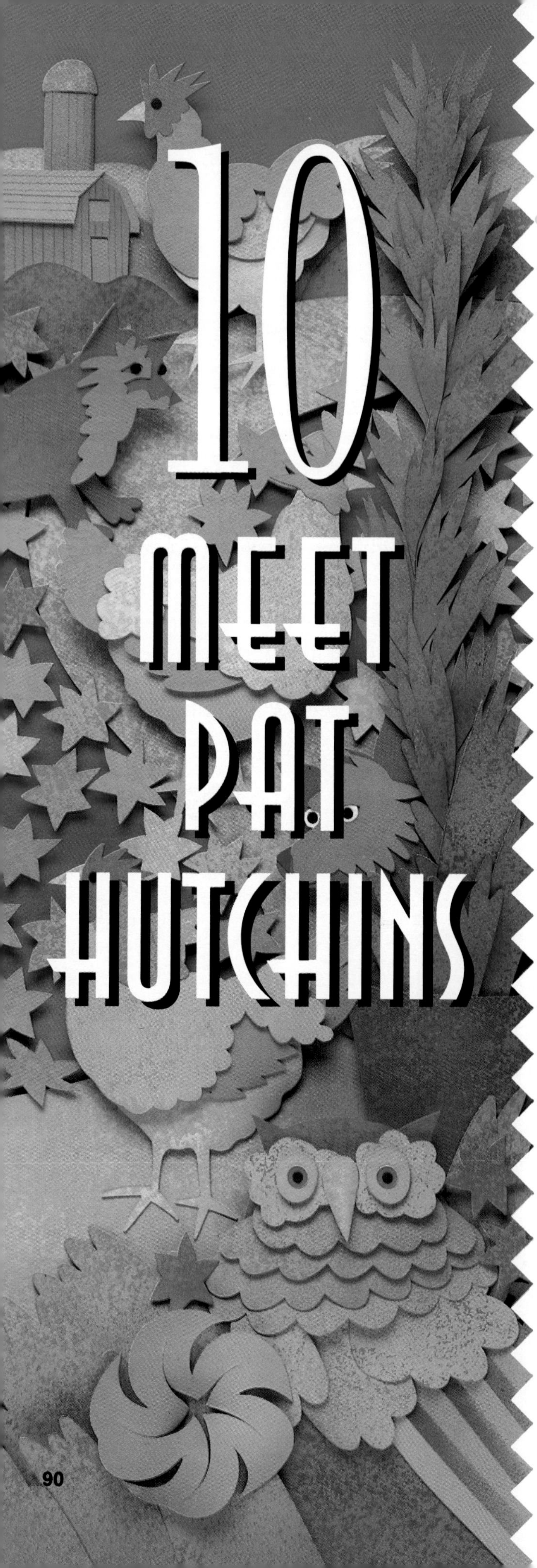

10 MEET PAT HUTCHINS

LITERATURE

Titch
by Pat Hutchins

Good-Night, Owl!
by Pat Hutchins

Rosie's Walk
by Pat Hutchins

Big Book of Songs:
Read a Book
by Marcy Marxer

Big Book of Poems:
Surprise
by Beverly McLoughland

SONGS AND STORIES
AUDIOCASSETTES
STORY SONGS: Read a Book

SING & READ BOOKS AND
AUDIOCASSETTES
Read a Book

Literature Activity Book: p. 81
Responding to Literature

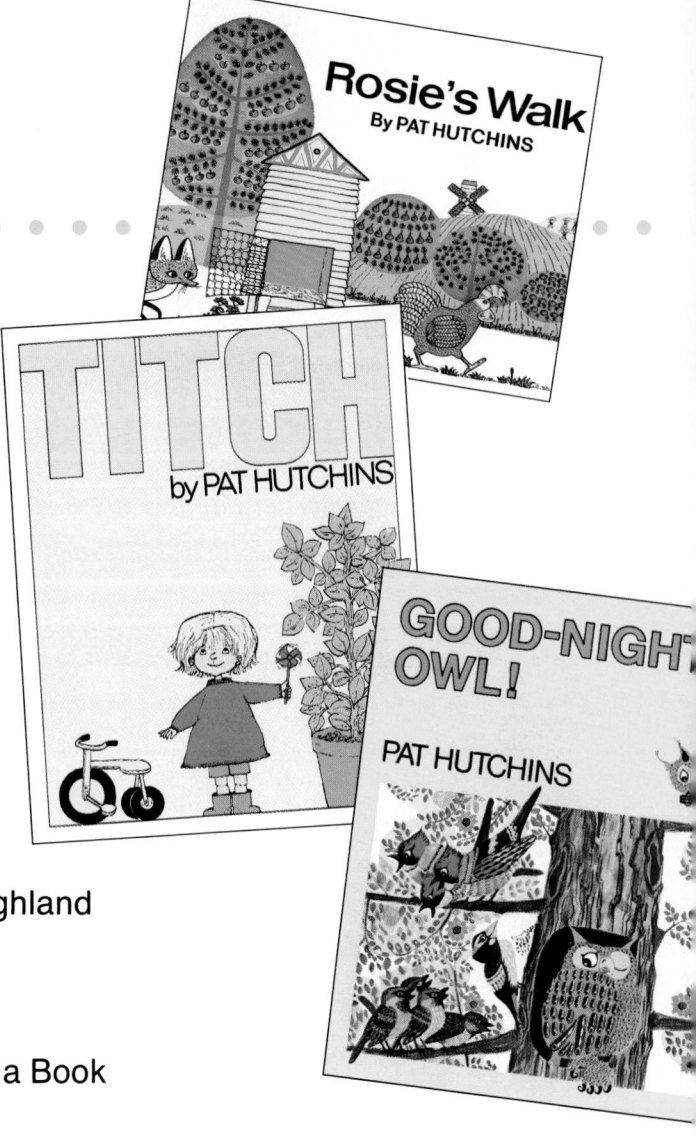

STAFF DEVELOPMENT A to EZ Handbook

- Pointing: p. 287
- Risk-Free Environment: p. 297

Performance Assessment Handbook

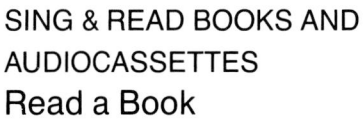

OTHER RESOURCES

- BIG BOOK POINTER
- BIG BOOK STAND
- JOURNALS

Sharing Time

Today's News

After you read and write Today's News, ask a volunteer to point out the form of the Theme Word, *writers.* Tell children that they will celebrate what they have learned about Pat Hutchins by finishing up the Pat Hutchins Corner.

We are writers, too!

Wrapping It Up

To remind children of the joys of reading, ask them to say with you the Theme Poem "Surprise" on pages 28–29 in the *Big Book of Poems.* Then invite them to sing along to the Theme Song "Read a Book."

♪ SONGS AND STORIES AUDIOCASSETTES
STORY SONGS: Read a Book

Display the song on pages 28–31 in the *Big Book of Songs.* Point to the words with the Big Book pointer as children sing along.

READ A BOOK

If you want adventure,
You want to unwind,
Pick up a good story,
Get out of that old grind,
And read a book!
(Read, read! Read, read a book!)
Read a book!
(Read, read! Read, read a book!)

Big Book of Songs, pages 28–29

READING AND WRITING

SHARING LITERATURE

LOOK IT OVER   Display the books *Titch; Good-Night, Owl!* and *Rosie's Walk*. Ask children to choose one of the three to reread.

REREAD THE STORY   As you reread the story children select, ask them to say with you the repetitive parts or other parts that they remember.

Review the letters *t* and *k* with children. Ask them to listen for any words that begin with *t* or *k* as you read. Then invite them to look through other Pat Hutchins books to find words that begin with those letters. For additional practice, you may wish to have children use the Phonics Activity Sheets on pages 109–110.

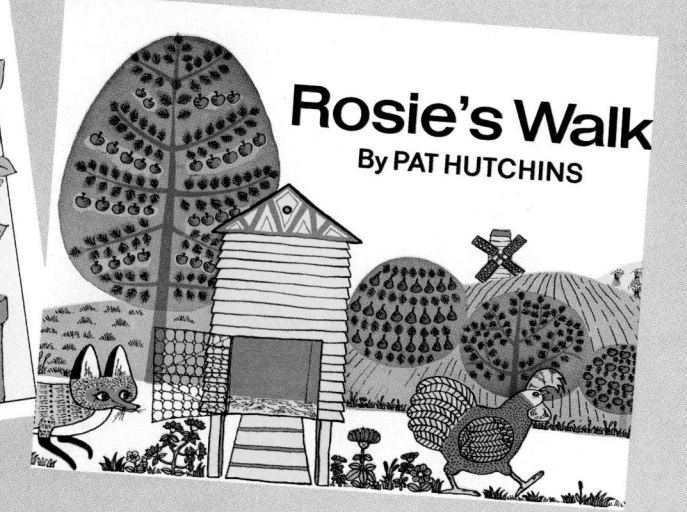

RESPONDING TO LITERATURE

BOOK TALK   Invite children to talk about the books they read in this theme and to discuss how the books are alike and different. You may wish to use the questions below to get the discussion started:

- *Which book did you like best? Why did you like it so much?*

- *Which book's pictures did you like most?*

- *Which book made you laugh?*

- *If you could ask Pat Hutchins to draw a picture for you, what would you want a picture of?*

- *If you could visit Pat Hutchins, what would you say to her? What questions would you like to ask her?*

- *Which characters had some of the same feelings that you have had?*

JOURNAL WRITING   Invite children to draw or write in their journals about their favorite book by Pat Hutchins. If they wish, they may write about a Hutchins book other than the three featured in this theme. Encourage children to use the word *writer* in their journal entries.

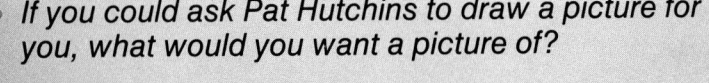

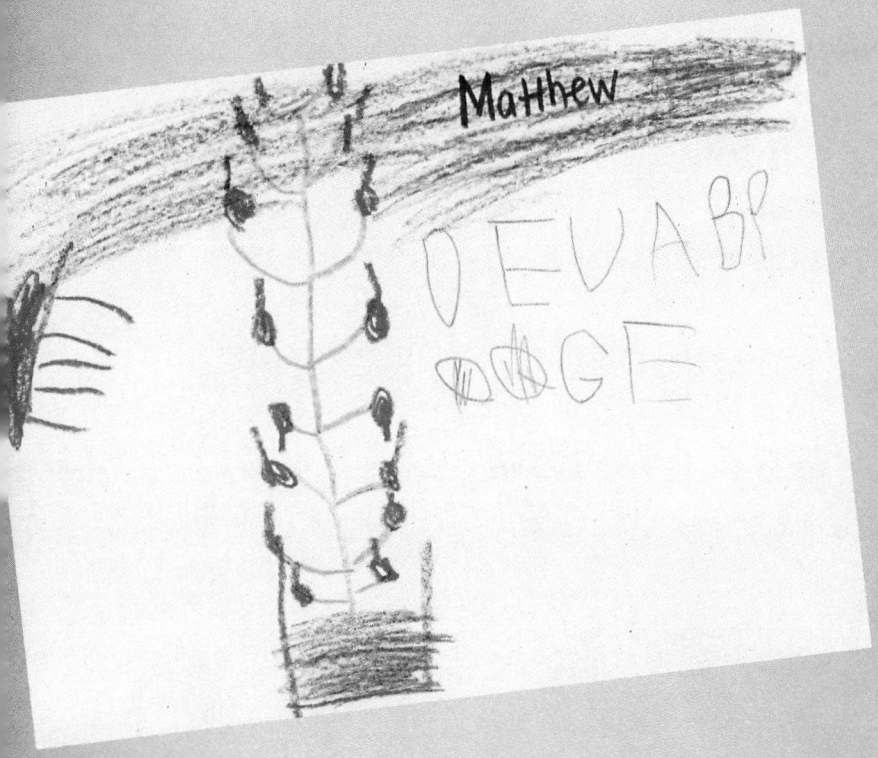

Matthew's letter forms are independent of sounds, phonemes, and words. They show developing print awareness. Matthew read his message like this: "This is the apple tree and it is going way up to the sky."

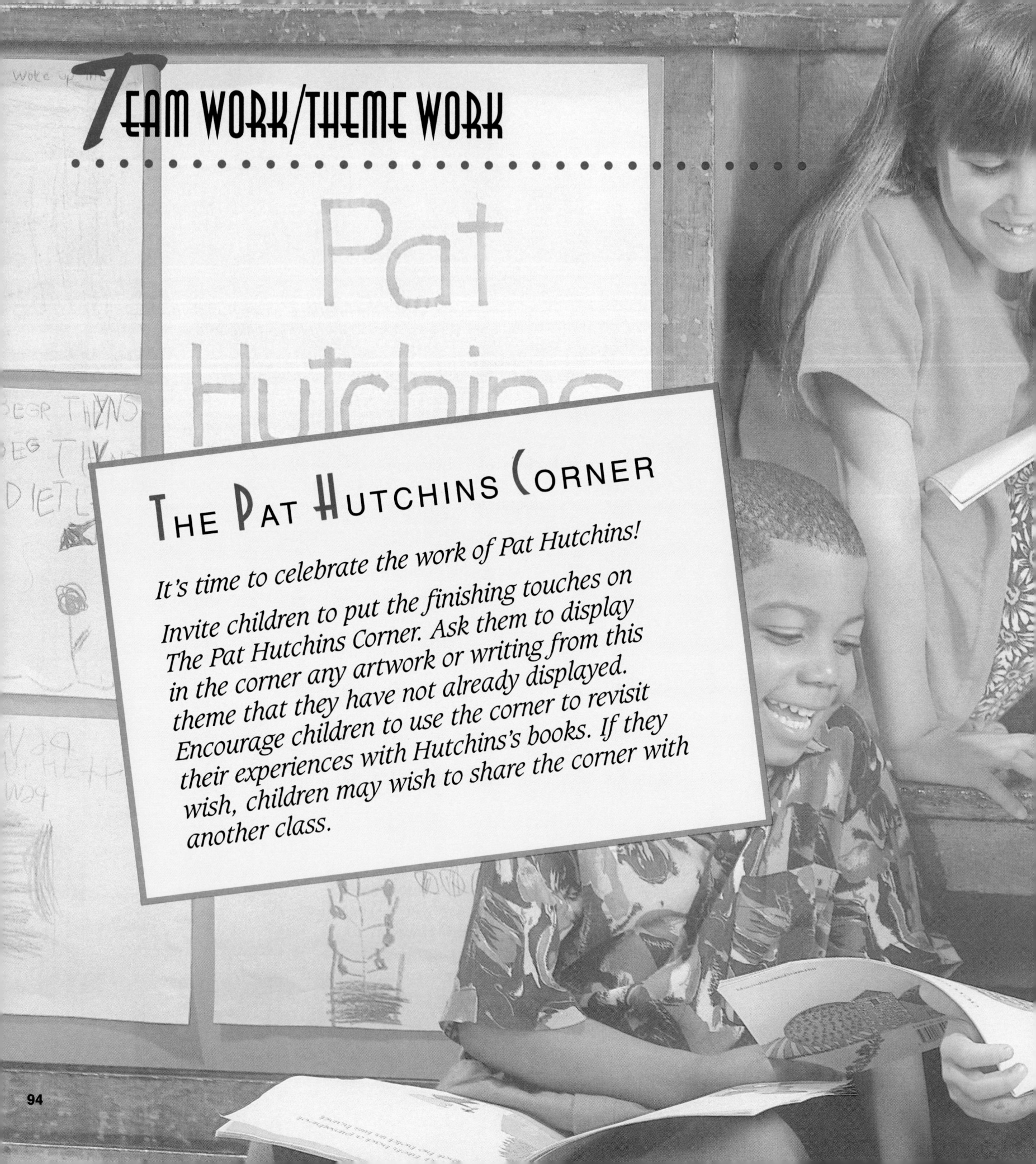

THE PAT HUTCHINS CORNER

It's time to celebrate the work of Pat Hutchins!

Invite children to put the finishing touches on The Pat Hutchins Corner. Ask them to display in the corner any artwork or writing from this theme that they have not already displayed. Encourage children to use the corner to revisit their experiences with Hutchins's books. If they wish, children may wish to share the corner with another class.

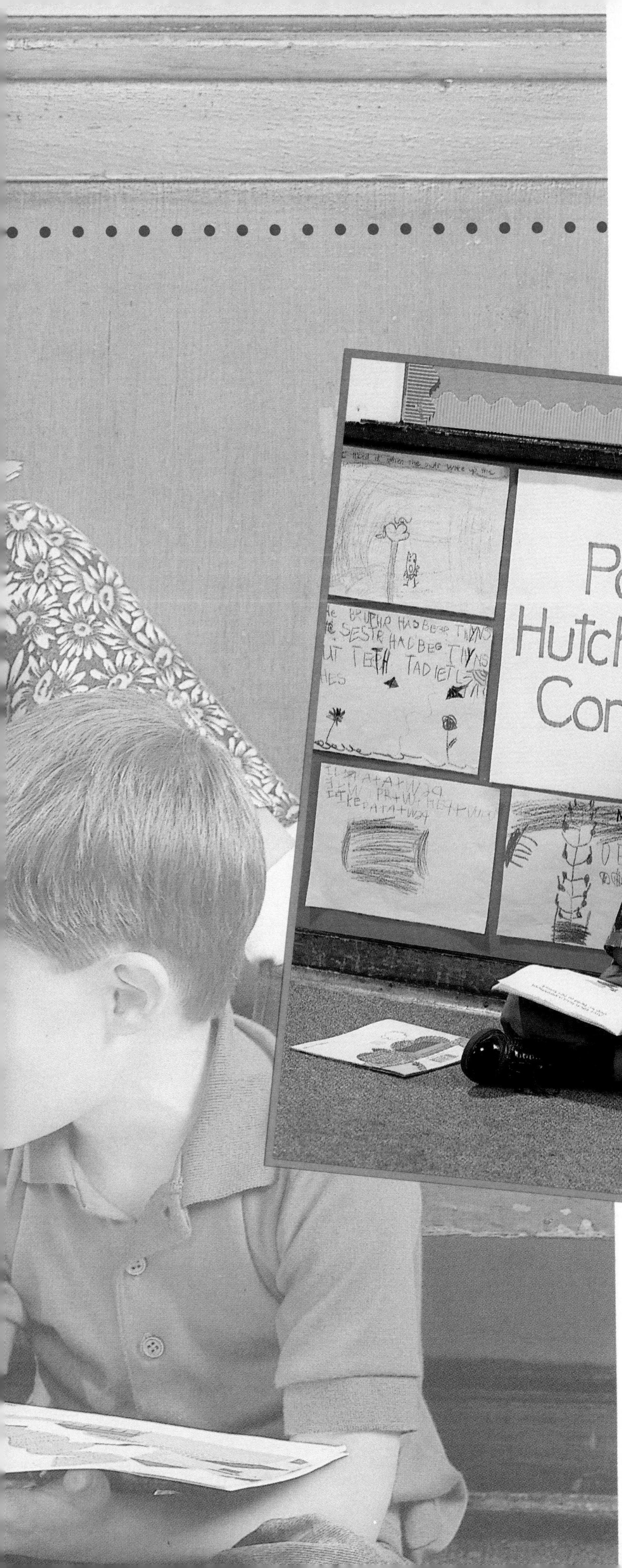

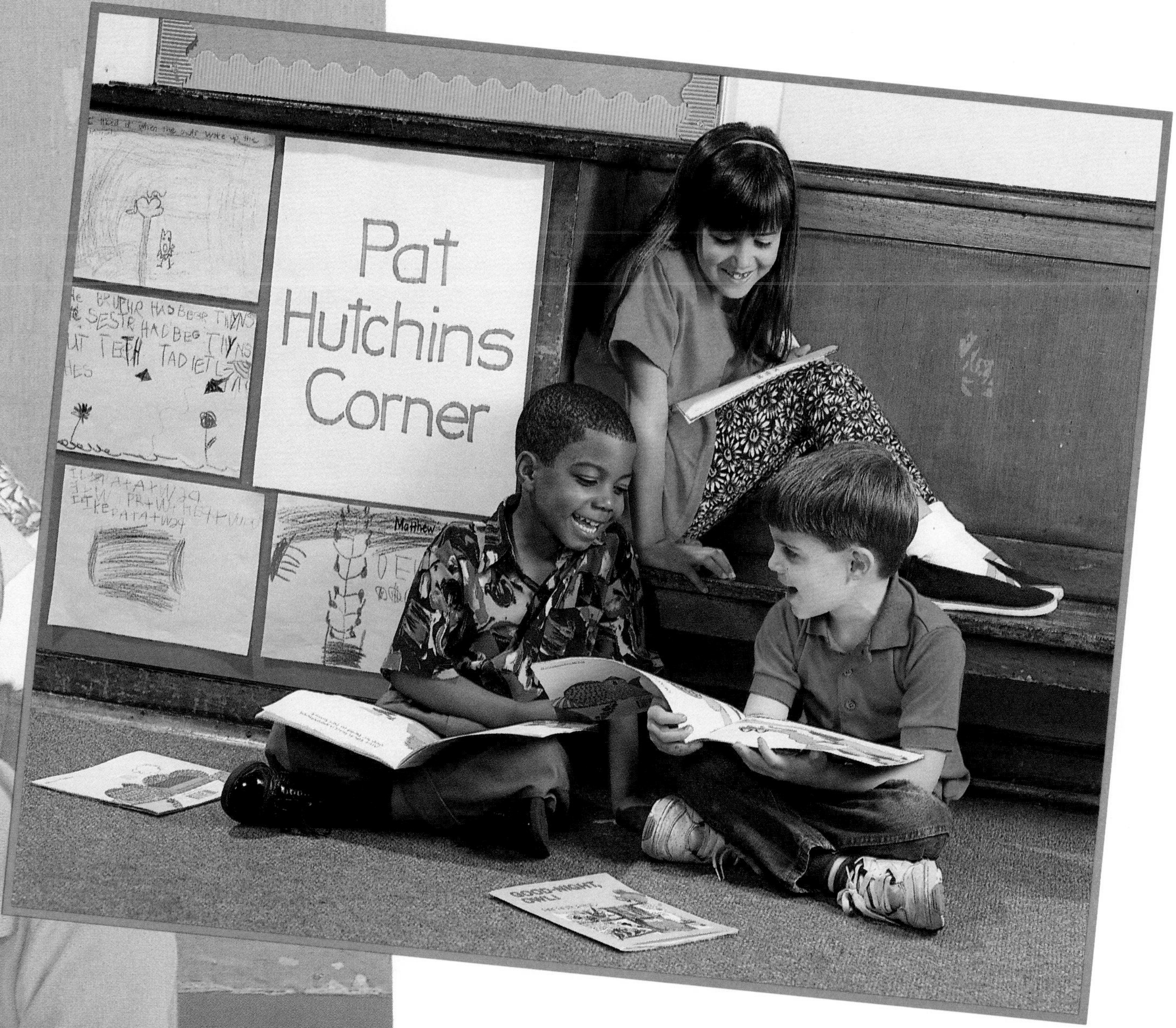
Pat
Hutchins
Corner
Matthew
GOOD-NIGHT, OWL!

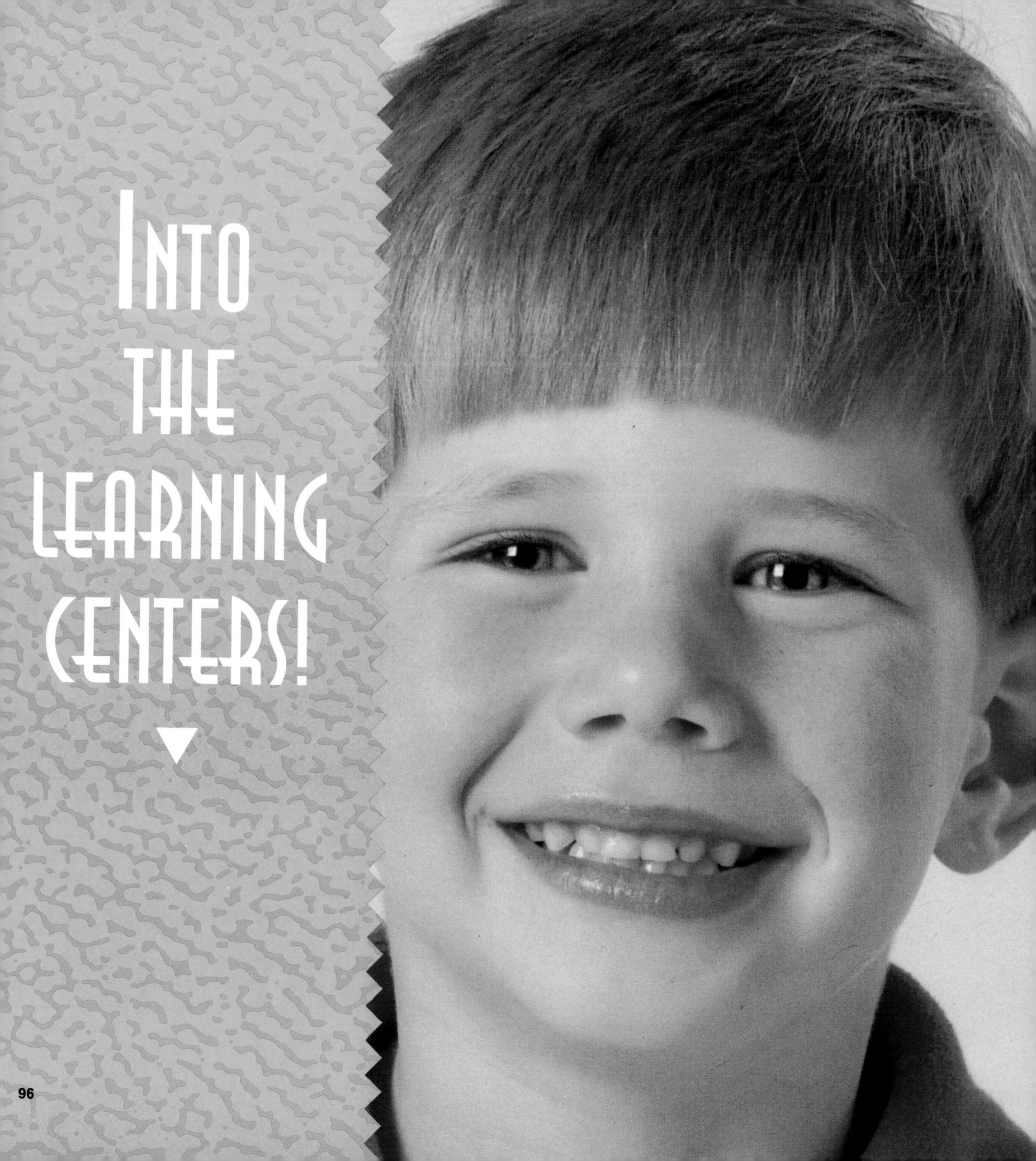

Into the Learning Centers!

▼

Learning Centers can be places where children learn independently, from one another, and from you! Engaging activities can motivate children to become literacy explorers!

A to EZ Handbook

READING CENTER

DRAMATIC PLAY CENTER

HANDS ON! LANGUAGE CENTER

WRITING CENTER

MATH CENTER

ART CENTER

SOCIAL STUDIES CENTER

SCIENCE CENTER

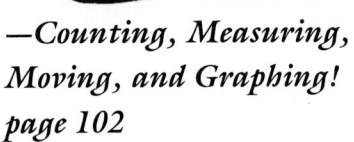

READING CENTER

Resources   ***Rosie's Walk * Good-Night Owl! * Big Book of Titch * Big Book of Songs * Big Book of Poems * Sing & Read Little Books * Listening Library Audiocassettes * Songs and Stories Audiocassettes *** theme-related books (See MORE BOOKS TO SHARE!, pages 32-33.) * brown wrapping paper or butcher paper * markers * green construction paper * scissors

Setting Up!   Display books for shared and emergent readings. Put up signs such as MEET PAT HUTCHINS and MORE BOOKS BY PAT HUTCHINS to encourage children to share the books in the Reading Center! You may also wish to start a book tree by drawing an outline of a tree with bare branches on chart paper. Cut out leaves from green construction paper. Write the titles *Rosie's Walk*; *Good-Night, Owl!* and *Titch* on the leaves, one title per leaf. Tell children that each time they read a book by Pat Hutchins, they can write the title on a leaf and add it to the book tree.

- Place the Sing & Read Little Book and Audiocassette for *Read a Book* by the tape recorder.

- Have the Listening Library Audiocassette for *Titch* available.

- Invite children to listen to "Rainbow Crow" on the SONGS AND STORIES AUDIOCASSETTES.

Centers in Action!   Invite children to explore the books and materials displayed. Continue to add books and materials to the center and invite children to do the same. Encourage children to compare the illustrations in Pat Hutchins's book and talk about how they are alike and different. Display the theme big books—and keep the Big Book pointer within easy reach so that children can model being teachers!

Our favorite books by Pat Hutchins!

Dramatic Play Center

Books! Books! Books!

Resources construction paper * crayons or markers * scissors * advertisements for books * posters about authors and books * books, including selections by Pat Hutchins * magazines * newspapers * reference books * play money * shoe boxes * index cards

Setting Up! Make a Dramatic Play Center by arranging boxes on a table so that books can be displayed on them as they are in a bookstore.

Centers in Action! Invite children to become bookstore managers, salespeople, and customers in a bookstore. Children can create their own bookstore or try the following suggestions:

- An inviting bookstore "window" advertising Pat Hutchins's books can be created, which beckons passersby to come into the bookstore.

- Children can hang posters about authors and books in the bookstore.

- Children may enjoy making their own advertisements for books to display in the bookstore.

- Encourage children to arrange the magazines and newspapers as well as the books about the bookstore. Special books, such as those by Pat Hutchins, should be arranged in the display center.

There are many opportunities for reading and writing in a bookstore!

- A MEET THE AUTHOR display can advertise a reading by none other than noted author Pat Hutchins. Children can take turns playing the role of Ms. Hutchins.

- The bookstore managers and salespeople may wish to write prices on index cards and display these cards by the books, magazines, and newspapers.

- The bookstore managers and salespeople may wish to write the title of each book, magazine, and newspaper on an index card and keep the cards in a shoe box, so that the "staff" of the bookstore can keep an inventory of the materials in the store.

- Customers in the bookstore can select their favorite books and buy them with the play money.

Hands On! Language Center

Resources **pocket chart and stand** * **ABC cards** * **slate board** * chalk * **sponge letters** * **letter stamps** * **linked letter cubes** * paper * pads * pencils * crayons * letter blocks * **magnetic letters**

Setting Up!   Children may explore language independently, but you may also wish to suggest the theme-related activities described under Centers in Action!

Centers in Action!

- Children can use sponge letters, letter stamps, and stencils to print and trace the letters in their names as well as Pat Hutchins's name.

- Children can work together to use sponge letters, letter stamps, and stencils to print and trace letters and words from *Rosie's Walk*, *Titch*, and *Good-Night, Owl!*

- Children may also enjoy using sponge letters, letter stamps, and stencils to print and trace the letters and words in their favorite Pat Hutchins books.

WRITING CENTER

Resources construction paper with 2 holes punched along the side for tying into a book * crayons * markers * pencils * hole punch * yarn

Setting Up! Point out to children that a biography is a true story about someone's life. Review the information from Team Work/Theme Work about Pat Hutchins to give children an example of what you mean. As children work in the Writing Center, you may also want to encourage them to choose their own topics to write about. Invite children to collaborate with partners and in small groups as well.

Centers in Action! Encourage children to participate in one or more of the following writing activities.

- **Write an Autobiographical Sketch** Invite children to write and illustrate facts about themselves on the pages of construction paper that you have prepared. Make a list of the kinds of things they might include in an autobiography, such as their names, where they live, where they were born, names of family members and friends, pets, and favorite activities.

  Children can continue to write and draw pictures about themselves as they move through the theme MEET PAT HUTCHINS. When they have completed their writings and drawings, they can combine their pages into a book by tying the pages together with yarn.

Providing the resources and the opportunities to write will send the message to children that they are writers!

- **Write a Letter to Pat Hutchins!** Children may also enjoy writing letters to Pat Hutchins to tell her what they think about her books. Her address is:
  Pat Hutchins
  75 Flask Walk
  London NW3 1ET   ENGLAND

- **Collect Writers' Tools** Brainstorm with children the types of tools a writer like Pat Hutchins might use in her work. Help children to assemble a writer's prop box in a briefcase or satchel. Include such tools as pencils, pens, markers, drawing and writing paper, letter templates and models, and a picture dictionary. Set up a sign-out system so children can take the writer's prop box home for an evening.

Math Center

Counting, Measuring, Moving, and Graphing!

Resources chart paper * markers or crayons * construction paper * a branch * clay * scissors * hole punch * yarn * large box open on each end * rope strung across two chairs * table * mat or small rug * chair * **Good-Night, Owl!** * **Rosie's Walk**

Setting Up!

- On construction paper, draw (or trace) and then cut out the outlines of the different kinds of birds found in *Good-Night, Owl!* Punch a hole in the top of each bird shape. Then thread each shape with a piece of yarn and tie it. Place the branch in a base of clay so that the branch resembles a bare tree.

- Arrange the chairs with the rope strung between them and the open-ended box in the learning center area, along with the table, mat, and chair. Write the directional words *across, around, over, past, through,* and *under* on the chart paper. Then discuss each word and its meaning with children.

Centers in Action! Invite children to take part in one or more of the following activities.

- **Count the Birds!** Children can hang the cutouts of the birds on the tree, then count them. How many of each kind of bird are in the tree? What is the total number of birds in the tree?

- **Measuring With Yarn** Children may enjoy experiencing the concepts of *big, bigger, little,* and *tiny* by measuring things in the classroom with pieces of yarn.

- **Experiencing Direction Words** Children can experience directional words by going across the learning center area, around a table or desk, over a rug or mat, past a chair, through a box, and under a rope.

- **Graphing Farm Animals** Invite children to count the number of each kind of animal shown in *Rosie's Walk.* Record this information and help children to create a graph such as the one shown.

Farm Animals

hens foxes frogs birds butter-flies mice goats bees

Math Center

Art Center

ALL KINDS OF ART!

Resources paper * feathers * construction paper * scissors * cotton * glue * index cards * crayons or markers * paintbrushes * paints * brown wrapping paper or grocery bags * scrap paper such as newspaper * salt play dough (1 cup water, 1/2 cup flour, 1 cup salt, saucepan, wax paper, rolling pin, food coloring optional) * toothpicks * straws * stapler

Setting Up!
- Fold pieces of the brown wrapping paper or grocery bags in half so that the paper is double in thickness.

- Staple the left side of pieces of paper to make blank books.

- If feathers are not available, cut different-colored pieces of construction paper into feather shapes.

- Mix water, flour, and salt in the saucepan and add the food coloring, if desired. Stir the mixture over low heat until it is thick and rubbery. Let it cool.

Centers in Action! Invite children to create their own artwork or try one of the following activities:

- **Make a Bird!** Children will enjoy making up their own kinds of birds by drawing pictures of them, then adding feathers and cotton to make them look real. Encourage children to write about their birds.

- **See How You Grow!** Children can press their hands in the salt play dough to make handprints. Help children to write their names beneath their handprints with a toothpick. When the impressions dry (in a few days), children can compare the handprint sizes.

- **Make a Character!** Children can also make stuffed characters by drawing, coloring, and painting big pictures of these characters on the folded brown paper. Then children can cut out the character shapes so that there is a front and a back piece for each. After children are helped to staple each front and back piece together, three-quarters of the way closed, they can stuff them with paper or cotton. Then the characters can be stapled closed.

You may wish to have children display their artwork in the Pat Hutchins Corner, which is described in Team Work/Theme Work. See pages 38–41 and 94–95.

Social Studies Center

Resources large pieces of butcher paper * crayons, markers, or paints and paintbrushes * construction paper * scissors * glue * boxes of different sizes (such as shoe boxes, cereal boxes, and milk cartons) * twigs * clay * cotton

Setting Up! Review the setting of *Rosie's Walk* with children. Then, if possible, take a walk through the school neighborhood with children and point out any birds, squirrels, or other wildlife that you see.

Centers in Action! Invite children to do one or more of the following activities.

- **Create a Story Setting!** Children can create the story scene for *Rosie's Walk* by covering boxes with construction paper, and then drawing or painting on the boxes to make them look like the buildings in the story. Children can draw or paint the farm's surface (grass, pond, and haystack, for example) on the large piece of butcher paper to make it look like the setting for *Rosie's Walk*. Trees can be made from small twigs and cotton painted green. Children can arrange the boxes and trees on the butcher paper to create the story setting for *Rosie's Walk*. Encourage children to retell the story using this story scene that they created.

- **Watching for Wildlife** After a walk around the school, children might enjoy drawing a picture of the neighborhood, including the wildlife that they saw during their walk. Encourage children to write about that wildlife, including the different noises that the animals make.

We can create the farm where Rosie takes her walk!

- **Look What I Can Do!** Children may enjoy writing and drawing pictures about things that they can do and things that they would like to be able to do, but cannot do yet. Invite children to draw pictures and write about what they can do, such as writing their names, drawing, sliding, climbing, and swinging. Then have children draw pictures and write about what they would like to do, such as riding a two-wheel bicycle, jumping rope, skipping, and playing an instrument. Children can put the pages together into a book.

Science Center

ALL ABOUT THE OUTDOORS!

Resources   chart paper * markers * books and magazines about animals * crayons * paints and paintbrushes * butcher paper * old magazines * scissors * cup with drainage holes or flowerpot * potting soil * flower seeds * paper * stapler

Setting Up!

- Start a chart by dividing the chart paper in half and labeling the first column *Animals* and the second column *The Sounds They Make.* Write *bees* in the first column and ask children what sound bees make. Write *buzz buzz* in the second column, under *The Sounds They Make.* Then write *hen* in the first column and ask children what sound they think a hen would make. Write children's response, or *cluck cluck,* in the second column, across from *hen.*

- Display pictures of farms in the Science Center. Encourage children to talk about what they know about farms. You may wish to review *Rosie's Walk* and to read other books about farms such as *Farm Animals,* a Dorling Kindersley Book (Aladdin Books, 1991), and *Old MacDonald Had a Farm,* illustrated by Carol Jones (Houghton Mifflin Company, 1988), to familiarize children with farms and farm life.

- Staple the left side of pieces of paper to make a journal. Write *Our Growth Journal* on the cover of the journal.

Centers in Action!   Invite children to do one or more of the following activities.

- **Match the Sound to the Animal** Children can continue the chart by writing the names or drawing pictures of the animals they have read about in *Rosie's Walk* and *Good-Night, Owl!* in the first column. Then children can make the sounds that each of those animals make and write those sounds in the second column.

- **Our Farm**   **Invite children to** draw and cut out pictures from magazines to make a mural of a farm. Then encourage children to write about their farm on pieces of paper. Display both the mural and the children's descriptions of it.

- **Growing, Growing, Grown!** Invite children to grow flower seeds! Have children fill a cup or flowerpot three-quarters full with potting soil, and then add three or four seeds. Children can then cover the seeds with soil, water them, and place the cup or pot on a sunny window sill to grow. Children should look at the cup or pot each day and water the seeds whenever the soil is dry. Encourage children to keep a growth journal in which they write about how the plants grow and change.

- **Good-Night, Animals!** Encourage children to draw pictures of and write about animals that sleep during the day and are awake during the night. You may wish to point out that raccoons and bats as well as owls are examples of animals that are awake throughout the night.

ACKNOWLEDGMENTS

The publisher gratefully acknowledges permission to reprint the following copyrighted material:

"Big, Bigger, Biggest," © 1976 words and music by Ella Jenkins, Ell-Bern Publishing Company, 1844 North Mohawk, Chicago.

"Feather or Fur" from NEW FEATHERS FOR THE OLD GOOSE by John Becker. Copyrighted by John Becker. Reprinted by permission of Haidee Kenedy.

"Mama Crow," © 1988 words and music by Sarah Pirtle, on THE WIND IS TELLING SECRETS, A Gentle Wind, Box 3103, Albany, NY 12203.

"Night Creature" from LITTLE RACCOON AND POEMS FROM THE WOODS by Lilian Moore. Copyright © 1975 by Lilian Moore. Reprinted by permission of Marian Reiner for the author.

"Read a Book," © 1989 words and music by Marcy Marxer, 2 Spoons Music (ASCAP).

"Surprise" by Beverly McLoughland. This appeared originally in CRICKET magazine, September 1985. Reprinted by permission of the author who controls all rights.

"Together Tomorrow," music and lyrics by John Forster and Tom Chapin. © 1988 by Limousine Music and The Last Music Company.

"Tommy" from BRONZEVILLE BOYS AND GIRLS by Gwendolyn Brooks. Copyright © 1956 by Gwendolyn Brooks Blakely. Reprinted by permission of HarperCollins Publishers.

Cover and Program Design: Michaelis/Carpelis Design Associates, Inc.

Additional Design: Textart, Inc.

Production: Textart, Inc.
Michaelis/Carpelis Design Associates, Inc.

Illustration

Cover Illustration: Carol Newsom

Back Cover Illustration: Patrick Merrell

Four-color airbrush: Brian Dugan, Mark Kaplan, Mary Ellen Senor

Poetry airbrush backgrounds: Mark Kaplan

Learning Center Logos: Rachel Geswaldo

Lesson Opener Panels: Josef Gast, 34, 66; Kathleen Kinkoff, 42, 72; Leo Monahan, 60, 90; Marti Shohet, 54, 84; Cindy Wrobel, 48, 78.

Four-color illustration: Pat Wong, 47, 50, 71, 103, 106.

Black line art: Network Graphics, 35, 43, 49, 55, 61, 67, 68, 73, 79, 81, 85, 102; Adam Weston, 59, 64, 65, 82, 88, 89.

Photography

All photographs are by Macmillan/McGraw-Hill School Division (MMSD) except as noted below.

35: Scott Harvey for MMSD. 37: Scott Harvey for MMSD. 39: Scott Harvey for MMSD. 41: Scott Harvey for MMSD. 43: Scott Harvey for MMSD. 45: Ken Karp for MMSD. 51: Scott Harvey for MMSD. 53: Ken Karp for MMSD. 56, 57: Ken Karp for MMSD. 59: Ken Karp for MMSD. 61: Scott Harvey for MMSD. 63: Ken Karp for MMSD. 65: Ken Karp for MMSD. 71: Ken Karp for MMSD. 73: Scott Harvey for MMSD. 75: Ken Karp for MMSD. 77: Ken Karp for MMSD. 78, 79: Scott Harvey for MMSD. 81: Scott Harvey for MMSD. 83: Ken Karp for MMSD. 85–87: Scott Harvey for MMSD. 89: Ken Karp for MMSD. 94, 95: Ken Karp for MMSD. 99–101: Ken Karp for MMSD. 102: Scott Harvey for MMSD. 103, 104: Ken Karp for MMSD. 105: Scott Harvey for MMSD.

INDEX

THE "T" TEAM OF TURTLES

T t
turtle

Write T and t.

Say the picture word on each turtle's team shirt.
If the picture word begins like <u>turtle</u> and <u>team</u>,
color the turtle and its shirt. Find out
which turtles belong on the "T" team!

A **K**ANGAROO'S POUCH FILLED WITH K's

K k

kangaroo

Write K and k.

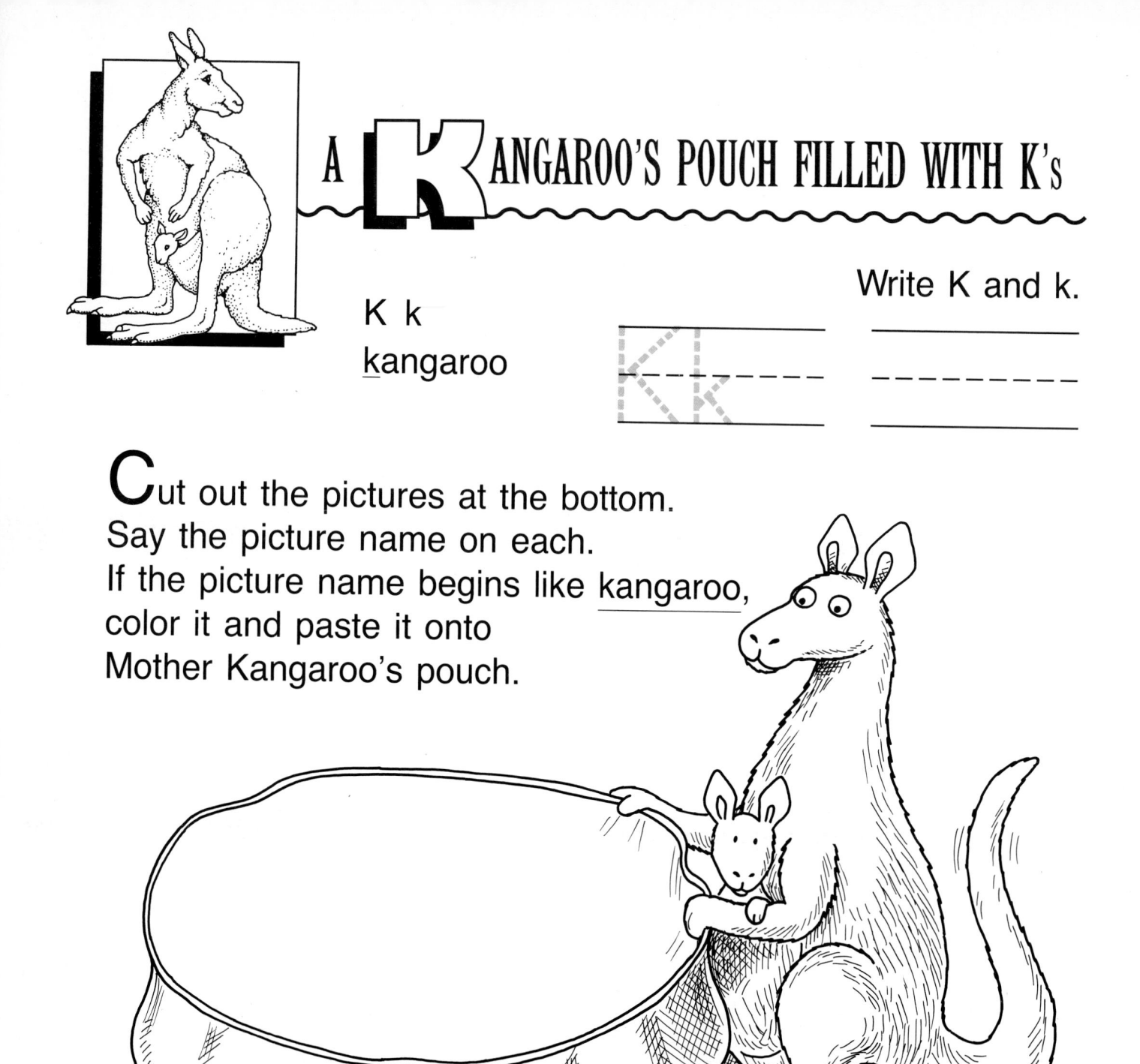

Cut out the pictures at the bottom.
Say the picture name on each.
If the picture name begins like kangaroo,
color it and paste it onto
Mother Kangaroo's pouch.

THEME 10

Share a Story!

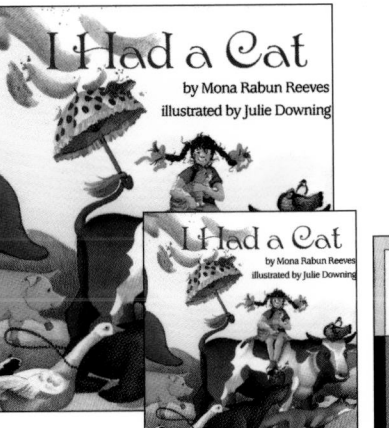

TRADE BOOK LITERATURE

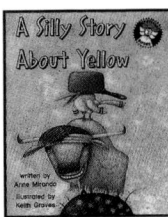

EARLY READERS

OTHER RESOURCES

- Big Book of Songs:
  pp. 32–33
- Big Book of Poems:
  pp. 30–31
- Big Book of Alphabet Rhymes
  and Chimes: pp. 12–13, 34
- Read Aloud Anthology:
  pp. 76–77, 78–79

- Songs and Stories
  Audiocassettes
    Story Songs: Tape 3, Side 1
    Storytelling: Tape 3, Side 1
- Sing a Sound
  Audiocassettes: Tape 1,
  Side 2; Tape 3, Side 6
- Listening Library
  Audiocassettes:
  Tape 5, Side 9

THEME OBJECTIVES

READING/WRITING LISTENING/SPEAKING

- shares ideas about stories and storytelling
- participates in creating and presenting a storytelling festival
- responds to others in a variety of ways
- reads, writes, and draws pictures about storytelling
- selects stories and books for personal interests
- appreciates the literary expression of our contemporary multicultural society and multicultural heritage
- recognizes cultural attitudes and customs in literary selections
- appreciates the artistic interpretation of literature through illustration, oral presentation, and other forms of expression
- retells stories
- shares writing
- participates in a variety of activities in response to literature

PHONICS AND DECODING

- discriminates the sound of letters: /f/*Ff*, /y/*Yy*
- identifies upper and lowercase letters: *Ff, Yy*
- recognizes sound/letter relationships: /f/*Ff*, /y/*Yy*
- writes upper and lowercase letters: *Ff, Yy*

CONCEPTS OF PRINT

- understands book concepts: cover, title, author, illustrator
- demonstrates awareness of directionality, letters, words, sentences, punctuation

Tell a Story/Sing a Song

AUTHORS

Elaine Mei Aoki

•

Virginia A. Arnold

•

James Flood

•

James V. Hoffman

•

Diane Lapp

•

Miriam Martinez

•

Annemarie Sullivan
Palincsar

•

Michael Priestley

•

Carl B. Smith

•

William H. Teale

•

Josefina Villamil
Tinajero

•

Arnold W. Webb

•

Karen D. Wood

Macmillan McGraw-Hill

New York   Farmington

AUTHORS, CONSULTANTS

MULTICULTURAL AND EDUCATIONAL CONSULTANTS

Yvonne Beamer, Joyce Buckner, Alma Flor Ada, Helen Gillotte,
Cheryl Hudson, Narcita Medina, Lorraine Monroe, James R. Murphy,
Sylvia Peña, Joseph B. Rubin, Ramon Santiago, Cliff Trafzer,
Hai Tran, Esther Lee Yao

LITERATURE CONSULTANTS

Ashley Bryan, Joan I. Glazer, Paul Janeczko, Margaret H. Lippert

INTERNATIONAL CONSULTANTS

Edward B. Adams, Barbara Johnson, Raymond L. Marshall

MUSIC AND AUDIO CONSULTANTS

John Farrell, Marilyn C. Davidson, Vincent Lawrence,
Sarah Pirtle, Susan R. Snyder,
Rick and Deborah Witkowski

Macmillan/McGraw-Hill

A Division of The McGraw-Hill Companies

Macmillan/McGraw-Hill
1221 Avenue of the Americas
New York, New York 10020

Printed in the United States of America

ISBN 0-02-181369-8 / K, U.10

2 3 4 5 6 7 8 9 BCM 02 01 00 99 98 97

Teacher's Planning Guide

Share a Story!

*To my mother,
who was my preschool teacher,
and who taught me that imagination is
our greatest resource.*

—Carl Smith

Contents

PRESENTING SHARE A STORY!

Share a Story!

An exploration of storytelling and dramatizations!
Theme Word: STORYTELLER
Theme Poem: "Worlds I Know"
 by Myra Cohn Livingston
Theme Song: "How About You?"
 by John Farrell

Contents

INTRODUCING TELL A STORY/SING A SONG

A New View of Kindergarten!

Welcome children to a print-rich, activity-based environment that nurtures emergent literacy!

19 BIG BOOKS!

48 TRADE BOOKS!

16 THEMES!

PROGRAM RESOURCES

BIG BOOK OF SONGS

BIG BOOK OF Cheep cheep cheep POEMS

Big Book of Songs
Theme Songs!

Big Book of Poems
Theme Poems!

THE MORE WE GET TOGETHER

The more we get together,
Together, together,
The more we get together,
The happier we'll be.

For your friends are my friends,
And my friends are your friends.
The more we get together,
The happier we'll be.

Traditional

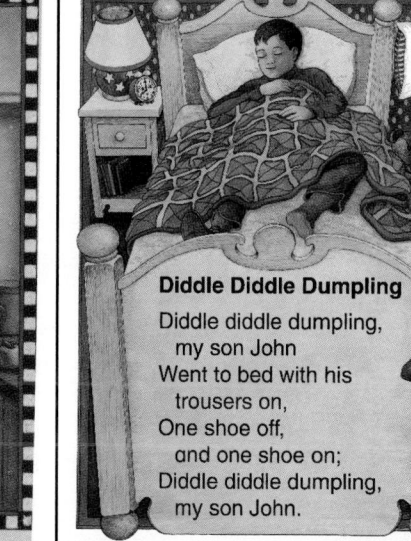

Cat's in the Cupboard

Great A, Little a,
Bouncing B!
The cat's in the cupboard
And can't see me.

Diddle Diddle Dumpling

Diddle diddle dumpling,
    my son John
Went to bed with his
    trousers on,
One shoe off,
    and one shoe on;
Diddle diddle dumpling,
    my son John.

Big Book of Alphabet Rhymes and Chimes
Verses for teaching the alphabet and concepts of print!
Plus the "Alphabet Song"!

Rhyme and Chime Strips
Each Rhyme and Chime on illustrated strips to use in pocket charts for Hands On! Language experiences!

| Cat's in the Cupboard |
| Great A, Little a, |
| Bouncing B! |
| The cat's in the cupboard |
| And can't see me. |

A a A a

B b B b

C c C c

Teacher's Read Aloud Anthology
32 Read Aloud selections from cultures around the world!

16 LITERATURE THEME PACKS

including 3 Trade Books (1 with a companion Big Book) and a Teacher's Planning Guide!

"Slither," said the snake in the cool morning air.

"Twitter," said the sparrows.
"Trot," said the mare.

"Paddle," Said the Swan

Written and illustrated
Gloria Kar...

IN THE ...
An Excursion in P...
by ESTHER H...
Pictures by EZRA J...

Big
Talk

By Miriam Schlein
Pictures by Joan Auclair

Big Book of *"Paddle," Said the Swan*

Also Available—

LISTENING LIBRARY AUDIOCASSETTES
for Big Books!

SONGS AND STORIES AUDIOCASSETTES
with Theme Songs, sound effects, and storytellings!

SING A SOUND AUDIOCASSETTES
with songs to encourage language play and to develop phonemic awareness!

TEACHER'S PLANNING GUIDE

SPEAK OUT!
MACMILLAN/McGRAW-HILL

Teacher's Planning Guide
for Speak Out!
Your resource for organizing activities—
• Sharing Time
• Reading and Writing
• Exploring Print
• Into the Learning Centers

ANCILLARIES

Alphabet Posters
26 full-color posters!

ABC Cards
Textured letter forms
for tactile learning!

Sing & Read Books and Audiocassettes
16 little books, one for each theme song,
with audiocassettes of children singing
and then reading the selection!

Literature Activity Book with

- Activities for introducing
  each theme
- Tell-a-Tale Take-Home Books
- Responding to Literature pages
- Exploring Print activities
- Just for Fun pages, too!

Also Available—

HomeWords:
Newsletters and more
to send home each month!

Sights & Sounds:
Interactive software for children to use in their
exploration of the sounds of language
and the letters that represent them!

Tell a Story / Sing a Song

PROGRAM THEMES	TRADE BOOKS	READ ALOUDS
1 GETTING TOGETHER	**BIG BOOK: *Getting Together*** by George Ancona ***What Will Mommy Do When I'm at School?*** by Dolores Johnson ***I'm Busy, Too*** by Norma Simon, illustrated by Dora Leder	**The Great Big Enormous Turnip** a Russian tale by Alexei Tolstoi **The Rabbit and the Elephant** a folk tale from Ghana retold by Ruthilde Kronberg and Patricia C. McKissack
2 SHARING WITH FRIENDS	**BIG BOOK: *Frog in the Middle*** by Susanna Gretz ***Will I Have a Friend?*** by Miriam Cohen, illustrated by Lillian Hoban ***Friends*** by Helme Heine	**The Lion and the Mouse** a fable by Aesop **The Three Friends** a folk tale from India retold by Isabel Wyatt
3 SPEAK OUT!	**BIG BOOK: *"Paddle," Said the Swan*** by Gloria Kamen ***In the Park*** by Esther Hautzig, illustrated by Ezra Jack Keats ***Big Talk*** by Miriam Schlein, illustrated by Joan Auclair	**The Long One** a Masai tale from East Africa by Verna Aardema **The Boy Who Cried Wolf** a fable by Aesop retold by Anne Terry White
4 LISTEN FOR SOUNDS!	**BIG BOOK: *Rain Talk*** by Mary Serfozo, illustrated by Keiko Narahashi ***Country Crossing*** by Jim Aylesworth, illustrated by Ted Rand ***Apt. 3*** by Ezra Jack Keats	**The Bremen Town Musicians** a German folk tale retold by Anne Rockwell **The Race Between Toad and Donkey** a Jamaican folk tale edited by Roger D. Abrahams

THEME WORDS	THEME SONGS	THEME POEMS	EXPLORING PRINT LESSONS
LPER	**The More We Get Together** a traditional song	**Together** by Paul Engle	Games and activities related to children's names
END	**Be a Friend** a traditional song	**Making Friends** by Eloise Greenfield	Games and activities related to friends and their names, and days of the week
EAKER	**The Buenas Song** a Hispanic song by Aaron Schroeder and David Grover	**Good Morning** by Muriel Sipe	Rhyme Time: Games, songs, and activities for rhyming
TENER	**The Little Red Caboose** Bernice Johnson Reagon's version of the traditional song	**Ears Hear** by Lucia and James L. Hymes, Jr.	*Big Book of Alphabet Rhymes and Chimes:* **Cc** Cat's in the Cupboard **Pp** Pease Porridge Hot

PROGRAM THEMES	TRADE BOOKS	READ ALOUDS
5 SING AND DANCE AWAY!	**BIG BOOK:** *Oh, A-Hunting We Will Go* by John Langstaff, illustrated by Nancy Winslow Parker *Max* by Rachel Isadora *The Little Band* by James Sage, illustrated by Keiko Narahashi	**The Twelve Dancing Princesses** a German fairy tale by the Brothers Grimm **The Clever Turtle** a Hispanic folk tale retold by Margaret H. Lippert
6 PAINT IT UP!	**BIG BOOK:** *Who Said Red?* by Mary Serfozo, illustrated by Keiko Narahashi *The little Bear Book* by Anthony Browne *circles, triangles and squares* by Tana Hoban	**The Black Cat** an American folk tale retold by Margaret H. Lippert **Ma Lien and the Magic Brush** a tale from China by Hisako Kimishima retold by Alvin Tresselt
7 EAT IT UP!	**BIG BOOK:** *Bread, Bread, Bread* by Ann Morris, photographs by Ken Heyman *Gregory, the Terrible Eater* by Mitchell Sharmat, illustrated by Jose Aruego and Ariane Dewey *What's on My Plate?* by Ruth Belov Gross, illustrated by Isadore Seltzer	**The Woman Who Flummoxed the Fairies** a Scottish folk tale retold by Sorche Nic Leodhas **Señor Billy Goat** a Hispanic folk tale retold by Pura Belpré
8 BUILD IT UP!	**BIG BOOK:** *Changes, Changes* by Pat Hutchins *I Read Signs* by Tana Hoban *Round Trip* by Ann Jonas	**The Three Little Pigs** an English fairy tale retold by Flora Annie Steel **Why the Moon Is in the Sky** an Ashanti folk tale from West Africa retold by Margaret H. Lippert

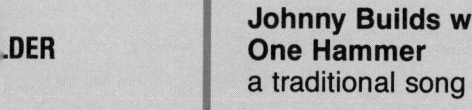
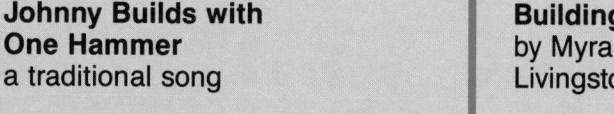
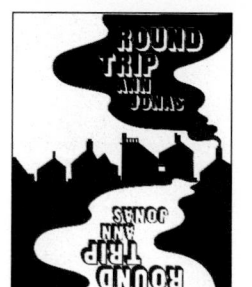
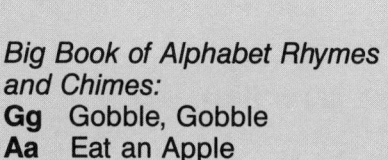

THEME WORDS	THEME SONGS	THEME POEMS	EXPLORING PRINT LESSONS
GER CER	**You'll Sing a Song and I'll Sing a Song** by Ella Jenkins	**Singing-Time** by Rose Fyleman	*Big Book of Alphabet Rhymes and Chimes:* **Hh** Hippity Hop to Bed **Mm** Miss Mary Mack
'IST	**I Know the Colors in the Rainbow** by Ella Jenkins	**Paints** by Ilo Orleans	*Big Book of Alphabet Rhymes and Chimes:* **Ss** Sing a Song of Sixpence **Bb** Bounce High, Bounce Low
K	**Short'ning Bread** a traditional Southern song	**Through the Teeth** a folk rhyme	*Big Book of Alphabet Rhymes and Chimes:* **Gg** Gobble, Gobble **Aa** Eat an Apple
DER	**Johnny Builds with One Hammer** a traditional song	**Buildings** by Myra Cohn Livingston	*Big Book of Alphabet Rhymes and Chimes:* **Rr** R Is for Ribbon **Ee** Engine, Engine, Number Nine

Program Themes	Trade Books	Read Alouds
9 MEET PAT HUTCHINS	**BIG BOOK:** *Titch* by Pat Hutchins *Rosie's Walk* by Pat Hutchins *Good-Night, Owl!* by Pat Hutchins	**It Could Always Be Worse** a Yiddish folk tale retold by Margot Zemach **Rainbow Crow** a Lenape tale retold by Nancy Van Laan
10 SHARE A STORY!	**BIG BOOK:** *I Had a Cat* by Mona Rabun Reeves, illustrated by Julie Downing *Little Red Hen* by Janina Domanska *Nessa's Fish* by Nancy Luenn, illustrated by Neil Waldman	**The Storytelling Stone** a Seneca tale retold by Joseph Bruchac **The Three Bears** an English folk tale retold by Margaret H. Lippert
11 ACT IT OUT!	**BIG BOOK:** *Handtalk Zoo* by George Ancona and Mary Beth *Stone Soup* by Marcia Brown *I'm Going on a Dragon Hunt* by Maurice Jones, illustrated by Charlotte Firmin	**The Three Billy Goats Gruff** a Norwegian folk tale retold by Margaret H. Lippert **The Terrible Tragadabas** a tale from Spanish New Mexico by Joe Hayes
12 WONDER ABOUT IT!	**BIG BOOK:** *White Is the Moon* by Valerie Greeley *Half a Moon and One Whole Star* by Crescent Dragonwagon, illustrated by Jerry Pinkney *The Park Bench* by Fumiko Takeshita, illustrated by Mamoru Suzuki	**The Spider Weaver** a folk tale from Japan retold by Florence Sakada **The One You Don't See Coming** a folk tale from Liberia retold by Harold Courlander and George Herzog

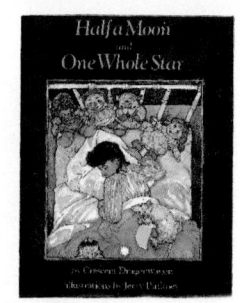

The Park Bench

Theme Words	Theme Songs	Theme Poems	Exploring Print Lessons
RITER	**Read a Book** by Marcy Marxer	**Surprise** by Beverly McLoughland	*Big Book of Alphabet Rhymes and Chimes:* **Tt** Toaster Time **Kk** A Kettle's for the Kitchen
RYTELLER	**How About You?** by John Farrell	**Worlds I Know** by Myra Cohn Livingston	*Big Book of Alphabet Rhymes and Chimes:* **Ff** Five Little Fishies **Yy** The Yak
OR	**Eency, Weency Spider** a traditional song	**On Our Way** by Eve Merriam	*Big Book of Alphabet Rhymes and Chimes:* **Qq** Quack, Quack, Quack **Zz** Zippety! Zippety! Zim, zim, zim!
NKER	**Twinkle, Twinkle, Little Star** a traditional song	**I Arise** an Eskimo song	*Big Book of Alphabet Rhymes and Chimes:* **Ii** If All the World Was Apple Pie **Xx** What Words Begin with X?

Tell a Story/Sing a Song

PROGRAM THEMES	TRADE BOOKS	READ ALOUDS
13 FIND IT OUT!	**BIG BOOK:** *What Do You See?* by Janina Domanska *Farm Animals* photographs by Philip Dowell and Michael Dunning *Changes* by Marjorie N. Allen and Shelley Rotner, photographs by Shelley Rotner	**Why Bears Have Short Tails** a Navajo legend from Arizona retold by Sandra Begay **The Plumage of the Owl/ El Plumaje del Mucaro** a Puerto Rican folk tale retold by Ricardo E. Alegría
14 MEET EZRA JACK KEATS	**BIG BOOK:** *Hi, Cat!* by Ezra Jack Keats *Kitten for a Day* by Ezra Jack Keats *Pet Show!* by Ezra Jack Keats	**Belling the Cat** a fable by Aesop retold by Joseph Jacobs **The Cat's Purr** a West Indian tale by Ashley Bryan
15 THINKING ABOUT ME	**BIG BOOK:** *All I Am* by Eileen Roe, illustrated by Helen Cogancherry *The Train to Lulu's* by Elizabeth Fitzgerald Howard, illustrated by Robert Casilla *Con Mi Hermano/With My Brother* by Eileen Roe, illustrated by Robert Casilla	**The Knee-High Man** an American black folk tale retold by Julius Lester **Anansi's Rescue from the River** a folk tale from West Africa retold by Harold Courlander
16 SETTING OUT!	**BIG BOOK:** *As the Crow Flies: A First Book of Maps* by Gail Hartman, illustrated by Harvey Stevenson *Look Out, Patrick!* by Paul Geraghty *Builder of the Moon* by Tim Wynne-Jones, illustrated by Ian Wallace	**Timimoto** a folk tale from Japan retold by Margaret H. Lippert **Jack and the Beanstalk** an English fairy tale retold by Virginia Haviland

THEME WORDS	THEME SONGS	THEME POEMS	EXPLORING PRINT LESSONS
SEARCHER	**Who Fed the Chickens?** by Ella Jenkins	**Who?** by Lilian Moore	*Big Book of Alphabet Rhymes and Chimes:* **Dd** Diddle Diddle Dumpling **Ww** Wee Willie Winkie
LUSTRATOR	**Library Song** by Michael Mark and Tom Chapin	**Picture People** by Myra Cohn Livingston	*Big Book of Alphabet Rhymes and Chimes:* **Ll** Lily's a Lady **Jj** Jack Be Nimble
LD	**I Am a Person** by Sarah Pirtle	**By Myself** by Eloise Greenfield	*Big Book of Alphabet Rhymes and Chimes:* **Nn** Nicholas Ned **Uu** Umbrellas
PLORER	**The Bear Went Over the Mountain** a traditional song	**Come Out** by Karla Kuskin	*Big Book of Alphabet Rhymes and Chimes:* **Oo** Polly, Put the Kettle On **Vv** Very Nice

Emergent Writing

MIRIAM MARTINEZ AND WILLIAM TEALE

The emergent literacy perspective is a powerful one because it lays the foundation for promoting children's literacy development through rich, exciting, and purposeful writing opportunities in the classroom.

1. **Drawing**

Scribble

2.

Children's Writing Strategies

In their early explorations of the writing system, young children typically do not write in conventional ways. Careful observations of children's emergent writing have revealed a general, but rather complicated, developmental pathway. As children move along this pathway, they typically use some or all of the following strategies:

1. **Drawing**

2. **Scribbling**

3. **Randomly Chosen Letters:** The child uses letters, but there is not a relationship between the letters chosen and the sounds in the words that are written.

4. **Words Copied from Environmental Print**

5. **Developmental Spelling:** There is a relationship between the letters used and the sounds in the words that are written, but only one or two of the sounds heard in words are represented. This behavior later develops to the point at which children are able to use a letter to represent every (or almost every) sound in the words that are written.

6. **Transitional Spelling:** Features of conventional spelling, like silent letters or doubling of consonants, begin to appear.

7. **Conventional Spelling**

Rich, Purposeful Writing Experiences

Young writers, like all writers, are most successful when they have interesting experiences to feed their writing. These include ''hands on'' activities, creative dramatics and art activities, content area experiences, explorations beyond the classroom, and opportunities to write about personal experiences beyond school.

Central to these efforts to ignite children's writing are rich literature experiences. One form that writing in response to literature takes is the journal. The journal is a place where children can record their thoughts, feelings, and reactions to a story they have just listened to or read.

Literature also nurtures children's own original story writing. Sometimes a storyline or story theme will serve as an invitation for the child to write about a similar experience. At other times, after reading a story with a distinctive predictable pattern, children may choose to use the same story pattern to organize their own writing.

Random Letters

REWRM
ERWDN
AEWR
AEWR

3.

Random Letters

YUVTOUSUCOt
CKOKOU
XOUOEUCI
OCUTCtCtC
2-6-85

3.

EMERGENT WRITING

Children's Growth as Writers

Three dimensions signal growth in children's writing. First is evidence that the child is using increasingly more sophisticated writing strategies (drawing, scribbling, developmental spellings, and so on.). However, as we observe children's movement along this developmental pathway, it's important to remember that not every child uses all strategies, nor will a child necessarily, as he or she begins to use a more sophisticated strategy, leave less sophisticated ones behind. If anything, many children tend to expand their repertoire of strategies, using different ones for different tasks.

The second dimension of children's growth as writers is what they say. It is particularly important to look for evidence that children are learning to organize their writing better, to develop their ideas more fully, and to use features that are associated with written language rather than oral language (Once upon a time...).

However, a word of warning is in order. As children begin to use more sophisticated writing strategies (in particular, as they concentrate on developmental spellings), the content and organization of their stories and journal entries may appear to become less sophisticated for a period of time. Rather than being taken as a cause for alarm, this state of affairs should be viewed as more of a natural trade-off. When children do get more control over sound-symbol relationships, they will again be able to attend more closely to what it is they want to say and to whom they want to say it.

4. **Copying Environmental Print**

5. **Early Developmental Spelling**

ly Developmental Spelling

W + C O p d B

Finally, it is important to remember that children's reading and writing development are integrally related, and this reading/writing connection must be taken into account in evaluating their growth as writers.

In particular, as a child reads what he or she has written, it is important to ask questions such as these:

• Does the child attend to the picture or the print in reading what she or he has written?

• Are the child's attempts to track the print successful?

• Does the child conventionally read what he or she has written?

• Does the child's intonation sound more like oral or written language?

As children move along the developmental pathway, their rereadings of their own writing become more print-based and sound increasingly like written language rather than oral language.

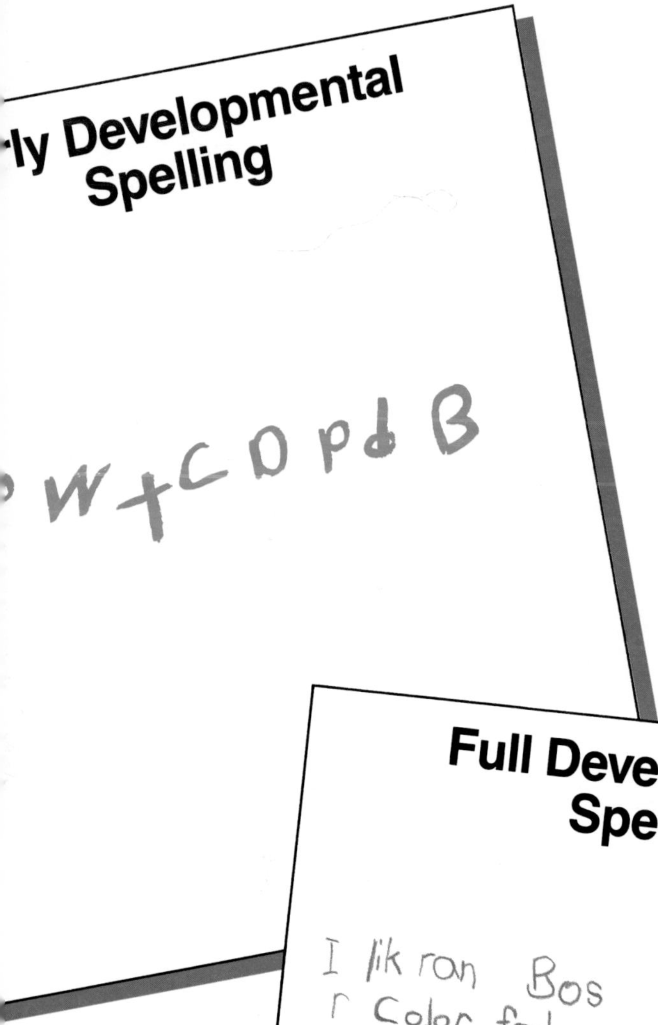

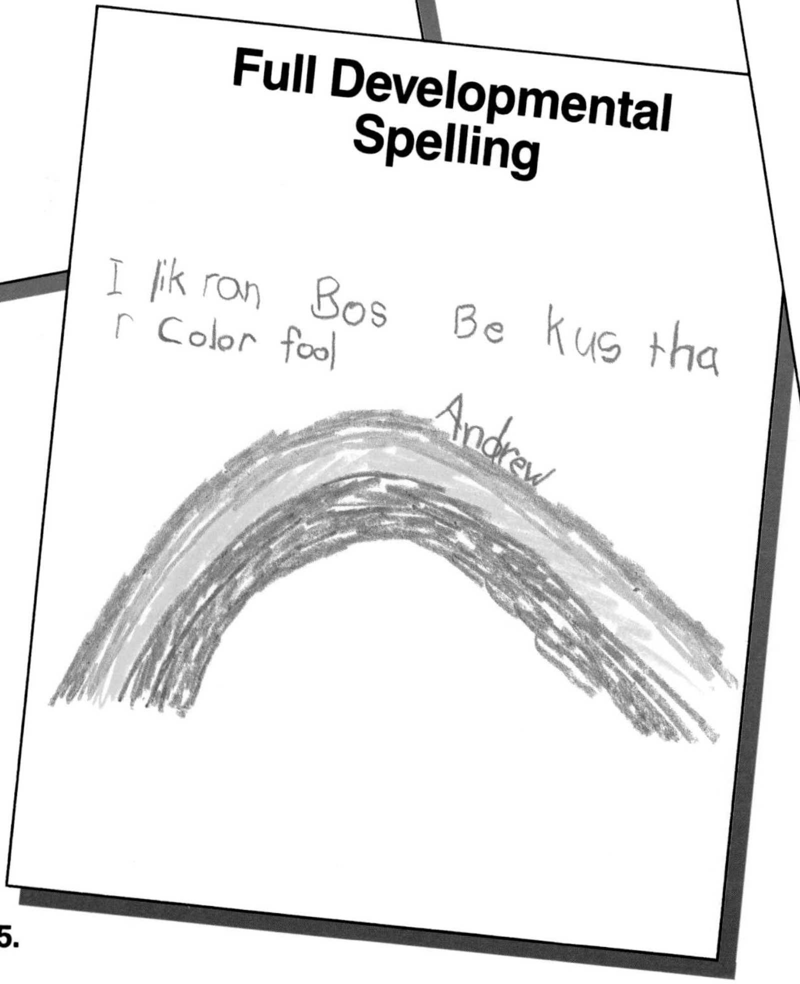

Full Developmental Spelling

I lik ron Bos   Be kus tha
r Color fool

Andrew

Transitional Spelling

5-2-85

Andrew

I llKe CooKes And
CaKs AndI theK
I Know To MaK theeM
uoosfian Wet And egg

5.

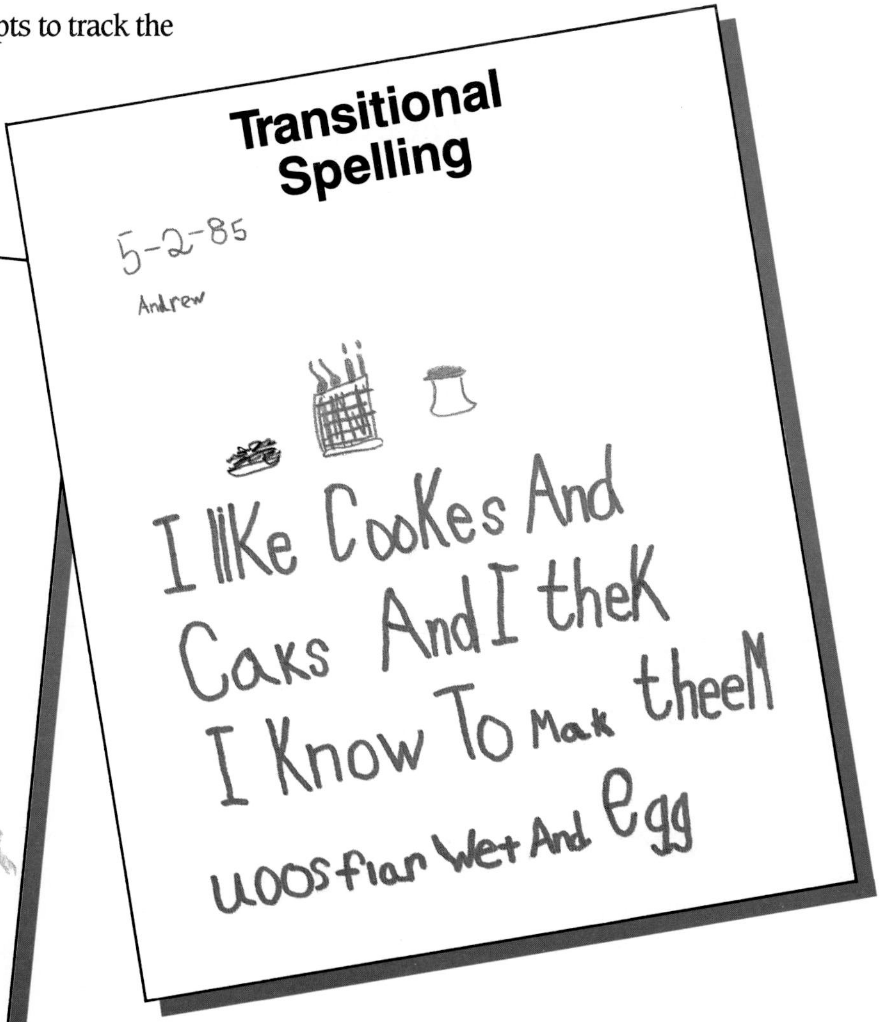

6.

STUDENTS ACQUIRING ENGLISH

EMERGENT LITERACY IN THE SECOND LANGUAGE

BY JOSEFINA VILLAMIL TINAJERO

The early childhood years are a remarkably active period for acquiring language and for learning about its written form. Classroom environments have a significant effect on children's language and literacy development. This is especially true for emergent readers and writers who are also acquiring English as a second language. The physical and social environment of the classroom, teacher beliefs and attitudes about language acquisition and emergent literacy, the types of activities planned, and the strategies and techniques used by teachers all affect the opportunities children have to emerge as readers and writers and to acquire a new language.

Supporting Kindergartners' Language Acquisition

It is our position that children *acquire* rather than *learn* a language in a natural progression of stages. As language is acquired, literacy in the new language develops. That is, current research suggests that the second language is acquired in the same manner as the first and that it is acquired most effectively in a highly interactive, total communication environment.

Children acquire language when they understand what people say to them or what is read. They acquire language by understanding messages and by responding to those messages in meaningful ways. Language must make sense to young children, and somehow it must be important for them to acquire it. Some of the best ways to encourage language development are to provide children with many opportunities to interact with other children, to encourage child's play, and to engage them in natural language activities. Songs, poems, stories, games, role-play, story theater, and dramatizations are especially effective because they allow students to hear natural English while providing a meaningful, motivating, and enjoyable context for learning.

Young SAEs need a favorable environment for language acquisition, an environment that is as natural and as language-rich as that within which they learned their first language. Kindergartners acquiring English, in particular, need many opportunities to hear and use English, to experiment with it, to take risks and try out their knowledge of the language. They need to be encouraged to express their ideas and feelings as they move along the pathway toward nativelike fluency.

When students offer responses, for example, their pronunciation may be poor and their grammatical construction may include elements from their first language. When this happens, teachers need to accept their responses, model the "correct" form in a tactful and unexaggerated way, and praise them for their contributions. Praising builds confidence and helps children feel valued as members of the class. They will also be much more motivated to "experiment" with the language and to take risks—that is, express their thoughts and ideas even if they are not yet fully fluent in the language.

Teachers can integrate the following techniques with activities planned for other children in the class.

Heterogeneous Grouping. One way to provide SAEs with opportunities to practice their English is to increase the frequency and variety of interactions among students. Pairing them with proficient English speakers for activities such as partner "reading" of Big Books and partner story retellings is one way

22

of increasing interaction. Grouping them with students of varying proficiencies for activities such as illustrating a new ending to a story or illustrating a character map is another. At other times, however, SAEs may be grouped together for activities such as listening to a story in their native language, working on a special project, or doing partner reading with other SAEs.

Cooperative Learning. Cooperative learning also increases the frequency and variety of second language practice through different types of interactions. It provides students with many opportunities to utilize newly acquired language and to "read and write" (scribbling and drawing are considered writing at this age) in English in a "safe" social situation where they don't feel threatened by error correction. Cooperative learning also provides students with opportunities to act as resources for each other and thus assume a more active role in learning.

When working with kindergartners acquiring English, it is also important to keep in mind that, as individuals, they are at different levels of English proficiency. Thus, when planning activities for them, teachers must be aware of the level of receptive and productive language they bring to the learning task. There may be some children who may not be ready to begin producing oral English. Some may be experiencing what is often referred to as the *"silent period" of language learning*. That is, second language learners go through a period of time during which they prefer to listen rather than to produce language. As with most second language learners, children's receptive language skills develop earlier than their productive ones (Rice, 1989).

It is important, however, to keep in mind that language learning is taking place during this time (Evans, 1990). Children don't always need to respond in order to learn new language skills. They can benefit greatly from the opportunity to absorb the conversations of others (Rice, 1989).

$\mathcal{U}$sing Literature to Nurture Children's Language Development

The best language lessons are good books and interesting discussions in which children are absorbed in the meaning of what is said to them or what is read.

For SAEs, literature cultivates language, provides language models, and facilitates language acquisition. As children listen to rhymes, poems, and patterned/predictable stories in English, they learn new language patterns and idiomatic usages, which are assimilated as children apply them to express their own thoughts and ideas during meaningful, well-planned lessons. Children with limited vocabulary can latch on to the "new" language they have heard, suddenly discovering that their former limited vocabulary takes on new dimensions.

$\mathcal{S}$torytelling with SAEs

Because storytelling encourages physical, visual, and aural/oral participation of students, it is an excellent context for teaching language and concepts to SAEs.

Listening and speaking skills, for example, are enriched through the use of puppetry, tapes, dramatic presentations, and the teacher's systematic reading to children. Children will also enjoy retelling stories they have been told or sharing stories from their own cultures, stories they may have learned at home or in their neighborhoods. Children's own creativity and ingenuity can also be encouraged and supported by allowing children to create, tell, and retell their own stories.

Following are some suggestions to take full advantage of storytelling activities to enhance language development for SAEs.

Oral Previewing. This technique adjusts the teacher's language input to children's language proficiency and comprehension level during storytelling. For SAEs, oral previewing takes the form of paraphrasing or telling the story "in your own words," both to make the story as comprehensible as possible and to facilitate language development. When using this technique, follow these guidelines.

First, screen the story, taking into account the language and experiential knowledge of students. Select areas of difficulty such as idiomatic language and difficult vocabulary. Become familiar with the story so that the retelling is as natural as possible, and so that you can be cognizant of facial expressions that might indicate whether or not SAEs are understanding the story.

Then hold up a copy of the book as you lead the children orally through the story, establishing plot and setting. Use gestures, body language, and facial expressions to help convey ideas and

Students Acquiring English

concepts. Use simple, well-formed sentences; limit sentence length and complexity while maintaining appropriate grammar and intonation.

Clarify the meaning of words, phrases, and idiomatic expressions using context clues, such as pointing to the illustrations or drawing simple pictures. Make frequent repetitions of key words and ideas. At times, incorporate role play to help children understand concepts and learn language through physical activity.

As you continue to go through the story, ask questions that require yes/no responses, a nod of the head, pointing to an illustration, or one- or two-word responses to check understanding. Also ask questions to relate the story situation to children's experiences. Remember that SAEs understand more than they can verbalize. As children respond using one or two words, repeat their utterances, use their words in an expanded comment. That is, use the *semantic expansion* technique, in which you as the teacher start with something the child said and elaborate to clarify or add to the response. Also, use structural expansion in which you as the teacher repeat an incorrect utterance correctly to model for the children. Finally, have children make predictions along the way to encourage language use and development of critical thinking skills. Remember to praise children for their contributions.

These types of teacher-child interactions with storybooks create a context for comprehending meaning, for making meaning. They help SAEs get past some of the difficult language so they can concentrate on the story line. Children also internalize new language related to the story they are about to hear.

The following storytelling variations help SAEs acquire language and make stories more comprehensible. Use them as often as possible. They are good for all children.

Puppetry. Puppets make stories come alive for children, and the actions associated with using them to tell or retell stories make language more comprehensible. Most important, however, SAEs are less reluctant to talk "when they take on other identities to perform. It is somehow less threatening to make a mistake as someone else; it becomes their mistake, not that of the student" (Evans, 1990).

Participation Stories. Certain stories invite children to participate actively as they respond to certain words that act as cues for actions like clapping or stamping their feet or shaking their heads. Before reading the story, the teacher introduces the cues. The children then act out the story as the teacher reads. These types of stories develop listening skills and facilitate language acquisition (Evans, 1990).

Pantomime. Through pantomime children use their whole bodies for making meaning as they participate in storytelling activities. Text becomes more comprehensible as characters come alive.

Story Retelling. Working with a partner, children retell stories to one another. Story retelling provides a great opportunity for children to use the language they have heard in the stories to express their own thoughts and ideas.

Tape Recordings. Tape recordings of stories are an excellent way to expose students to good literature that may be beyond their reading abilities but within their listening abilities. Children will also enjoy making their own recordings of

stories. These recordings also serve as good diagnostic tools.

Choral Reading. Choral readings of stories, with a mix of SAEs and proficient English speakers, give shy learners a safe way to practice formal speaking. Remember, the desire of SAEs to produce language varies greatly—allow them to join in when they're ready.

Shared Reading and SAEs

Another excellent way to provide SAEs with rich literature experiences is to conduct shared reading with books that contain repetitive language and/or predictable outcomes. The repetitive characteristics of the texts facilitate the natural acquisition of vocabulary, pronunciation, and language structures. Big Books are particularly effective for group study and for exposing children to print.

The repeated readings help children to read more efficiently, gain confidence, practice using their reading skills, and increase their sight vocabulary. And since the illustrations in the books are closely tied to the text, children get visual support for the rapid development of a wide range of vocabulary. The reading and rereading of stories also allow SAEs to hear and practice, in an informal setting, the rhythm and structure of English.

As children recite and participate in shared reading activities using rhymes, poems, songs, and pattern stories, they learn new language patterns. They internalize these patterns and then use them to express their own thoughts and ideas. Furthermore, through shared reading, children are exposed to the written and oral forms of language and are offered

numerous opportunities to develop listening, speaking, reading, and writing skills at the "teachable moment."

Shared reading activities also establish the kind of low-anxiety environment essential to language acquisition and provide SAEs at varying/lower levels of English proficiency with the opportunity to participate with the rest of the class. It is also a pleasurable experience that helps SAEs develop a positive attitude toward acquiring English and learning to read in a second language.

In selecting materials to use with SAEs, select those with texts containing features such as rhyme, rhythmic language, predictable or repetitive plots and language patterns, or illustrations that closely parallel the text. Screen materials carefully for overload of idiomatic language and situations that are culturally unfamiliar. Finally, select materials at the appropriate instructional level that foster students' appreciation of reading and develop positive attitudes toward learning to read in English.

Language Experience Activities

The language experience approach is particularly suitable for use with SAEs because the children's language proficiency, no matter how limited, is valued and used as a starting point for further development. And because SAEs' proficiency in English often varies significantly, language experience activities help build a common knowledge and language base for them. The approach also integrates children's ideas, interests, experiences, and natural language, using them to motivate students to read.

Through language experience, SAEs are also able to acquire the basic skills of reading and writing with familiar material—their own. Thus, the text is rich in comprehensible content that further develops children's language proficiency.

Establishing Partnerships with Parents

A primary way in which we can provide more supportive learning environments for all children is to involve their parents, working with them as colleagues, inviting them to participate as valuable resources of information and perspectives, and sharing with them ways in which parents enhance education at home.

Parents can assist teachers in creating more supportive and nurturing learning environments that offer the security needed for SAEs to participate in a culturally different setting. Parents can be invited to the classroom to tell stories from the oral tradition, to read stories, read or recite poetry, share "how to" information, and present topics that have inspired and informed their lives.

Parents often think that they cannot help their children at home if they do not speak English. Teachers need to make an effort to assure them that working with their children in their native language is of benefit because concepts learned in the native language will transfer to English.

The Challenge

Kindergarten is a critical point for students acquiring English. Beyond their needs for skills in academic growth, SAEs also have motivational and emotional needs that must be met. These needs are often magnified in importance where there are cultural and linguistic differences between the school and the home. They include children's need to feel a sense of identity, to belong, to be understood by and communicate with significant others, and to succeed in environments in which they are accepted and respected. Kindergarten teachers can make a difference in the lives of these children. By simply applying some of the basic principles discussed here, teachers can provide a nurturing and intellectually stimulating environment where students acquiring English can succeed and thrive.

References

Auerbach, E. (1989). Toward a social-contextual approach to family literacy. Harvard Educational Review, 59, No. 2, pp. 165–181.

Early, M. (1991). Using wordless picture books to promote second language learning. ELT Journal. Volume 45/3. July. pp. 245–250.

Evans, L. S. (1990). Storytelling and oral language development in ESL classrooms. TESOL Newsletter. October. pp. 3, 16, 18, 30.

Flood, J.; Lapp, D.; Tinajero, J.; and Nagel, G. Parents and teachers: Partners in developing literacy for multicultural students. (unpublished manuscript).

Nurss, J. R. and Hough, R. A. (1985). Story reading: Language arts for limited English speakers. TESOL Newsletter. Vol. 8, No. 1. pp. 1–2.

Rice, M. (1989). Children's language acquisition. American Psychologist. Volume 4. February. pp. 149–156.

*I*NTRODUCING **SHARE A STORY!**

Invite children to explore storytelling through trade books, read aloud selections, poetry, and songs!

TRADE BOOKS

BIG BOOK

I Had a Cat
by *Mona Rabun Reeves,*
illustrated by Julie Downing
A girl's house is filled with animals of all kinds—a cat, a dog, an ape, an elk, a bear, and more! So many animals that they won't fit in her house! They all go on a trip to find new homes!
Available as a Big Book and a little book, and included on the
LISTENING LIBRARY AUDIOCASSETTE

Little Red Hen
by *Janina Domanska*
Little Red Hen finds a grain of wheat. Will her friends help her plant and harvest it? Who will eat the bread she makes from the wheat?

Nessa's Fish
by *Nancy Luenn, illustrated by Neil Waldman*
A little girl named Nessa and her grandmother walk half a day to reach a fishing pond. After catching lots of fish, the grandmother gets sick. Nessa must save the fish and her grandmother from hungry animals: a fox, wolves, and a bear!

READ ALOUDS

TEACHER'S READ ALOUD ANTHOLOGY

The Storytelling Stone
a *Seneca tale retold by Joseph Bruchac*
A tale about how storytelling came to be! It all begins with a story telling stone.

The Three Bears
an *English folk tale retold by Margaret H. Lippert*
Little Wee Bear, Middle-sized Bear, and Great Huge Bear take a walk to let their porridge cool. What happens when the Bears get home?

G BOOKS

BIG BOOK OF POEMS
Worlds I Know
by Myra Cohn Livingston

BIG BOOK OF SONGS
How About You?
by John Farrell

Also Available—

SING & READ BOOKS AND AUDIOCASSETTES
How About You?

SONGS AND STORIES AUDIOCASSETTES
Story Songs—including the
Theme Song—and Storytellings!

EXPLORING PRINT

BIG BOOK OF ALPHABET RHYMES AND CHIMES
PLUS RHYME AND CHIME STRIPS

- **Ff** Five Little Fishies

- **Yy** The Yak

Also Available—

SING A SOUND AUDIOCASSETTES
Songs for language play and for
developing phonemic awareness!

THEME 10: SHARE A STORY!
Overview for Week 1

LITERATURE	SHARING TIME	READING AND WRITING
1 THEME POEM "Worlds I Know"	**Today's News** and becoming storytellers p. 35	Reading the Theme Poem "Worlds I K and Responding through **Poem Talk** Telling Stories from Pictures pp. 36-37
2 READ ALOUD "The Storytelling Stone"	**Today's News** and talking about where stories come from p. 41	Reading "The Storytelling Stone" and Responding through **Book Talk**, Journal Writing, and Making a Story E pp. 42-43
3 NESSA'S FISH	**Today's News** and sharing information about Inuits and the Arctic p. 47	Reading *Nessa's Fish* and Responding through **Book Talk**, Journal Writing, and Story Theater pp. 48-49
4 NESSA'S FISH	**Today's News** and reading the poem "Adventures of Isabel" p. 53	Rereading *Nessa's Fish* and Responding through **Book Talk** and Making a Story Elements Chart pp. 54-55
5 I HAD A CAT	**Today's News** and singing the song "The Animal Fair" p. 59	Reading *I Had a Cat* and Responding through **Book Talk**, Journal Writing, and Taking a Field Trip or Inviting a Guest Speaker pp. 60-61

THEME WORD: STORYTELLER

ch theme helps children see themselves from a different
rspective. This theme helps children see themselves as
rytellers.

XPLORING PRINT

:oding and Phonics
ers *F, f*
nd/Letter Relationships /f/ *F, f*
NG: "I've Been Workin' on the Railroad"
44-45

:oding and Phonics
ers *F, f*
nd/Letter Relationships /f/ *F, f*
BOOK OF ALPHABET RHYMES AND CHIMES:
e Little Fishies"
50-51

:cepts of Print
ctionality, Words
YME AND CHIME STRIPS:
e Little Fishies"
56-57

:oding and Phonics
ers *F, f*
nd/Letter Relationships /f/ *F, f*
:cepts of Print
ctionality, Words, Letters
YME AND CHIME STRIPS:
e Little Fishies"
62-63

THEME GOALS AND OUTCOMES

The literature and activities in this theme were
carefully selected and reviewed by the program
authors and by the multicultural, literature, and
educational consultants who worked together to
develop the program goals and outcomes.

MULTICULTURAL PERSPECTIVES

Appreciate and value diverse points of view

Become aware of cultural backgrounds,
experiences, emotions, and ideas of self and
others through literature

Appreciate the literary expression of our
contemporary multicultural society and
multicultural heritage

Appreciate the universality of literary themes in
many cultures and in many different times

Appreciate the significance of traditional
literature within a culture

Recognize cultural attitudes and customs in
literary selections

PERSONAL INTERESTS AND ATTITUDES

Develop an awareness of the classroom as a
community of learners that values cooperation,
fair play, and respect for others and for oneself

Select stories and books for personal interests

Develop personal reading and writing interests

Make connections between one's personal life
and literature

Choose to read and write for a variety of
purposes

Share, review, and recommend books to others

Participate in reading, writing, listening, and
viewing activities

Appreciate the artistic interpretation of literature
through film, illustration, photography, dance,
oral presentations, and other forms of expression

LITERATURE	SHARING TIME	READING AND WRITING
6 *I HAD A CAT*	**Today's News** and singing the Theme Song "How About You?" p. 65	Rereading *I Had a Cat* and Responding through **Book Talk** and Being a Storyteller pp. 66-67
7 *LITTLE RED HEN*	**Today's News** and reading the poem "Five Little Chickens" p. 71	Reading *Little Red Hen* and Responding through **Book Talk** and Journal Writing pp. 72-73
8 *LITTLE RED HEN*	**Today's News** and creating verses for the song "The Mulberry Bush" p. 77	Rereading *Little Red Hen* and Responding through **Book Talk** and Creating a Big Book pp. 78-79
9 **READ ALOUD** "The Three Bears"	**Today's News** and reading the rhyme "Bears, Bears, Everywhere" p. 83	Reading "The Three Bears" and Responding through **Book Talk**, Journal Writing, and Story Theater pp. 84-85
10 *NESSA'S FISH* *I HAD A CAT* *LITTLE RED HEN*	**Today's News** and singing the Theme Song "How About You?" and rereading the Theme Poem "Worlds I Know" p. 89	Reviewing the trade books in the theme and Responding through **Book Talk** and Journal Writing pp. 90-91

Integrating Language Arts and Other Curriculum Areas

Into the Learning Centers!

MORE BOOKS TO SHARE

The books on these pages can be shared with children throughout the theme. The books can also be put into the Reading Center so children can read and enjoy them.

MORE BOOKS ABOUT SHARING A STORY

■ THE MITTEN

adapted by Jan Brett (G. P. Putnam's Sons, 1991). In this delightful retelling of a Ukrainian folk tale, a young boy drops a mitten in the snow. One by one, animals of the forest seek shelter within it, stretching it as they crawl in. Oblivious to what is happening, the boy plays happily throughout the day. All ends well when the oversized mitten is returned to him in an extraordinary manner.

■ ONCE A MOUSE . . . A FABLE CUT IN WOOD

by Marcia Brown (Aladdin, 1981). From ancient India comes this tale about big and little and the dangers of becoming too prideful about one's position in life. Marcia Brown won a Caldecott Honor Medal for the magnificent woodcuts that accompany the story.

■ AUNT ISABEL TELLS A GOOD ONE

by Kate Duke (Dutton, 1991). Aunt Isabel and Penelope, two enchantingly depicted mice, get together for a storytelling session. As Aunt Isabel lists the ingredients of a good story—main characters, setting, conflict—Penelope fills in the details. Reading the book aloud (really two stories in one) provides an opportunity to discuss storytelling and story elements.

■ MILLIONS OF CATS

by Wanda Gag (Scholastic, 1956, originally published in 1928). One of the precursors of the contemporary picture book, this Newbery Honor book still amuses readers with its humorous situations and touching ending. A good choice to demonstrate how using a refrain can heighten the storyteller's art.

■ TREASURE NAP

by Juanita Havill, illus. by Elivia Savadier (Houghton Mifflin, 1992). "It's too hot to take a nap, Mamá," Alicia complains. So Mamá places Alicia and baby Ramón before the cooling breeze of an electric fan and tells them the story of her own great-grandmother Rita who journeyed from Mexico to the United States many years ago. In her arms, Rita carried her two treasures: a bird cage and a *pito*, gifts from her grandfather that are still treasured by her descendants today.

■ TELL ME A STORY, MAMA

by Angela Johnson, illus. by David Soman (Orchard, 1989). A young girl and her mother share the familiar and much-loved stories from Mama's own childhood. A warm and sensitive story about continuity among three generations of a loving family.

■ FREDERICK

by Leo Lionni (Pantheon, 1967). All summer long, the industrious mice warn Frederick that he, too, must gather food for the long winter ahead. But Frederick is gathering his own supply of sustenance—words. Before long he is able to demonstrate that the storyteller has an important role to play in our society.

■ THE ROUGH-FACE GIRL

by Rafe Martin, illus. by David Shannon (G. P. Putnam's Sons, 1992). Variations of the Cinderella story are found throughout the folklore of the world. In this version from the Algonquin nation retold by professional storyteller Rafe Martin, the youngest daughter in a poor family is forced to tend the fire continually, the cinders of which roughen and scar her skin. Ultimately her goodness and beauty are recognized by the Invisible Being who chooses her for his wife.

■ **THE STORY OF JUMPING MOUSE: A NATIVE AMERICAN LEGEND**
retold by John Steptoe (Lothrop, Lee & Shepard, 1984). In this powerful Caldecott Honor book, Jumping Mouse yearns to visit the far-off land beyond his own familiar desert home. The journey is long and difficult, but the little mouse keeps hope alive in his breast even as he gives away his most precious possessions—his sight and sense of smell—to others in need. Rewarded for his compassion, Jumping Mouse is turned into an eagle to fly freely in the far-off land forever.

■ **THE BIG FAT WORM**
by Nancy Van Laan, illus. by Marisabina Russo (Knopf, 1987). This circular story with its repetitive, predictable text and vibrant illustrations will captivate kindergartners as one bigger and fatter animal after another threatens to eat the preceding creature. Of course, the circle comes around and it all begins anew.

MORE VARIANT TALES

Three tales about controlling the weather from Africa, Europe, and Asia:

■ **BRINGING THE RAIN TO KAPITI PLAIN: A NANDI TALE**
by Verna Aardema, illus. by Beatriz Vidal (Dial, 1981).

■ **HOW THE SUN WAS BROUGHT BACK TO THE SKY**
adapted from a Slovenian folk tale by Mirra Ginsburg, illus. by Jose Aruego and Ariane Dewey (Macmillan, 1975).

■ **BAWSHOU RESCUES THE SUN**
by Chun-Chan Yeh and Allan Baillie, illus. by Michelle Powell (Scholastic, 1991).

A variation of the Theme Book *Little Red Hen:*

■ **THE LITTLE RED HEN**
by Paul Galdone (Clarion, 1973).

A variation of the selection in the Read Aloud Anthology:

■ **GOLDILOCKS AND THE THREE BEARS**
retold by James Marshall (Dial, 1988).

Three versions of "Little Red Riding Hood":

■ **RED RIDING HOOD**
retold in verse by Beatrice Schenk de Regniers, illus. by Edward Gorey (Aladdin, 1972).

■ **RED RIDING HOOD**
retold by James Marshall (Dial, 1987).

■ **LON PO PO: A RED-RIDING HOOD STORY FROM CHINA**
translated by Ed Young (Philomel, 1989).

MORE BOOKS BY THEME AUTHORS AND ILLUSTRATORS

■ **IF ALL THE SEAS WERE ONE SEA**
etchings by Janina Domanska (Macmillan, 1987, originally published in 1971). A Caldecott Honor book, this version of the familiar nursery rhyme comes alive through Domanska's striking four-color etchings.

■ **MOTHER EARTH**
by Nancy Luenn, illus by Neil Waldman (Atheneum, 1992). An ecological message is introduced to the reader through Luenn's lyrical text and Waldman's luminous paintings.

■ **THE SPOOKY EERIE NIGHT NOISE**
by Mona Rabun Reeves, illus. by Paul Yalowitz (Bradbury, 1989). A young girl hears a spooky noise as she lies in bed. Is it a monster? With the help of a flashlight held by her obliging parents, the noisemakers—two hungry skunks—are revealed!

1 SHARE A STORY!

LITERATURE
Big Book of Poems:
Worlds I Know
   by Myra Cohn Livingston

Big Book of Songs:
How About You? by John Farrell

 SONGS AND STORIES
AUDIOCASSETTES
STORY SONGS: How About You?

 SING & READ BOOKS AND
AUDIOCASSETTES
How About You?

Literature Activity Book: pp. 82–83
   Share a Story!

STAFF DEVELOPMENT A to EZ Handbook

   • Retelling: p. 295

   • Risk-Free Environment: p. 297

Performance Assessment Handbook

HomeWords: Home-School Resources

OTHER RESOURCES

• BIG BOOK STAND
• BIG BOOK POINTER
• CHART PAPER
• MARKERS
• OVERSIZED BOOK
   COVERS, POSTERS,
   PHOTOGRAPHY
   BOOKS, OR
   CALENDARS

LITERACY SUPPORT:
*B*UILDING LANGUAGE
AND CONCEPTS

**For children acquiring English and/or
needing more intensive support, you
may wish to incorporate the following
suggestions into the basic lesson plan.**

Explain that a storyteller tells a story without reading a book.
Model the storytelling process by telling a favorite tale or family
story. Encourage children to tell a favorite story to a partner.
Emphasize that some cultures, including African and Native
American, have very strong oral traditions.

SHARING TIME

TODAY'S NEWS

Gather children together and then write and read Today's News, tracking each word as you read it. Ask children to pair up to talk about their favorite stories.

What stories do you like? Can you be a storyteller?

CREATING INTEREST AND BUILDING BACKGROUND

Because motivation matters!

Introduce the theme SHARE A STORY! by inviting children to name some of their favorite stories. List the stories on chart paper and read the chart with children. Keep the chart on display to add children's suggestions throughout the theme.

FAVORITE STORIES

Brer Rabbit tales

The Peach Boy

Little Red Riding Hood

Johnny Appleseed

Max

The Little Mermaid

Invite children to talk about their favorite stories. Where did they first hear the story? Why is it a favorite? Have they ever shared the story with anyone else?

Write the Theme Word *storyteller* and discuss its meaning. Share with children that people have been telling stories since ancient times. The first stories were not written down in books, but were passed along orally by storytellers. Good storytellers memorized *dozens* of stories to share with their audiences.

People still work as professional storytellers today. Although books have been widely available for five hundred years, most people still love to hear someone "spin a good yarn."

Share with children that they will be exploring the theme of storytelling together. Encourage them to think of themselves as storytellers throughout this theme. Whenever children finish telling a story, reinforce the notion that they are storytellers.

Sharing Literature
"Worlds I Know"

LISTEN TO THE SOUNDS OF POETRY   Invite children to listen to the Theme Poem "Worlds I Know." You may want to familiarize yourself with the pacing and rhymes of the poem ahead of time.

Reread the poem slowly and expressively. You may even wish to "act out" the poem with a book prop. As you read, encourage children to try to see in their minds what the poem says.

SEE THE POEM IN PRINT   Display the Theme Poem "Worlds I Know" on pages 30–31 in the *Big Book of Poems.* Explain that the poem children have been listening to is the poem they can see in the Big Book.

Read the poem again, tracking the print with the Big Book pointer. Invite children to join in on the rhyming words.

WORLDS I KNOW

I can read the pictures
by myself
in the books that lie
on the lowest shelf.
I know the place
where the stories start
and some I can even say
by heart,
and I make up adventures
and dreams and words
for some of the pages
I've never heard.

Myra Cohn Livingston

30

31

Big Book of Poems, pages 30–31

RESPONDING TO LITERATURE

POEM TALK   Encourage children to share personal reactions to the poem. You may want to begin by sharing your reaction in order to provide a model for personal involvement with literature.

Build on this sharing of responses with a discussion of the poem. You may want to present some of the prompts below to get the discussion started.

- *The poet talks about "reading pictures." What do you think she means? Have you ever made up words to go along with the pictures that you see in a book?*

- *When the poet says "in the books that lie/on the lowest shelf," where do you think she is talking about? Where do you get books?*

- *Which kind of story do you like to tell, one you've heard before or one you've made up?*

TELL A STORY WITH A PICTURE   Invite children to tell a story from a picture! Display a few large, intriguing pictures and book covers, both familiar and unfamiliar, such as Big Book covers, nature magazines, photography books, and calendars. After identifying a few of the objects in a chosen picture, invite volunteers to make up or retell a story about the picture. You may wish to model the first storytelling yourself.

TEAM WORK/THEME WORK A STORYTELLING FESTIVAL!

Introducing the Project: We Share Stories!
Generate excitement for a Storytelling Festival by asking children to think about the Theme Word *storyteller* and inviting them to choose their favorite stories and storytelling experiences.

Refer back to the Theme Word *storyteller*. Encourage children to talk about why they like certain storytellers. Is it their actions? The tones of their voices? Their puppets, music, or other props? Explain that in this theme children will have the chance to be the storytellers. Share with them that they will use their imaginations and experiences as they work together on a Storytelling Festival. During the festival, children will have the opportunity to entertain their families and friends with their tales!

Sing Out!
Invite children to listen to the Theme Song "How About You?" Play the song on the STORY SONGS AUDIOCASSETTE a few times until children feel comfortable singing along. You may wish to display the song on pages 32–33 of the *Big Book of Songs.*

♪ SONGS AND STORIES AUDIOCASSETTES
STORY SONGS: How About You?

Brainstorming and Sharing Ideas
Begin talking about the Storytelling Festival that children will plan and participate in. You may want to display familiar folk tales, inviting children to talk about the tales and discuss the ones they know. Encourage children who can to share stories in languages other than English and stories that reflect various cultures.

How About You?

Songs are meant to be sung.
Tales are meant to be told.
Everyone has a story to tell.
There's a story for everyone I know.
There's a story for everyone!

CHORUS
How about you? How about you?
Do you have a tale you'd like to tell?
How about you? How about you?
Do you have a tale to tell?

John Farrell

Big Book of Songs, pages 32–33

Refer children to their list of favorite stories and remind them that they can add to the list throughout the theme. Invite individuals or pairs of children to choose the stories they would like to tell at the Storytelling Festival. Add the storytellers' names to the list as the planning progresses.

FAVORITE STORIES	STORYTELLER
Brer Rabbit tales	Janice
The Peach Boy	Greg
Little Red Riding Hood	Toni and Chris
Johnny Appleseed	Jenni
Max	Billy
The Little Mermaid	Steve and Gina

Planning

As you work through the theme with children, add to the chart stories that they learn. Encourage each child or pair of children to choose a favorite story to tell at the Storytelling Festival.

You may wish to suggest that the class as a whole open the Storytelling Festival by singing the Theme Song "How About You?" Discuss with children the order in which they will each tell a story. You may want to suggest that a couple of children play the roles of emcees and introduce their classmates to the audience. Then ask children to think about who they might like to invite to their Storytelling Festival.

Set aside time for children to practice their storytelling with each other. Listening to and telling stories may be even more special throughout the theme if there is a comfortable, inviting corner of the classroom set up for this purpose.

INTO THE LEARNING CENTERS
You may wish to place the Sing & Read Book and its audiocassette for "How About You?" in the Reading Center and invite children to listen to the tape as they read the book. See page 96.

To help children prepare for the Storytelling Festival, you may wish to suggest that they begin work in the Learning Centers described on pages 95–103.

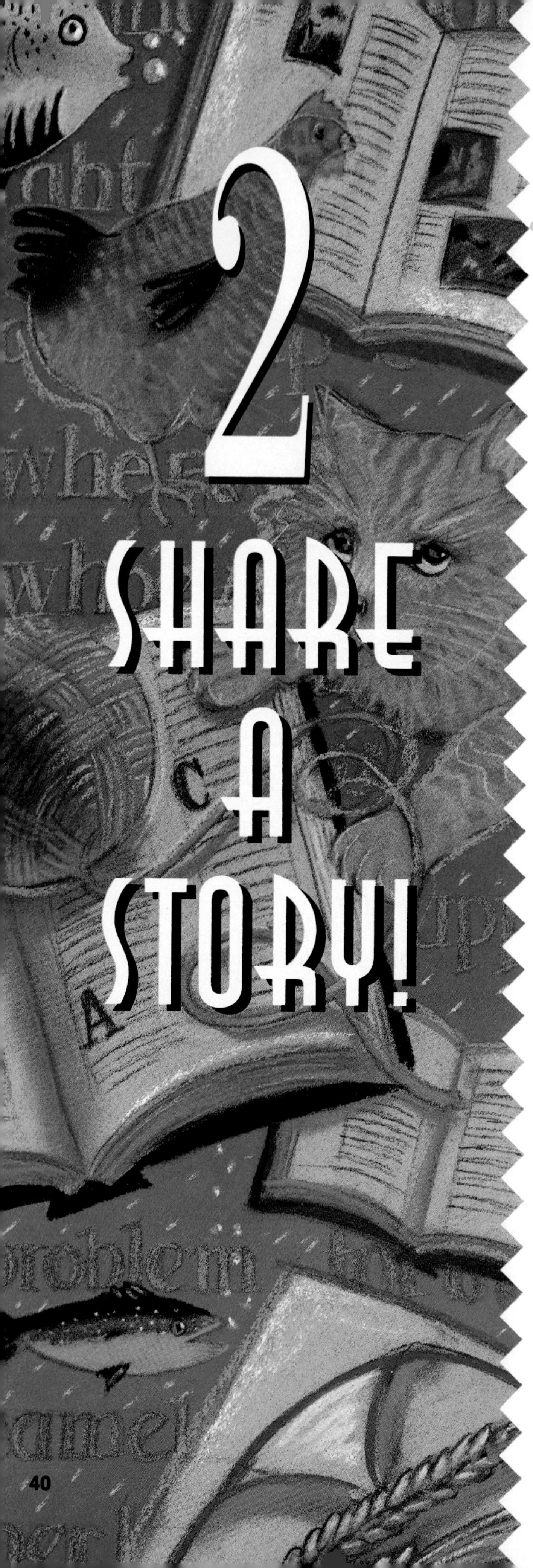

2 SHARE A STORY!

Teacher's
READ·ALOUD
ANTHOLOGY

MACMILLAN/McGRAW-HILL

OTHER RESOURCES

• CHART PAPER
• MARKERS
• TO MAKE JOURNALS:
    STAPLER
    UNLINED PAPER
    CONSTRUCTION
    PAPER
• TO MAKE STORY BAG:
    PLASTIC, CLOTH, OR
    PAPER BAG
    SMALL OBJECTS
    THAT REPRESENT
    STORIES
• WORD MASK

SHARING TIME

TODAY'S NEWS

Write and read Today's News, pointing to each word as you read. Ask children to think about the question.

Where do stories come from?

CREATING INTEREST AND BUILDING BACKGROUND

Because motivation matters!

Thousands of stories exist, and thousands more have yet to be told. Where do all these stories come from? Invite children to share their thoughts about where storytellers get their stories. Chart their responses on chart paper and then read them together.

Where do stories come from?
books
imagination
dreams
everyday happenings
conversations

Explain to children that today's story "The Storytelling Stone" was told by Native Americans to explain how stories came to be.

Today's News
Where do stories come from?

41

READING AND WRITING

SHARING LITERATURE
"The Storytelling Stone"

■ **Read Aloud Anthology:** pages 78–79

SHARE THE STORY Encourage children to be good story listeners as you read the Seneca tale "The Storytelling Stone." Suggest to them that they listen to see if any of their ideas about where stories come from are used in this story.

About the Story

Developing Multicultural Awareness

The Seneca were one of six Native American groups that made up the Iroquois federation. The Iroquois lived in *longhouses,* long rectangular buildings housing several families. Traditionally, a *Hageota* (hä gē′ ō də), or Iroquois storyteller, would tell stories inside the longhouses during the cold winter months. The Hageota carried a story bag. Each article in the bag represented a story. After an item was pulled out of the bag and shown to the audience, the story would begin.

Great Stone
Naho

RESPONDING TO LITERATURE

BOOK TALK   Have children share their personal reactions to "The Storytelling Stone." To begin the discussion, you may wish to offer your own reaction to the story with comments and questions like these.

- *I like the idea of people giving thanks when a storyteller finishes a tale. What do you think of that idea?*

- *Do you think this story really tells where stories come from? Why?*

- *The storytelling stone ends its tale with the word* Naho, *meaning "I have spoken." "The End" is another way stories are sometimes ended. If you could choose any words to end a story, what might you say?*

- *One detail I found interesting was the boy calling the stone "Grandfather." I think he must have used that name to show respect. What do you think?*

JOURNAL WRITING   What stories would children like the Great Stone to tell? Encourage children to draw pictures and write letters in their journals to request a story from the storytelling stone. If possible, display a large rock and label it "Great Stone."

Provide theme journals for children by stapling approximately ten sheets of paper together or have children bring in journals to use.

MAKE A STORY BAG   Make a classroom story bag! (See page 42.) Each child can make or bring in a small object to put in the bag. Brainstorm some possibilities with children.

Later, children can take turns pulling an object out of the bag, identifying the story it signifies, and then telling the story.

43

Exploring Print — LEARNING THE CODE

In the Exploring Print lessons for this theme, children will learn about F, f and Y, y and the sounds they represent. Take advantage of opportunities to point out these letters and the sounds they represent as you share Today's News, as you talk with children about their writing, and as you reread the theme-related trade books.

DECODING AND PHONICS

LETTERS: F, f
SOUND/LETTER RELATIONSHIPS: /f/F, f

Developing Phonemic Awareness
In "The Storytelling Stone," the boy hurried home to tell the Great Stone's stories to his family. Did you know that a song can tell a story, too? Share with children that workers who built the nation's railroads often "sang" stories as they worked. Then sing or play "I've Been Workin' on the Railroad." Encourage children to sing along. You may want to write the song on chart paper and place it on display in the Music Center.

I've Been Workin' on the Railroad

I've been workin' on the railroad,
All the livelong day,
I've been workin' on the railroad,
Just to pass the time away.
Don't you hear the whistle blowin',
Rise up so early in the morn;
Don't you hear the captain shoutin',
"Dinah, blow your horn!"

Dinah, won't you blow,
Dinah, won't you blow,
Dinah, won't you blow your horn,
Dinah, won't you blow,
Dinah, won't you blow,
Dinah, won't you blow your horn!

Someone's in the kitchen with Dinah,
Someone's in the kitchen, I know,
Someone's in the kitchen with Dinah,
Strummin' on the old banjo
And singin',

Fee, Fi, Fiddlee-i-o,
Fee, Fi, Fiddlee-i-o,
Fee, Fi, Fiddlee-i-o,
Strummin' on the old banjo.

SING A SOUND AUDIOCASSETTES
I've Been Workin' on the Railroad

44

Sing the song again, and encourage children to clap in rhythm when singing. Ask children to name the words in the song that begin with the same sound as the word family.

Developing Print Awareness

Write the line "Fee, Fi, Fiddlee-i-o" on the chalkboard or on chart paper, and encourage children to repeat the words with you as you point to each word.

With a word mask, frame a capital *F*.

• *Let's look at some f's together. Here is a capital, or uppercase, F in the word Fee. Say Fee with me. Can you find another word in the line that begins with a capital F?*

Next, write a lowercase *f* on the board. Display the Alphabet Poster for Ff nearby.

• *Here is a lowercase f I have written on the board. Can you find a lowercase f on the Alphabet Poster?*

Encourage children to come forward to point to and to trace over with their fingers the uppercase and lowercase *f*'s.

Invite children to replace the initial consonant sound of their names with the sound represented by the letter *f*. For example, "Tom" would be "Fom," "Anna" would be "Fanna," and "Rita" would be "Fita." Then have children draw a picture of themselves and label it with their nonsense name. You might wish to make a bulletin board or word wall of the new names and label it "Fee, Fi, Fiddlee-i-o."

3

SHARE A STORY!

LITERATURE

Nessa's Fish by Nancy Luenn, illustrated by Neil Waldman

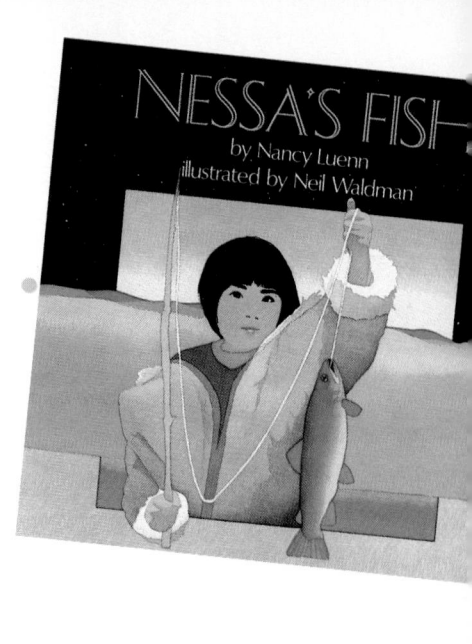

NESSA'S FISH
by Nancy Luenn
illustrated by Neil Waldman

SING & READ BOOKS AND AUDIOCASSETTES
How About You?

EXPLORING PRINT

Big Book of Alphabet Rhymes and Chimes:
   Five Little Fishies

Alphabet Poster for Ff

ABC cards

Literature Activity Book: p. 84
   Learning the Code: F, f

Practice Book: p. 48

BRWL: Letterbook F(10)

STAFF DEVELOPMENT A to EZ Handbook
   • Invented Spelling: p. 260
   • Phonemic Awareness: p. 281

Performance Assessment Handbook

OTHER RESOURCES

• MAP OR GLOBE
• STORY THEATER PROPS
   COATS
   ROCKS
• BIG BOOK STAND
• BIG BOOK POINTER
• UNLINED INDEX CARDS
• PENCILS

LITERACY SUPPORT:
BUILDING LANGUAGE AND CONCEPTS

For children acquiring English and/or needing more intensive support, you may wish to incorporate the following suggestions into the basic lesson plan.

This story has a rich vocabulary. During the reading, discuss each page using your own words, and use the illustrations to clarify concepts. You can further aid comprehension by inviting volunteers to act out the role of Nessa, the wolf, and the bear as you read.

After the reading, pair children and have them retell the story to each other.

SHARING TIME

TODAY'S NEWS

Gather children together and write and read Today's News, pointing to each word as you read. Encourage children to talk about stories with adventures in them, and tell about any adventures they've had.

Do you like adventure stories?

CREATING INTEREST AND BUILDING BACKGROUND

Because motivation matters!

To prepare children for a story about an Inuit girl and her grandmother, share the following information. Show pictures and nonfiction books on the Arctic, if possible. You may wish to point out the Arctic on a map or globe.

- *The Inuits live in one of the coldest and harshest areas of the world: the Arctic.*

- *The land areas are huge plains called the tundra. This land is frozen during most of the year.*

- *Rivers and lakes are covered by ice most of the time. Sometimes Inuits cut a hole in the ice and catch fish through the hole.*

- *Animals found in the Arctic include foxes, wolves, reindeer, caribou, bears, whales, and seals.*

Tell children that in the next story an Inuit girl goes on a fishing trip with her grandmother and has quite an adventure!

Reading and Writing

SHARING LITERATURE
Nessa's Fish

LOOK IT OVER   Hold up the cover of *Nessa's Fish* and track the words in the title as you read each one. Point to the apostrophe and the *s* in the title and tell children that these two things together mean that the fish belong to Nessa. Then read and track the name of the author, Nancy Luenn, and the illustrator, Neil Waldman. Encourage children to look at the front and back covers and predict what might happen in the story.

SHARE THE STORY   You may want to pause after Nessa is confronted with each of the animals and invite children to predict what she might do to solve the problem.

About the Author

Nancy Luenn grew up in Los Angeles, California. Her family had a big backyard where she and her brothers and sisters could dig holes and use their imaginations in creating new worlds. They did not have a TV, so her mother read stories aloud each evening. Some of Nancy's favorite stories were fantasies.

About the Illustrator

Neil Waldman has been an illustrator for magazines, advertisements, book covers, and record album covers for over twenty years. He has also designed and illustrated postage stamps for ten different countries! Although well known for his bold and colorful illustrations, it is only recently that he has begun to illustrate children's books.

At autumn camp, Nessa and her grandmother walked inland half a day to fish in the stony lake.

They jigged for fish all afternoon and evening. They caught more than they could carry home. They caught enough to feed everyone in camp.

Nessa and her grandmother stacked up the fish. They piled stones over them to keep away the foxes. Then, tired out, they fell asleep.

6

7

RESPONDING TO LITERATURE

BOOK TALK Invite children to share their personal reactions to the book. Talk about your own response to get the sharing started. You may want to present some of these prompts.

- *I thought it was exciting when Nessa faced the fox, the wolves, and the bear. What did you like about the story?*

- *Do you think people can really "talk" to animals?*

- *Did you like the pictures in the book? Which picture is your favorite?*

- *What would you tell a friend about this story?*

JOURNAL WRITING Invite children to draw and write about the story in their journals. As children write, you may wish to model writing in your own journal. Ask children if they would like to share what they wrote with the group. You may wish to use the following prompts to help students begin.

- *Why were the fish important?*

- *What would you say to Nessa if you could speak to her?*

STORY THEATER Children can play the roles of Nessa, her parents, her grandparents, the fox, the wolves, and the bear. Simple props might include coats, construction-paper claws, sock or rope tails, and rocks. Encourage children to improvise the actions and dialog. You may want to reread the story to children before they act it out.

INTO THE LEARNING CENTERS
Invite children to the Art Center where they can make background scenery, props, costumes, and puppets for Story Theater or their Storytelling Festival! See page 101.

TEAM WORK/THEME WORK
You may want to encourage children to continue the planning and work on their Storytelling Festival. See pages 38–39 and 92–93.

A WLFe WUSEN THe Book AND THe BeRe WUEN Too

Lauren is a capable writer whose spelling is easily read by adults. However, in this instance, she relied more on her illustration than her written message to convey her interpretation of the bear's character.
Lauren read her message like this: "A wolf was in the book and a bear was too."

Exploring Print

HANDS ON LANGUAGE

DECODING AND PHONICS

LETTERS: *F, f*
SOUND/LETTER RELATIONSHIPS: /f/*F, f*

Developing Phonemic Awareness

In *Nessa's Fish,* Nessa and her grandmother caught many fish. Invite children to listen as you read "Five Little Fishies" on pages 12–13 in the *Big Book of Alphabet Rhymes and Chimes*, a rhyme about five fish Nessa and her grandmother would have had trouble catching. As you come to words that begin with *f,* slightly emphasize the initial sound.

- *Listen to the sound you hear at the beginning of* five, fishies, first, fourth, fifth, *and* fishing. *What other words do we know that begin with the same sound?*

Repeat the rhyme a few times, encouraging children to chime in.

Developing Print Awareness

Display "Five Little Fishies" on pages 12–13 of the *Big Book of Alphabet Rhymes and Chimes* and say the rhyme with children. Use the Big Book pointer to point out words that begin with *f.* Explain that the letter *f* stands for /f/ in the words *five, fishies, first, fourth, fifth,* and *fishing.*

Try rereading the rhyme in a call-and-response format. Divide children into five groups, and have each group repeat and act out the response of the appropriate fish after you have read the call line.

Five Little Fishies

Five little fishies
swimming in a pool.

First one said,
"This pool is cool."

Second one said,
"This pool is deep."

Third one said,
"I want to sleep."

Fourth one said,
"Let's dive and dip."

Fifth one said,
"I spy a ship."

Fishing boat comes,
Line goes Ker-splash,

Away the five little
fishies dash.

Ff

Big Book of Alphabet Rhymes and Chimes,
pages 12–13

Ff

fish

Then display the Alphabet Poster and ABC cards for Ff, or write the letters on the chalkboard and on cards of your own.

Have children compare the *F*'s on the Big Book page with the letters on the poster and card. Encourage children to talk about the fish pictured on the poster.

Invite pairs of children to go on a Word Hunt around the room to find words on charts, signs, and in books that begin with the same sound and letter as *five, fishies, first, fourth, fifth,* and *fishing.* Have them copy the words on cards and then share and display them within an outline of a fish on a Word Wall or bulletin board.

■ **Literature Activity Book:** page 84

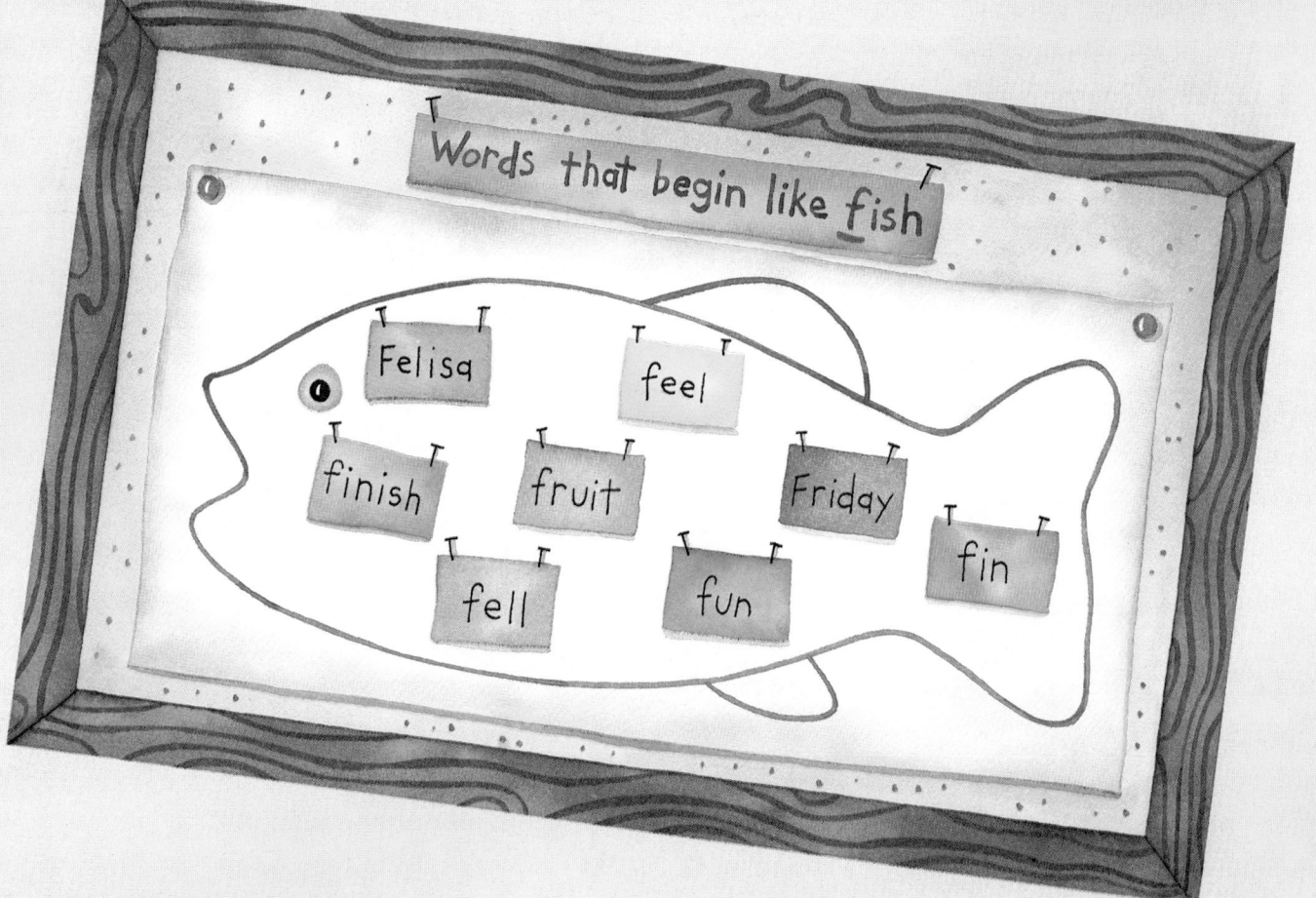

Words that begin like fish

Felisa   feel

finish   fruit   Friday   fin

fell   fun

4. SHARE A STORY!

LITERATURE
Nessa's Fish by Nancy Luenn,
   illustrated by Neil Waldman

SING & READ BOOKS AND
AUDIOCASSETTES
How About You?

EXPLORING PRINT
*Big Book of Alphabet Rhymes
and Chimes:*
   Five Little Fishies

Rhyme and Chime Strips:
   Five Little Fishies

Learning the Code: F, f

BRWL: Letterbook F(10)

 **STAFF DEVELOPMENT** A to EZ Handbook
   • Concepts of Print: p. 248
   • Language Experience Writing: p. 268

Performance Assessment Handbook

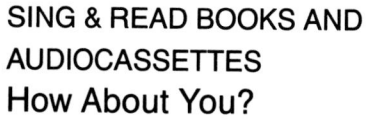

OTHER RESOURCES

• CHART PAPER
• MARKERS
• LARGE DRAWING PAPER
• PENCILS
• CRAYONS
• PAINTS
• BIG BOOK STAND
• BIG BOOK POINTER
• POCKET CHART AND
  STAND

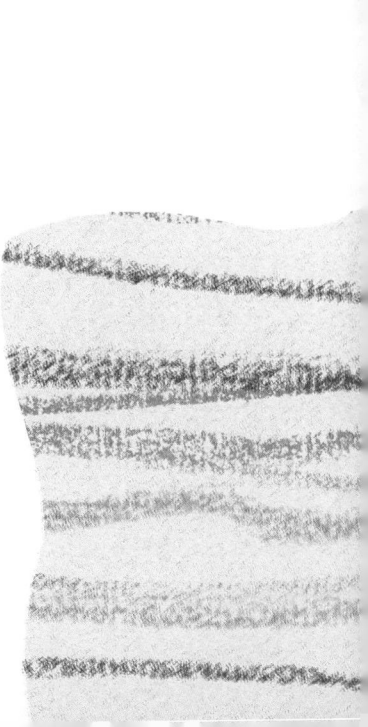

SHARING TIME

TODAY'S NEWS

Write and read Today's News, tracking each word as you read. Encourage children to talk about other bear stories they have read and enjoyed.

Do you like stories about bears?

CREATING INTEREST AND BUILDING BACKGROUND

Because motivation matters!

Invite children to listen to the first verse, or part, of the poem "Adventures of Isabel" by Ogden Nash. This verse is about a girl who, like the character in *Nessa's Fish,* meets up with a bear. You may wish to copy the poem onto chart paper to display to the class.

ADVENTURES OF ISABEL

Isabel met an enormous bear,
Isabel, Isabel, didn't care;
The bear was hungry, the bear was ravenous,
The bear's big mouth was cruel and cavernous.
The bear said, Isabel, glad to meet you,
How do, Isabel, now I'll eat you!
Isabel, Isabel, didn't worry,
Isabel didn't scream or scurry.
She washed her hands and she straightened
   her hair up,
Then Isabel quietly ate the bear up.

—Ogden Nash

Read the verse again and encourage children to join in saying Isabel's name when you prompt them. You may wish to allow children to act out the verse. Invite children to compare Isabel's and Nessa's responses to the bears.

REANING AND WRITING

SHARING LITERATURE
Nessa's Fish

REREAD THE STORY   Invite children to listen again to *Nessa's Fish*. On this rereading, you may wish to suggest to children that they imagine themselves in Nessa's place and think about how she feels when her grandmother gets sick and when each animal approaches.

PRINT AWARENESS

Direction
Encourage children to watch your finger movements as you trace the words on each page in a left-to-right progression and move back to the left and down to continue the next line.

PHONEMIC AWARENESS

Initial Sounds: /f/f
Ask children to listen for words that begin with /f/ as in *fish* as you reread page 22 of the story. Read the page again and tell them to clap each time they hear a word that begins like *fish (father, feel, foolish, fur, and falling)*. Encourage children to name other words with the same beginning sound as *fish*.

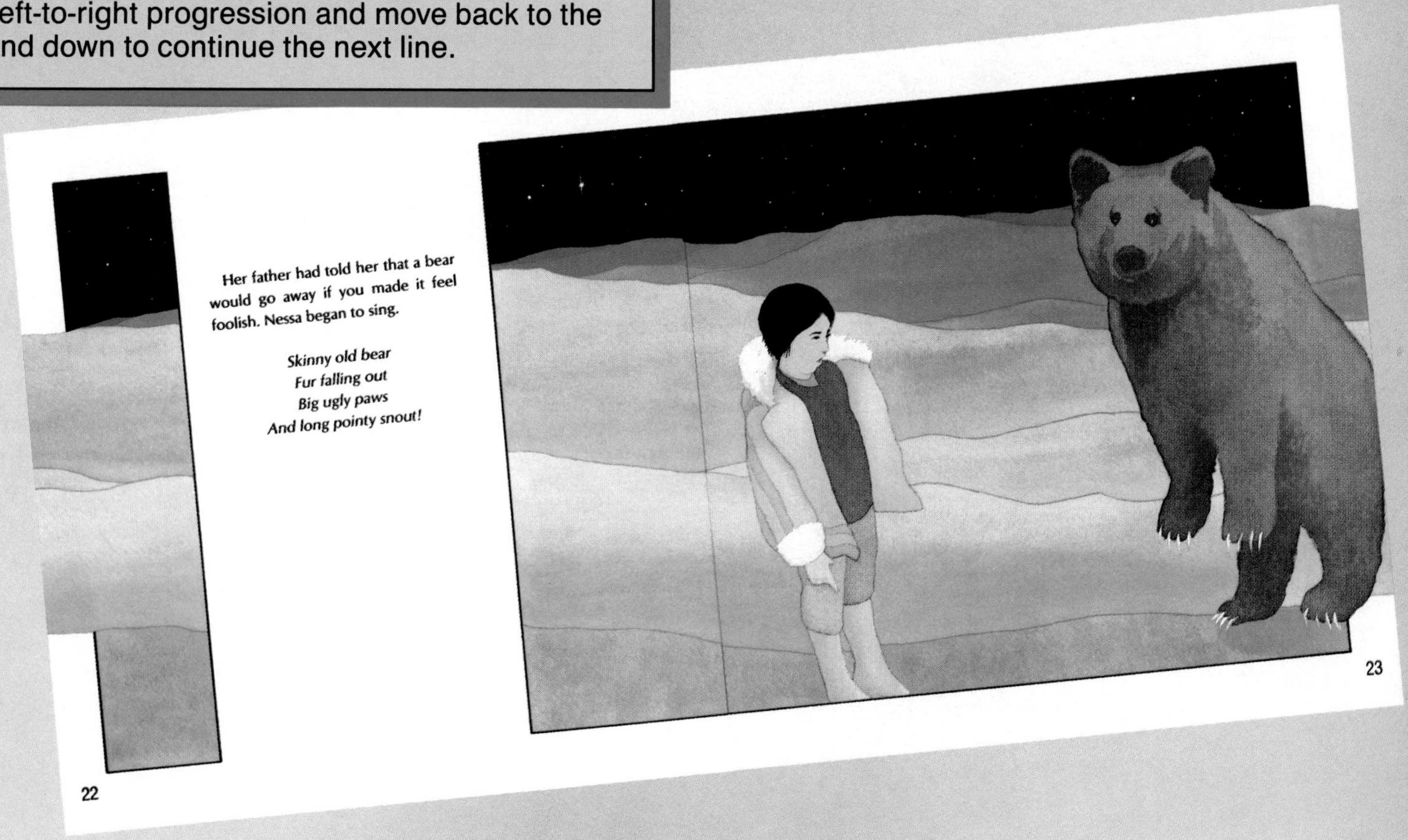

Her father had told her that a bear would go away if you made it feel foolish. Nessa began to sing.

Skinny old bear
Fur falling out
Big ugly paws
And long pointy snout!

22

23

RESPONDING TO LITERATURE

BOOK TALK   After children have shared personal reactions to the rereading of *Nessa's Fish,* ask them to think about Nessa's feelings at different points in the story.

- *How do you think Nessa felt when her grandmother became ill?*

- *How did Nessa feel when she first saw the fox, wolves, and bear? Show us what her expression may have looked like after she scared away each of the animals.*

- *What were Nessa's feelings at the end of the story?*

STORY ELEMENTS   Work together to create a chart outlining the major story elements. Encourage children to refer back to the story as needed or upon completion of the chart to verify their information.

INTO THE LEARNING CENTERS
Children can welcome home Nessa and her grandmother by making a banner in the Writing Center! See page 98.

The fish are hopping in the Math Center where children will enjoy "fishing" for numbers and shapes! See page 100.

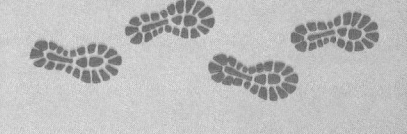

NESSA'S FISH

Characters	Nessa
	Grandmother
	fox, wolves, bear
	Grandfather, Mother, Father
Setting	lake
	Arctic

Plot

Who came?	What happened?
fox	Nessa made it go away.
wolves	Nessa made them go away.
bear	Nessa made it go away.
Grandfather, Mother, Father	They took Nessa, Grandmother, and the fish home.

Using the Rhyme and Chime Strips gives children a Hands On! Language experience that allows them to explore important concepts of print.

CONCEPTS OF PRINT
Directionality, Words

Developing Print Awareness
Display pages 12–13 in the *Big Book of Alphabet Rhymes and Chimes* and encourage children to recite the rhyme with you as you use the Big Book pointer to point to each word.

Cut the Rhyme and Chime Strips for "Five Little Fishies" to build the rhyme in the pocket chart. Invite children to recite the rhyme with you.

Five Little Fishies

Five little fishies
swimming in a pool.

First one said,
"This pool is cool."

Second one said,
"This pool is deep."

Third one said,
"I want to sleep."

Fourth one said,
"Let's dive and dip."

Fifth one said,
"I spy a ship."

Fishing boat comes,
Line goes Ker-splash,

Away the five little
fishies dash.

Ff

Big Book of Alphabet Rhymes and Chimes,
pages 12–13

Cut the word cards from the second set of Rhyme and Chime Strips for *Five, fishies, First, Fourth, Fifth,* and *Fishing.* Invite children to say the words with you as you emphasize /f/ at the beginning of the words.

Five little fishies	swimming in a pool.
First one said,	"This pool is cool."
Second one said,	"This pool is deep."
Third one said,	"I want to sleep."
Fourth one said,	"Let's dive and dip."
Fifth one said,	"I spy a ship."
Fishing boat comes,	line goes Ker-splash,
Away the five little	fishies dash.

Place the word cards in the pocket chart over the matching words in the phrases. Invite children to recite the rhyme with you again. Encourage children to find the two words in the last line that start with the same sound. Use the picture cards to have children match the pictures of the various fish and the fishing boat to the appropriate word or phrase.

INTO THE LEARNING CENTERS
Encourage children to use the *Big Book of Alphabet Rhymes and Chimes,* the Rhyme and Chime Strips, and the word and picture cards to build the rhyme "Five Little Fishies" in the pocket chart in the Hands On! Language Center. See page 97.

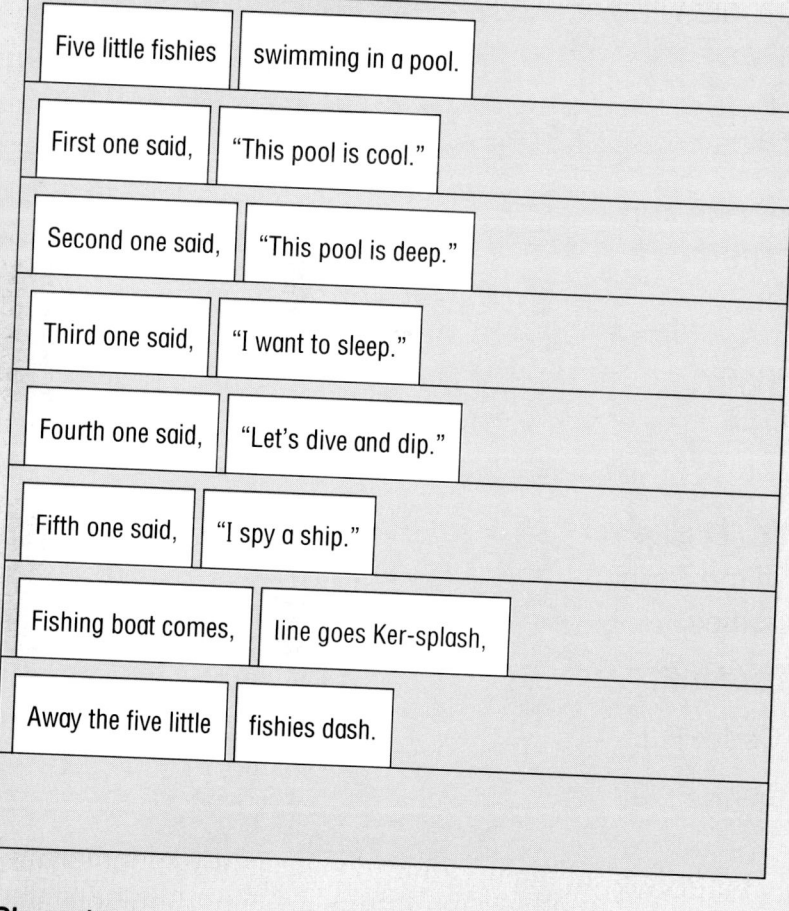

FIVE LITTLE FISHIES

Five little fishies swimming in a pool.

First one said, "This pool is cool."

Second one said, "This pool is deep."

Third one said, "I want to sleep."

Fourth one said, "Let's dive and dip."

Fifth one said, "I spy a ship.

Fishing boat comes, line goes Ker-splash,

Away the five little fishies dash.

5

SHARE A STORY!

LITERATURE **BIG BOOK**

I Had a Cat
by Mona Rabun Reeves,
illustrated by Julie Downing

SONGS AND STORIES
AUDIOCASSETTES
STORY SONGS:
The Animal Fair

SING & READ BOOKS AND
AUDIOCASSETTES
How About You?

LISTENING LIBRARY
AUDIOCASSETTES
I Had a Cat

EXPLORING PRINT
Rhyme and Chime Strips:
 Five Little Fishies

Alphabet Poster for Ff

Learning the Code: F, f

BRWL: Letterbook F(10)

STAFF DEVELOPMENT  A to EZ Handbook
 • Big Books: p. 246
 • Shared Reading: p. 299

Performance Assessment Handbook

OTHER RESOURCES

• BIG BOOK STAND
• BIG BOOK POINTER
• WORD MASK
• POCKET CHART AND
  STAND

LITERACY SUPPORT:

BUILDING LANGUAGE AND CONCEPTS

For children acquiring
English and/or needing
more intensive support,
you may wish to
incorporate the following
suggestions into the
basic lesson plan.

Before reading, build background on farm, zoo, and domestic
animals using the animals shown on the front and back covers.
During reading, invite children to find each animal in the pictures.
After reading, have children draw favorite animals and classify
the animals as farm, zoo, or domestic.

SHARING TIME

TODAY'S NEWS

Write and read Today's News, pointing to each word as you read. Ask children to talk about favorite stories. If they were going to be an animal, which one would it be?

Imagine you are an animal. What animal are you?

CREATING INTEREST AND BUILDING BACKGROUND

Because motivation matters!

Invite children to listen to a song about animals. Read the title to them and ask what they think the song will be about. What do they think an Animal Fair is? What animals might be there?

The Animal Fair

I went to The Animal Fair,
The birds and the beasts were there,
The big baboon, by the light of the moon,
Was combing his auburn hair;
You ought to have seen the monk,
He jumped on the elephant's trunk;
The elephant sneezed and fell on his knees
And what became of the monk?

♪ SONGS AND STORIES AUDIOCASSETTES
STORY SONGS: The Animal Fair

Invite children to sing the song and use gestures to show what the animals did. Then ask children if they think this is a song about what animals in real life might do. Why or why not? Encourage them to create their own tale or story by telling what they think "became of the monk."

Tell children they are going to hear a story a girl tells about other animals—many other animals.

Reading and Writing

I Had a Cat

BIG BOOK

LOOK IT OVER   Display the front and back covers of the Big Book for *I Had a Cat* and track the words in the title as you read each one. Invite children to predict what the girl's story might be about. Where do they think the animals walking along the road are going? Do they think this is a story about real animals? Do they think this is a story about something that could really have happened? Let children know that you will put a little version of the book in the Reading Center that they can look at on their own.

SHARE THE STORY   Invite children to listen to the story to verify their predictions about the girl's story. You might want to stop after reading pages 8–9 to ask if this is a story about things animals in real life can do.

About the Author

Mona Rabun Reeves, the author of *I Had a Cat,* said that this book is "probably a takeoff on my own life experience! At one point my children owned over 35 animals, and we found good homes for most of them eventually; the rest we kept."

About the Illustrator

As a child, illustrator Julie Downing "loved to read, draw, and put on plays in [her] backyard" and now feels fortunate to have a career that "combines all of [her] favorite things." Very interested in theater, she feels that "illustrating children's books is a wonderful combination of artist, director, set designer and costume designer."

There was no room left in the house,
Not even for a tiny mouse.
There was no food left in the shed.
The animals could not be fed.
I did not know what else to do;

16

17

RESPONDING TO LITERATURE

BOOK TALK Invite children to share their personal reactions to the book and to the illustrations. You may want to model a personal response to begin the sharing.

- *That was quite a story! Can you imagine having all those animals and having to find homes for them? Have you or someone you know ever had to find a home for an animal?*

- *The girl returned home to find the cat still there. If I could choose, I would keep the dog. Which would you keep?*

- *I especially like the picture on pages 14–15 where the animals are having breakfast. Which is your favorite?*

- *Would you like to have the girl in the story as a friend?*

JOURNAL WRITING Invite children to draw or write about the book in their journals. You might provide the following prompts as ways to help children begin thinking about writing and drawing:

- *My favorite animal was* _____.

- *The silliest picture was* _____.

- *I would have kept the (goat) because* _____.

FIELD TRIP Children are sure to enjoy a field trip to a local zoo, farm, pet store, or animal shelter. They would also enjoy hearing a guest from one of these places speak about animals that make good pets, that live in the zoo, and/or that can be found on farms.

INTO THE LEARNING CENTERS
Children can use what they have discovered about animals to write animal riddles in the Writing Center. See page 98.

Young children frequently do not reread what they have written. However, Jenilee has begun to reread, and in this instance when she reread and found something not to her liking, she chose to rewrite her sentence in its entirety.
Jenilee read her message like this: "I like the funny cat in the story. The funny cat jumped off the table."

DECODING AND PHONICS

LETTERS: *F, f*
SOUND/LETTER RELATIONSHIPS: */f/F, f*

CONCEPTS OF PRINT
Directionality, Words, Letters

Developing Phonemic Awareness
Remind children that they have been learning about the sound heard at the beginning of words like *fish, feed, foxes, father, fast, family, fire, five,* as well as many others (words found in *Nessa's Fish,* "The Storytelling Stone," and *I Had a Cat,* as well as "Five Little Fishies" on pages 12–13 in the *Big Book of Alphabet Rhymes and Chimes*). Ask children to suggest other words that have the same beginning sound.

Developing Print Awareness
Display the Alphabet Poster for Ff and point to the word *fish.* Frame the letter *f* in the word. Remind children that the letter *f* stands for the sound heard at the beginning of the word *fish.*

Use the Rhyme and Chime Strips for "Five Little Fishies" to build the rhyme in the pocket chart as shown.

Five little fishies	swimming in a pool.
First one said,	"This pool is cool."
Second one said,	"This pool is deep."
Third one said,	"I want to sleep."
Fourth one said,	"Let's dive and dip."
Fifth one said,	"I spy a ship."
Fishing boat comes,	line goes Ker-splash,
Away the five little	fishies dash.

Five li**f** fishies | swimming in a pool.

Firs one said, | "This pool is cool."

ond one said, | "This pool is deep."

nird one said, | "I want to sleep."

Fourth one said, | "Let's dive and dip."

Fifth one said, | "I spy a ship."

ishing boat comes, | line goes Ker-splash,

way the five little | fishies dash.

Encourage children to say the rhyme with you as you point to each word with a Big Book pointer. Have children clap each time they hear a word with the same sound as they hear at the beginning of *fish*. Insert a word card for each of these words.

Frame the first letter in each word card and have children name it as an *f*. Emphasize that the letter *f* stands for the sound heard at the beginning of the words *five, fishies, first, fourth, fifth,* and *fishing*.

Use letter cards for *F* and *f* to match the beginning letters in the words that begin with those letters.

Review charts and other print resources in the classroom to find words that begin with the same sound and letter as *fish*.

INTO THE LEARNING CENTERS

Using letter stamps, sponge letters, and magnetic letters in the Hands On! Language Center is a motivating way for children to experiment with print. See page 97.

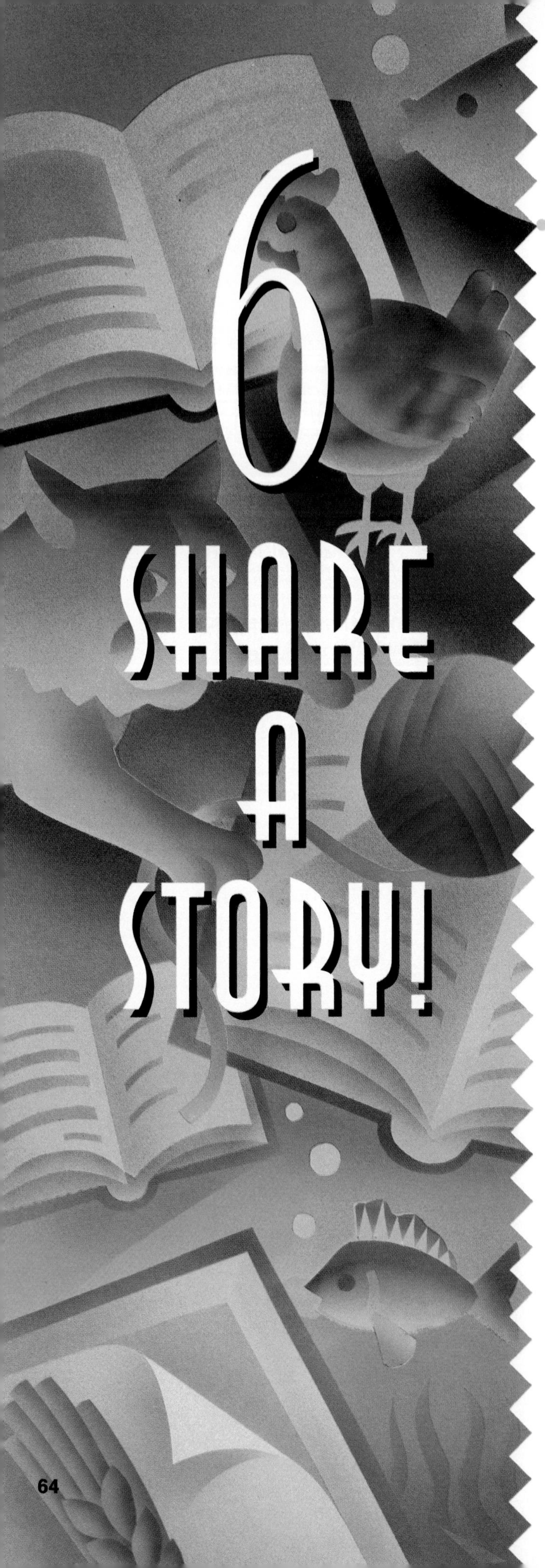

6 SHARE A STORY!

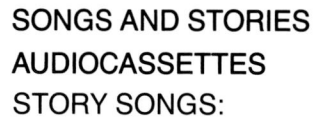
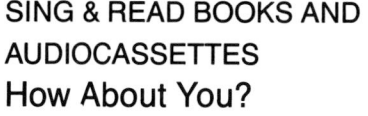

OTHER RESOURCES

• BIG BOOK STAND
• BIG BOOK POINTER
• WORD MASK
• PAPER
• CRAYONS OR PENCILS

SHARING TIME

TODAY'S NEWS

Write and read Today's News, pointing to each word as you read. Ask a volunteer to point to the variation of the Theme Word, *storyteller*. Explain that the letter *s* at the end means "more than one." Talk with children about what storytellers do.

We can be storytellers, too!

CREATING INTEREST AND BUILDING BACKGROUND

Because motivation matters!

Invite children to sing the Theme Song "How About You?" Children should be familiar with this song from other lessons. Tell them that as the song says, everyone has a song to sing and a story to tell. After singing "How About You?" share with children that they will listen to a story, and then tell their own story, as the girl did in *I Had a Cat.*

♪ SONGS AND STORIES AUDIOCASSETTES
STORY SONGS: How About You?

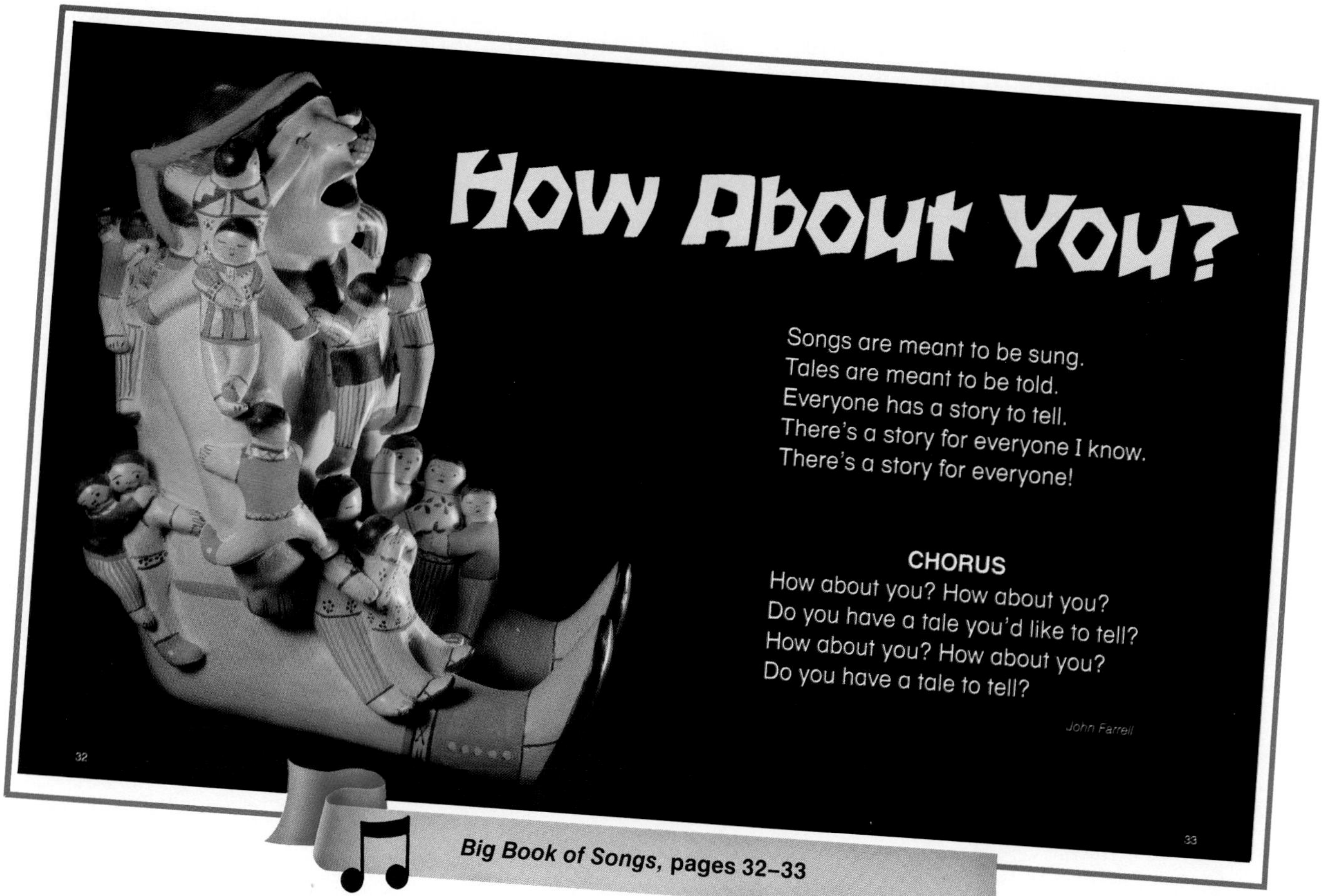

HOW ABOUT YOU?

Songs are meant to be sung.
Tales are meant to be told.
Everyone has a story to tell.
There's a story for everyone I know.
There's a story for everyone!

CHORUS
How about you? How about you?
Do you have a tale you'd like to tell?
How about you? How about you?
Do you have a tale to tell?

John Farrell

Big Book of Songs, **pages 32–33**

Reading and Writing

Sharing Literature
I Had a Cat

REREAD THE STORY Invite children to listen again to *I Had a Cat*. Tell children that in many stories, a story character has a problem and finds a way to solve it. Ask children to listen carefully and look at the illustrations as you turn the pages of the Big Book. Invite them to call out "Oh, no!" when you read what the girl's problem is, and then when you read the ways she solves the problem, they can call out "Yea!"

Phonemic Awareness

Initial Sounds: /y/y
Display page 13 and ask children to identify the different animals. Elicit that one of the animals is a yak. Repeat the word *yak* emphasizing the initial sound of *y*. Turn to page 20 and read that page, asking children if they hear another word that begins with the same sound as *yak*.

Print Awareness

Typesize Variations
Focus on the changes in typesize of the print. Help children recognize that the print starts out large and bold, when the girl is happy and feeling good about the animals she has (page 7). The print becomes smaller as she realizes that she has too many of them (page 16). Explain that the print becomes large and bold again when she has figured out what to do with the animals and realizes that she still has the cat (page 30).

As you read, help children notice variations in typesize, and ask them what these changes might suggest about the girl's feelings. Ask them whether they think that even though the girl has found ways to solve her problem, she may feel bad about having to part with the animals. Children might enjoy suggesting how the girl might have sounded as she told each part of her story.

Responding to Literature

BOOK TALK After children have shared personal reactions to the rereading of *I Had a Cat*, invite them to take a close look at the art. Page through the book as you talk about the illustrations.

- *The illustrator, Julie Downing, drew some very funny pictures. On pages 6–7, what are the ape, the bird, the frog, and the girl doing? Which pictures do you think are really funny? Why?*

- *Which picture best shows what the girl's problem is? What would you have drawn to show that she had too many animals?*

- *Imagine that this is your story. What would you do about having so many animals?*

- *What did you like about the story? What would you change about it?*

WRITE A STORY   Invite children to be storytellers as they write and illustrate other creative ways to solve the girl's problem, or as they create their own stories such as "I Had a Hippo" or "I Had a Kangaroo." Children may work in small groups to collaborate. Encourage children to tell their stories.

INTO THE LEARNING CENTERS
Invite children into the Writing Center where they may enjoy writing and illustrating their stories, and making them into books. See page 98.

TEAM WORK/THEME WORK
This is a good opportunity to have children develop a story for the Storytelling Festival. See pages 38–39 and 92–93.

EXPLORING PRINT LEARNING THE CODE

In the Exploring Print lessons for this theme, children will learn about the letters F, f and Y, y and the sounds they represent. Take advantage of opportunities to point out these letters and the sounds they represent as you share Today's News, as you talk with children about their writing, and as you reread the theme-related trade books.

DECODING AND PHONICS

LETTERS: *Y, y*
SOUND/LETTER RELATIONSHIPS: /y/Y, y

Developing Phonemic Awareness
Remind children that they are learning about the sounds of language and the letters that stand for those sounds. Explain that these letters and sounds make up the words that storytellers use to tell stories and songwriters use in songs. Then tell children that they will learn a song that has been popular for many, many years.

Sing or play "Yankee Doodle," suggesting that children stand and march or step along to the music. Children might enjoy adding gestures for riding a pony and sticking the feather in the cap. Sing the song again and invite children to join in.

Now sing the song and have children clap when they hear the word *Yankee*. Point out that the word *Yankee* begins with the same sound as they hear at the beginning of the word *yak*. Say *Yankee* again, emphasizing the beginning sound.

Yankee Doodle

Yankee Doodle went to town
A riding on a pony,
He stuck a feather in his cap
And called it macaroni.

Yankee Doodle, keep it up,
Yankee Doodle dandy,
Mind the music and the step
And with the girls be handy.

♪ SING A SOUND AUDIOCASSETTES
Yankee Doodle

Developing Print Awareness
Write the title of the song "Yankee Doodle" on chart paper or the chalkboard. Point to the title of the song. Encourage children to say the words with you as you point to each one.

Use a word mask or your hands to frame the capital Y in the word *Yankee*.

- *Let's look at some y's together. Here is a capital, or uppercase, Y in the word* Yankee *in the title of the song. Say* Yankee *with me.*

Then frame the lowercase y in the word *yak* on the Alphabet Poster.

- *Here is a lowercase y in the word* yak, *one of the animals in the story* I Had a Cat. *Say the word* yak *with me.*

Encourage children to come forward to point to and trace over with their fingers the uppercase and lowercase y's in these words.

Explain that the letter y stands for the sound heard at the beginning of the word Yankee. Have children name other words that begin with this sound.

Begin a Word Wall titled "Spin a Yarn with Y" in letters made from yarn. (If you have established a Storyteller's Corner in the room, you may wish to create the Word Wall there.) Invite children to draw pictures of things that begin with the same sound as Yankee, such as yard, yarn, yellowbird, yolk (of an egg), yo-yo, and yucca. Encourage children to title their pictures and attach them to the Word Wall.

Then invite children to visit the storyteller's corner to "spin yarns." Share with them that a yarn is a story that is made-up, and their yarns or stories can be as silly as they wish. Have children look at the pictures and include in their stories as many words that begin with /y/ as they can.

7

SHARE A STORY!

OTHER RESOURCES

• BIG BOOK STAND
• BIG BOOK POINTER

LITERACY SUPPORT:
BUILDING LANGUAGE AND CONCEPTS

**For children acquiring English and/or
needing more intensive support, you
may wish to incorporate the following
suggestions into the basic lesson plan.**

Before reading, describe how we get bread by beginning with a
seed. Explain unfamiliar vocabulary from the text, such as
threshing, grinding, and *mill.* If possible, show a real seed and
pictures of wheat fields.

After reading, invite children to discuss what the Little Red Hen
did first, second, third, and so on.

SHARING TIME

TODAY'S NEWS

Write and read Today's News, pointing to the words as you read. Lead children in a discussion about why it's good to work together to get things done.

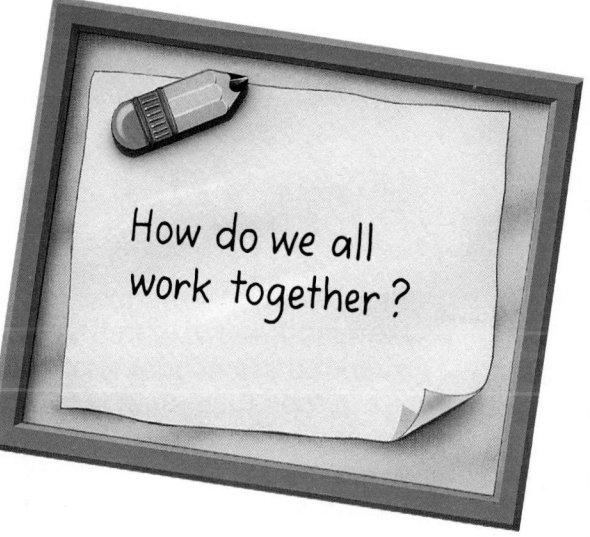

How do we all work together?

CREATING INTEREST AND BUILDING BACKGROUND

Because motivation matters!

Invite children to listen to the poem "Five Little Chickens" to discover what the mother hen thinks her chicks need to do to get what they want.

Encourage children to join you in reciting the poem. Divide the children into two groups. Invite one group to recite the line " I wish I could find" and the other group to provide the last line in each stanza. The last word in the line rhymes with the last word in line two. The last line names what the little chicken wants to find.

Tell children that in the next story, they will meet another hen who believes in working for what you need.

You may want to take a moment to focus children's attention on words in the poem that begin with /f/ as in *fish* by having them clap when they hear one. Another suggestion is to read the third stanza slowly, asking children to shout out "Yes!" when they hear a word that begins with the same sound as *yak* and *yes*.

Five Little Chickens

Said the first little chicken,
    With a queer little squirm,
"I wish I could find
    A fat little worm."

Said the next little chicken,
    With an odd little shrug,
"I wish I could find
    A fat little slug."

Said the third little chicken,
    With a sharp little squeal,
"I wish I could find
    Some nice yellow meal."

Said the fourth little chicken,
    With a small sigh of grief,
"I wish I could find
    A little green leaf."

Said the fifth little chicken,
    With a faint little moan,
"I wish I could find
    A wee gravel stone."

"Now, see here," said the mother,
    From the green garden patch,
"If you want your breakfast,
    Just come here and scratch."

—Anonymous

READING AND WRITING

SHARING LITERATURE
Little Red Hen

LOOK IT OVER   Read the title and the illustrator's name, tracking each word. Show children the front and back covers, pointing out the shapes and patterns in the art.

Invite children to identify the animals on the covers. Who do children think the book will be mainly about? Will this be a *story* about or *facts* about a hen? How can children tell?

SHARE THE STORY   As you read, you may want to engage children in pointing out the characters and details in this animated and very stylized art. Children will enjoy predicting the responses of the cat, goose, and rat to each of Little Red Hen's questions.

About the Author/Illustrator

Share with children that Janina Domanska was born in Warsaw, Poland, where she grew up and attended the Academy of Fine Arts. Her paintings are in the Museum of Modern Art in Warsaw and in several private art galleries in Rome.

Domanska has illustrated more than thirty children's books. In the basement of her home in Connecticut, she operates a small printing press on which she made the original engravings for *Under the Green Willow* and *If All the Seas Were One Sea*, a Caldecott Honor winner.

"Who will plant this?" she asked.
"Not I," said the cat.
"Not I," said the goose.
"Not I," said the rat.
"Then I will," said Little Red Hen.

10

11

RESPONDING TO LITERATURE

BOOK TALK Invite children to share their personal reactions to the book. You may wish to present some of the prompts below to begin discussion, or you may want to talk about your reactions to the story.

- *Do you like the way the story ends? Do you think it was right for the hen to keep the bread for herself and her chicks?*

- *Little Red Hen is a hard worker! Does she remind you of any characters in other stories or of anyone you know?*

- *The art has so many shapes and patterns in it! Do you like the art? What did you notice about the animals?*

JOURNAL WRITING Invite children to draw or write about their favorite parts of the book or what they didn't like. You may want to try to use the Theme Word *storyteller* in your journal writing. Share with children what you wrote and ask if they would like to share what they wrote.

INTO THE LEARNING CENTERS
Children will be excited about planting their own seeds in the Science Center. See page 102.

In the Art Center on page 101, children can create patterned pictures using tissue paper.

TEAM WORK/THEME WORK
Little Red Hen is a tale children will delight in dramatizing during their Storytelling Festival. See pages 38–39 and 92–93.

In his developmental spellings, Mitch represented all (or almost all) of the sounds he heard in the words he wrote.
Mitch read his message like this: "The little red hen asked, 'Who will thresh the wheat?'"

EXPLORING PRINT LEARNING THE CODE

DECODING AND PHONICS

LETTERS: *Y, y*
SOUND/LETTER RELATIONSHIPS: /y/*Y, y*

Developing Phonemic Awareness

Ask children if they think any of the animals in *I Had a Cat* would have been willing to help Little Red Hen plant the grain, thresh the wheat, go to the mill, and bake the bread. Would the silly goose or the fuzzy fox or maybe the snow-white lamb have been willing to help? Mention the yak, and then invite children to listen as you read "The Yak" by Jack Prelutsky on page 34 in the *Big Book of Alphabet Rhymes and Chimes.* As you come to words that begin with *y*, slightly emphasize the initial sound.

- *Listen to the sound you hear at the beginning of* yak, yickity-yackity, *and* yickity-yak. *What other words do we know that begin with the same sound?*

Repeat the rhyme a few times, encouraging children to chime in.

Developing Print Awareness

Display "The Yak" on page 34 of the *Big Book of Alphabet Rhymes and Chimes* and say the rhyme with children. Use the Big Book pointer to point out the words that begin with *y.*

Yy

The Yak

Yickity-yackity, yickity-yak,
the yak has a scriffily,
scraffily back;
some yaks are brown yaks
and some yaks are black,
yickity-yackity, yickity-yak.

Jack Prelutsky

**Big Book of Alphabet Rhymes and Chimes,
page 34**

Then display the Alphabet Poster and the ABC cards for Yy, or write the letters on the chalkboard and on cards of your own.

yak

Have children compare the *Y*'s on the Big Book page with the letters on the poster and the card. Encourage children to compare the various pictures of yaks they have seen: the Alphabet Poster, the illustration accompanying "The Yak" on page 34 of the *Big Book of Alphabet Rhymes and Chimes,* and the illustration on pages 12–13 of *I Had a Cat.*

Invite pairs of children to go on a Word Hunt around the room to find words on charts, signs, and in books that begin with the same sound and letter as *yickity-yak* and *yak*. Have them copy the words on cards and then share and display them on a Word Wall or bulletin board.

■ **Literature Activity Book:** page 85

INTO THE LEARNING CENTERS
Encourage children to visit the Hands On! Language Center for more activities with sounds and letters. See page 97.

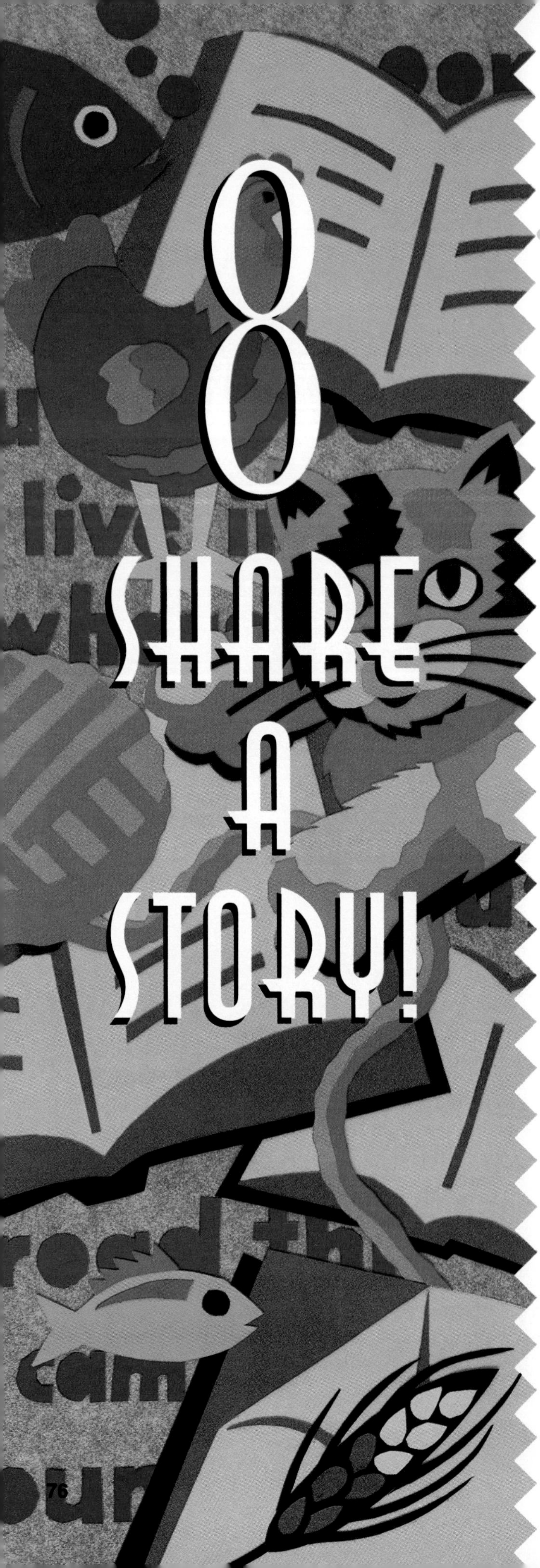

8
SHARE A STORY!

LITERATURE
Little Red Hen
  by Janina Domanska

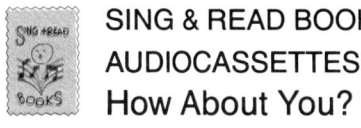 SING & READ BOOKS AND
AUDIOCASSETTES
How About You?

EXPLORING PRINT
*Big Book of Alphabet Rhymes
and Chimes:* The Yak

Rhyme and Chime Strips:
  The Yak

Learning the Code: Y, y

BRWL: Letterbook Y(23)

 A to EZ Handbook
  • Hands On! p. 258
  • Predictable Books: p. 289

Performance Assessment Handbook

OTHER RESOURCES

- BIG BOOK STAND
- BIG BOOK POINTER
- POCKET CHART AND
  STAND
- CHART PAPER
- MARKERS
- WORD MASK
- MURAL PAPER
- CRAYONS

SHARING TIME

TODAY'S NEWS

Write and read Today's News, tracking each word. Invite children to discover the words that begin with the same sound as *yak*. Ask a volunteer to trace each *y* and to tell which one is a capital letter.

Can you sing while you work? Yes, you can!

CREATING INTEREST AND BUILDING BACKGROUND

Because motivation matters!

Encourage children to talk about when and why people sing. Tell children that people do sometimes sing while they work, and invite them to create lyrics for "The Mulberry Bush" that Little Red Hen could sing. Children will enjoy developing actions to go with their lyrics.

The Mulberry Bush

Chorus
Here we go 'round the Mulberry bush,
   the Mulberry bush, the Mulberry bush,
Here we go 'round the Mulberry bush,
   so early in the morning.

This is the way we plant the grain,
   plant the grain, plant the grain,
This is the way we plant the grain,
   so early in the morning.
2. ...cut the wheat   5. ...carry the flour
3. ...thresh the wheat   6. ...make the bread
4. ...carry the wheat   7. ...eat the bread

You may want to write the song on chart paper and then read it through once with the children before you all sing it.

READING AND WRITING

SHARING LITERATURE
Little Red Hen

REREAD THE STORY   Invite children to listen again to *Little Red Hen*. With this rereading, encourage children to chime in on the predictable dialog. At the appropriate points, engage children in singing the song lyrics they created for "The Mulberry Bush."

PHONEMIC AWARENESS

Repetition/Rhyming
Invite children to identify the repetitive phrases in the story, asking volunteers to name the animals who always use these phrases. You may want to encourage them to name the two animals whose names rhyme and the two that sound completely different.

Ask children to listen as you read Little Red Hen's response to the "Not I" dialog of the cat, goose, and rat. What one word does she always say that is the same as what the other three animals say?

PRINT AWARENESS

Quotation Marks
On page 10, mask the hen's question and show children the quotation marks and the question mark, pointing out their purposes. Ask volunteers to locate the quotation marks used with the words the cat, goose, and rat speak. Use similar opportunities to work with these print clues on pages 16, 22, 28, and 32.

RESPONDING TO LITERATURE

BOOK TALK Invite children to think about what Little Red Hen does with the grain and what she is like.

- *Do you think what Little Red Hen does with her grain and wheat plant is the same as what people do to get bread?*

- *If the hen found another seed, what would she do? What would the other animals do?*

FROM STORY MAP TO BIG BOOK Encourage children to work with you to chart the sequence of events in the story. Read the chart together when it is complete. Then children can gather in groups to draw a large picture of each event. The pictures can be put into a Big Book for retelling the story.

Animals' Actions

Hen	Cat Goose Rat
	did nothing
planted grain	did nothing
cut, threshed wheat	did nothing
took wheat to mill	did nothing
carried flour home	did nothing
baked bread	did nothing
ate the bread	

Flour
xxxxx

INTO THE LEARNING CENTERS
In the Art Center on page 101, children can make puppets to use in the Dramatic Play Center on page 99.

79

Using the Rhyme and Chime Strips gives children a Hands On! Language experience that allows them to explore important concepts of print.

CONCEPTS OF PRINT
Directionality, Words

Developing Print Awareness
Display page 34 in the *Big Book of Alphabet Rhymes and Chimes* and encourage children to recite the rhyme with you as you use the Big Book pointer to point to each word.

Yy

The Yak
Yickity-yackity, yickity-yak,
the yak has a scriffily,
scraffily back;
some yaks are brown yaks
and some yaks are black,
yickity-yackity, yickity-yak.

Jack Prelutsky

Big Book of Alphabet Rhymes and Chimes, page 34

Use a word mask to frame the words in the first line. Explain to children that the spaces between the words separate the letters that make up one word from the letters that make up another word.

Use the strips and word cards from the Rhyme and Chime Strips for "The Yak" to build the rhyme in the pocket chart as shown, and encourage children to recite it with you. You may want to show children how you move from left to right and then down to the next line, moving left to right again, as you put the cards in the pockets and as you read the rhyme.

Yickity–yackity,	yickity–yak,			
the	yak	has	a	scriffily,
scraffily	back;			
some	yaks	are	brown	yaks
and	some	yaks	are	black,
yickity–yackity,	yickity–yak.			

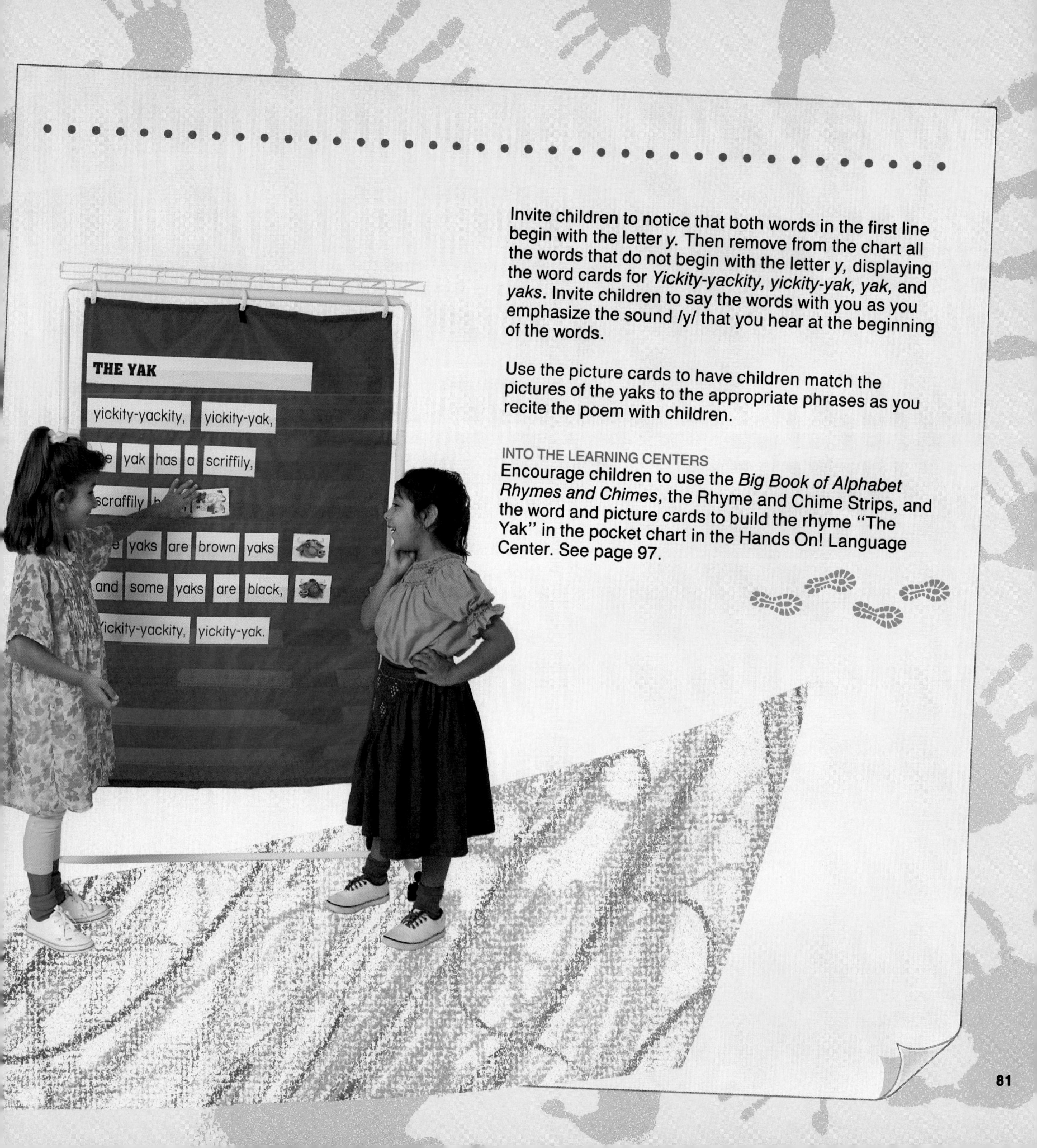

THE YAK

yickity-yackity,   yickity-yak,

...e yak has a scriffily,

scraffily b...

...e yaks are brown yaks

and some yaks are black,

...ickity-yackity,   yickity-yak.

Invite children to notice that both words in the first line begin with the letter *y*. Then remove from the chart all the words that do not begin with the letter *y*, displaying the word cards for *Yickity-yackity, yickity-yak, yak,* and *yaks*. Invite children to say the words with you as you emphasize the sound /y/ that you hear at the beginning of the words.

Use the picture cards to have children match the pictures of the yaks to the appropriate phrases as you recite the poem with children.

INTO THE LEARNING CENTERS
Encourage children to use the *Big Book of Alphabet Rhymes and Chimes*, the Rhyme and Chime Strips, and the word and picture cards to build the rhyme "The Yak" in the pocket chart in the Hands On! Language Center. See page 97.

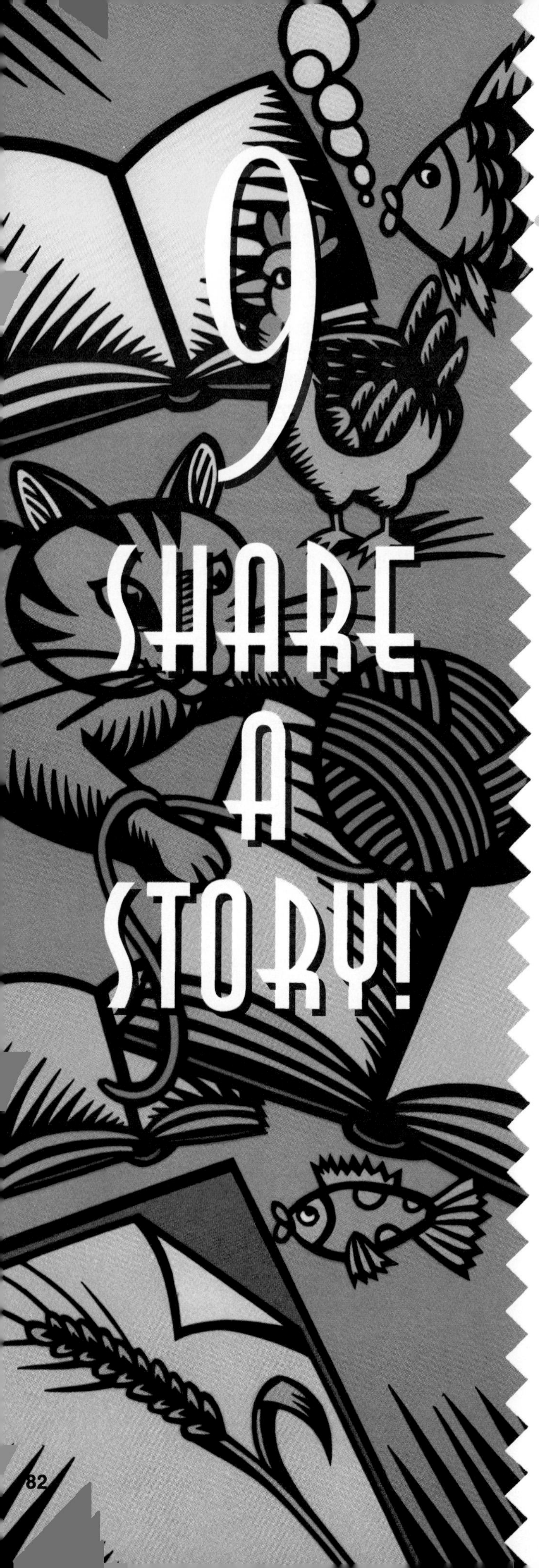

9

SHARE A STORY!

LITERATURE

Read Aloud Anthology
  "The Three Bears"
  An English folk tale
  retold by Margaret H. Lippert

SONGS AND STORIES
AUDIOCASSETTES
STORYTELLINGS:
The Three Bears

SING & READ BOOKS AND
AUDIOCASSETTES
How About You?

EXPLORING PRINT

Rhyme and Chime Strips:
  The Yak

Alphabet Poster for Yy

Learning the Code: Y, y

BRWL: Letterbook Y(23)

 A to EZ Handbook
  • Hands On! p. 258
  • Pocket Chart: p. 285

Performance Assessment Handbook

OTHER RESOURCES

• CHART PAPER
• MARKERS
• POCKET CHART AND
  STAND
• STORY THEATER PROP
  STUFFED OR
    CARDBOARD BEAR
  PLASTIC OR PAPER
    BOWLS
  DOLL
• WORD MASK
• BIG BOOK POINTER

Sharing Time

TODAY'S NEWS

Write and read Today's News, tracking each word as you read. Discuss with children what bears they know about.

What famous bears do you know about?

CREATING INTEREST AND BUILDING BACKGROUND

Because motivation matters!

Share the rhyme "Bears, Bears, Everywhere" with children and turn your classroom into a den full of bears! You may wish to write the poem on chart paper to display to the children and point to each word as you read the poem together. When you reread the rhyme, have children pantomime the bears' actions. You may want to try rereading the rhyme progressively faster for three or four rounds.

Bears, Bears, Everywhere
Bears, bears, everywhere!
Climbing stairs
Sitting on chairs
Collecting fares
Painting squares
Bears, bears, everywhere!

Share with children that today they will be listening to "The Three Bears," and encourage them to discuss what they know about the tale.

READING AND WRITING

SHARING LITERATURE
"The Three Bears"

SHARE THE STORY   Invite children to listen as you read or play the story on the STORYTELLINGS AUDIOCASSETTE. Encourage children to compare this version of the story to versions they may have heard previously.

The predictable nature of the events and the dialog may inspire children to spontaneously chime in on retellings. For one retelling, children can work in four groups, with each group supplying dialog for one of the characters. Encourage children to imagine what Goldilocks might have said for each event and to use facial and vocal expressions to indicate how Goldilocks and the three bears felt.

♪ SONGS AND STORIES AUDIOCASSETTES
STORYTELLINGS: The Three Bears

About the Story — *Developing Multicultural Awareness*

"The Three Bears" is an English folk tale. The earliest known version of the tale was written in 1831. In it, the intruder in the bears' house was a wicked, old woman. In later retellings, the old woman was changed to a young, blonde-haired girl.

■ **Read Aloud Anthology:** pages 78–79

RESPONDING TO LITERATURE

BOOK TALK   Have children share their personal reactions to "The Three Bears." To begin the discussion, you may wish to offer your own reactions to the story with comments and questions like these.

- *Whenever I hear this story, I want to tell Goldilocks to stay out of other people's houses! Would you do what Goldilocks did?*

- *How do you think Goldilocks felt when she was awakened by the three bears?*

- *This is a story of threes. Let's discover how many things occur in threes.*

JOURNAL WRITING   Invite children to put themselves in Goldilocks's shoes! Encourage them to draw and write in their journals about how Goldilocks felt before she saw the bears and how she felt *after* she saw the bears.

STORY THEATER With its simple structure and repetitive dialog, children will love to dramatize "The Three Bears." They can use their imaginations to visualize each scene, or they can use props such as stuffed or cardboard bears, plastic or paper bowls, and a doll.

INTO THE LEARNING CENTERS

The concept of comparisons is a key element in "The Three Bears." Encourage children to visit the Math Center today to compare various objects. See page 100.

TEAM WORK/THEME WORK

Allow time for children to make their final preparations for the Storytelling Festival. See pages 38–39 and 92–93.

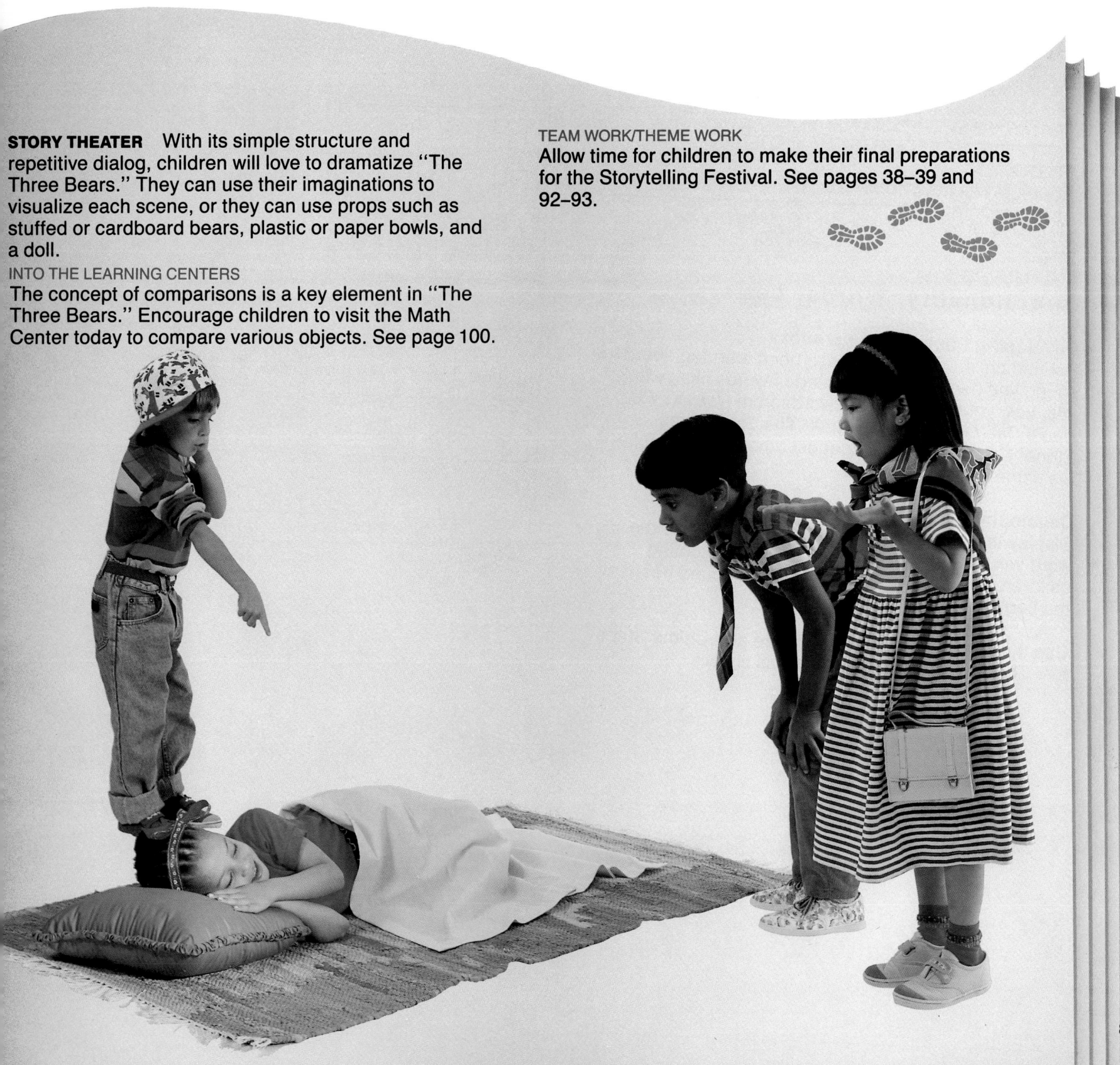

DECODING AND PHONICS

LETTERS: *Y, y*
SOUND/LETTER RELATIONSHIPS: */y/Y, y*

CONCEPTS OF PRINT
Directionality, Words, Letters

Developing Phonemic Awareness
Remind children that they have been learning about the sound you hear at the beginning of words like *yellow, you, yak, yours,* and *years* (words from *Nessa's Fish, I Had a Cat, Little Red Hen,* and "The Storytelling Stone"). Ask children to suggest other words that have the same beginning sound.

Developing Print Awareness
Display the Alphabet Poster for Yy and point to the word *yak.* Frame the letter *y* in the word. Remind children that the letter *y* stands for the sound heard at the beginning of the word *yak.*

Use the word cards from the Rhyme and Chime Strips for "The Yak" to build the rhyme as shown.

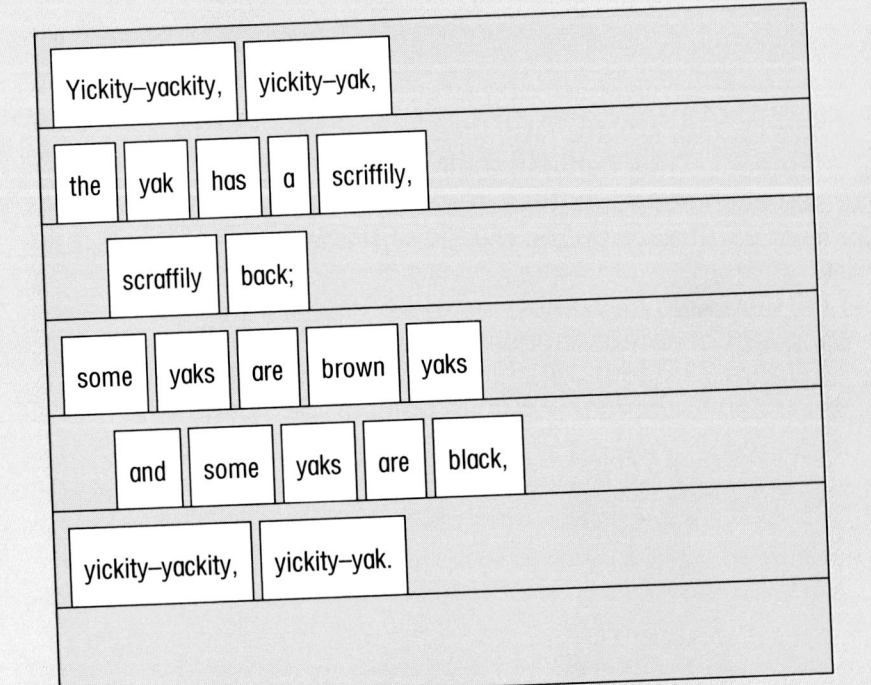

Yickity–yackity, | yickity–yak,

the | yak | has | a | scriffily,

scraffily | back;

some | yaks | are | brown | yaks

and | some | yaks | are | black,

yickity–yackity, | yickity–yak.

As you point to each word with the Big Book pointer, encourage children to say the rhyme with you. Have children stamp their feet each time they hear a word that begins with /y/, the same beginning sound as in *yak*.

Ask volunteers to come up and take a word card that begins with the sound /y/.

Review all the charts and other print resources in the classroom to find words that begin with the same sound and letter as *yak*.

INTO THE LEARNING CENTERS
Encourage print exploration! Invite children to the Hands On! Language Center to work with letter stamps, sponge letters, and magnetic letters. See page 97.

10 SHARE A STORY!

LITERATURE

Nessa's Fish by Nancy Luenn,
   illustrated by Neil Waldman

I Had a Cat
   by Mona Rabun Reeves,
   illustrated by Julie Downing

Little Red Hen
   by Janina Domanska

Big Book of Poems:
Worlds I Know
   by Myra Cohn Livingston

Big Book of Songs:
How About You?
   by John Farrell

 SONGS AND STORIES
AUDIOCASSETTES
STORY SONGS:
How About You?

 SING & READ BOOKS AND
AUDIOCASSETTES
How About You?

Literature Activity Book: p. 89
   Responding to Literature

STAFF DEVELOPMENT A to EZ Handbook

   • Emergent Literacy: p. 253

   • Observation: p. 279

Performance Assessment Handbook

OTHER RESOURCES

• BIG BOOK STAND
• BIG BOOK POINTER

SHARING TIME

TODAY'S NEWS

Read and write Today's News, tracking each word as you read. Ask a child to point out the Theme Word, *storyteller.* Then ask children to think about what stories they might like to tell at their Storytelling Festival.

Storyteller, storyteller, what story will you tell ?

WRAPPING IT UP

To create a festive mood, reintroduce the Theme Song "How About You?" from the *Big Book of Songs,* pages 32–33. Invite children to sing the song.

Afterward, you may wish to reread the Theme Poem "Worlds I Know" on pages 30–31 of the *Big Book of Poems* with children.

♪ SONGS AND STORIES AUDIOCASSETTES
STORY SONGS: How About You?

How About You?

Songs are meant to be sung.
Tales are meant to be told.
Everyone has a story to tell.
There's a story for everyone I know.
There's a story for everyone!

CHORUS
How about you? How about you?
Do you have a tale you'd like to tell?
How about you? How about you?
Do you have a tale to tell?

John Farrell

32   33

Big Book of Songs, pages 32–33

Reading and Writing

SHARING LITERATURE

LOOK IT OVER   Display the books *Nessa's Fish, I Had A Cat,* and *Little Red Hen.* Invite children to select one book to reread and encourage them to give a reason for their choice.

REREAD THE STORY   If children choose *Nessa's Fish,* encourage them to act out Nessa's actions as she talks to the animals. If they request *Little Red Hen,* ask children to join in on the repetitive dialog in the story. For *I Had a Cat,* children may be able to chime in with some of the animals' names.

Review the letters children learned about this week by asking children to find and listen for words that begin with *f* and *y.* For additional practice, you may wish to use the Phonics Activity Sheets on pages 108–109.

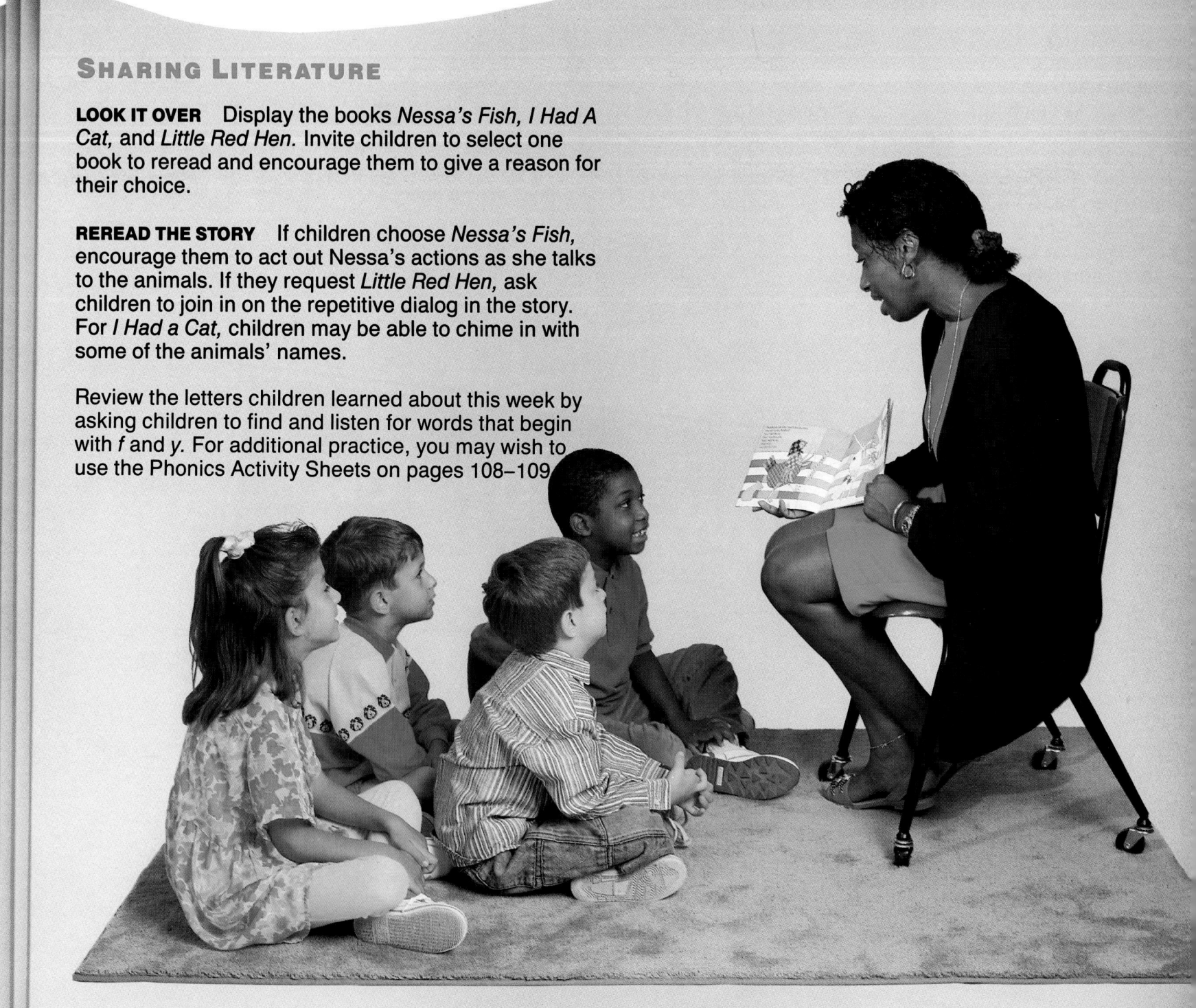

RESPONDING TO LITERATURE

BOOK TALK   Invite children to share their reactions to the books, and encourage them to talk about how the books are alike and different. You may want to use the questions below to get the discussion started.

- *Which book's pictures did you like best? What did you like about them?*

- *What advice do you think Nessa would have given the girl in* I Had a Cat *for getting rid of all those animals?*

- *How are the animals in the three books alike? How are they different?*

- *Which story would you most like to retell to a friend? Why?*

JOURNAL WRITING   Invite children to write and draw in their journals about the book they liked best. Encourage children to share their journals with the group.

INTO THE LEARNING CENTERS

If children would like to do more reading and writing about the theme books, invite them to visit both the Reading Center and the Writing Center. See pages 96 and 98.

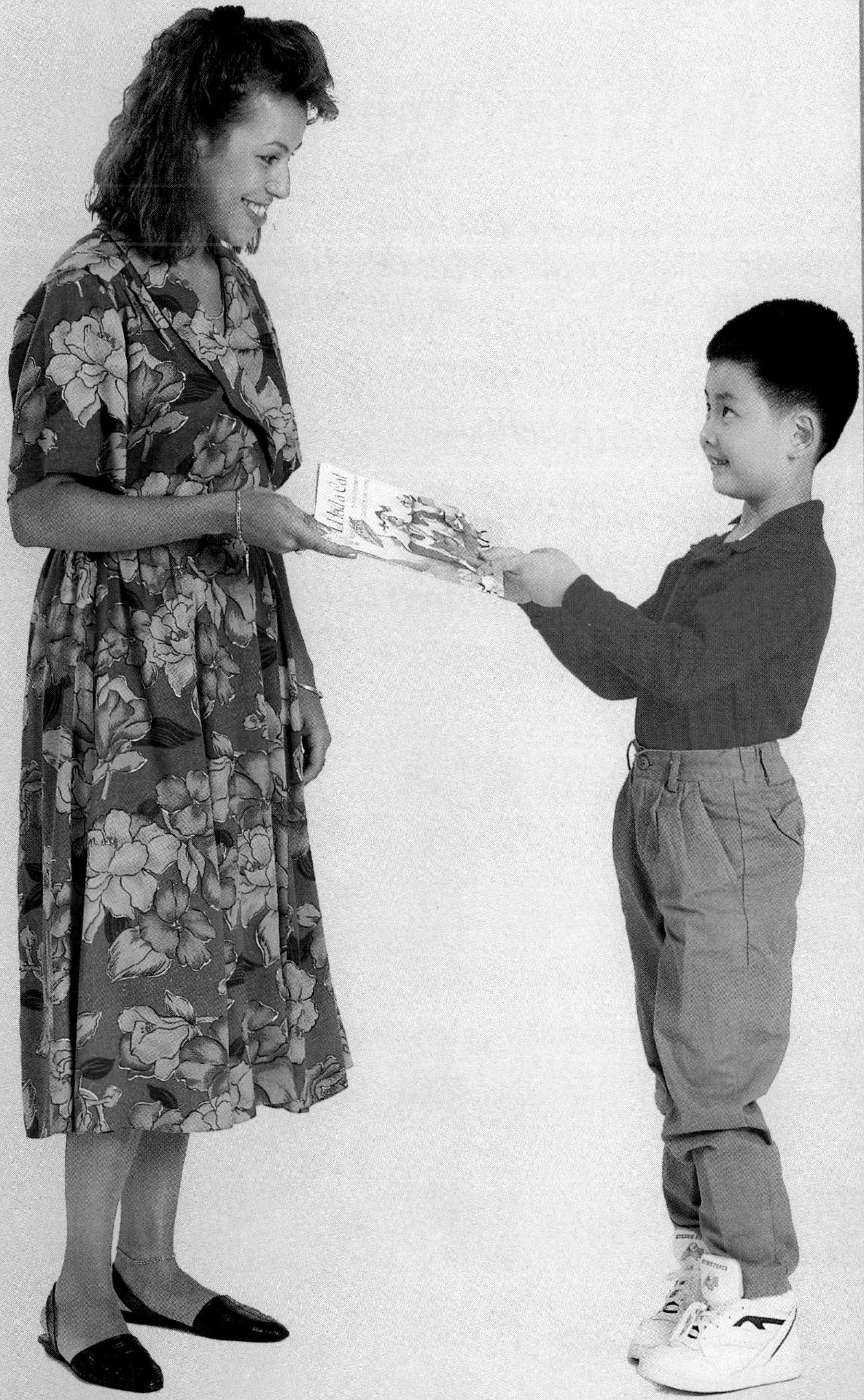

TEAM WORK/THEME WORK

Storytelling Festival
Program

Stories	Storytellers
Anansi the Spider	Talisha, Billy, Jenni
The Peach Boy	Greg
The Story of Brer Rabbit	Janice, Steve
Johnny Appleseed	

A STORYTELLING FESTIVAL!

And now the enchantment begins! Invite everyone in; settle down for a warm, entertaining Storytelling Festival! Children will share their stories and their imaginations, weaving wonders for all to behold!

You may want to videotape or tape-record the festival and place the tapes in the Listening Corner so children can listen to themselves and their classmates at their leisure.

g Festival!

Storytelling Festival
Program
Part 1
Stories
Anansi the Spider
The Peach Boy
The Story of Brer Rabbit
Johnny Appleseed
Storytellers
Talisha, Billy, Jenni
Greg
Janice, Steve
Arturo
Sharing Our Stories!
A Storytelling Festival!
Storyteller

INTO THE LEARNING CENTERS!

▼

Learning Centers can be places where children learn independently, from one another, and from you! Engaging activities can motivate children to become literacy explorers!

STAFF DEVELOPMENT **A to EZ Handbook**
• Learning Centers: page 270

READING CENTER

—Sharing Stories! page 96

MATH CENTER

—Numbers and More! page 100

HANDS ON! LANGUAGE CENTER

—Exploring Language through Manipulatives! page 97

ART CENTER

—Getting Creative! page 101

WRITING CENTER

—Encouraging Emergent Writers! page 98

SCIENCE CENTER

—Growing Plants! page 102

DRAMATIC PLAY CENTER

—Act It Out! page 99

MUSIC CENTER

—Singing About Animals! page 103

Reading Center

(See MORE BOOKS TO SHARE pages 32–33.)

SHARING STORIES!

Resources *Nessa's Fish * I Had a Cat * Little Red Hen * Big Book of Songs * Big Book of Poems * Big Book pointer * Sing & Read Little Books * Listening Library Audiocassettes * Songs and Stories Audiocassettes* * theme-related books (See MORE BOOKS TO SHARE pages 32–33.)

Setting Up! Display books for shared and emergent readings. To encourage small groups of children to explore the books and material together, create a "storytelling circle" in the center. Arrange four or five chairs or floor mats in a semicircle.

- Place the Sing & Read Book and Audiocassette for "How About You?" by the tape recorder.

- Have the Listening Library Audiocassette for *I Had a Cat* available.

- Invite children to listen to "How About You?" on the SONGS AND STORIES AUDIOCASSETTES.

Centers in Action! Invite children to explore the books and materials in the center. Continue to add favorite stories to the center, inviting children to do the same. Suggest that children add any audiocassettes of their favorite stories, songs, or poems.

Children might enjoy retelling one of the stories they know from the display to a small group of friends. Display the theme Big Books and keep the Big Book pointer accessible to children so that they can act as teachers!

To be storytellers, children need to read and listen to lots of stories.

Hands On! Language Center

EXPLORING LANGUAGE THROUGH MANIPULATIVES

Resources *Rhyme and Chime Strips ("Five Little Fishies" for Week One; "The Yak" for Week Two)* * *pocket chart and stand* * *alphabet posters for Ff and Yy* * *chalkboard* and chalk or chart paper and markers * *sponge letters* * *letter stamps* * paper * pads * pencils * crayons * *magnetic letters* * *magnetic board* * letter blocks

Setting Up! In the Hands On! Language Center, children may explore language independently. You may also wish to suggest theme-related activities as described under Centers in Action!

Centers in Action!

- Invite children to use magnetic letters or sponge letters to spell the name of each animal in *Nessa's Fish.*

- Children can print the names of all their favorite animals in *I Had a Cat* on the chalkboard.

- Invite children to discover the rhyming words in *I Had a Cat* and to write them in lists.

- Children may enjoy creating letter posters. Ask children to find words that begin with *F, f* or *Y, y* in *I Had a Cat, Little Red Hen,* and *Nessa's Fish.* They can use sponge letters or letter stamps to print the words and then illustrate them. Children may want to add other words they know that begin with the letters *F, f* and *Y, y.*

The theme books are excellent resources for exploring language.

WRITING CENTER

ENCOURAGING EMERGENT WRITERS!

Resources paper * pencils * crayons * markers * drawing paper * *I Had a Cat* * *Little Red Hen* * *Nessa's Fish* * stapler

Setting Up! As children work in the Writing Center, encourage them to choose their own topics to write about. Invite children to collaborate with partners and in small groups as well.

Centers in Action!

Animals, Animals! Children may enjoy creating their own animal alphabet book. Provide copies of the books *I Had a Cat, Little Red Hen,* and *Nessa's Fish.* Ask children to make separate lists for the animal names that begin with the same letter. Children can add drawings to their lists. The lists can then be stapled together in alphabetical order to create books. Encourage children to make colorful covers for their books.

Story Spin-Off! Children can keep the action of a favorite story going by writing a story spin-off. Invite children to write about and draw pictures telling what happened to one group of animals in *I Had a Cat* that the young girl found a new home for. Encourage children to share their stories at the Storytelling Festival.

Animal Riddles! Invite children to create their own animal riddles. Have children choose an animal from *I Had a Cat, Little Red Hen,* or *Nessa's Fish* and write a riddle like the following:

I am furry. I hop a lot. Who am I?

Ask children to write the answers to their riddles on the backs of their papers. Children may want to combine their riddles in a class book that everyone can share!

Nessa's Banner! Children may enjoy making a banner that welcomes Nessa home from her fishing trip. Encourage them to make their banners colorful.

Announcing the Storytelling Festival! Children can create eye-catching invitations announcing the date, time, and place of their Storytelling Festival. They can write programs with story titles and storytellers' names.

Children's writing can be compiled into books that they can share in the Reading Center.

98

Dramatic Play Center

ACT IT OUT!

Resources *I Had a Cat* * *Little Red Hen* * *Nessa's Fish* * background mural * large box * costumes * puppets * story props * hats, caps, scarves, costume jewelry, or any other items appropriate for costumes

Setting Up! Cut out the back and a front window from a large box to serve as a puppet theater. Children may want to use supplies in the Art Center to decorate the theater.

Centers in Action!

Putting On a Play Invite children to read their favorite stories and work with groups of friends to act them out. Help children assign roles for each story character.

A Puppet Show Children may enjoy turning one of the stories into a puppet show. They can use the puppet theater and the puppets that they create in the Art Center. See page 101.

The plays and the puppet shows can be incorporated into the Team Work/Theme Work project, a Storytelling Festival. See pages 38–39 and 92–93.

Children will read their favorite stories and act them out!

Math Center

Resources construction paper * string or yarn * clothespins * sets of three classroom objects, such as balls, dolls, and stuffed animals * boxes

Setting Up! For the "Going Fishing" activity, cut out two sets of 10 fish shapes from construction paper. Number one set from 1 to 10. Tape each numbered fish to the top of a clothespin. Then hang string or yarn as a clothesline, and attach the clothespins in consecutive order. On each of the fish shapes in the second set write the word name for one of the ten numbers. Draw the corresponding amount of dots or stars on the fish.

You may want to create additional sets of fish shapes that use geometric shapes or different sets of numbers.

For the "How Do They Compare?" activity, fill boxes with three similar objects of different sizes, such as 3 balls, 3 dolls, and 3 stuffed animals.

Math games provide opportunities for children to see content-area words in print.

Centers in Action!

- **Going Fishing** Place the set of fish shapes with the drawings and the word names in a container. Invite children to go fishing by reaching into the container and pulling out a fish. Children must clip their "catch" to the matching fish on the clothesline.

- **How Do They Compare?** Invite children to order the objects in each box according to size. Ask them to describe each object as big, bigger, biggest; small, smaller, smallest; tall, taller, tallest; or short, shorter, shortest. Perhaps they would like to discuss which objects are just the right size for baby bear, mama bear, or papa bear!

Art Center

Getting Creative!

Resources poster board * construction paper * butcher paper * crayons, markers, and paints * yarn * ribbon * cotton balls * string * pieces of felt * paper bags, socks, gloves * shoe boxes * empty spools of thread * refrigerator box * old pieces of cloth * modeling clay * tissue paper * string * glue

Setting Up! Organize supplies in different containers on a table!

Centers in Action!

- **Puppets and a Puppet Theater** Children can use paints and markers to title and to decorate the window side of the refrigerator box for the Dramatic Play Center, page 99. Old pieces of cloth can be attached to the inside of the window to be used as theater curtains.

   Old socks, gloves, and different-sized paper bags can be turned into puppets for puppet shows. Children can decorate their puppets with yarn, construction paper, crayons, markers, and paints.

- **Beautiful Scenery** Children may enjoy creating a farm mural to help them act out the story of *Little Red Hen*. Those children who choose to act out *Nessa's Fish* can create a snowy tundra. The inside of the puppet theater can be transformed into a house for acting out *I Had a Cat*.

Labeling art projects offers children more opportunities for writing.

- **Stories in a Box** Invite children to make scenes from their favorite stories come to life in dioramas. Have children decorate the inside of a shoe box with construction paper, markers, and paints. They can use clay figures, empty thread spools, and other materials to create their scenes.

- **Pattern Animals** Have children glue string or yarn in the outline of a favorite animal onto a piece of drawing paper. Children can glue pieces of different-colored tissue paper to the inside of the animal. Ask children to write the names of their animals when they are finished.

Science Center

Growing Plants!

Resources 2 lima beans per child * clear plastic cups * soil * water * masking tape * chart paper * markers

Setting Up! Tape two lima beans to the inside of each plastic cup.

Centers in Action! Remind children of the grain of wheat that the Little Red Hen planted. Tell them that they can plant their own seeds and watch them grow, too. Have children follow these directions:

1. Write your name on a strip of masking tape. Attach it around the bottom of the cup.
2. Fill the cup with soil.
3. Put the lima beans in near the top. Cover them with soil.
4. Add water to the soil.
5. Put the cup in a sunny area in the classroom.
6. Add water to the soil every day.

Have children make notes in a chart or draw pictures of the plants every few days to record what happens.

Observing and recording data gives children experience with different types of print, such as charts.

Music Center

SINGING ABOUT ANIMALS!

Resources   *I Had a Cat * Little Red Hen * Nessa's Fish* * tape recorder

Setting Up!   Place floor mats in a circle.

Centers in Action!
- **"Old MacDonald"**   Invite children to sing "Old MacDonald" using some of the animals that they have read about. With each new verse, children take turns standing in the middle of the circle and imitating the sound of the animal that is named.

- **Sound Effects**   Invite children to create sound effects for a storytelling they might do. They may choose to imitate some of the animal sounds if they are retelling *I Had a Cat,* for example.

- **Creating a Song**   Children can create a song from a story or poem in this theme. Invite children to clap to the rhythm of the song they create. Then, encourage them to sing the words to the rhythm that they discover. Children can tape-record their song for others to hear.

Children play with language as they sing and act out songs.

ACKNOWLEDGMENTS

The publisher gratefully acknowledges permission to reprint the following copyrighted material:

Verse 1 from "Adventures of Isabel" from BAD PARENTS' GARDEN OF VERSES by Ogden Nash. Copyright 1936 by Ogden Nash. Reprinted by permission of Little, Brown and Company.

"Bears, Bears, Everywhere!" from FIRST SONGS & ACTION RHYMES compiled by Jenny Wood. Copyright © 1990 by Conran Octopus Limited. Reprinted with permission of Aladdin Books, an imprint of Macmillan Publishing Company and Conran Octopus Limited.

"How About You?" © 1992 words and music by John Farrell, Hope River Music.

"Worlds I Know" excerpted from "Worlds I Know" in WORLDS I KNOW AND OTHER POEMS by Myra Cohn Livingston. Copyright © 1985 by Myra Cohn Livingston. Reprinted with permission of Margaret K. McElderry Books, an imprint of Macmillan Publishing Company.

Cover and Program Design: Michaelis/Carpelis Design Associates, Inc.

Additional Design: Textart, Inc.

Production: Textart, Inc.
Michaelis/Carpelis Design Associates, Inc.

Illustration

Cover Illustration: Bob Pepper

Back Cover Illustration: Patrick Merrell

Four-color airbrush: Brian Dugan, Mark Kaplan, Mary Ellen Senor

Poetry airbrush backgrounds: Mark Kaplan

Learning Center Logos: Rachel Geswaldo

Lesson Opener Panels: Fanny Mellet Berry, 58, 88; Kathleen Kinkoff, 40, 70; Nicolai Punim, 34, 66; Marti Shohet, 46, 76; Andrea Wisnewski, 52, 82.

Four-color illustration: Pat Wong, 45, 51, 79B, 100.

Black line art: Network Graphics, 35, 38, 41, 47, 53, 55, 59, 65, 69, 77, 79, 83, 89; Adam Weston, 56, 62, 80, 86.

Photography

All photographs are by Macmillan/McGraw-Hill School Division (MMSD) except as noted below.

35: Scott Harvey for MMSD. 39: Scott Harvey for MMSD. 42: RMIP/Richard Haynes for MMSD. 47: Scott Harvey for MMSD. 69: Scott Harvey for MMSD. 75: Ken Karp for MMSD. 77–90: Scott Harvey for MMSD. 92, 93: Scott Harvey for MMSD. 94: Bruce Berman for MMSD. 96, 97: Scott Harvey for MMSD. 99: Scott Harvey for MMSD. 100–103: Scott Harvey for MMSD.

Index

A FOUNTAIN OF FISH

F f

<u>f</u>ish

Write F and f.

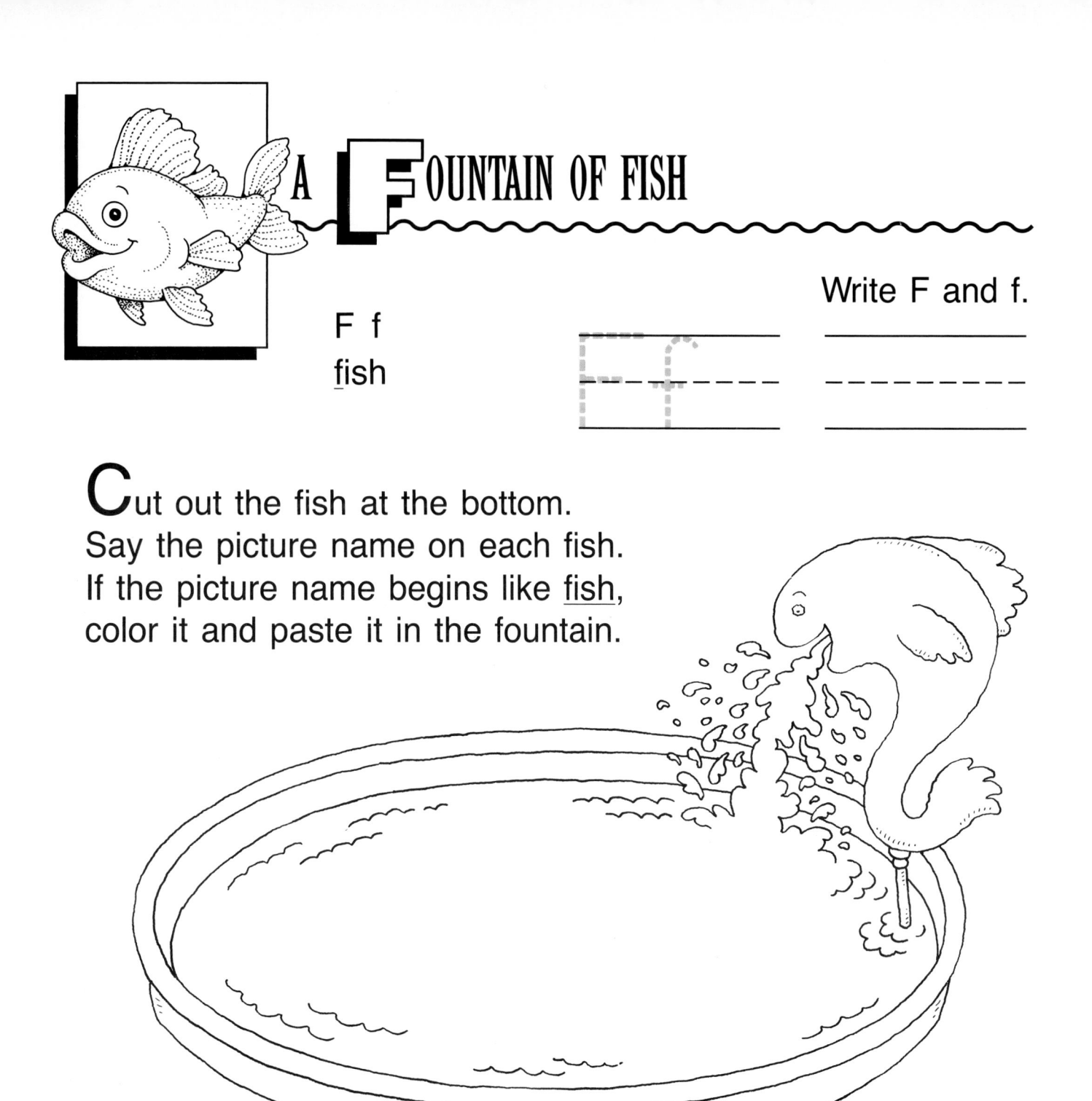

Cut out the fish at the bottom.
Say the picture name on each fish.
If the picture name begins like <u>fish</u>,
color it and paste it in the fountain.

Macmillan/McGraw-Hill

A **Y**ARD OF YAKS

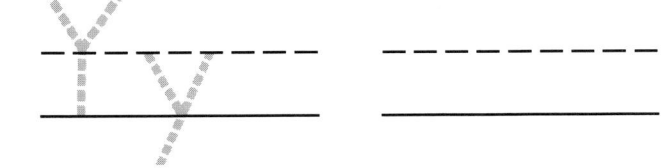

Y y

<u>y</u>ak

Write Y and y.

Y y

Cut out the pictures at the bottom.
Say each picture name.
If the picture name inside each yak
begins like <u>y</u>ak, paste it into the yard.

Act It Out!

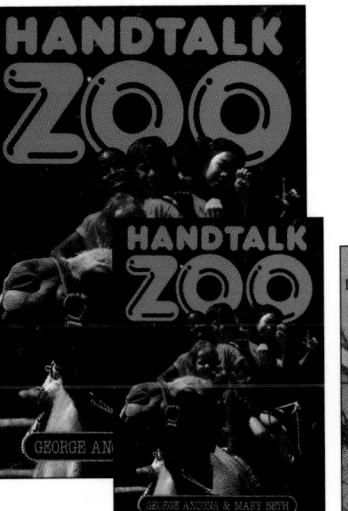
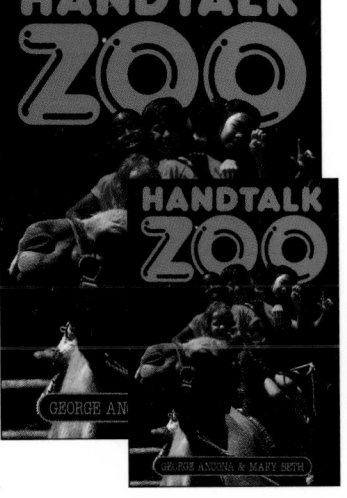

TRADE BOOK LITERATURE

EARLY READERS

THEME OBJECTIVES

READING/WRITING LISTENING/SPEAKING

- shares ideas about dramatic performance
- participates in creating and presenting a dramatic performance
- works together with others
- reads, writes, and draws pictures about dramatization
- selects stories and books for personal interests
- appreciates the literary expression of our contemporary multicultural society and multicultural heritage
- recognizes cultural attitudes and customs in literary selections
- appreciates the artistic interpretation of literature through illustration, oral presentation, and other forms of expression
- retells stories
- participates in a variety of activities in response to literature

PHONICS AND DECODING

- discriminates the sound of letters: /z/*Zz*, /kw/*Qu, qu*
- identifies upper and lowercase letters: *Zz, Qq*
- recognizes sound/letter relationships: /z/*Zz*, /kw/*Qu, qu*
- writes upper and lowercase letters: *Zz, Qq*

CONCEPTS OF PRINT

- understands book concepts: cover, title, author, illustrator
- demonstrates awareness of directionality, letters, words, sentences, punctuation

OTHER RESOURCES

- Big Book of Songs: pp. 34–37
- Big Book of Poems: pp. 32–33
- Big Book of Alphabet Rhymes and Chimes: pp. 35, 24
- Read Aloud Anthology: pp. 80-81, 82-89

- Songs and Stories Audiocassettes
  Story Songs: Tape 3, Side 2
  Storytellings: Tape 3, Side 2
- Sing a Sound Audiocassettes:
  Tape 3, Side 6;
  Tape 2, Side 4

Tell a Story / Sing a Song

AUTHORS

Elaine Mei Aoki

•

Virginia A. Arnold

•

James Flood

•

James V. Hoffman

•

Diane Lapp

•

Miriam Martinez

•

Annemarie Sullivan
Palincsar

•

Michael Priestley

•

Carl B. Smith

•

William H. Teale

•

Josefina Villamil
Tinajero

•

Arnold W. Webb

•

Karen D. Wood

Macmillan McGraw-Hill

New York   Farmington

Authors, Consultants

Multicultural and Educational Consultants

Yvonne Beamer, Joyce Buckner, Alma Flor Ada, Helen Gillotte,
Cheryl Hudson, Narcita Medina, Lorraine Monroe, James R. Murphy,
Sylvia Peña, Joseph B. Rubin, Ramon Santiago, Cliff Trafzer,
Hai Tran, Esther Lee Yao

Literature Consultants

Ashley Bryan, Joan I. Glazer, Paul Janeczko, Margaret H. Lippert

International Consultants

Edward B. Adams, Barbara Johnson, Raymond L. Marshall

Music and Audio Consultants

John Farrell, Marilyn C. Davidson, Vincent Lawrence,
Sarah Pirtle, Susan R. Snyder,
Rick and Deborah Witkowski

Macmillan/McGraw-Hill

A Division of The McGraw-Hill Companies

Copyright © 1997 Macmillan/McGraw-Hill, a Division of the Educational and
Professional Publishing Group of The McGraw-Hill Companies, Inc.

Macmillan/McGraw-Hill
1221 Avenue of the Americas
New York, New York 10020

Printed in the United States of America

ISBN 0-02-181370-1 / K, U.11

2 3 4 5 6 7 8 9 BCM 02 01 00 99 98 97

Teacher's Planning Guide

Act It Out!

*To the 1984–1985 kindergarten students
and kindergarten teachers
at Braun Station Elementary School
in San Antonio, Texas.
You were the pioneers—or the guinea pigs—
who first helped us put into practice
our ideas about emergent literacy,
and for that we thank you.*

—*Bill Teale*

Contents

PRESENTING ACT IT OUT!

Act It Out!

A theme about acting and actors!
Theme Word: ACTOR
Theme Poem: "On Our Way"
 by Eve Merriam
Theme Song: "Eency, Weency Spider"
 a traditional song

Contents

_I_NTRODUCING TELL A STORY/SING A SONG

A New View of Kindergarten!

Welcome children to a print-rich, activity-based environment that nurtures emergent literacy!

19 BIG BOOKS!

48 TRADE BOOKS!

16 THEMES!

PROGRAM RESOURCES

Big Book of Songs
Theme Songs!

Big Book of Poems
Theme Poems!

The more we get together,
Together, together,
The more we get together,
The happier we'll be.

For your friends are my friends,
And my friends are your friends.
The more we get together,
The happier we'll be.

Traditional

THE MORE WE GET TOGETHER

Cc

Cat's in the Cupboard

Great A, Little a,
Bouncing B!
The cat's in the cupboard
And can't see me.

Dd

Diddle Diddle Dumpling

Diddle diddle dumpling,
  my son John
Went to bed with his
  trousers on,
One shoe off,
  and one shoe on;
Diddle diddle dumpling,
  my son John.

Big Book of Alphabet Rhymes and Chimes
Verses for teaching the alphabet and concepts of print!
Plus the "Alphabet Song"!

Rhyme and Chime Strips
Each Rhyme and Chime
on illustrated strips to use in
pocket charts for
Hands On! Language
experiences!

| Cat's in the Cupboard |
| Great A, Little a, |
| Bouncing B! |
| The cat's in the cupboard |
| And can't see me. |

A a A a

B b B b

C C C c

Teacher's Read Aloud Anthology
32 Read Aloud selections
from cultures around
the world!

Plus —

STAFF DEVELOPMENT

A to EZ Handbook:
Staff Development Guide

Performance Assessment Handbook

Early Literacy Assessment

7

16 LITERATURE THEME PACKS

including 3 Trade Books (1 with a companion Big Book) and a Teacher's Planning Guide!

"Slither," said the snake in the cool morning air.

"Twitter," said the sparrows.
"Trot," said the mare.

Big Book of "Paddle," Said the Swan

"Paddle," Said the Swan

Written and illust[...] Gloria Kan[...]

IN THE [...]
An Excursion in Poet[...]
BY ESTHER HA[...]
Pictures by EZRA JA[...]

Big Talk

By Miriam Schlein
Pictures by Joan Auclair

Also Available—

LISTENING LIBRARY AUDIOCASSETTES
for Big Books!

SONGS AND STORIES AUDIOCASSETTES
with Theme Songs, sound effects, and storytellings!

SING A SOUND AUDIOCASSETTES
with songs to encourage language play and to develop phonemic awareness!

TEACHER'S PLANNING GUIDE

SPEAK OUT!
MACMILLAN/MCGRAW-HILL

Teacher's Planning Guide
for Speak Out!
Your resource for organizing activities—
• Sharing Time
• Reading and Writing
• Exploring Print
• Into the Learning Centers

NCILLARIES

ABC Cards
Textured letter forms
for tactile learning!

Alphabet Posters
26 full-color posters!

Sing & Read Books and Audiocassettes
16 little books, one for each theme song,
with audiocassettes of children singing
and then reading the selection!

Literature Activity Book with

- Activities for introducing
  each theme
- Tell-a-Tale Take-Home Books
- Responding to Literature pages
- Exploring Print activities
- Just for Fun pages, too!

Also Available —

HomeWords:
Newsletters and more
to send home each month!

Sights & Sounds:
Interactive software for children to use in their
exploration of the sounds of language
and the letters that represent them!

Tell a Story/Sing a Song

PROGRAM THEMES	TRADE BOOKS	READ ALOUDS
1 GETTING TOGETHER	**BIG BOOK:** *Getting Together* by George Ancona *What Will Mommy Do When I'm at School?* by Dolores Johnson *I'm Busy, Too* by Norma Simon, illustrated by Dora Leder	**The Great Big Enormous Turnip** a Russian tale by Alexei Tolstoi **The Rabbit and the Elephant** a folk tale from Ghana retold by Ruthilde Kronberg and Patricia C. McKissack
2 SHARING WITH FRIENDS	**BIG BOOK:** *Frog in the Middle* by Susanna Gretz *Will I Have a Friend?* by Miriam Cohen, illustrated by Lillian Hoban *Friends* by Helme Heine	**The Lion and the Mouse** a fable by Aesop **The Three Friends** a folk tale from India retold by Isabel Wyatt
3 SPEAK OUT!	**BIG BOOK:** *"Paddle," Said the Swan* by Gloria Kamen *In the Park* by Esther Hautzig, illustrated by Ezra Jack Keats *Big Talk* by Miriam Schlein, illustrated by Joan Auclair	**The Long One** a Masai tale from East Africa by Verna Aardema **The Boy Who Cried Wolf** a fable by Aesop retold by Anne Terry White
4 LISTEN FOR SOUNDS!	**BIG BOOK:** *Rain Talk* by Mary Serfozo, illustrated by Keiko Narahashi *Country Crossing* by Jim Aylesworth, illustrated by Ted Rand *Apt. 3* by Ezra Jack Keats	**The Bremen Town Musicians** a German folk tale retold by Anne Rockwell **The Race Between Toad and Donkey** a Jamaican folk tale edited by Roger D. Abrahams

Theme Words	Theme Songs	Theme Poems	Exploring Print Lessons
LPER	**The More We Get Together** a traditional song	**Together** by Paul Engle	Games and activities related to children's names
IEND	**Be a Friend** a traditional song	**Making Friends** by Eloise Greenfield	Games and activities related to friends and their names, and days of the week
EAKER	**The Buenas Song** a Hispanic song by Aaron Schroeder and David Grover	**Good Morning** by Muriel Sipe	Rhyme Time: Games, songs, and activities for rhyming
STENER	**The Little Red Caboose** Bernice Johnson Reagon's version of the traditional song	**Ears Hear** by Lucia and James L. Hymes, Jr.	*Big Book of Alphabet Rhymes and Chimes:* **Cc** Cat's in the Cupboard **Pp** Pease Porridge Hot

PROGRAM THEMES	TRADE BOOKS	READ ALOUDS
5 SING AND DANCE AWAY!	**BIG BOOK: *Oh, A-Hunting We Will Go*** by John Langstaff, illustrated by Nancy Winslow Parker ***Max*** by Rachel Isadora ***The Little Band*** by James Sage, illustrated by Keiko Narahashi	**The Twelve Dancing Princesses** a German fairy tale by the Brothers Grimm **The Clever Turtle** a Hispanic folk tale retold by Margaret H. Lippert
6 PAINT IT UP!	**BIG BOOK: *Who Said Red?*** by Mary Serfozo, illustrated by Keiko Narahashi ***The little Bear Book*** by Anthony Browne ***circles, triangles and squares*** by Tana Hoban	**The Black Cat** an American folk tale retold by Margaret H. Lippert **Ma Lien and the Magic Brush** a tale from China by Hisako Kimishima retold by Alvin Tresselt
7 EAT IT UP!	**BIG BOOK: *Bread, Bread, Bread*** by Ann Morris, photographs by Ken Heyman ***Gregory, the Terrible Eater*** by Mitchell Sharmat, illustrated by Jose Aruego and Ariane Dewey ***What's on My Plate?*** by Ruth Belov Gross, illustrated by Isadore Seltzer	**The Woman Who Flummoxed the Fairies** a Scottish folk tale retold by Sorche Nic Leodhas **Señor Billy Goat** a Hispanic folk tale retold by Pura Belpré
8 BUILD IT UP!	**BIG BOOK: *Changes, Changes*** by Pat Hutchins ***I Read Signs*** by Tana Hoban ***Round Trip*** by Ann Jonas	**The Three Little Pigs** an English fairy tale retold by Flora Annie Steel **Why the Moon Is in the Sky** an Ashanti folk tale from West Africa retold by Margaret H. Lippert

Theme Words	Theme Songs	Theme Poems	Exploring Print Lessons
...NGER ...NCER	**You'll Sing a Song and I'll Sing a Song** by Ella Jenkins	**Singing-Time** by Rose Fyleman	*Big Book of Alphabet Rhymes and Chimes:* **Hh** Hippity Hop to Bed **Mm** Miss Mary Mack
...RTIST	**I Know the Colors in the Rainbow** by Ella Jenkins	**Paints** by Ilo Orleans	*Big Book of Alphabet Rhymes and Chimes:* **Ss** Sing a Song of Sixpence **Bb** Bounce High, Bounce Low
...OK	**Short'ning Bread** a traditional Southern song	**Through the Teeth** a folk rhyme	*Big Book of Alphabet Rhymes and Chimes:* **Gg** Gobble, Gobble **Aa** Eat an Apple
...ILDER	**Johnny Builds with One Hammer** a traditional song	**Buildings** by Myra Cohn Livingston	*Big Book of Alphabet Rhymes and Chimes:* **Rr** R Is for Ribbon **Ee** Engine, Engine, Number Nine

Program Themes	Trade Books	Read Alouds
9 MEET PAT HUTCHINS	**BIG BOOK:** *Titch* by Pat Hutchins *Rosie's Walk* by Pat Hutchins *Good-Night, Owl!* by Pat Hutchins	**It Could Always Be Worse** a Yiddish folk tale retold by Margot Zemach **Rainbow Crow** a Lenape tale retold by Nancy Van Laan
10 SHARE A STORY!	**BIG BOOK:** *I Had a Cat* by Mona Rabun Reeves, illustrated by Julie Downing *Little Red Hen* by Janina Domanska *Nessa's Fish* by Nancy Luenn, illustrated by Neil Waldman	**The Storytelling Stone** a Seneca tale retold by Joseph Bruchac **The Three Bears** an English folk tale retold by Margaret H. Lippert
11 ACT IT OUT!	**BIG BOOK:** *Handtalk Zoo* by George Ancona and Mary Beth *Stone Soup* by Marcia Brown *I'm Going on a Dragon Hunt* by Maurice Jones, illustrated by Charlotte Firmin	**The Three Billy Goats Gruff** a Norwegian folk tale retold by Margaret H. Lippert **The Terrible Tragadabas** a tale from Spanish New Mexico by Joe Hayes
12 WONDER ABOUT IT!	**BIG BOOK:** *White Is the Moon* by Valerie Greeley *Half a Moon and One Whole Star* by Crescent Dragonwagon, illustrated by Jerry Pinkney *The Park Bench* by Fumiko Takeshita, illustrated by Mamoru Suzuki	**The Spider Weaver** a folk tale from Japan retold by Florence Sakada **The One You Don't See Coming** a folk tale from Liberia retold by Harold Courlander and George Herzog

THEME WORDS	THEME SONGS	THEME POEMS	EXPLORING PRINT LESSONS
WRITER	**Read a Book** by Marcy Marxer	**Surprise** by Beverly McLoughland	*Big Book of Alphabet Rhymes and Chimes:* **Tt** Toaster Time **Kk** A Kettle's for the Kitchen
STORYTELLER	**How About You?** by John Farrell	**Worlds I Know** by Myra Cohn Livingston	*Big Book of Alphabet Rhymes and Chimes:* **Ff** Five Little Fishies **Yy** The Yak
ACTOR	**Eency, Weency Spider** a traditional song	**On Our Way** by Eve Merriam	*Big Book of Alphabet Rhymes and Chimes:* **Qq** Quack, Quack, Quack **Zz** Zippety! Zippety! Zim, zim, zim!
THINKER	**Twinkle, Twinkle, Little Star** a traditional song	**I Arise** an Eskimo song	*Big Book of Alphabet Rhymes and Chimes:* **Ii** If All the World Was Apple Pie **Xx** What Words Begin with X?

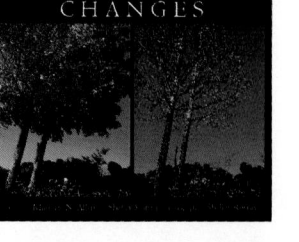

Program Themes	Trade Books	Read Alouds
13 FIND IT OUT!	**BIG BOOK: *What Do You See?*** by Janina Domanska ***Farm Animals*** photographs by Philip Dowell and Michael Dunning ***Changes*** by Marjorie N. Allen and Shelley Rotner, photographs by Shelley Rotner	**Why Bears Have Short Tails** a Navajo legend from Arizona retold by Sandra Begay **The Plumage of the Owl/ El Plumaje del Mucaro** a Puerto Rican folk tale retold by Ricardo E. Alegría
14 MEET EZRA JACK KEATS	**BIG BOOK: *Hi, Cat!*** by Ezra Jack Keats ***Kitten for a Day*** by Ezra Jack Keats ***Pet Show!*** by Ezra Jack Keats	**Belling the Cat** a fable by Aesop retold by Joseph Jacobs **The Cat's Purr** a West Indian tale by Ashley Bryan
15 THINKING ABOUT ME	**BIG BOOK: *All I Am*** by Eileen Roe, illustrated by Helen Cogancherry ***The Train to Lulu's*** by Elizabeth Fitzgerald Howard, illustrated by Robert Casilla ***Con Mi Hermano/With My Brother*** by Eileen Roe, illustrated by Robert Casilla	**The Knee-High Man** an American black folk tale retold by Julius Lester **Anansi's Rescue from the River** a folk tale from West Africa retold by Harold Courlander
16 SETTING OUT!	**BIG BOOK: *As the Crow Flies: A First Book of Maps*** by Gail Hartman, illustrated by Harvey Stevenson ***Look Out, Patrick!*** by Paul Geraghty ***Builder of the Moon*** by Tim Wynne-Jones, illustrated by Ian Wallace	**Timimoto** a folk tale from Japan retold by Margaret H. Lippert **Jack and the Beanstalk** an English fairy tale retold by Virginia Haviland

16

Theme Words	Theme Songs	Theme Poems	Exploring Print Lessons
SEARCHER	**Who Fed the Chickens?** by Ella Jenkins	**Who?** by Lilian Moore	*Big Book of Alphabet Rhymes and Chimes:* **Dd** Diddle Diddle Dumpling **Ww** Wee Willie Winkie
LUSTRATOR	**Library Song** by Michael Mark and Tom Chapin	**Picture People** by Myra Cohn Livingston	*Big Book of Alphabet Rhymes and Chimes:* **Ll** Lily's a Lady **Jj** Jack Be Nimble
IILD	**I Am a Person** by Sarah Pirtle	**By Myself** by Eloise Greenfield	*Big Book of Alphabet Rhymes and Chimes:* **Nn** Nicholas Ned **Uu** Umbrellas
PLORER	**The Bear Went Over the Mountain** a traditional song	**Come Out** by Karla Kuskin	*Big Book of Alphabet Rhymes and Chimes:* **Oo** Polly, Put the Kettle On **Vv** Very Nice

EMERGENT WRITING

MIRIAM MARTINEZ AND WILLIAM TEALE

The emergent literacy perspective is a powerful one because it lays the foundation for promoting children's literacy development through rich, exciting, and purposeful writing opportunities in the classroom.

Children's Writing Strategies

In their early explorations of the writing system, young children typically do not write in conventional ways. Careful observations of children's emergent writing have revealed a general, but rather complicated, developmental pathway. As children move along this pathway, they typically use some or all of the following strategies:

1. **Drawing**

2. **Scribbling**

3. **Randomly Chosen Letters:** The child uses letters, but there is not a relationship between the letters chosen and the sounds in the words that are written.

4. **Words Copied from Environmental Print**

5. **Developmental Spelling:** There is a relationship between the letters used and the sounds in the words that are written, but only one or two of the sounds heard in words are represented. This behavior later develops to the point at which children are able to use a letter to represent every (or almost every) sound in the words that are written.

6. **Transitional Spelling:** Features of conventional spelling, like silent letters or doubling of consonants, begin to appear.

7. **Conventional Spelling**

1. Drawing

2. Scribble

18

Random Letters

Random Letters

REWRM
ERWDN
AEWR
AEWR

Rich, Purposeful Writing Experiences

Young writers, like all writers, are most successful when they have interesting experiences to feed their writing. These include ''hands on'' activities, creative dramatics and art activities, content area experiences, explorations beyond the classroom, and opportunities to write about personal experiences beyond school.

Central to these efforts to ignite children's writing are rich literature experiences. One form that writing in response to literature takes is the journal. The journal is a place where children can record their thoughts, feelings, and reactions to a story they have just listened to or read.

Literature also nurtures children's own original story writing. Sometimes a storyline or story theme will serve as an invitation for the child to write about a similar experience. At other times, after reading a story with a distinctive predictable pattern, children may choose to use the same story pattern to organize their own writing.

YUVTOUSUCOt
CKOKOU
OUOEUCI
OCUTCtCtC

2-6-85

3.

3.

Emergent Writing

Children's Growth as Writers

Three dimensions signal growth in children's writing. First is evidence that the child is using increasingly more sophisticated writing strategies (drawing, scribbling, developmental spellings, and so on.). However, as we observe children's movement along this developmental pathway, it's important to remember that not every child uses all strategies, nor will a child necessarily, as he or she begins to use a more sophisticated strategy, leave less sophisticated ones behind. If anything, many children tend to expand their repertoire of strategies, using different ones for different tasks.

The second dimension of children's growth as writers is what they say. It is particularly important to look for evidence that children are learning to organize their writing better, to develop their ideas more fully, and to use features that are associated with written language rather than oral language (Once upon a time...).

However, a word of warning is in order. As children begin to use more sophisticated writing strategies (in particular, as they concentrate on developmental spellings), the content and organization of their stories and journal entries may appear to become less sophisticated for a period of time. Rather than being taken as a cause for alarm, this state of affairs should be viewed as more of a natural trade-off. When children do get more control over sound-symbol relationships, they will again be able to attend more closely to what it is they want to say and to whom they want to say it.

4. Copying Environmental Print

5. Early Developmental Spelling

...ly Developmental Spelling

w t c o p d B

Finally, it is important to remember that children's reading and writing development are integrally related, and this reading/writing connection must be taken into account in evaluating their growth as writers.

In particular, as a child reads what he or she has written, it is important to ask questions such as these:

- Does the child attend to the picture or the print in reading what she or he has written?

- Are the child's attempts to track the print successful?

- Does the child conventionally read what he or she has written?

- Does the child's intonation sound more like oral or written language?

As children move along the developmental pathway, their rereadings of their own writing become more print-based and sound increasingly like written language rather than oral language.

Full Developmental Spelling

I lik ron Bos   Be kus tha
r color fool

Andrew

5.

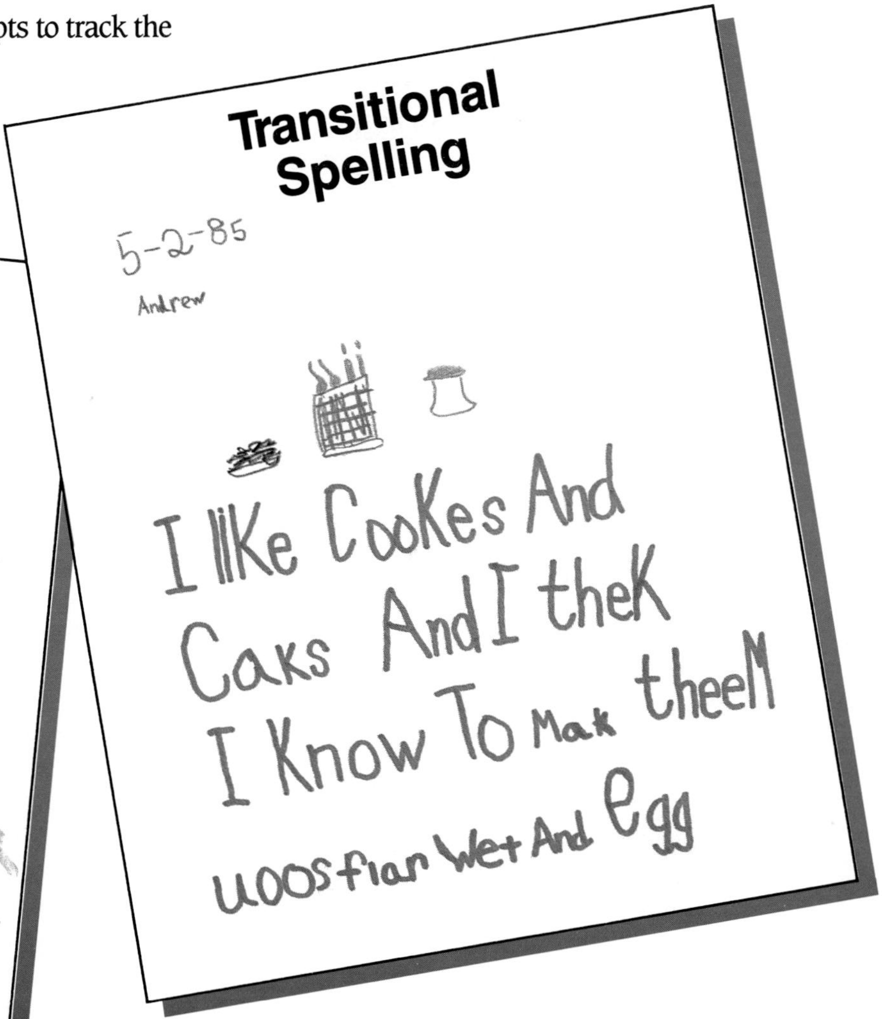

Transitional Spelling

5-2-85

Andrew

I llKe CooKes And Caks And I theK I Know To MaK theeM uoos fian Wet And egg

6.

STUDENTS ACQUIRING ENGLISH

EMERGENT LITERACY IN THE SECOND LANGUAGE

BY JOSEFINA VILLAMIL TINAJERO

The early childhood years are a remarkably active period for acquiring language and for learning about its written form. Classroom environments have a significant effect on children's language and literacy development. This is especially true for emergent readers and writers who are also acquiring English as a second language. The physical and social environment of the classroom, teacher beliefs and attitudes about language acquisition and emergent literacy, the types of activities planned, and the strategies and techniques used by teachers all affect the opportunities children have to emerge as readers and writers and to acquire a new language.

Supporting Kindergartners' Language Acquisition

It is our position that children *acquire* rather than *learn* a language in a natural progression of stages. As language is acquired, literacy in the new language develops. That is, current research suggests that the second language is acquired in the same manner as the first and that it is acquired most effectively in a highly interactive, total communication environment.

Children acquire language when they understand what people say to them or what is read. They acquire language by understanding messages and by responding to those messages in meaningful ways. Language must make sense to young children, and somehow it must be important for them to acquire it. Some of the best ways to encourage language development are to provide children with many opportunities to interact with other children, to encourage child's play, and to engage them in natural language activities. Songs, poems, stories, games, role-play, story theater, and dramatizations are especially effective because they allow students to hear natural English while providing a meaningful, motivating, and enjoyable context for learning.

Young SAEs need a favorable environment for language acquisition, an environment that is as natural and as language-rich as that within which they learned their first language. Kindergartners acquiring English, in particular, need many opportunities to hear and use English, to experiment with it, to take risks and try out their knowledge of the language. They need to be encouraged to express their ideas and feelings as they move along the pathway toward nativelike fluency.

When students offer responses, for example, their pronunciation may be poor and their grammatical construction may include elements from their first language. When this happens, teachers need to accept their responses, model the "correct" form in a tactful and unexaggerated way, and praise them for their contributions. Praising builds confidence and helps children feel valued as members of the class. They will also be much more motivated to "experiment" with the language and to take risks—that is, express their thoughts and ideas even if they are not yet fully fluent in the language.

Teachers can integrate the following techniques with activities planned for other children in the class.

Heterogeneous Grouping. One way to provide SAEs with opportunities to practice their English is to increase the frequency and variety of interactions among students. Pairing them with proficient English speakers for activities such as partner "reading" of Big Books and partner story retellings is one way

22

of increasing interaction. Grouping them with students of varying proficiencies for activities such as illustrating a new ending to a story or illustrating a character map is another. At other times, however, SAEs may be grouped together for activities such as listening to a story in their native language, working on a special project, or doing partner reading with other SAEs.

Cooperative Learning. Cooperative learning also increases the frequency and variety of second language practice through different types of interactions. It provides students with many opportunities to utilize newly acquired language and to "read and write" (scribbling and drawing are considered writing at this age) in English in a "safe" social situation where they don't feel threatened by error correction. Cooperative learning also provides students with opportunities to act as resources for each other and thus assume a more active role in learning.

When working with kindergartners acquiring English, it is also important to keep in mind that, as individuals, they are at different levels of English proficiency. Thus, when planning activities for them, teachers must be aware of the level of receptive and productive language they bring to the learning task. There may be some children who may not be ready to begin producing oral English. Some may be experiencing what is often referred to as the *"silent period" of language learning*. That is, second language learners go through a period of time during which they prefer to listen rather than to produce language. As with most second language learners, children's receptive

language skills develop earlier than their productive ones (Rice, 1989).

It is important, however, to keep in mind that language learning is taking place during this time (Evans, 1990). Children don't always need to respond in order to learn new language skills. They can benefit greatly from the opportunity to absorb the conversations of others (Rice, 1989).

$\mathcal{U}$sing Literature to Nurture Children's Language Development

The best language lessons are good books and interesting discussions in which children are absorbed in the meaning of what is said to them or what is read.

For SAEs, literature cultivates language, provides language models, and facilitates language acquisition. As children listen to rhymes, poems, and patterned/predictable stories in English, they learn new language patterns and idiomatic usages, which are assimilated as children apply them to express their own thoughts and ideas during meaningful, well-planned lessons. Children with limited vocabulary can latch on to the "new" language they have heard, suddenly discovering that their former limited vocabulary takes on new dimensions.

$\mathcal{S}$torytelling with SAEs

Because storytelling encourages physical, visual, and aural/oral participation of students, it is an excellent context for teaching language and concepts to SAEs.

Listening and speaking skills, for example, are enriched through the use of puppetry, tapes, dramatic presentations, and the teacher's systematic reading to children. Children will also enjoy retelling stories they have been told or sharing stories from their own cultures, stories they may have learned at home or in their neighborhoods. Children's own creativity and ingenuity can also be encouraged and supported by allowing children to create, tell, and retell their own stories.

Following are some suggestions to take full advantage of storytelling activities to enhance language development for SAEs.

Oral Previewing. This technique adjusts the teacher's language input to children's language proficiency and comprehension level during storytelling. For SAEs, oral previewing takes the form of paraphrasing or telling the story "in your own words," both to make the story as comprehensible as possible and to facilitate language development. When using this technique, follow these guidelines.

First, screen the story, taking into account the language and experiential knowledge of students. Select areas of difficulty such as idiomatic language and difficult vocabulary. Become familiar with the story so that the retelling is as natural as possible, and so that you can be cognizant of facial expressions that might indicate whether or not SAEs are understanding the story.

Then hold up a copy of the book as you lead the children orally through the story, establishing plot and setting. Use gestures, body language, and facial expressions to help convey ideas and

Students Acquiring English

concepts. Use simple, well-formed sentences; limit sentence length and complexity while maintaining appropriate grammar and intonation.

Clarify the meaning of words, phrases, and idiomatic expressions using context clues, such as pointing to the illustrations or drawing simple pictures. Make frequent repetitions of key words and ideas. At times, incorporate role play to help children understand concepts and learn language through physical activity.

As you continue to go through the story, ask questions that require yes/no responses, a nod of the head, pointing to an illustration, or one- or two-word responses to check understanding. Also ask questions to relate the story situation to children's experiences. Remember that SAEs understand more than they can verbalize. As children respond using one or two words, repeat their utterances, use their words in an expanded comment. That is, use the *semantic expansion* technique, in which you as the teacher start with something the child said and elaborate to clarify or add to the response. Also, use structural expansion in which you as the teacher repeat an incorrect utterance correctly to model for the children. Finally, have children make predictions along the way to encourage language use and development of critical thinking skills. Remember to praise children for their contributions.

These types of teacher-child interactions with storybooks create a context for comprehending meaning, for making meaning. They help SAEs get past some of the difficult language so they can concentrate on the story line. Children also internalize new language related to the story they are about to hear.

The following storytelling variations help SAEs acquire language and make stories more comprehensible. Use them as often as possible. They are good for all children.

Puppetry. Puppets make stories come alive for children, and the actions associated with using them to tell or retell stories make language more comprehensible. Most important, however, SAEs are less reluctant to talk "when they take on other identities to perform. It is somehow less threatening to make a mistake as someone else; it becomes their mistake, not that of the student" (Evans, 1990).

Participation Stories. Certain stories invite children to participate actively as they respond to certain words that act as cues for actions like clapping or stamping their feet or shaking their heads. Before reading the story, the teacher introduces the cues. The children then act out the story as the teacher reads. These types of stories develop listening skills and facilitate language acquisition (Evans, 1990).

Pantomime. Through pantomime children use their whole bodies for making meaning as they participate in storytelling activities. Text becomes more comprehensible as characters come alive.

Story Retelling. Working with a partner, children retell stories to one another. Story retelling provides a great opportunity for children to use the language they have heard in the stories to express their own thoughts and ideas.

Tape Recordings. Tape recordings of stories are an excellent way to expose students to good literature that may be beyond their reading abilities but within their listening abilities. Children will also enjoy making their own recordings of

stories. These recordings also serve as good diagnostic tools.

Choral Reading. Choral readings of stories, with a mix of SAEs and proficient English speakers, give shy learners a safe way to practice formal speaking. Remember, the desire of SAEs to produce language varies greatly—allow them to join in when they're ready.

Shared Reading and SAEs

Another excellent way to provide SAEs with rich literature experiences is to conduct shared reading with books that contain repetitive language and/or predictable outcomes. The repetitive characteristics of the texts facilitate the natural acquisition of vocabulary, pronunciation, and language structures. Big Books are particularly effective for group study and for exposing children to print.

The repeated readings help children to read more efficiently, gain confidence, practice using their reading skills, and increase their sight vocabulary. And since the illustrations in the books are closely tied to the text, children get visual support for the rapid development of a wide range of vocabulary. The reading and rereading of stories also allow SAEs to hear and practice, in an informal setting, the rhythm and structure of English.

As children recite and participate in shared reading activities using rhymes, poems, songs, and pattern stories, they learn new language patterns. They internalize these patterns and then use them to express their own thoughts and ideas. Furthermore, through shared reading, children are exposed to the written and oral forms of language and are offered

numerous opportunities to develop listening, speaking, reading, and writing skills at the "teachable moment."

Shared reading activities also establish the kind of low-anxiety environment essential to language acquisition and provide SAEs at varying/lower levels of English proficiency with the opportunity to participate with the rest of the class. It is also a pleasurable experience that helps SAEs develop a positive attitude toward acquiring English and learning to read in a second language.

In selecting materials to use with SAEs, select those with texts containing features such as rhyme, rhythmic language, predictable or repetitive plots and language patterns, or illustrations that closely parallel the text. Screen materials carefully for overload of idiomatic language and situations that are culturally unfamiliar. Finally, select materials at the appropriate instructional level that foster students' appreciation of reading and develop positive attitudes toward learning to read in English.

Language Experience Activities

The language experience approach is particularly suitable for use with SAEs because the children's language proficiency, no matter how limited, is valued and used as a starting point for further development. And because SAEs' proficiency in English often varies significantly, language experience activities help build a common knowledge and language base for them. The approach also integrates children's ideas, interests, experiences, and natural language, using them to motivate students to read.

Through language experience, SAEs are also able to acquire the basic skills of reading and writing with familiar material—their own. Thus, the text is rich in comprehensible content that further develops children's language proficiency.

Establishing Partnerships with Parents

A primary way in which we can provide more supportive learning environments for all children is to involve their parents, working with them as colleagues, inviting them to participate as valuable resources of information and perspectives, and sharing with them ways in which parents enhance education at home.

Parents can assist teachers in creating more supportive and nurturing learning environments that offer the security needed for SAEs to participate in a culturally different setting. Parents can be invited to the classroom to tell stories from the oral tradition, to read stories, read or recite poetry, share "how to" information, and present topics that have inspired and informed their lives.

Parents often think that they cannot help their children at home if they do not speak English. Teachers need to make an effort to assure them that working with their children in their native language is of benefit because concepts learned in the native language will transfer to English.

The Challenge

Kindergarten is a critical point for students acquiring English. Beyond their needs for skills in academic growth, SAEs also have motivational and emotional needs that must be met. These needs are often magnified in importance where there are cultural and linguistic differences between the school and the home. They include children's need to feel a sense of identity, to belong, to be understood by and communicate with significant others, and to succeed in environments in which they are accepted and respected. Kindergarten teachers can make a difference in the lives of these children. By simply applying some of the basic principles discussed here, teachers can provide a nurturing and intellectually stimulating environment where students acquiring English can succeed and thrive.

References

Auerbach, E. (1989). Toward a social-contextual approach to family literacy. Harvard Educational Review, 59, No. 2, pp. 165–181.

Early, M. (1991). Using wordless picture books to promote second language learning. ELT Journal. Volume 45/3. July. pp. 245–250.

Evans, L. S. (1990). Storytelling and oral language development in ESL classrooms. TESOL Newsletter. October. pp. 3, 16, 18, 30.

Flood, J.; Lapp, D.; Tinajero, J.; and Nagel, G. Parents and teachers: Partners in developing literacy for multicultural students. (unpublished manuscript).

Nurss, J. R. and Hough, R. A. (1985). Story reading: Language arts for limited English speakers. TESOL Newsletter. Vol. 8, No. 1. pp. 1–2.

Rice, M. (1989). Children's language acquisition. American Psychologist. Volume 4. February. pp. 149–156.

INTRODUCING ACT IT OUT!

Invite children to explore the fun and excitement of acting through trade books, read aloud selections, poetry, and songs!

TRADE BOOKS

Handtalk Zoo
by George Ancona and Mary Beth
A visit to the zoo is described in sign language and fingerspelling. Available as a Big Book and little book.

I'm Going on a Dragon Hunt
by Maurice Jones,
illustrated by Charlotte Firmin
A boy on a dragon hunt faces some formidable obstacles, including a wide river, a deep ravine, and a tall tree, in this variation of the traditional chant.

Stone Soup
by Marcia Brown
In this classic tale, three soldiers induce some miserly villagers to share their food by convincing them that they can make soup from stones.

READ ALOUDS

TEACHER'S READ ALOUD ANTHOLOGY
The Three Billy Goats Gruff
a *Norwegian folk tale* retold by *Margaret H. Lippert*
A troll prevents three goats from crossing a bridge to eat tasty grass, until they figure out how to outwit him.

The Terrible Tragadabas
a tale from *Spanish New Mexico*
retold by *Joe Hayes*
The terrible tragadabas lays siege to the store and frightens everyone with noisy threats until a lowly bee chases him away.

BIG BOOK OF POEMS
On Our Way
by Eve Merriam

BIG BOOK OF SONGS
Eency, Weency Spider
a traditional song

EXPLORING PRINT

**BIG BOOK OF ALPHABET RHYMES AND CHIMES
PLUS RHYME AND CHIME STRIPS**

• **Zz** Zippety! Zippety! Zim, zim, zim!

• **Qq** Quack, Quack, Quack

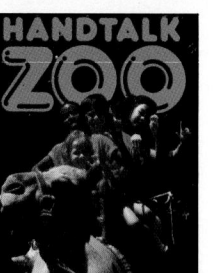

THEME 11: ACT IT OUT!
Overview for Week 1

LITERATURE	SHARING TIME	READING AND WRITING
1 THEME POEM "On Our Way"	**Today's News** and acting out nursery rhymes p. 35	Reading the Theme Poem and Responding through **Poem Talk,** Making a Class Big Book, and Poem Theatre pp. 36-37
2 HANDTALK ZOO	**Today's News** and singing "Time to Wake Up!" p. 41	Reading *Handtalk Zoo* and Responding through **Book Talk,** Journal Writing, and Signing pp. 42-43
3 HANDTALK ZOO	**Today's News** and singing and acting out "Let's Pretend" p. 47	Rereading *Handtalk Zoo* and Responding through **Book Talk,** Sign Language Cards, and Fingerspellings pp. 48-49
4 READ ALOUD "The Three Billy Goats Gruff"	**Today's News** and singing "Big, Bigger, Biggest" p. 53	Reading "The Three Billy Goats Gruff" and Responding through **Book Talk,** Journal Writing, and Dramatization pp. 54-55
5 I'M GOING ON A DRAGON HUNT	**Today's News** and singing "Oh, A-Hunting We Will Go" p. 59	Reading *I'm Going on a Dragon Hunt* and Responding through **Book Talk,** Journal Writing, and a Story Mural pp. 60-61

ch theme helps children see themselves from a different
spective. This theme helps children see themselves as
ors.

EXPLORING PRINT

coding and Phonics
ters *Z, z*
und/Letter Relationships /z/ *Z, z*
NG: "Going to the Zoo"
  44-45

coding and Phonics
ters *Z, z*
und/Letter Relationships /z/ *Z, z*
BOOK OF ALPHABET RHYMES AND CHIMES:
ppety! Zippety! Zim, zim, zim!"
  50-51

ncepts of Print
ectionality, Words
YME AND CHIME STRIPS:
ppety! Zippety! Zim, zim, zim!"
  56-57

coding and Phonics
ters *Z, z*
und/Letter Relationships /z/ *Z, z*
ncepts of Print
ectionality, Words, Letters
YME AND CHIME STRIPS:
ppety! Zippety! Zim, zim, zim!"
  62-63

THEME GOALS AND OUTCOMES

The literature and activities in this theme were
carefully selected and reviewed by the program
authors and by the multicultural, literature, and
educational consultants who worked together to
develop the program goals and outcomes.

MULTICULTURAL PERSPECTIVES

Appreciate and value diverse points of view

Become aware of cultural backgrounds,
experiences, emotions, and ideas of self and
others through literature

Appreciate the literary expression of our
contemporary multicultural society and
multicultural heritage

Appreciate the universality of literary themes in
many cultures and in many different times

Appreciate the significance of traditional
literature within a culture

Recognize cultural attitudes and customs in
literary selections

PERSONAL INTERESTS AND ATTITUDES

Develop an awareness of the classroom as a
community of learners that values cooperation,
fair play, and respect for others and for oneself

Select stories and books for personal interests

Develop personal reading and writing interests

Make connections between one's personal life
and literature

Choose to read and write for a variety of
purposes

Share, review, and recommend books to others

Participate in reading, writing, listening, and
viewing activities

Appreciate the artistic interpretation of literature
through film, illustration, photography, dance,
oral presentations, and other forms of expression

LITERATURE	SHARING TIME	READING AND WRITING
6 *I'M GOING ON A DRAGON HUNT*	**Today's News** and enjoying the poem "Make Believe" p. 65	Rereading *I'm Going on a Dragon Hunt* and Responding through **Book Talk**, Additional Episodes, and Chanting the Traditional Oral Version pp. 66-67
7 **READ ALOUD** "The Terrible Tragadabas"	**Today's News** and sharing the poem "Beware, My Child" p. 71	Reading "The Terrible Tragadabas" and Responding through **Book Talk**, Journal Writing, a Class Big Book, and Dramatization pp. 72-73
8 *STONE SOUP*	**Today's News** and talking about favorite soups p. 77	Reading *Stone Soup* and Responding through **Book Talk**, Journal Writing, Dramatization, and Collecting Ingredie... pp. 78-79
9 *STONE SOUP*	**Today's News** and singing "Sitting in the Soup" p. 83	Rereading *Stone Soup* and Respondin... through **Book Talk**, Thank-You Notes, and Cooking Soup and Writing Recipe... pp. 84-85
10 *HANDTALK ZOO* *I'M GOING ON A DRAGON HUNT* *STONE SOUP*	**Today's News,** and saying the Theme Poem "On Our Way" and singing the Theme Song "Eency, Weency Spider" p. 89	Reviewing the theme trade books and Responding through **Book Talk** and Journal Writing pp. 90-91

INTEGRATING LANGUAGE ARTS AND OTHER CURRICULUM AREAS

Into the Learning Centers!

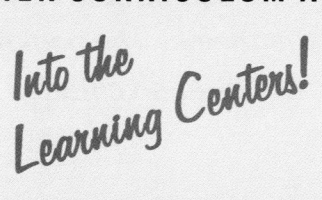

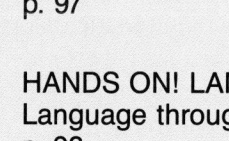
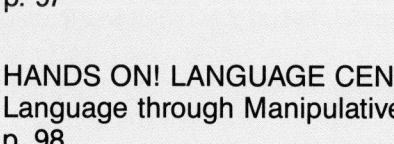

MORE BOOKS TO SHARE

The books on these pages can be shared with children throughout the theme. The books can also be put into the Reading Center so children can read and enjoy them.

MORE BOOKS ABOUT ACTING IT OUT

■ **WHO'S IN RABBIT'S HOUSE? A MASAI TALE**
retold by Verna Aardema, illus. by Leo and Diane Dillon (Dial, 1977). A comic play, complete with masks, is performed before a crowd of Masai villagers. Kindergartners will enjoy enacting the simple plot, wearing masks of their own creation.

■ **WILD WILD SUNFLOWER CHILD ANNA**
by Nancy White Carlstrom, illus. by Jerry Pinkney (Macmillan, 1987). The morning is filled with activity as Anna dances through sunlit fields, hops from rock to rock across a creek, pretends to be the captain of a ship sailing high in a tree, and finally, exhausted, falls asleep in the soft grass. Children will act out Anna's morning with all the joy and expressiveness of young children.

■ **CLAP YOUR HANDS**
by Lorinda Bryan Cauley (G. P. Putnam's Sons, 1992). "Clap your hands,/Stomp your feet./Shake your arms,/then take a seat." So begins this irresistible rhyme filled with humor and exhilarating activity. Children will want to jump right up and join the fun.

■ **THE GREAT KAPOK TREE: A TALE OF THE AMAZON RAIN FOREST**
by Lynne Cherry (HBJ, 1990). In the Amazon rain forest, a man is sent to chop down a great kapok tree. Tired out from his labors, he falls asleep before completing the task. As he sleeps, the animals who live in the tree entreat him to spare their home. Performers can speak each animal's lines as an adult reads the narration.

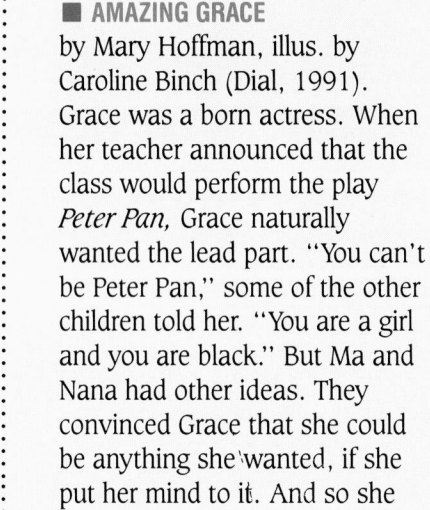

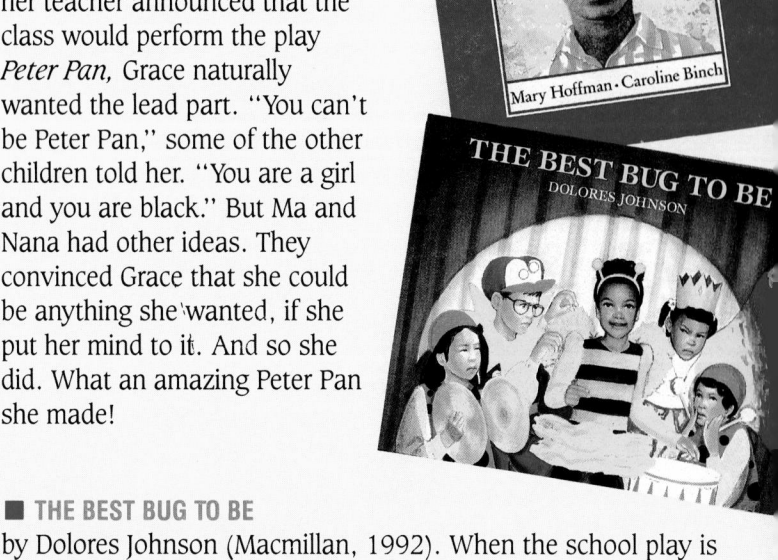

■ **AMAZING GRACE**
by Mary Hoffman, illus. by Caroline Binch (Dial, 1991). Grace was a born actress. When her teacher announced that the class would perform the play *Peter Pan,* Grace naturally wanted the lead part. "You can't be Peter Pan," some of the other children told her. "You are a girl and you are black." But Ma and Nana had other ideas. They convinced Grace that she could be anything she wanted, if she put her mind to it. And so she did. What an amazing Peter Pan she made!

■ **THE BEST BUG TO BE**
by Dolores Johnson (Macmillan, 1992). When the school play is announced, Kelly fully anticipates that she will be given a starring role. Instead she is assigned the part of a bumblebee. Bumblebees don't sing or dance; they just buzz. Disappointed, she shares her feelings with her parents. "Whatever you're asked to do, sweetheart, you should do your absolute best," her father tells her. Kelly works hard on her buzz and, on opening night, the other children have to agree: A bumblebee is the best bug to be.

■ **CHICKA CHICKA BOOM BOOM**
by Bill Martin, Jr., and John Archambault, illus. by Lois Ehlert (Simon & Schuster, 1989). This classroom favorite is easily turned into a play that involves twenty-six participants as the letters of the alphabet climb to the top of the coconut tree and fall back down again. Chicka chicka BOOM BOOM!

■ PRETEND YOU'RE A CAT

by Jean Marzollo, illus. by Jerry Pinkney (Dial, 1990). Simple verses encourage children to mimic the actions of familiar animals. Jerry Pinkney's engaging illustrations of children and animals performing similar movements add to the reader's enjoyment.

■ THE STORY OF CHICKEN LICKEN

by Jan Ormerod (Lothrop, Lee & Shepard, 1985). As a group of children perform the play *The Story of Chicken Licken* on a well-lit stage, another performance is taking place in the darkened theater.

■ UNCLE NACHO'S HAT/EL SOMBRERO DEL TÍO NACHO

adapted by Harriet Rohmer, illus. by Veg Reisberg, Spanish version by Rosalma Zubizarreta (Children's Book Press, 1989). This story, told in English and Spanish, is based on a Nicaraguan folk tale and adapted from a script used by the Puppet Workshop of Nicaraguan National Television. Written mainly as a dialog, it can be converted easily back into a script. Encourage children to stage the play using puppets.

■ WE'RE GOING ON A BEAR HUNT

retold by Michael Rosen, illus. by Helen Oxenbury (Margaret K. McElderry, 1989). This appealing book is a variation of a traditional chant. Children can make believe they are splashing across a river or sloshing through oozy mud, chanting the evocative sound words as they proceed, while a narrator reads the text.

■ THE HOUSE THAT JACK BUILT

illus. by Jenny Stow (Dial, 1992). The words are the same, but the landscape has been changed in Stow's version of this cumulative nursery rhyme. Jack has built a house amidst the lush foliage of the Caribbean, which has been brought to life by the vibrantly colored collage illustrations.

■ CAPS FOR SALE: A TALE OF A PEDDLER, SOME MONKEYS AND THEIR MONKEY BUSINESS

by Esphyr Slobodkina (Harper Trophy, 1987, originally published in 1940) and **FIFTY RED NIGHT-CAPS** by Inga Moore (Chronicle, 1988). These two versions of the classic story of monkeys who steal a batch of hats and then frustrate the hats' owner by imitating his every movement are a natural for large group dramatization as a narrator reads the story. As many children as are eager to participate can be incorporated into the play.

■ ALBERT'S PLAY

by Leslie Tryon (Atheneum, 1992). Albert, a duck and the Pleasant Valley School's carpenter, helps the students stage a play based on "The Owl and the Pussy Cat." The poem is printed at the back of the book, and if your children are not familiar with it, you may want to read it aloud before beginning *Albert's Play*. The text and the detailed illustrations provide a good jumping-off place for discussing how a play is produced.

Mᴏʀᴇ ʙᴏᴏᴋs ʙʏ ᴛʜᴇᴍᴇ ᴀᴜᴛʜᴏʀs ᴀɴᴅ ɪʟʟᴜsᴛʀᴀᴛᴏʀs

■ CINDERELLA, OR THE LITTLE GLASS SLIPPER

translated by Marcia Brown (Aladdin, 1954). Marcia Brown's traditional version of Cinderella won the Caldecott Medal in 1955. After hearing the story read several times, children can improvise dialog and perform their own version.

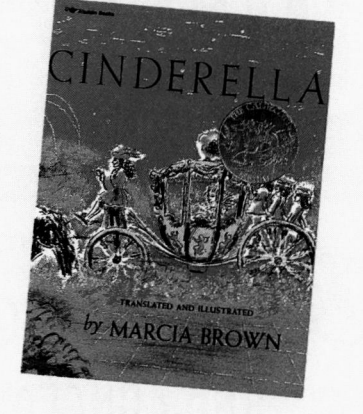

■ HANDTALK SCHOOL

by Mary Beth Miller and George Ancona, photographs by George Ancona (Four Winds, 1991). The authors have followed a group of residential students at the New York School for the Deaf as they prepare for their Thanksgiving play. Through photographs, children speak to the reader using American Sign Language (ASL). The third in the Handtalk series, this book helps kindergartners comprehend the universality of communication.

1

ACT IT OUT!

LITERATURE

Big Book of Poems:
On Our Way
  by Eve Merriam

Big Book of Songs:
Eency, Weency Spider
Traditional

SONGS AND STORIES
AUDIOCASSETTES
STORY SONGS:
Eency, Weency Spider

 SING & READ BOOKS AND
AUDIOCASSETTES
Eency, Weency Spider

Literature Activity Book: pp. 90–91
  Act It Out!

STAFF DEVELOPMENT A to EZ Handbook

• Masking: p. 273

• Nursery Rhymes: p. 276

Performance Assessment Handbook

HomeWords: Home-School Resources

OTHER RESOURCES

• BIG BOOK STAND
• BIG BOOK POINTER
• CHART PAPER
• MARKERS
• TO MAKE A BIG BOOK:
  BUTCHER PAPER
  CRAYONS
  STAPLER

LITERACY SUPPORT:
Building Language and Concepts

For children acquiring English and/or needing more intensive support, you may wish to incorporate the following suggestions into the basic lesson plan.

Review names of animals. Then have children "act out" various animals by playing charades. As children move and make the sounds of an animal, have them ask the class, "What am I?" The class responds by saying, "Are you a _____?" Build vocabulary by having children "act out" directions. For example, the teacher says, "Let's be actors by pretending to eat spaghetti."

Sharing Time

TODAY'S NEWS

Write and read Today's News, pointing to each word as you read. Mask the Theme Word, *actor.* Encourage children to think about being actors and share who they would like to pretend to be.

Everyone can be an actor. Let's pretend!

CREATING INTEREST AND BUILDING BACKGROUND

Because motivation matters!

Introduce the theme ACT IT OUT! by inviting children to act out a familiar nursery rhyme. The following rhymes present good opportunities for dramatization. You may want to write the rhymes on chart paper to display in the Reading Center.

Miss Muffet

Little Miss Muffet
Sat on a tuffet,
Eating her curds and whey;
There came a big spider,
Who sat down beside her
And frightened Miss Muffet away.

Humpty Dumpty

Humpty Dumpty sat on a wall,
Humpty Dumpty had a great fall;
All the King's horses, and all the King's men
Cannot put Humpty Dumpty together again.

Jack and Jill

Jack and Jill went up the hill,
　To fetch a pail of water;
Jack fell down, and broke his crown,
　And Jill came tumbling after.

Then up Jack got and off did trot,
　As fast as he could caper,
To old Dame Dob, who patched his nob
　With vinegar and brown paper.

After children have dramatized several rhymes, write the Theme Word *actor* on the chalkboard. Explain that *actor* is the Theme Word because throughout the theme, children will be actors who play many different roles.

Reading and Writing

SHARING LITERATURE
"On Our Way"

LISTEN TO THE SOUNDS OF POETRY   Invite children to listen as you read the Theme Poem "On Our Way."

SEE THE POEM IN PRINT   Display the Theme Poem "On Our Way" in the *Big Book of Poems.* Use the Big Book pointer or your finger to track each word as you read the poem title and the author's name. Explain that the poem shown in the Big Book is the poem you just read.

Read the poem again, tracking the print with the Big Book pointer or your finger.

On Our Way

What kind of walk
    shall we take today?
Leap like a frog?
    Creep like a snail?
Scamper like a squirrel
    with a furry tail?

Flutter like a butterfly?
Chicken peck?
Stretch like a turtle with
a poking-out neck?

Trot like a pony,
clip clop clop?
Swing like a monkey
    in a treetop?

Scuttle like a crab?
    Kangaroo jump?
Plod like a camel with an
    up-and-down hump?

We could even try
    a brand-new way—
Walking down the street
On our own two feet.

Eve Merriam

32   33

Big Book of Poems, pages 32–33

RESPONDING TO LITERATURE

POEM TALK Encourage children to share their personal reactions to the poem. You might begin by sharing any of your own comments or thoughts in order to provide a model for personal involvement with literature. The following questions might also be used to encourage individual response.

- *Which kind of walk would you most like to take today? Show us how that animal would walk.*

- *I was a bit surprised by the poem's ending. Was anyone else surprised by it? Let's reread the last three lines and talk about what they mean.*

- *I thought this was a good poem to introduce the theme* ACT IT OUT! *Do you agree? Why or why not?*

CLASS BIG BOOK As you reread the poem, help children list all the animals mentioned in the poem. Read the list aloud together when it is completed.

frog	pony
snail	monkey
squirrel	crab
butterfly	kangaroo
chicken	camel
turtle	person

Form small groups and, using butcher paper, have them illustrate each animal's way of walking. When the illustrations are complete, write the appropriate line of the poem onto each sheet. Then create a title page and a page for the first line and bind the pages in sequence to create a Big Book of the poem.

POEM THEATER Form a line of twelve children. Reread the poem, pausing after each new animal is described, and have one child act out the movements of each animal in turn.

TEAM WORK/THEME WORK A DRAMATIC PERFORMANCE

Introducing the Project: A Dramatic Performance
Share with children that to celebrate the theme ACT IT OUT! they will be putting on a dramatic performance of their own choosing. Each person will act in the performance and/or help get ready for the performance in some way.

Review the Theme Word *actor* and display it in a prominent place.

> Actor

Invite children to talk about what an actor does. Focusing on an actor's role in a television show or in a movie may help children relate to this idea. Encourage children to recognize that actors often prepare for their roles by rehearsing things to say and do in a performance.

Brainstorming and Sharing Ideas
Start planning the performance by inviting children to list things that need to be done to make the performance a success. Record these tasks on chart paper.

Performance Checklist

Decide what to act out

Assign parts

Rehearse

Make costumes

Write invitations

Create a program

Videotape the performance for
   family members who can't come

Sing Out!
Introduce the Theme Song "Eency, Weency Spider" as a song dramatized with hand movements that might be included in the performance.

Play the Theme Song on the SONGS AND STORIES AUDIOCASSETTE. Then display the words to the song in the *Big Book of Songs* and track the print with the Big Book pointer as children sing and perform the motions.

♪ SONGS AND STORIES AUDIOCASSETTES
STORY SONGS: Eency, Weency Spider

eency, weency spider

Eency, weency spider
Went up the water spout.

Down came the rain
And washed the spider out.

34

35

Big Book of Songs, pages 34–37

Planning

As you progress through the theme, involve children in all aspects of planning for their performance. Writing invitations, announcements, programs, signs, and thank-you notes are all ways to involve children in purposeful literary activities in a meaningful context.

Start a list of possible ideas for dramatizations to include in the performance. Add to the list as other possibilities are presented throughout the theme.

INTO THE LEARNING CENTER
You may wish to place the Sing & Read Book and its audiocassette for "Eency, Weency Spider" in the Reading Center and invite children to listen to the tape as they read the book. See page 96.

On Our Way
Eency, Weency Spider
Time to Wake Up!
Where Is Thumbkin?
Let's Pretend
The Three Billy Goats Gruff
I'm Going on a Dragon Hunt

The Terrible Tragadabas
Stone Soup

Theme Poem
Theme Song
a song with sign language
a finger play
a song to imitate animals
a folk tale
a book accompanied by
  hand motions
a folk tale
a folk tale retold in a book

2 ACT IT OUT!

LITERATURE

Handtalk Zoo
   by George Ancona
   and Mary Beth

GEORGE ANCONA & MARY BETH

SONGS AND STORIES
AUDIOCASSETTES
STORY SONGS:
Eency, Weency Spider
Time to Wake Up!

SING & READ BOOKS AND AUDIOCASSETTES
Eency, Weency Spider

EXPLORING PRINT

SING A SOUND AUDIOCASSETTES
Going to the Zoo
Learning the Code: Z, z
Practice Book: p. 53
BRWL: Letterbook Z(24)

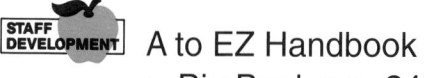

A to EZ Handbook
   • Big Books: p. 246
   • Journals: p. 264

Performance Assessment Handbook

OTHER RESOURCES

- BIG BOOK STAND
- BIG BOOK POINTER
- TO MAKE JOURNALS:
    STAPLER
    UNLINED PAPER
    CONSTRUCTION
    PAPER
- WORD MASK
- CHART PAPER
- MARKERS

For children acquiring English and/or needing more intensive support, you may wish to incorporate the following suggestions into the basic lesson plan.

LITERACY SUPPORT:
BUILDING LANGUAGE AND CONCEPTS

Prepare children for *Handtalk Zoo* by discussing the different ways in which people who are hearing impaired communicate. Preview page 31 to introduce children to fingerspelling. If possible, invite someone who knows sign language to the classroom. During reading, review names of the common foods on pages 18–19.

SHARING TIME

TODAY'S NEWS

After you read and write Today's News, invite children to use their hands to communicate such ideas as "good-bye," "be quiet," "stop," and "come here." They might also enjoy using their hands to act out the Theme Song "Eency, Weency Spider."

Today we will learn to talk with our hands.

♪ SONGS AND STORIES AUDIOCASSETTES
STORY SONGS: Eency, Weency Spider

CREATING INTEREST AND BUILDING BACKGROUND

Because motivation matters!

Share with children that today's story is entitled *Handtalk Zoo* and portrays a method of talking with one's hands called sign language. When signing, a person uses his or her hands to make a sign for each word or idea.

Introduce the song "Time to Wake Up!" on the STORY SONGS AUDIOCASSETTE. Then teach children how to sign "time" and "wake up" and invite them to use the signs when those words appear in the song. You may want to write the words to the song on chart paper and display it in the Music Center.

Time to Wake Up!

It's time to play! Time to wake up!
Outside to stay! Time to wake up!
A sunny day, Time to wake up!
Will come at last. Time to wake up!
Time to wake up! Time to wake up! Wake up!

—Barbara Staton

Encourage children to look for the uses of the sign for "time" in *Handtalk Zoo.*

♪ SONGS AND STORIES AUDIOCASSETTES
STORY SONGS: Time to Wake Up!

READING AND WRITING

SHARING LITERATURE
Handtalk Zoo

LOOK IT OVER   Display the Big Book for *Handtalk Zoo.* Explain to children that the Big Book will help them see the words as you read. Place a little version of the book in the Reading Center so children can explore the book independently.

Use the Big Book pointer or your finger to track each word as you read the title on the cover of *Handtalk Zoo.* Read the names of the author/photographer team and display their photograph on the back cover. Invite children to speculate what the sign George Ancona and Mary Beth are making in the photograph might mean.

Invite children to notice what the children on the cover are doing. Share that the formations they are making with their hands are fingerspellings. In sign language, each sign represents a whole word or idea, while in fingerspelling, each sign represents one letter, so that words are spelled out letter by letter. Help children use the fingerspelling alphabet on page 31 to find out what word the children are spelling. (camel)

SHARE THE STORY   Introduce *Handtalk Zoo* as a story told in photographs, sign language, and fingerspellings. It is about a trip Mary Beth and a group of children took to the Bronx Zoo in New York City. As you read, use the Big Book pointer to highlight sign language, fingerspellings, and printed text. Invite volunteers to discuss what characteristic of each animal is portrayed by its sign.

About the Author/Photographer

Mary Beth (Miller) was born in Louisville, Kentucky, to deaf parents. She learned to sign before she was even one year old and has communicated with deaf people all over the world as a member of the National Theater of the Deaf.

George Ancona, who is Mexican-American, lives in Santa Fe, New Mexico. Other books for which he has taken photographs include *Turtle Watch,* which he also wrote, and *Harry's Helicopter* by Joan Anderson.

George Ancona and Mary Beth have worked together on other books that show signing, including *Handtalk* and *Handtalk Birthday.*

RESPONDING TO LITERATURE

BOOK TALK   Invite children to share any personal comments or questions about the story. You may want to talk about your reactions to the unique format of the book, in order to model for children how readers respond to particular aspects of a selection. The following questions might get the discussion started.

- *Did you think this book was like most other books we have read or somewhat different? Why?*

- *Sometimes I found it hard to know where to look because both pictures and hand signs were shown on one page. Did anyone else feel that way?*

- *I liked the sign for zebra because it meant a horse with stripes. Which sign did you like best?*

JOURNAL WRITING Provide journals for children to use throughout the theme by stapling together sheets of paper. Invite children to draw their favorite animal from *Handtalk Zoo* and to show the sign for that animal. You may wish to model writing in your own journal, so children will see the importance of written response. After writing, invite volunteers to share their work.

Vernon wrote about the splashes from fish in his father's aquarium. He drew people looking down at the fish and wrote his message of "splash."

SIGNING Invite individual children to look through the Big Book or little book version of *Handtalk Zoo* and choose a sign to make. The other children can then identify the animal or idea being communicated and make the sign themselves.

TEAM WORK/THEME WORK
You may want to practice singing "Eency, Weency Spider" with hand motions in preparation for the upcoming Dramatic Performance. See pages 38–39 and 92–93.

INTO THE LEARNING CENTERS
You might want to set up a puppet theater in the Dramatic Play Center. Model for children how to use their hands as puppets in fingerplays such as "Where Is Thumbkin?" See page 97. You may wish to write the words to this fingerplay on chart paper and display it in the Dramatic Play Center.

Where is Thumbkin? Where is Thumbkin?
Here I am, here I am; (Bring out one thumb
    and then the other.)
How are you today, sir? Very well, I thank you,
    (Nod one thumb and then the other.)
Run away, run away. (Hide thumbs and repeat
    with fingers: pointer, tallie, ring man, pinkie.)

EXPLORING PRINT LEARNING THE CODE

In the Exploring Print Lessons for this theme, children will learn about the letters Z, z and Qu, qu and the sounds they represent. Take advantage of opportunities to point out these letters and the sounds they represent as you share Today's News, as you talk with children about their writing, and as you reread the theme-related trade books.

DECODING AND PHONICS

LETTERS: *Z, z*
SOUND/LETTER RELATIONSHIPS: /z/Z, z

Developing Phonemic Awareness

Remind children of the setting of *Handtalk Zoo*. Here is a song about a trip to the zoo. Sing or play "Going to the Zoo" and encourage children to join in on the chorus.

Going to the Zoo

We're going to the zoo, zoo, zoo.
How about you, you, you?
You can come too, too, too.
We're going to the zoo, zoo, zoo.

—Tom Paxton

SING A SOUND AUDIOCASSETTES
Going to the Zoo

Sing the song again and have children clap each time they hear the word *zoo*. Point out that the name of one common zoo animal, the zebra, begins with the same sound as *zoo*. Say these words again, accenting the beginning sound.

Developing Print Awareness

Write the song title and the first line of "Going to the Zoo" on the chalkboard or on chart paper. Encourage children to say the title and first line with you and to follow along as you point to each word.

Going to the Zoo

We're going to the zoo, zoo, zoo.

Use a word mask to frame a capital and lowercase z in the title and first line.

- *Let's look at some z's together. Here is a capital, or uppercase, Z at the beginning of the word Zoo.*

- *Here is a lowercase z at the beginning of the word zoo. What other words can you find in this line that begin with a lowercase z?*

- *The letter z stands for the sound you hear at the beginning of the words zebra and zoo. Say "zoo" with me.*

Encourage children to point to uppercase and lowercase z's in the title or first line and trace over them with their fingers.

You might want to create a "Z Zoo" bulletin board using construction paper. Encourage children to draw and label other pictures whose names begin with z and add them to the zoo scene.

45

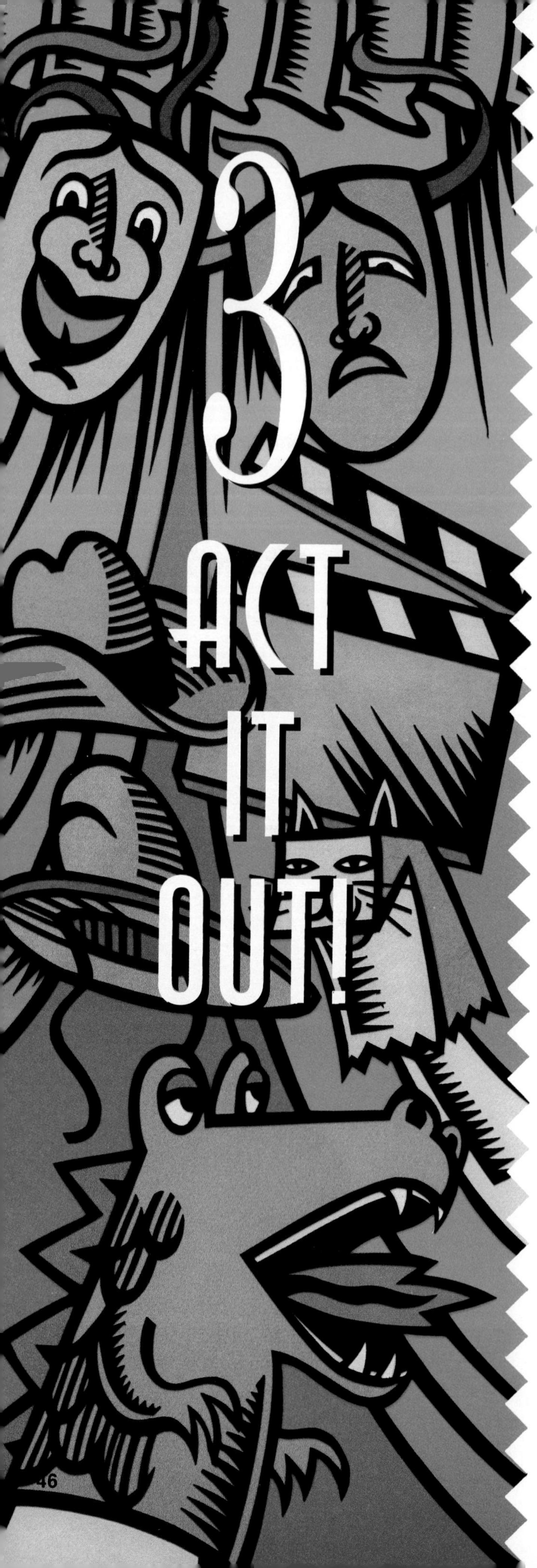

3

ACT IT OUT!

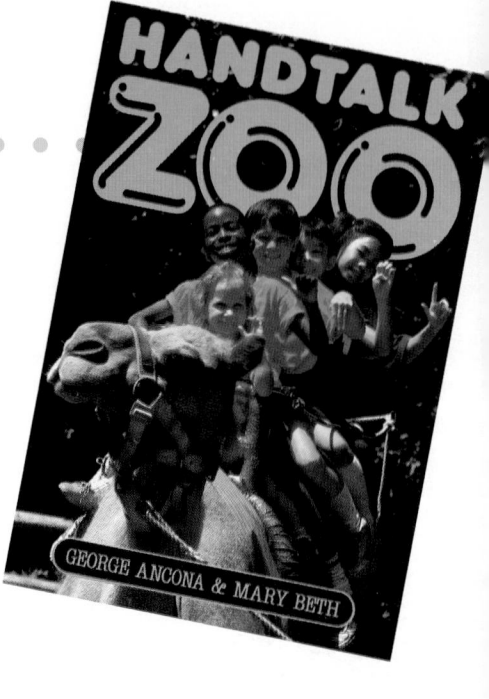

LITERATURE

Handtalk Zoo
by George Ancona
and Mary Beth

 SONGS AND STORIES
AUDIOCASSETTES
STORY SONGS:
Let's Pretend

Big Book of Poems:
On Our Way
by Eve Merriam

EXPLORING PRINT
*Big Book of Alphabet Rhymes
and Chimes:*
Zippety! Zippety! Zim, zim, zim!

Alphabet Poster for Zz

ABC cards

Literature Activity Book: p. 92
Learning the Code: Z, z

Practice Book: p. 54

BRWL: Letterbook Z(24)

 A to EZ Handbook
• Phonemic Awareness: p. 281
• Shared Reading: p. 299

Performance Assessment Handbook

Sharing Time

Today's News

After you write and read Today's News, invite the class to choose one animal from *Handtalk Zoo* and fingerspell that animal's name together. Some children might also enjoy using the fingerspelling alphabet on page 31 of the Big Book of *Handtalk Zoo* to form the letters of their own name.

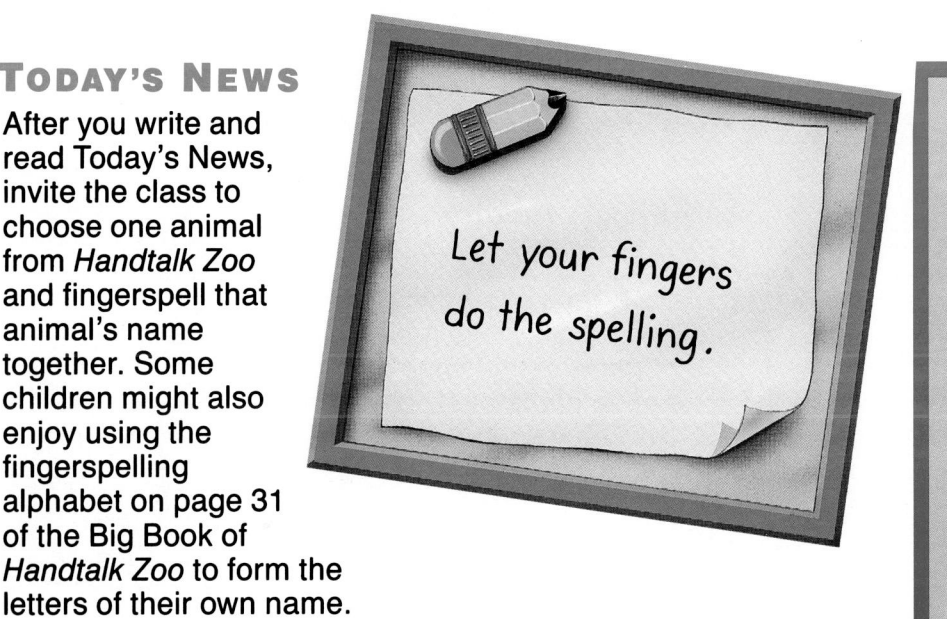

Let your fingers do the spelling.

Creating Interest and Building Background

Because motivation matters!

Talk with children about the different animals seen in *Handtalk Zoo.* Then introduce the song "Let's Pretend" by playing it on the STORY SONGS AUDIOCASSETTE. This song invites children to pantomime the actions of two of the animals in the book.

The SONGS AND STORIES AUDIOCASSETTE for this song has the first two verses in addition to the last two shown here.

You may want to write the song on chart paper to display in the Music Center.

Let's Pretend

Chorus
Let's pretend, just you and me,
Be whatever we want to be.
You will be my special friend,
And we'll play let's pretend.

Let's be a monkey, a monkey, a monkey.
Let's be a monkey now.
Hanging up in the monkey tree,
Make a funny face and scratch your knee.
Best little monkey that you ever did see.
Let's be a monkey now.

Chorus

Let's be a gray wolf, a gray wolf, a gray wolf.
Let's be a gray wolf now.
Growling around on four gray feet,
Mean and ugly and not very sweet.
Looking for something nice to eat.
Let's be a gray wolf now.

Chorus: two times

—Tom Paxton

Children might also enjoy creating additional verses about other animals. Rereading the Theme Poem "On Our Way" might serve as a source of ideas.

♪ SONGS AND STORIES AUDIOCASSETTES
STORY SONGS: Let's Pretend

Reading and Writing

SHARING LITERATURE
Handtalk Zoo

BIG BOOK

REREAD THE STORY As you turn the pages of the Big Book, invite children to use the photographs to name each of the animals. Encourage them to form the sign or fingerspelling for each animal.

PRINT AWARENESS

Letters
Highlight how the number of letters in the fingerspelling matches the number of letters in the animal's name. Encourage children to use this knowledge to determine which animal names are longer or shorter.

PHONEMIC AWARENESS

Initial Sounds: Review /p/p
- Invite children to name the two foods that begin with the same sound on pages 18–19 and to name the two animals that begin with the same sound on pages 26–27.

Initial Sounds: /z/z
- Invite children to figure out the animal names on the sign at the zoo on page 5. Ask children to identify the two words that begin with the letter *z*. Then ask them to find the animal name that begins with the same sound as *zoo*.

RESPONDING TO LITERATURE

BOOK TALK   Invite children to share any comments or questions they may have had about *Handtalk Zoo* since their last reading. You might then take this opportunity to explore issues related to deafness. The questions below might get the discussion started.

- *People who are born unable to hear have a harder time learning to speak the way we learned to speak. They can learn to talk with their hands using sign language or fingerspellings. Can you think of anyone you have seen on television or in real life who talks using his or her hands?*

- *In what ways would your life be different if you could only talk using sign language or fingerspellings? In what ways would your life be the same?*

- *Why would it be useful for a hearing person to know how to use sign language?*

SIGN LANGUAGE CARDS   Teach children the signs for "I love you." Invite them to make a card using those signs to give to a family member.

FINGERSPELLINGS   Display the fingerspelling alphabet shown in *Handtalk Zoo* and help each child form one letter to re-create the alphabet.

TEAM WORK/THEME WORK
Children might like to practice "Let's Pretend" (page 47) as a possible song to include in their Dramatic Performance. See pages 38–39 and 92–93.

INTO THE LEARNING CENTERS
Today would be a good day to invite children to create a sign language picture dictionary in the Writing Center. See page 99.

EXPLORING PRINT   LEARNING THE CODE

DECODING AND PHONICS

LETTERS: *Z, z*
SOUND/LETTER RELATIONSHIPS: */z/Z, z*

Developing Phonemic Awareness
Remind children that they are learning about the sounds of language and the letters that stand for those sounds. Invite them to listen as you read ''Zippety! Zippety! Zim, zim, zim!'' on page 35 of the *Big Book of Alphabet Rhymes and Chimes*.

As you come to words that begin with *z,* slightly emphasize the initial sound.

Repeat the rhyme a few times encouraging children to chime in.

- *Listen to the sound you hear at the beginning of* zippety *and* zim. *What other words do we know that begin with the same sound?*

Zippety! Zippety! Zim, zim, zim!
Zippety, zim! Zippety, zim!
Zippety! Zippety! Zim, zim, zim!
Zippety! Zippety! Zoop-a-laa!
Bernice Wells Carlson

Big Book of Alphabet Rhymes and Chimes,
page 35

Developing Print Awareness
Display ''Zippety! Zippety! Zim, zim, zim!'' on page 35 of the *Big Book of Alphabet Rhymes and Chimes* and repeat the rhyme with children. Use the Big Book pointer or a word mask to point out or frame words that begin with uppercase or lowercase z.

Then display the Alphabet Poster and ABC cards for Zz, or write the letters on the chalkboard and on cards of your own.

■ **Literature Activity Book:** page 92

zebra

Have children compare the *z*'s on the Big Book page with the letters on the poster and cards. Encourage children to talk about the zebra pictured on the poster.

Invite children to go on a Word Hunt around the room to find words on charts, signs, and in books that begin with the same sound and letter as *zoo* and *zebra*. Have them copy the words on cards and then share and display them on the bulletin board.

INTO THE LEARNING CENTERS
Encourage children to visit the Hands On! Language Center to use the resources there for more activities with sounds and letters. See page 98.

4 ACT IT OUT!

LITERATURE
Read Aloud Anthology
   "The Three Billy Goats Gruff"
   a Norwegian folk tale
   retold by Margaret H. Lippert

 SONGS AND STORIES
AUDIOCASSETTES
STORY SONGS:
Big, Bigger, Biggest

 SING & READ BOOKS AND
AUDIOCASSETTES
Eency, Weency Spider

EXPLORING PRINT
*Big Book of Alphabet Rhymes
and Chimes:*
   Zippety! Zippety! Zim, zim, zim!

Rhyme and Chime Stripes:
   Zippety! Zippety! Zim, zim, zim!

Learning the Code: Z, z

BRWL: Letterbook Z(24)

STAFF DEVELOPMENT A to EZ Handbook
   • Concepts of Print: p. 248
   • Retelling: p. 295

Performance Assessment Handbook

OTHER RESOURCES

• WORLD MAP OR GLOBE
• BIG BOOK STAND
• BIG BOOK POINTER
• POCKET CHART AND
  STAND
• WORD MASK
• JOURNALS

Sharing Time

Today's News

Gather children together and write and read Today's News, pointing to the words as you read. Tell children that today they will act out "The Three Billy Goats Gruff," a Norwegian folk tale about three goats and their experience with an ugly troll.

Trip, trap. Trip, trap. Here come three billy goats.

Creating Interest and Building Background

Because motivation matters!

After children listen to Ella Jenkins's song "Big, Bigger, Biggest," invite them to create a verse about three different-sized billy goats. You may want to write this song on chart paper to display for the class.

Big, Bigger, Biggest

I saw a **big** dog.
I saw a **bigger** dog.
I saw the **biggest** dog of all.

I saw a **tiny** bug.
I saw a **tinier** bug.
I saw the **tiniest** bug of all.

I saw a **small** bird.
I saw a **smaller** bird.
I saw the **smallest** bird of all.

I ate a **good** apple.
I ate a **better** apple.
I ate the **best** apple of all.

I saw a **nice** play.
I saw a **nicer** play.
I saw the **nicest** play of all.

I wore a **warm** sweater.
I wore a **warmer** sweater.
I wore the **warmest** sweater of all.

—Ella Jenkins

♪ SONGS AND STORIES AUDIOCASSETTES
STORY SONGS: Big, Bigger, Biggest

READING AND WRITING

SHARING LITERATURE
"The Three Billy Goats Gruff"

SHARE THE STORY Explain that while some stories are told with words and pictures, other stories are told without pictures, so that listeners have to make pictures in their minds. Encouraging children to form a picture of a troll and to share their images before you begin telling the story will help promote such visualizations.

As much as possible, tell the story from memory. Use different voices for the three billy goats and the troll. Invite children to slap their hands on their knees as each goat crosses the bridge to simulate the "Trip, trap. Trip, trap."

■ **Read Aloud Anthology:** pages 80–81

RETELL THE STORY Invite children to chime in on the repetitive dialog:

"Who's that going over my bridge?"

"It is I, the _____ Billy Goat Gruff."

"I'm coming to eat you up."

This might work well done in two groups, with one representing the troll and the other representing the billy goats.

About the Story

Point out the continent of Europe and the country of Norway on a world map or globe. Share that "The Three Billy Goats Gruff" was originally written down in that country by P. C. (Peter Christen) Asbjornsen. This version of the tale is a retelling by Margaret Lippert, an American storyteller who likes both "to tell stories and to write them down."

RESPONDING TO LITERATURE

BOOK TALK   Invite children to share their personal reactions to the story. You may want to comment on how this particular version of the story is the same as or different from other versions you have heard and encourage children to do the same.

You may want to use the following prompts to get the discussion started.

- *What was the problem the three billy goats had?*

- *How did they solve their problem?*

- *Can you think of other ways the billy goats might have solved their problem without hurting the troll?*

JOURNAL WRITING   Invite children to draw their favorite part of the folk tale while you model drawing or writing in your journal. Labeling the characters in your drawing may encourage some children to do the same.

DRAMATIZING   Invite groups of four to choose characters and to establish areas of the classroom to serve as a bridge and a meadow. After the groups have practiced their renditions, invite several groups to present the story for the rest of the class.

TEAM WORK/THEME WORK

Do children want to act out "The Three Billy Goats Gruff" in the upcoming Dramatic Performance? See pages 38–39 and 92–93.

INTO THE LEARNING CENTERS

For explorations of size comparisons, encourage children to visit the Science Center. To help children develop an understanding of the number three, invite them to the Math Center. Add the three billy goat puppets to the Dramatic Play Center. See pages 97, 103, and 104.

Using the Rhyme and Chime Strips gives children a Hands On! Language experience that allows them to explore important concepts of print.

CONCEPTS OF PRINT
Directionality, Words

Zippety! Zippety! Zim, zim, zim!
Zippety, zim! Zippety, zim!
Zippety! Zippety! Zim, zim, zim!
Zippety! Zippety! Zoop-a-laa!

Bernice Wells Carlson

Big Book of Alphabet Rhymes and Chimes,
page 35

Developing Print Awareness

Display page 35 in the *Big Book of Alphabet Rhymes and Chimes* and encourage children to recite the rhyme with you as you point to each word with the Big Book pointer.

Use a word mask to frame each word in the first line. Point out the spaces between the words. Explain that the spaces help readers see where one word ends and another begins.

Use the word cards cut from the Rhyme and Chime Strips for "Zippety! Zippety! Zim, zim, zim!" to build the rhyme in the pocket chart as shown. Recite the rhyme as you build it in the chart and encourage children to recite it with you.

Zippety!	Zippety!	Zim,	zim,	zim!
Zippety,	zim!	Zippety,	zim!	
Zippety!	Zippety!	Zim,	zim,	zim!
Zippety!	Zippety!	Zoop-a-laa!		

Talk about words in the rhyme that are the same and point to them. Take the word cards for *Zippety* out of the pocket chart and ask eight children to hold them. Have each child count the number of letters in the word after you model the process.

Display the word cards for *Zippety* and *Zim*. Ask children what they notice about these two words. Which word has more letters? Which word is longer?

Point out the exclamation mark after the words *Zippety* and *zim*. Ask children to say those words in a way that shows great excitement.

As you replace all word cards in the pocket chart, invite children to recite the rhyme with you again.

INTO THE LEARNING CENTERS
Allow children to use the *Big Book of Alphabet Rhymes and Chimes*, the Rhyme and Chime Strips, and the word cards to build the rhyme "Zippety! Zippety! Zim, zim, zim!" in the pocket chart in the Hands On! Language Center. See page 98.

5
ACT IT OUT!

LITERATURE
I'm Going on a Dragon Hunt
by Maurice Jones,
illustrated by Charlotte Firmin

SING & READ BOOKS AND
AUDIOCASSETTES
Eency, Weency Spider

EXPLORING PRINT
Rhyme and Chime Strips:
Zippety! Zippety! Zim, zim, zim!

Alphabet Poster for Zz

Learning the Code: Z, z

BRWL: Letterbook Z(24)

STAFF DEVELOPMENT A to EZ Handbook
• Invented Spelling: p. 260
• Zone of Proximal Development: p. 303

Performance Assessment Handbook

OTHER RESOURCES

• CHART PAPER
• MARKERS
• MAP OR GLOBE
• BUTCHER PAPER
• POCKET CHART AND
  STAND
• JOURNALS

LITERACY SUPPORT:
BUILDING LANGUAGE AND CONCEPTS

For children acquiring English and/or needing more intensive support, you may wish to incorporate the following suggestions into the basic lesson plan.

Read the title of the book and explain that the word *hunt* can mean "to look for something." Build background on dragons by encouraging children to describe the way a dragon looks and acts. Then ask children to visualize a dragon in their heads. Help children conclude that dragons are make-believe animals.

SHARING TIME

· ·

TODAY'S NEWS

As you write and read Today's News, point to the word *dragon* each time it appears. Display the cover of the book *I'm Going on a Dragon Hunt* and invite children to identify the words in Today's News that are the same as two words in the title of the book. Encourage children to say what is different about the words.

A dragon hunt.
A dragon hunt.
Today we're going on a dragon hunt!

CREATING INTEREST AND BUILDING BACKGROUND

Because motivation matters!

Share with children that today's story is entitled *I'm Going on a Dragon Hunt.* Then invite children to sing verses of the well-known traditional song about a hunt for different animals, "Oh, A-Hunting We Will Go." You may want to write the song on chart paper and display it in the Music Center.

Oh, A-Hunting We Will Go

Oh, a-hunting we will go,
A-hunting we will go;
We'll catch a fox and put him in a box,
And then we'll let him go!

After children have sung several verses using different animal names, invite them to create a verse about a hunt for a dragon.

Oh, a-hunting we will go,
A-hunting we will go;
We'll catch a dragon and put him in a wagon,
And then we'll let him go!

READING AND WRITING

SHARING LITERATURE
I'm Going on a Dragon Hunt

LOOK IT OVER   Read the book title while tracking the print with your finger. Point to the author's name, Maurice Jones, and the words "pictures by Charlotte Firmin."

Talk with children about what they notice on the title page. Encourage them to question the boy's choice of a butterfly net for a dragon hunt and to notice the dragon footprint on which he is standing.

SHARE THE STORY   Invite children to simulate the boy's movements as he charges through the grass, sails across the river, climbs up the tree, swings across the ravine, and squelches through the mud.

REREAD THE STORY   Invite children to chime in on the repeated line "Hello, what's this?" They might also shade their eyes with their hands on each of these lines to simulate looking out.

About the Author and Illustrator

Maurice Jones lives in England. He wrote this book as a variation of a traditional chant he had learned as a child. He has since written *I'm Going on a Gorilla Hunt.* He also works as a social worker and enjoys playing the guitar.

Charlotte Firmin also lives in England. You may want to point out the continent of Europe and the country of England on a map or globe. Firmin is one of six daughters of a famous English television producer, Peter Firmin. She has also illustrated *Aren't They Wonderful?* (in praise of dads) and *Isn't She Clever?* (in praise of moms).

RESPONDING TO LITERATURE

BOOK TALK   Invite children to share any personal questions or comments about the book. You may want to share any of your reactions to the story as a way of modeling how readers actively respond to literature. Prompts such as the following might help get the discussion started.

- *I was afraid when the boy went into the cave all by himself. Did anyone else feel that way?*

- *I thought the way the boy got across the river was clever. Let's look and see how he did it.*

- *The boy had to think of ways to get past several other difficult places on his hunt for the dragon. Which one of his ideas did you like the best?*

JOURNAL WRITING   Ask children to think of all the difficult things the boy met on his dragon hunt. Have them record their favorite parts of the story. You may wish to write your favorite parts in your own journal as children think of their favorite parts. Share journal entries by listing the places the boy went and graphing the number of times each place was chosen by children.

tall grass	tall tree	wide river	deep ravine	thick mud	sofa

STORY MURAL   Form six groups, one for each of the obstacles the boy encountered and one for the dragon. Give each group one sheet of butcher paper on which to illustrate their episode. As groups share their completed works, refer to the book to determine the sequence in which the sheets of butcher paper should be mounted to create a story mural.

INTO THE LEARNING CENTERS
In the Writing Center, children might like to create a new story based on the pattern in *I'm Going on a Dragon Hunt.* See page 99.

Anthony wanted to draw the boy back at home. When he wrote the word *like*, he spelled it *lk*, but Katie (another child) corrected him and he added the *i* and the *e*.

Anthony read his message like this: "I like the part when he was at home on the sofa."

DECODING AND PHONICS

LETTERS: *Z, z*
SOUND/LETTER RELATIONSHIPS: /z/*Z, z*

CONCEPTS OF PRINT
Directionality, Words, Letters

Developing Phonemic Awareness
Remind children that they have been learning about the sound you hear at the beginning of words like *zoo, zebra,* and *zippety* (words found in *Handtalk Zoo* and "Zippety! Zippety! Zim, zim, zim!" on page 35 in the *Big Book of Alphabet Rhymes and Chimes*). Invite children to suggest other words that have the same beginning sound.

Developing Print Awareness
Display the Alphabet Poster for Zz and point to the word *zebra.* Frame the letter *z* in the word. Remind children that the letter *z* stands for the sound they hear at the beginning of the word *zebra.*

Use the word cards from the Rhyme and Chime strips for "Zippety! Zippety! Zim, zim, zim!" to build the rhyme in the pocket chart as shown below.

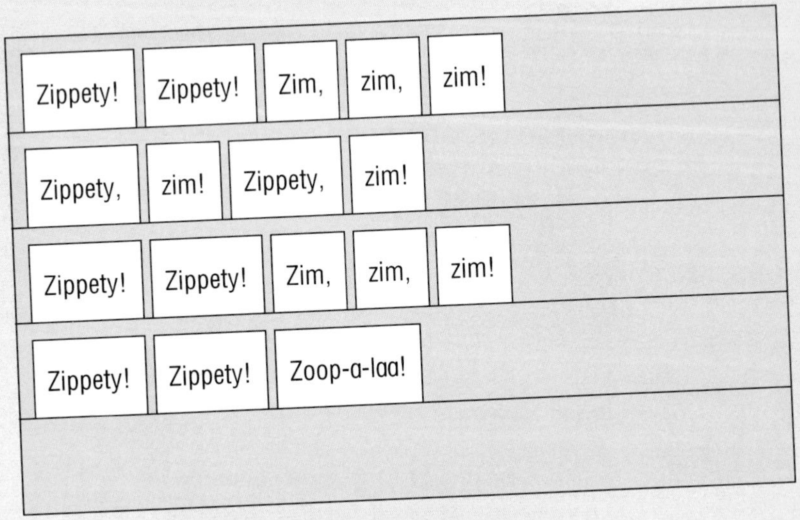

Zippety!	Zippety!	Zim,	zim,	zim!
Zippety,	zim!	Zippety,	zim!	
Zippety!	Zippety!	Zim,	zim,	zim!
Zippety!	Zippety!	Zoop-a-laa!		

Encourage children to say the rhyme with you as you point to each word with the Big Book pointer. Have children clap each time they hear a word that begins with the same sound as *zebra*.

Ask children to recite the rhyme and clap again. This time remove any word card for which they did not clap. Note that there are no word cards removed.

Zippety!	Zippety!	Zim,	zim,	zim!		
Zippety,	zim!	Zippety,	zim!			
Zippety!	Zippety!	Zim,	zim,	zim!		
Zippety!	Zippety!	Zoop-a-laa!				

Frame the first letter in each word and have children identify it as a *z*. Emphasize that the letter *z* stands for the sound heard at the beginning of the words *zippety* and *zim*. Use letter cards for *Z* and *z* from the Rhyme and Chime Strips and match them to the words that begin with those letters.

Review any charts and other print resources in the classroom to find words that begin with the same sound and letter as *zippety*.

INTO THE LEARNING CENTERS
Using letter stamps, sponge letters, and magnetic letters in the Hands On! Language Center is a motivating way for children to experiment with print. See page 98.

6

ACT IT OUT!

LITERATURE

I'm Going on a Dragon Hunt
  by Maurice Jones,
  illustrated by Charlotte Firmin

Big Book of Songs:
Eency, Weency Spider
  Traditional

 SONGS AND STORIES
AUDIOCASSETTES
STORY SONGS:
Eency, Weency Spider

 SING & READ BOOKS AND
AUDIOCASSETTES
Eency, Weency Spider

EXPLORING PRINT

SING A SOUND AUDIOCASSETTES
Six Little Ducks

Learning the Code: Qu, qu

Practice Book: p. 55

BRWL: Letterbook Q(21)

STAFF DEVELOPMENT A to EZ Handbook
  • Phonics: p. 283
  • Pointing: p. 287

Performance Assessment Handbook

OTHER RESOURCES

• CHART PAPER
• MARKERS
• WORD MASK

Sharing Time

Today's News

After you write and read Today's News, highlight the word *act* and invite children to note how it is different from the Theme Word *actor*. Invite volunteers to pretend to be the boy and the dragon.

Let's pretend to be the boy and the dragon today! Act out the story!

Creating Interest and Building Background

Because motivation matters!

Introduce a poem about pretending. Encourage children to form pictures in their minds of what the poem describes. You may want to write the poem on chart paper and display it in the Reading Center.

Make Believe

I made believe fly
A bird so blue
It glowed like sky—
   And up it flew!

I made believe grow
A tree in a wood
With petals of snow—
   And there it stood!

I'd love to pretend
A dragon for fun,
Or an ogre—but if
   I saw one I'd run!

So I'll make up a very
Small elf instead
To sing in the moonlight
   Beside my bed.

—Harry Behn

Invite children to recite the third stanza with you and to describe how it is similar to *I'm Going on a Dragon Hunt.* You might conclude by singing the Theme Song "Eency, Weency Spider," about another individual's exciting expedition.

🎵 SONGS AND STORIES AUDIOCASSETTES
STORY SONGS: Eency, Weency Spider

READING AND WRITING

SHARING LITERATURE
I'm Going on a Dragon Hunt

REREAD THE STORY   Read pages 19–23—when the boy goes into the cave—with a feeling of suspense. Then invite children to provide the narrative to describe the boy's hasty retreat as shown on the pages without text, pages 26–31. They might also chime in on the concluding "Phew! Safe at last."

PHONEMIC AWARENESS

Initial Sounds: Review /t/t
Compare the sentences *It's tall grass* (page 4) and *It's a tall tree* (page 10). Invite children to decide which description has two words that begin with the same sound and to repeat those words.

PRINT AWARENESS

Matching
- Point out how the author's and illustrator's names are printed in red on the book cover and invite children to find those names on the title page.

Word Repetition
- Many words and phrases are repeated within the story pattern. Write any of these words on chart paper and invite children to find the repetitions within the text.

  Can't—pages 5, 8, 10, 13, 16 (twice on each page)

  Hello, what's this?—pages 4, 7, 10, 15, 18, 20

RESPONDING TO LITERATURE

BOOK TALK   Invite children to share any thoughts or questions they may have had about the story since their last reading of it. Share any new perceptions of your own.

You might then use the following questions to focus on the sequence of events within the story.

- *In what order did the boy find himself by the mud, grass, tree, river, and ravine? Let's look in the book to see if we're right.*

- *In what order did he see those things as he ran away from the dragon?*

ADDITIONAL EPISODES   Invite children to write a new episode for the story in which the boy experiences another obstacle.

TRADITIONAL ORAL VERSION   You may want to write the song on chart paper and then read it through once with the children before you all sing it. Create a steady beat by slapping one thigh and then the other, as you recount the story events in sequence.

Dragon Hunt

Chorus:

Going on a dragon hunt! (Going on a dragon hunt!)

I'm not scared! (I'm not scared!)

Got my hat on my head. (Got my hat on my head.)

Got my boots on my feet. (Got my boots on my feet.)

Coming to some tall grass! (Coming to some tall grass.)

Can't walk round it! (Can't walk round it.)

Can't leap over it! (Can't leap over it.)

Have to charge through. (Have to charge through.)

(Brush palms together.)

Use the book to create the remaining verses of the chant. Perform the hand motions to accompany the following lines:

"Have to sail across it"—Hold onto imaginary mast.
"Have to climb up it"—Move hands as if climbing.

"Have to swing across it"—Clasp hands and swing across.
"Have to squelch through it"—Move hands as if stepping in mud.

End the chant with:

Coming to a dark cave.
Take a look inside.
Looks like the tail of a . . .
Feels like the tail of a . . .
OH NO, IT'S A DRAGON!

On this verse, have children move their hands as if they are running feet, then repeat all the other movements as fast as possible in reverse order. Finally, have them wipe their brows with the backs of their hands as they chime in on "Phew! Safe at last."

TEAM WORK/THEME WORK
Do children want to perform the traditional oral version of *I'm Going on a Dragon Hunt* and act out the expedition with their hands, as part of their Dramatic Performance? See pages 38–39 and 92–93.

EXPLORING PRINT   LEARNING THE CODE

In the Exploring Print lessons for this theme, children will learn about the letters Z, z and Qu, qu and the sounds they represent. Take advantage of opportunities to point out these letters and the sounds they represent as you share Today's News, as you talk with children about their writing, and as you reread the theme-related trade books.

DECODING AND PHONICS

LETTERS: *Qu, qu*
SOUND/LETTER RELATIONSHIPS: /kw/*Qu, qu*

Developing Phonemic Awareness
Discuss with children some other animals that the boy in *I'm Going on a Dragon Hunt* could have been searching for. Invite children to imitate the different sounds those animals might make. Here is a song about the sounds a duck makes. Sing or play "Six Little Ducks" and encourage children to join in.

Six Little Ducks

Six little ducks that I once knew,
Fat ones, skinny ones, fair ones too.
But the one little duck with the feather on his
   back,
He led the others with his quack, quack, quack!
Quack, quack, quack. Quack, quack, quack.
He led the others with his quack, quack, quack!

SING A SOUND AUDIOCASSETTES
Six Little Ducks

Sing the song again and have children form duck beaks with their hands in front of their mouths. Encourage them to open and close their beaks each time they hear the word *quack*. Point out that *quack* begins with the same sound as *queen*. Say these words again, accenting the beginning sound.

Developing Print Awareness
Write the fifth line of "Six Little Ducks" on the chalkboard or on chart paper. Encourage children to say the line with you as you point to each word.

Quack, quack, quack. Quack, quack, quack.

68

Use a word mask to frame a capital and lowercase *q* in the line.

- Let's look at some *q*'s together. Here is a capital, or uppercase, Q at the beginning of the word Quack. What other word can you find in this line that begins with a capital Q?

- Here is a lowercase *q* at the beginning of the word quack. What other words can you find in this line that begin with a lowercase *q*?

- *Qu* stands for the sound you hear at the beginning of the words queen *and* quack. *Say "quack" with me.*

Encourage children to point to uppercase and lowercase *q*'s in the line "Quack, quack, quack" and to trace over them with their fingers.

You might want to create a "Quilt" Word Wall using construction paper. Encourage children to draw and label other pictures whose names begin with *qu* and place them on top of the quilt.

7

ACT IT OUT!

LITERATURE

Read Aloud Anthology
  "The Terrible Tragadabas"
  a tale from Spanish New Mexico
  retold by Joe Hayes

 SONGS AND STORIES
AUDIOCASSETTES
STORYTELLINGS:
The Terrible Tragadabas

 SONGS AND STORIES
AUDIOCASSETTES
STORY SONGS: Big, Bigger, Biggest

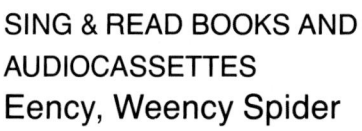 SING & READ BOOKS AND
AUDIOCASSETTES
Eency, Weency Spider

Literature Activity Book: pp. 95–96
  Tell a Tale

EXPLORING PRINT

*Big Book of Alphabet Rhymes
and Chimes:* Quack, Quack, Quack

Alphabet Poster for Qq

ABC cards

Literature Activity Book: p. 93
  Learning the Code: Q, q

Practice Book: p. 56

BRWL: Letterbook Q(21)

 A to EZ Handbook
  • Environmental Print: p. 255
  • Technology: p. 301

Performance Assessment Handbook

OTHER RESOURCES

• UNITED STATES MAP
• BUTCHER PAPER
• BIG BOOK POINTER
• BIG BOOK STAND
• JOURNALS
• INDEX CARDS

SHARING TIME

TODAY'S NEWS

Write and read Today's News, pointing to the words as you read. Tell children that today they will hear a folk tale from Spanish New Mexico about a scary creature called *The Terrible Tragadabas*.

It's scary and it's big. The Terrible Tragadabas is here!

CREATING INTEREST AND BUILDING BACKGROUND

Because motivation matters!

Share with children that today's folk tale is entitled "The Terrible Tragadabas." Then use this poem about another fearsome beast to set the tone for the tale.

Beware, My Child

Beware, my child,
of the snaggle-toothed beast.
He sleeps till noon,
then makes his feast
on Hershey bars
and cakes of yeast
and anyone around—o.

So when you see him,
sneeze three times
and say three loud
and senseless rhymes
and give him all your
saved-up dimes,
or else you'll ne'er be found—o.

—Shel Silverstein

Since today's folk tale employs a size-based repetitive pattern similar to "The Three Billy Goats Gruff," children might also enjoy singing "Big, Bigger, Biggest." Children should be familiar with this song from Lesson 4. (See page 53.)

♪ SONGS AND STORIES AUDIOCASSETTES
STORY SONGS: Big, Bigger, Biggest

Reading and Writing

SHARING LITERATURE
"The Terrible Tragadabas"

SHARE THE STORY   Play the STORYTELLINGS
AUDIOCASSETTE of "The Terrible Tragadabas." Remind
children that when stories are told without pictures,
listeners can create their own pictures in their minds.

As the story is told, encourage children to simulate
each door-knocking by rapping on the floor.

RETELL THE STORY   Invite children to chime in on the
repetitive dialog.

"WHO IS IT?"

"I'm _____."

"
_____, _____,
DON'T YOU COME INSIDE.
I'M THE TRAGADABAS,
AND I'LL SWALLOW YOU ALIVE!"

"Tragadabas? What's a Tragadabas?"

This might work well in two groups, with one group
representing the Tragadabas and the other
representing the three girls and grandma.

♪ SONGS AND STORIES AUDIOCASSETTES
STORYTELLINGS: The Terrible Tragadabas

■ **Read Aloud Anthology:** pages 82–89

About the Story — Developing Multicultural Awareness

Point out the state of New Mexico on a map. Share
that "The Terrible Tragadabas" is a Spanish tale
that was originally told in New Mexico. This version
of the tale is told in both its original Spanish and in
English by Southwestern storyteller Joe Hayes.

Joe Hayes has written down many of the region's
tales from varied cultures. His first book, *The Day It
Snowed Tortillas,* recounts tales from Spanish New
Mexico, while *Coyote E.* retells Native American
tales and *A Heart Full of Turquoise* retells Pueblo
Indian tales.

RESPONDING TO LITERATURE

BOOK TALK   Invite children to share any reactions to
the story. You might begin the discussion by sharing
any of your personal reactions.

Extend this discussion into a comparison between "The
Terrible Tragadabas" and "The Three Billy Goats
Gruff" using such questions as the following.

● *Did this story remind you of any other story we've
read in this theme?*

● *Let's make a chart to compare the parts of those
two stories.*

	Three Billy Goats	The Terrible Tragadabas
Characters	3 billy goats troll	3 girls grandma Tragadabas bee storekeeper
Problem	couldn't get over the bridge	couldn't get into the store
Solution	the big billy goat pushed the troll	the bee stung the Tragadabas

JOURNAL WRITING   Remind children that since both the Tragadabas and the troll are made-up creatures, no one can know what they look like. Invite them to record their images of either character in their journals and then to share these images with each other.

CLASS BIG BOOK   Challenge children to determine the major story events and then to work in small groups to illustrate each event on butcher paper. These sheets can then be stapled together in sequence to form a Big Book of the story.

DRAMATIZATION   Invite groups of seven to draw three backdrops to depict the three story settings: the house, the store, and the tree. Each group can then choose roles, practice their story dramatizations in front of their backdrops, and then perform their renditions for the class.

INTO THE LEARNING CENTERS
This would be a good day to reinforce children's understanding of size comparisons by sending them to the Science Center or to emphasize their understanding of three by sending them to the Math Center. See pages 103–104.

You might also want to cue the SONGS AND STORIES AUDIOCASSETTE at the beginning of "The Terrible Tragadabas" and place it in the Reading Center. See page 96.

73

DECODING AND PHONICS

LETTERS: *Qu, qu*
SOUND/LETTER RELATIONSHIPS: /kw/*Qu, qu*

Developing Phonemic Awareness
Ask children to listen as you read "Quack, Quack, Quack" on page 24 in the *Big Book of Rhymes and Chimes*. As you come to words that begin with *qu*, slightly emphasize the initial sound.

- *Listen to the sound you hear at the beginning of quack. What other words do we know that begin with the same sound?*

Repeat the rhyme a few times, encouraging children to chime in.

Developing Print Awareness
Display "Quack, Quack, Quack" on page 24 in the *Big Book of Alphabet Rhymes and Chimes* and say the rhyme with children. Use the Big Book pointer or a word mask to point out or frame words that begin with *qu*.

Qq   Quack, Quack, Quack

Gobble, gobble, gobble
Quack, quack, quack.
A turkey says gobble,
And a duck says quack.

Big Book of Alphabet Rhymes and Chimes,
page 24

Then display the Alphabet Poster and ABC cards for Qq, or write the letters on the chalkboard or on cards of your own. Have children compare the *q*'s on the Big Book page with the letters on the poster and cards. Encourage children to talk about the quail pictured on the poster.

■ **Literature Activity Book:** page 93

quail

Invite pairs of children to go on a Word Hunt around the room to find words on charts, signs, and in books that begin with the same sound and letters as *queen* and *quack*. Have them copy the words on cards and then share and display them on the bulletin board.

INTO THE LEARNING CENTERS
Encourage children to visit the Hands On! Language Center to use the resources there for more activities with sounds and letters. See page 98.

8 ACT IT OUT!

STONE SOUP

by Marcia Brown

LITERATURE
Stone Soup
  by Marcia Brown

SING & READ BOOKS AND
AUDIOCASSETTES
Eency, Weency Spider

Literature Activity Book: p. 94
  Just for Fun

EXPLORING PRINT
*Big Book of Alphabet Rhymes
and Chimes:*
  Quack, Quack, Quack

Rhyme and Chime Strips:
  Quack, Quack, Quack

Learning the Code: Qu, qu

BRWL: Letterbook Q(21)

STAFF
DEVELOPMENT A to EZ Handbook
  • Dramatization: p. 252
  • Pocket Chart: p. 285

Performance Assessment Handbook

OTHER RESOURCES

- CHART PAPER
- MARKERS
- TO DRAMATIZE THE
  STORY:
    LARGE POT
    BUCKETS
    3 ROUND STONES
    SOUP INGREDIENTS
- BIG BOOK POINTER
- BIG BOOK STAND
- POCKET CHART AND
  STAND
- JOURNALS

**For children acquiring English and/or
needing more intensive support, you
may wish to incorporate the following
suggestions into the basic lesson plan.**

LITERACY SUPPORT:
BUILDING LANGUAGE AND CONCEPTS

Before reading, show children the cover of the book and say
the title aloud. Have children describe or define *stones.* If
possible, show children some real stones. During reading,
pause after each page to discuss and elaborate on the text's
complex dialog. Substitute familiar words or phrases wherever
necessary to ensure comprehension.

SHARING TIME

TODAY'S NEWS

As children gather around to watch you write and hear you read the message, invite them to repeat the question. Point to the question mark and explain that it shows a question is being asked. Then encourage children to answer the question.

> Carrots, potatoes, cabbage, and a stone. Did you ever hear of stone soup?

CREATING INTEREST AND BUILDING BACKGROUND

Because motivation matters!

Make sure children understand the process by which soup is made by using questions such as the following.

- *What kinds of soup have you eaten? Which kind is your favorite?*

- *Now people can buy soup already made in a can. Does anyone know how the soup is made before it is put into the can or how to make soup without using a can?*

- *What kinds of cooking equipment and ingredients would you need to make soup?*

READING AND WRITING

SHARING LITERATURE
Stone Soup

LOOK IT OVER   Display the title page and read the title. Then read and track the words "an old tale—told and pictured by Marcia Brown." Help children understand that Marcia Brown did not make up the story, but rather retold an old French tale she had heard.

SHARE THE STORY   Invite children to listen to the story to find out how to make stone soup. As you read, highlight the repetitive pattern by asking children to predict what will happen each time the soldiers ask for just a little bit of something for the soup.

REREAD THE STORY   Focus children's attention on aspects of the story that help them realize that it occurred long ago, such as the peasants' clothing.

About the Author/Illustrator

Marcia Brown was born in 1918 in Rochester, New York. Her interest in retelling folk and fairy tales developed as she worked at the New York Public Library telling stories to young children.

Many of Marcia Brown's books have received awards. She received her first children's literature award in 1948, when *Stone Soup* was chosen as a runner-up for the Caldecott Medal. Between 1950 and 1954, she wrote five books, all of which were retellings of folk or fairy tales and all of which were chosen as runners-up for the Caldecott Medal. She eventually received the Caldecott Medal in 1955 for her retelling of *Cinderella*.

It took many buckets of water to fill the pot. A fire was built on the village square and the pot was set to boil.

RESPONDING TO LITERATURE

BOOK TALK Invite children to share their comments or questions regarding the story. You may model such personal response to literature by sharing any of your own reactions or by using such comments as the following.

- *Why do you think the peasants hid their food from the soldiers?*

- *The story said that the peasants hid their food because they were afraid of strangers. Why were they afraid of strangers?*

- *How did the peasants feel about the strangers by the end of the story? Why did their feelings change? Have your feelings about someone ever changed as you got to know them?*

JOURNAL WRITING Share with children that later they will be acting out *Stone Soup* together. Encourage them to think about what part they might like to play and to record their feelings in their journals.

DRAMATIZATION As you revisit the book, work together to list all of the ingredients the peasants brought to help make the soup. Use the children's stated role preferences to assign each child a part in a story dramatization. Then encourage children to use the list to make any necessary props and costumes and to perform their play. Read the list aloud with children.

large pot	carrots
buckets of water	cabbage
3 round stones	beef and potatoes
salt and pepper	barley and a cup of milk

COLLECTING INGREDIENTS Share with children that they will be making their own stone soup on another day. Invite them to bring to school any ingredients that might be added to the soup.

TEAM WORK/THEME WORK
Will children choose to act out *Stone Soup* as part of the Dramatic Performance? See pages 38–39 and 92–93.

INTO THE LEARNING CENTERS
Children might like to make stone wishes and write soup recipes in the Writing Center. See page 99.

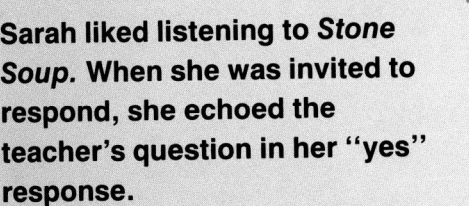

Sarah liked listening to *Stone Soup*. When she was invited to respond, she echoed the teacher's question in her "yes" response.

79

Using the Rhyme and Chime Strips gives children a Hands On! Language experience that allows them to explore important concepts of print.

CONCEPTS OF PRINT
Directionality, Words

Qq

Quack, Quack, Quack

Gobble, gobble, gobble
Quack, quack, quack.
A turkey says gobble,
And a duck says quack.

Big Book of Alphabet Rhymes and Chimes, page 24

Developing Print Awareness

Display page 24 in the *Big Book of Alphabet Rhymes and Chimes* and encourage children to recite the rhyme with you as you point to each word with the Big Book pointer.

Use a word mask to frame each word in the title. Point out the spaces between the words. Explain that the spaces help readers see where one word ends and another begins.

Use the word cards cut from the Rhyme and Chime Strips for "Quack, Quack, Quack" to build the rhyme in the pocket chart as shown. Recite the rhyme as you build it in the chart and encourage children to recite it with you.

Gobble,	gobble,	gobble,		
Quack,	quack,	quack.		
A	turkey	says	gobble,	
And	a	duck	says	quack.

Then use the picture cards to have children match the pictures of the turkey and the duck as you and the children recite the appropriate phrases.

Talk about words that are the same and point to them. Take the word cards for *quack* out of the pocket chart and ask three children to hold them. Have each child count the number of letters in each word he or she is holding.

Display the word cards for *Quack* and *quack*. Ask children what they notice about these two words. Which word starts with a capital *Q*? Which word starts with a lowercase *q*?

As you replace all word cards in the pocket chart, invite children to recite the rhyme with you again.

INTO THE LEARNING CENTERS
Allow children to use the *Big Book of Alphabet Rhymes and Chimes*, the Rhyme and Chime Strips, and the word and picture cards to build the rhyme "Quack, Quack, Quack" in the pocket chart in the Hands On! Language Center. See page 98.

Gobble, gobble, gobble

Quack, quack, quack.

A turkey says gobble,

And a duck says quack.

9
ACT IT OUT!

LITERATURE
Stone Soup
   by Marcia Brown

♪ SONGS AND STORIES
AUDIOCASSETTES
STORY SONGS:
Sitting in the Soup

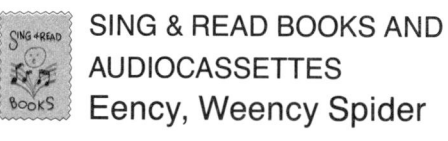 SING & READ BOOKS AND
AUDIOCASSETTES
Eency, Weency Spider

EXPLORING PRINT
Alphabet Poster for Qq

Rhyme and Chime Strips:
   Quack, Quack, Quack

Learning the Code: Qu, qu

BRWL: Letterbook Q(21)

STAFF DEVELOPMENT A to EZ Handbook
   • Language Experience
     Writing: p. 268
   • Music and Movement: p. 274

Performance Assessment Handbook

OTHER RESOURCES

• TO MAKE SOUP:
     POT
     CHICKEN OR BEEF
        BROTH OR
        BOUILLON CUBES
     SALT AND PEPPER
     VARIETY OF
        VEGETABLES
     BARLEY, RICE,
        OR NOODLES
     PEELERS
     KNIVES
     STOVE
• CHART PAPER
• MARKERS
• POCKET CHART AND
     STAND

Sharing Time

TODAY'S NEWS

As you write Today's News, point out the Theme Word *actor*. Then invite children to speculate on what they might cook today.

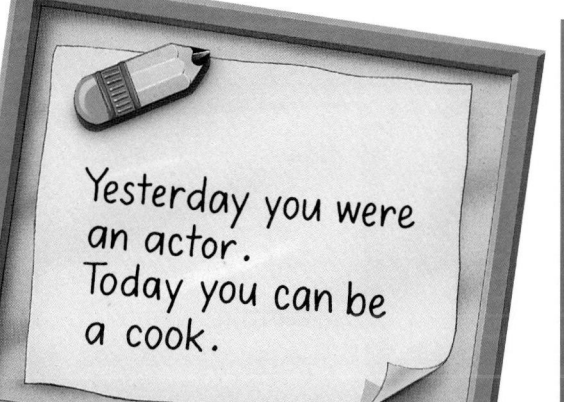

Yesterday you were an actor.
Today you can be a cook.

CREATING INTEREST AND BUILDING BACKGROUND

Because motivation matters!

Introduce a song by Sarah Pirtle about another soup with something special in it. Encourage children to add movements as they sing.

Sitting in the Soup

Chorus
Here we are, sitting in the soup,
   sitting in the soup on Sunday.

Now jump like jumping beans, jump like
   jumping beans.
Turn on the stove, boil those beans, and jump
   like jumping beans.

The beans are jumping in the pot,
Start to giggle, start to shout,
Spin around and they all jump out,
Run come a-giggle on home.

Chorus

Now shake yourself like salt, shake yourself
   like salt.
Turn on the stove to sizzle up hot and shake
   yourself like salt.
And twist that pepper out, twist that pepper
   out.
Twist and twist and twist again, and twist that
   pepper out.

—Sarah Pirtle

SONGS AND STORIES AUDIOCASSETTES
STORY SONGS: Sitting in the Soup

Reading and Writing

Stone Soup

REREAD THE STORY   Before rereading, share the dedication "to my mother and father" and have children decide to whom they might dedicate a book. During the rereading, invite children to create their own dialog for the peasants' responses each time the soldiers ask for a specific ingredient for the soup.

PHONEMIC AWARENESS

Initial Sounds: /kw/ *qu*
- Invite children to listen for the word that begins with the sound of *qu* as you read this sentence from page 11:

  They spread old quilts over the carrot bins.

PRINT AWARENESS

Matching
- Invite children to point to the two words on the book cover that begin with the same letter and to identify that letter. Challenge a volunteer to point to the two words that begin with that letter in the first sentence.

Stone Soup

chicken broth	frozen peas
carrots	cooked red beans
potatoes	noodles
onions	1 smooth clean stone

1. Heat chicken broth in a large pot.
2. Wash, peel, and slice carrots, potatoes, and onions.
3. Add carrots, potatoes, onions, peas, beans, and stone to broth.
4. Simmer for about 20 minutes.
5. Add noodles.
6. Simmer for about 10 minutes more.

RESPONDING TO LITERATURE

BOOK TALK   After inviting children to share personal reactions to the story, focus their attention on the unstated facts about the soup using the following questions.

- *The villagers thought the soldiers could make soup using only stones. Do you think they really could?*

- *What would the soup have been like if the peasants had not brought food to add to it?*

- *What lesson might the villagers have learned?*

At Vincent and Marie's the answer was the same. It had been a poor harvest and all the grain must be kept for seed.

So it went all through the village. Not a peasant had any food to give away. They all had good reasons. One family had used the grain for feed. Another had an old sick father to care for. All had too many mouths to fill.

THANK-YOU NOTES   Invite children to write thank-you notes from the soldiers to the peasants or from the peasants to the soldiers. Place two labeled mailboxes in the Writing Center for the correspondence.

COOKING SOUP AND WRITING RECIPES   Involve children in making soup by helping them wash, peel, and slice the vegetables that they brought from home and place them in a pot containing chicken or beef broth or chicken or beef bouillon cubes and water. Simmer for about 30 minutes until vegetables are tender.

Work together to record the ingredients and each step on a Language Experience Chart to create a recipe for your group's concoction. You might recopy and duplicate the recipe for children to take home.

TEAM WORK/THEME WORK
Have children made a program to show what will be performed and by whom in their Dramatic Performance? See pages 38–39 and 92–93.

INTO THE LEARNING CENTERS
Do children want to create personal soup recipes in the Writing Center? See page 99.

EXPLORING PRINT

LEARNING THE CODE
DEVELOPING CONCEPTS OF PRINT

HANDS ON LANGUAGE

DECODING AND PHONICS

LETTERS; *Qu, qu*
SOUND/LETTER RELATIONSHIPS: /kw/*Qu, qu*

CONCEPTS OF PRINT
Directionality, Words, Letters

Developing Phonemic Awareness
Remind children that they have been learning about the sound at the beginning of words like *quilt, quail,* and *quack* (words from *Stone Soup* and "Quack, Quack, Quack" on page 24 in the *Big Book of Alphabet Rhymes and Chimes).* Invite children to suggest other words that have the same beginning sound.

Developing Print Awareness
Display the Alphabet Poster for Qq and point to the word *quail.* Frame the letters *qu* in the word. Remind children that the letters *qu* stand for the sound heard at the beginning of the word *quail.*

Use the word cards from the Rhyme and Chime Strips for "Quack, Quack, Quack" to build the rhyme in the pocket chart as shown below.

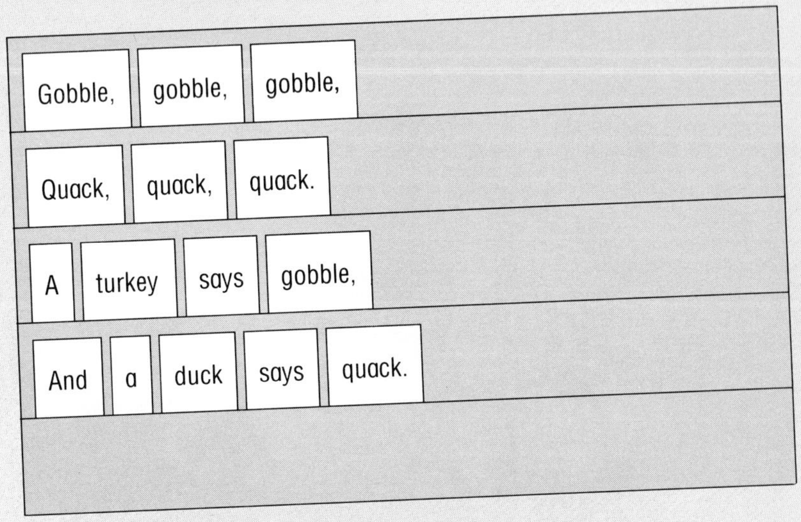

Gobble, gobble, gobble,
Quack, quack, quack.
A turkey says gobble,
And a duck says quack.

Encourage children to say the rhyme with you as you point to each word with the Big Book pointer. Have children clap each time they hear a word that begins with the same sound as *quail.*

Ask children to recite the rhyme and clap again. This time remove any card for which the children did not clap.

Frame the first letter in each word and have children identify it as a *q*. Emphasize that the letters *qu* stand for the sound heard at the beginning of the words *quail* and *quack*. Use letter cards for *Q* and *q* from the Rhyme and Chime Strips and match them to the words that begin with those letters.

Quack,	quack,	quack.		
		quack.		

Review all the charts and other print resources in the classroom to find words that begin with the same sound and letters as *quack*.

INTO THE LEARNING CENTERS
Using letter stamps, sponge letters, and magnetic letters in the Hands On! Language Center is a motivating way for children to experiment with print. See page 98.

87

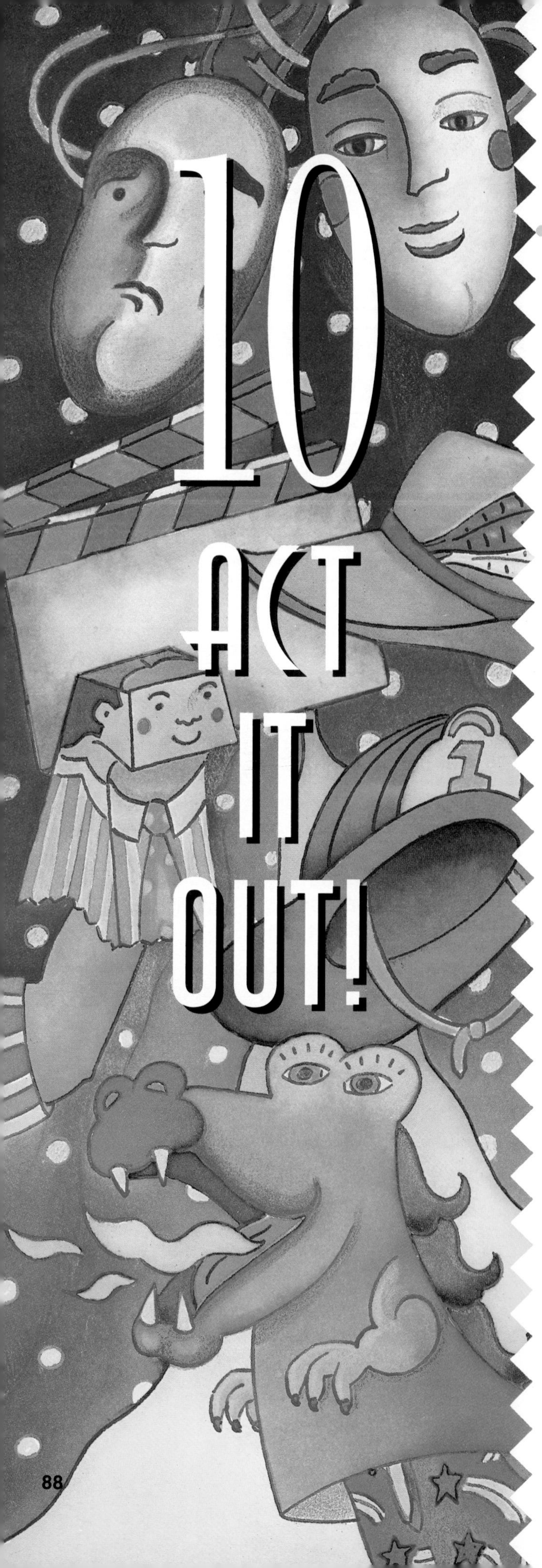

10 ACT IT OUT!

LITERATURE

Handtalk Zoo
by George Ancona
and Mary Beth

I'm Going on a Dragon Hunt
by Maurice Jones,
illustrated by Charlotte Firmin

Stone Soup
by Marcia Brown

Big Book of Poems:
On Our Way
by Eve Merriam

Big Book of Songs:
Eency, Weency Spider
Traditional

SONGS AND STORIES AUDIOCASSETTES
STORY SONGS:
Eency, Weency Spider

SING & READ BOOKS AND AUDIOCASSETTES
Eency, Weency Spider

Literature Activity Book: p. 97
Responding to Literature

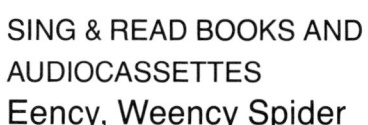

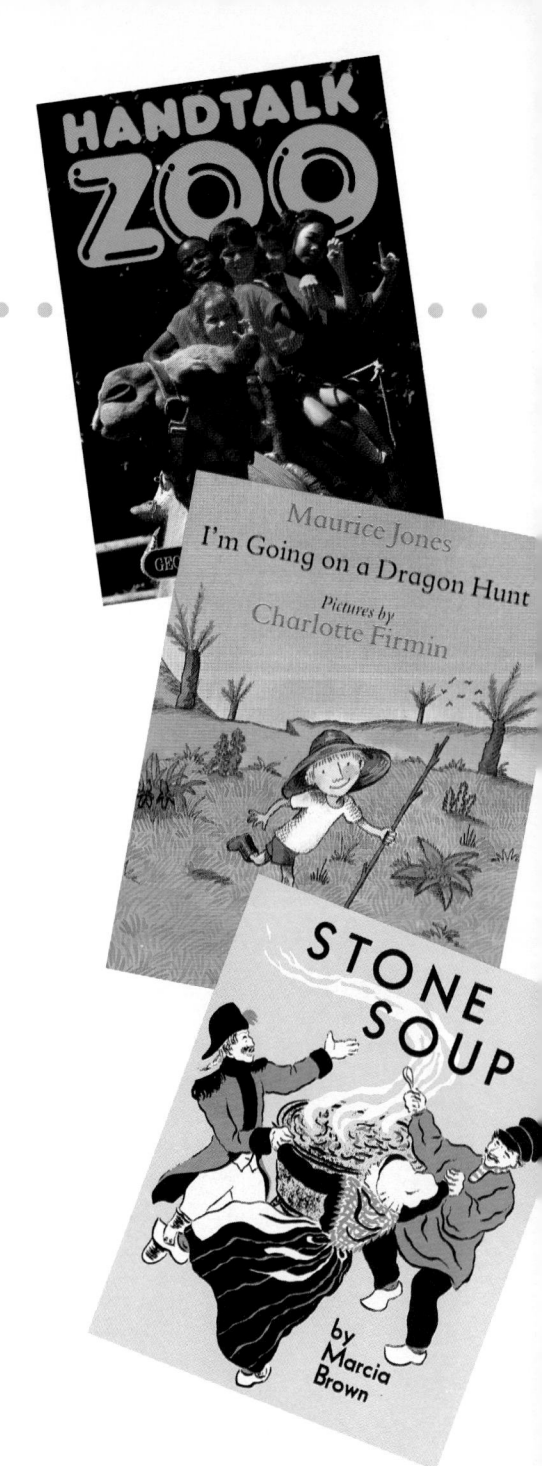

STAFF DEVELOPMENT A to EZ Handbook

- Observation: p. 279
- Risk-Free Environment: p. 297

Performance Assessment Handbook

OTHER RESOURCES

- Big Book Pointer
- Big Book Stand
- Journals

SHARING TIME

TODAY'S NEWS

After you write and read Today's News, highlight the word *actors* and invite children to note how it is different from the Theme Word *actor*. Children can then discuss any tasks that need to be accomplished before the performance.

Actors, are you ready for our performance?

WRAPPING IT UP

To get children in the mood for the Dramatic Performance, reread the Theme Poem "On Our Way," pausing for volunteers to act out each animal's movements. Children might also sing the Theme Song "Eency, Weency Spider" on pages 34–37 of *The Big Book of Songs* and accompany it with the hand motions. Reintroduce the Theme Word *actor* by asking children to name the times that they acted out, or dramatized, activities with each story.

♪ SONGS AND STORIES AUDIOCASSETTES
STORY SONGS: Eency, Weency Spider

On Our Way

What kind of walk
shall we take today?
Leap like a frog?
Creep like a snail?
Scamper like a squirrel
with a furry tail?

Flutter like a butterfly?
Chicken peck?
Stretch like a turtle with
a poking-out neck?

Trot like a pony,
clip clop clop?
Swing like a monkey
in a treetop?

Scuttle like a crab?
Kangaroo jump?
Plod like a camel with an
up-and-down hump?

We could even try
a brand-new way—
Walking down the street
On our own two feet.

Eve Merriam

32   33

Big Book of Poems, pages 32–33

Reading and Writing

SHARING LITERATURE

LOOK IT OVER   Display all of the theme books (*Handtalk Zoo, I'm Going on a Dragon Hunt,* and *Stone Soup*) and read the titles. Hold up each book and invite volunteers to share what they remember about it. Ask the class to choose one book for you to reread.

REREAD THE STORY   Reread the chosen selection. Help set a purpose for listening by inviting children to think about why the characters in the book might be described as actors.

Review the letters *z* and *q* that children learned about by noting words that begin with these letters. Point out concepts of print introduced earlier in the theme as appropriate. To give children additional practice, you may wish to use the Phonics Activity Sheets on pages 109–110.

90

RESPONDING TO LITERATURE

BOOK TALK   Invite children to share their reactions to any of the three stories. Be sure to share your questions and responses, too.

Encourage children to talk about how the books are the same and how they are different. The following questions may be used to extend this comparative discussion:

- *In which book did the characters act with their hands? Which book did we act out with our hands?*

- *Why might the soldiers in* Stone Soup *be described as actors?*

- *Which of the books did you most like acting out?*

JOURNAL WRITING   Point to the Theme Word *actor* where you wrote it at the beginning of the theme or rewrite it on the chalkboard. Talk with children about their experiences being actors during this theme.

Provide a sense of closure to the theme by inviting children to record in their journals any of their experiences as actors. Provide a model for journal writing by recording any of your responses to the children as actors. Conclude by inviting volunteers to share their entries with the class.

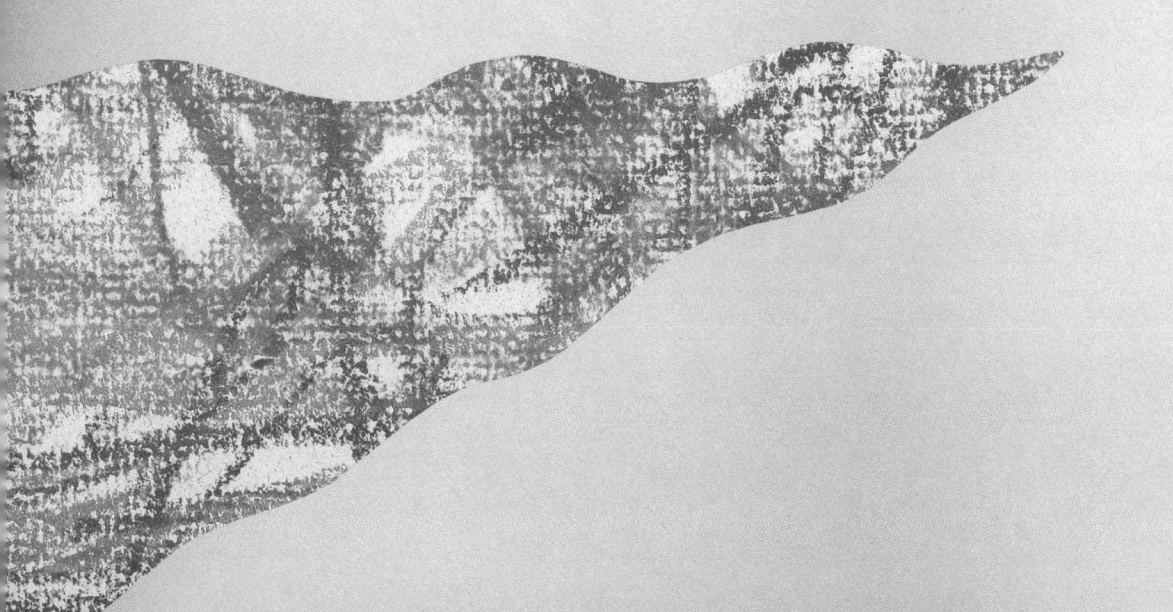

A Dramatic Performance

Raise the curtain and turn on the spotlights!

Invite some children, perhaps wearing paper boutonnieres, to usher the audience to their seats before the performance begins. This is an important day and children should feel a sense of pride and ownership as they share the results of their dramatic endeavors with family and friends.

If possible, videotape or photograph the performance for any family members who are unable to attend. Invite guests to examine the writing and art that children have produced in this theme.

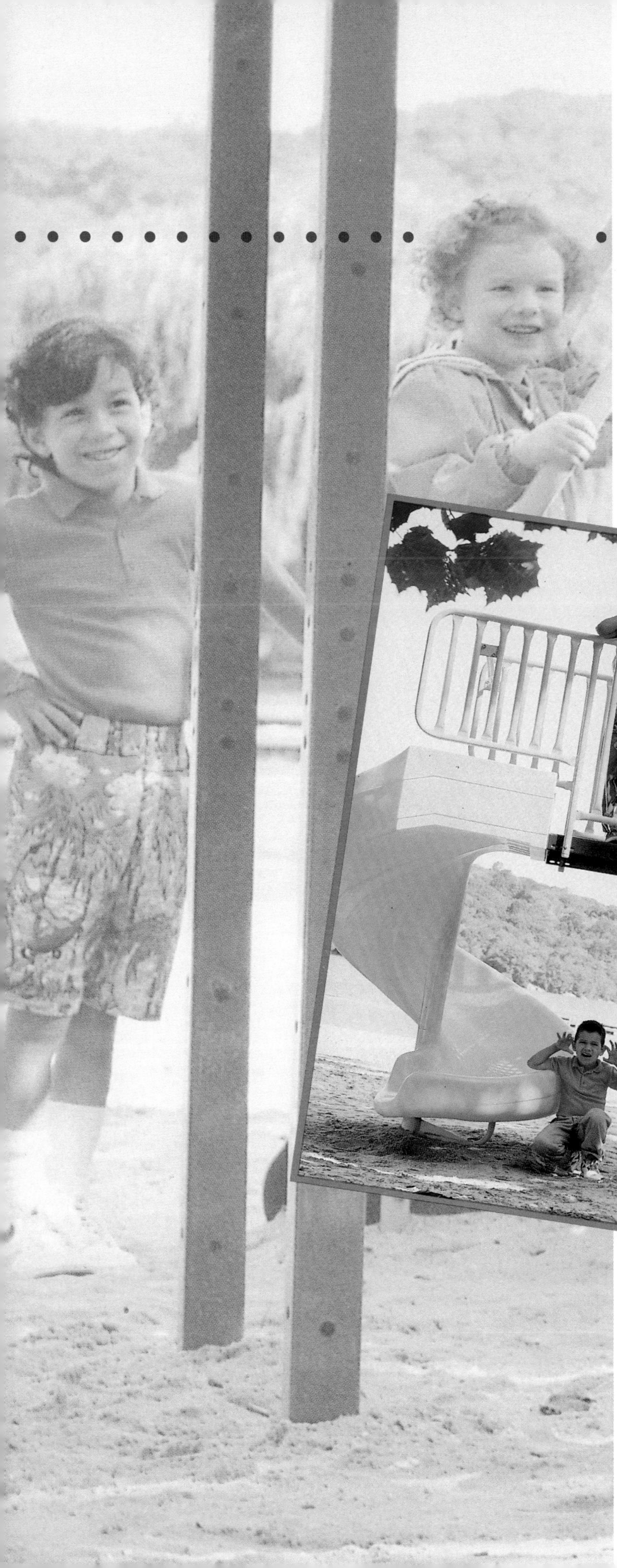

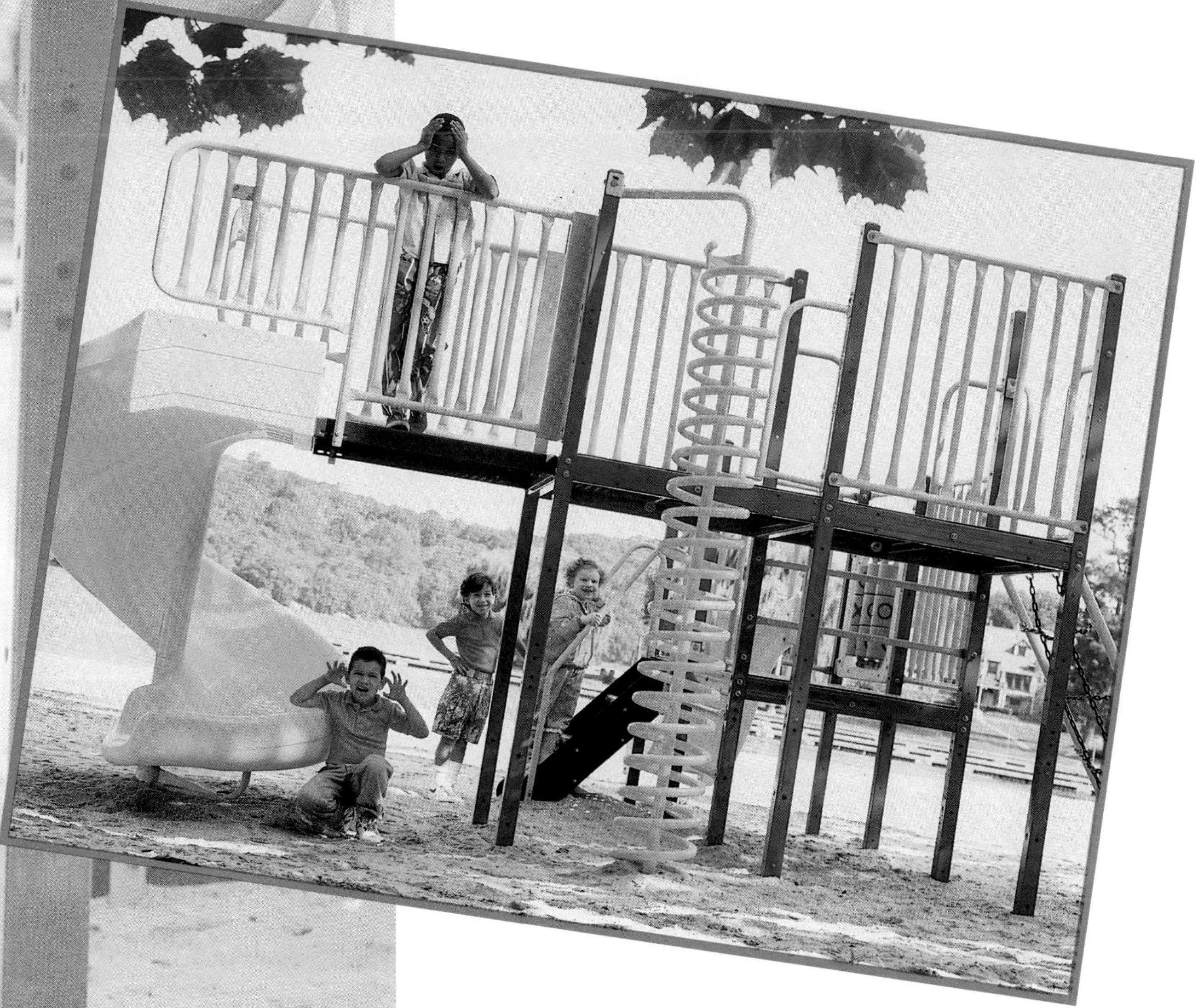

Into the Learning Centers!

▼

94

*L*earning Centers can be places where children learn independently, from one another, and from you! Any of these engaging activities can motivate children to become literacy learners.

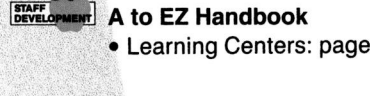
A to EZ Handbook
• Learning Centers: page 270

READING CENTER

—*Acting Out Books! page 96*

DRAMATIC PLAY CENTER

—*Put on a Puppet Show! page 97*

HANDS ON! LANGUAGE CENTER

—*Exploring Language through Manipulatives! page 98*

WRITING CENTER

—*Promoting Emergent Writing! page 99*

MUSIC CENTER

—*Acting Out Feelings through Song! page 100*

ART CENTER

—*Create Trolls, Dragons, and the Tragadabas! page 101*

GAMES CENTER

—*Play Variations of "In Grandma's Trunk"! page 102*

MATH CENTER

—*All About Three! page 103*

SCIENCE CENTER

—*Animal, Vegetable, and Mineral! page 104*

READING CENTER

ACTING OUT BOOKS!

Resources   ***I'm Going on a Dragon Hunt * Stone Soup * Big Book of Handtalk Zoo * Big Book of Poems * Big Book of Songs * Sing & Read Little Books and Audiocassettes * Songs and Stories Audiocassettes ***** theme-related books (See MORE BOOKS TO SHARE!, pages 32-33.) * tape recorder

Setting Up!   Display the books in an inviting manner for shared and emergent readings. Encourage dramatizations of the stories by providing story-related props such as a large pot and three round stones or a large straw hat and a net. You might also wish to make story characters of oaktag or flannel (for a flannel board).

• Place the Sing & Read Little Book and Audiocassette for "Eency, Weency Spider" by the tape recorder.

• Invite children to listen to "The Terrible Tragadabas" on the SONGS AND STORIES AUDIOCASSETTES.

Centers in Action!   Invite children to explore the books and materials displayed. Keep adding books and materials to the center throughout the theme and encourage children to do the same. Display the theme Big Books and keep the Big Book pointer near them so that children can model being teachers! You may also wish to note which books children enjoy the most and reread those books to the class or to small groups.

DRAMATIC PLAY CENTER

PUT ON A PUPPET SHOW!

Resources large cardboard box * oaktag * crayons or markers * glue * tongue depressors * construction paper * stapler * play money * the theater section of a newspaper * programs from professional or amateur productions

Setting Up!

- Cut out one side and a window from a large cardboard box to make a theater.

- Draw or trace the three billy goats and the troll on pieces of oaktag. Cut these characters out and tape each of them to a tongue depressor to make stick puppets.

- Cut pieces of the construction paper into 3″ × 2″ rectangular tickets.

- Staple pieces of construction paper along the long, left side to make booklets.

- Arrange chairs for the audience in front of the puppet theater.

Centers in Action!
Encourage children to become puppeteers, a narrator, ushers, and members of an audience at a puppet theater. Children may wish to include one or more of the following activities in their dramatic play.

- Children can decorate the theater for the play by displaying posters, announcements, and programs.

Children will be motivated to read and write as they participate in the production of the puppet show.

- Children can write and illustrate their own programs to distribute before the play that tell about the story and the children involved in the production.

- Children can tape pieces of construction paper together to make theater posters announcing the production of "The Three Billy Goats Gruff."

- The ushers can write *ticket* on each 3″ × 2″ piece of construction paper and sell the tickets to the audience.

- The ushers can escort the members of the audience to their seats.

- The narrator can introduce the puppeteers as well as narrate the story.

Modeling some of the behaviors described above will increase the likelihood of children incorporating them into their own play.

HANDS ON! LANGUAGE CENTER

EXPLORING LANGUAGE THROUGH MANIPULATIVES!

Resources *Rhyme and Chime Strips ("Zippety! Zippety! Zim, zim, zim!" and "Quack, Quack, Quack")* * pocket chart and stand * *Alphabet Posters for Zz and Qq* * *ABC cards* * *slate board* * chalk * *sponge letters* * *letter stamps* * *linked letter cubes* * letter blocks * *magnetic letters* * paper * pads * pencils * crayons

Setting Up! You may wish to set up this center near the Word Walls suggested in the Exploring Print lessons. Encourage children to explore language independently and periodically suggest the theme-related activities described under Centers in Action!

Centers in Action!

- Children can use sponge letters and letter stamps to trace and print the letters *Z, z,* and *Q, q.*

- Children may like to draw pictures of striped zebras, zoos, or zippers, then write about their pictures. For the letters *Q, q,* children can draw pictures of quiet places, queens, or quails, and then write about them.

- Children can also create Zany Zoos by printing letters with letter stamps, then drawing on the letters to turn them into animals.

- Invite children to draw and label pictures from *I'm Going on a Dragon Hunt, Stone Soup,* and *Handtalk Zoo.*

Z is in zebra and q is in queen!

Writing Center

Resources paper * construction paper * crayons * pencils * markers * stone * cooking pot

Setting Up! Encourage each child to write independently or with partners or small groups about topics of their own choosing or suggest any of the theme-related activities listed in Centers in Action!

Centers in Action!

- **Picture Dictionary** Invite children to draw pictures of hand signs and write their meanings. Children may use the signs shown in *Handtalk Zoo* as a model. When the pictures and writing have been completed, children can combine their pages into a picture dictionary of hand signs and their meanings.

- **Story Innovation** What would happen if the main character in *I'm Going on a Dragon Hunt* could not remember how to get home after finding the dragon? Invite children to write and illustrate their own variations of this story or write and illustrate their own story based on this one.

Children have many reasons to write in the Act It Out! Writing Center.

- **Magic Stone Wishes** Provide a round stone similar to the "magic" stone in *Stone Soup.* Then invite children to hold it, make wishes, and record these wishes on paper. Wishes can then be tossed into a pot labeled "Wishes Soup."

- **Soup Recipes** Invite children to write and draw pictures for their own recipes showing the ingredients and steps to follow for making a soup they would like.

- **Newspaper Articles** Children can record any of the story events in a newspaper article. Children might like to describe the class field trip to the zoo, the hunt and escape from a dragon, or the three soldiers' triumphant concoction of stone soup. You may also wish to encourage children to draw pictures to accompany their article.

Provide time for children to write invitations, announcements, programs, signs, and thank-you notes for the dramatic performance in Team Work/Theme Work. See pages 38–39 and 92–93.

Music Center

Resources chart paper * butcher paper * crayons * markers * stapler * blank audiocassette * tape recorder

Setting Up! Write out the words for "If You're Happy and You Know It" on the chalkboard or on chart paper. Sing the song once, then sing it again with children. If possible, make a tape recording of children singing the first verse and place this recording along with a tape recorder and the copy of the words in the Music Center.

Centers in Action! Invite children to act out being happy as they sing this song again. Then suggest that children make up verses for this song about other feelings such as mad, sad, or tired. Encourage children to sing these verses and act out the feelings they are singing about. Children can also write each verse that describes a different feeling on a piece of chart paper, illustrate that feeling, then combine all the pages into a big book.

Children can express themselves through music.

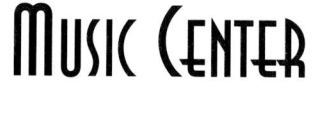

If You're Happy and You Know It

If you're happy and you know it, clap your hands. (Clap, clap)
If you're happy and you know it, clap your hands. (Clap, clap)
If you're happy and you know it, then your face
will surely show it.
If you're happy and you know it, clap your hands. (Clap, clap)

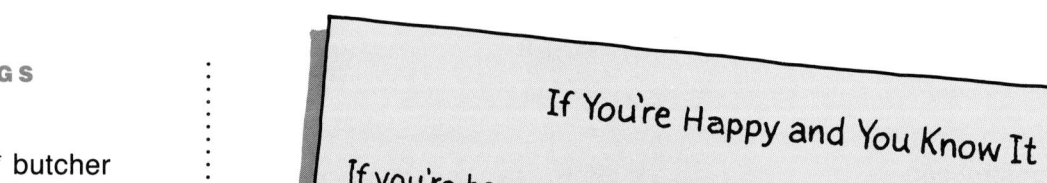

100

Art Center

CREATE TROLLS, DRAGONS, AND THE TRAGADABAS!

Resources clay or salt modeling dough (½ cup flour, 1 cup water, 1 cup salt, a saucepan, wax paper, food coloring, and an airtight container) * construction paper * paint * paintbrushes * crayons * markers * paper clips or bobby pins * buttons * yarn * glue

Setting Up!
- **Salt Modeling Dough:** Mix the flour, water, salt, and food coloring in a saucepan and stir it over a low heat. When the mixture becomes thick and rubbery, remove it from the heat and spoon it onto a floured sheet of wax paper. Let it cool before use. The dough can be stored in an airtight container or dried in a few days if left out in the open air.

- Arrange the buttons, paper clips or bobby pins, and yarn on the table. Then discuss trolls, dragons, and tragadabases and remind children that these creatures are make-believe.

Centers in Action! Invite children to create their own trolls, dragons, or tragadabases out of clay or salt modeling dough. Children can employ their own methods or try one of the following ideas:

- Use a paper clip or bobby pin to scratch a pattern of scales or hair in the clay or modeling dough.

- Use buttons to create eyes like the troll's, which were described as being "as big as saucers."

- Use yarn to create hair.

Using shoe boxes, children may also like to create the troll's bridge, the store in which the terrible tragadabas stayed, or the cave of the dragon. Children can paint the shoe boxes and decorate them with construction paper to make them look like bridges, stores, and caves.

Games Center

PLAY VARIATIONS OF "IN GRANDMA'S TRUNK"!

Resources chart paper * markers

Setting Up! Review the game "In Grandma's Trunk" in which children take turns adding to the sentence *In Grandma's trunk I packed _____.* One child begins the game by repeating the sentence and completing it by naming an appropriate item. The next child repeats the same sentence with the previously named item, and adds another appropriate item. The game continues with each child repeating the phrase with all previously named items and then adding a new one.

Then tell children that they can play different versions of this game based on what they have read in ACT IT OUT! Write the following lines on the chalkboard or on chart paper:

(For *Handtalk Zoo*)	I went to the zoo and I saw a _____.
(For *I'm Going on a Dragon Hunt*)	I went on a hunt and I came to a _____.
(For *Stone Soup*)	In my stone soup, I put _____.

Centers in Action!

- **Follow the Leader** Ask a volunteer to play the part of the leader and to lead the other children about the Games Center as he or she describes the obstacles in the center. For example, the leader might say "Hello, what's this? It's a desk. Can't jump over it. Can't go through it. Have to go around it." Children can continue this game until each of them has had an opportunity to be the leader.

- **In Grandma's Trunk** Invite groups of children to sit in a circle and play a version of "In Grandma's Trunk" by using one of the lines you have written. Then encourage children to try to play this game using each of the other lines that you wrote.

- **What Am I?** Children can take turns acting out the role of animals such as those found in *Handtalk Zoo* as other children try to guess what animal is being acted out. The child acting out the animal may wish to answer questions such as *Do you swim in water?* or *Do you have stripes?*

Math Center

Developing a concrete understanding of the number 3!

ALL ABOUT THREE!

Resources pennies * beans * beads * pebbles * shells * seeds * pasta bows * marbles * paper cups * glue * glitter, sand, or salt * construction paper * crayons or markers

Setting Up! Invite children to name what there were three of in the stories *Stone Soup*, "The Three Billy Goats Gruff," and "The Terrible Tragadabas."

Centers in Action! To help children develop a concrete feel for the number 3, invite them to participate in one or more of the following activities.

- **Counting Three** Invite children to divide the pennies, beans, beads, pebbles, shells, seeds, pasta bows, or marbles into groups of three. Then have a volunteer hide all, some, or none of each group of items under a cup; the remaining items from the group should be placed on top of the cup. Encourage the other children to guess how many of these counters are on top of the cup and how many are hidden underneath it. When the children have guessed, they can pick up the cup to see if they answered correctly.

- **Drawing in Threes** Children can draw pictures of three friends, family members, or pets. Encourage children to write about their drawings and to sign their work.

- **Hunting for Three** Children can go on a hunt about the Math Center and classroom for three of anything. Some examples of things children might find three of include blocks, containers, paintbrushes, crayons, pages, and books. Encourage children to display their collections in the Math Center.

- **Number Cards** Children can write the number 3 on the front of a piece of folded construction paper, trace over that number with glue, then sprinkle glitter, salt, or sand over the glue. When the glue is dry, children can shake off the excess glitter, salt, or sand, then trace over the number 3 lightly with their fingers. On the inside of the card, children can glue three beans, beads, pennies, pebbles, seeds, or pasta bows.

Science Center

ANIMAL, VEGETABLE, AND MINERAL!

Resources butcher paper * large sheets of paper with three holes punched in the left side of each sheet * yarn * crayons or markers * scale * shoe-box lids or polystyrene meat trays * glue * stones of different sizes

Setting Up!
- On a piece of butcher paper, start a chart of animals that swim in water. Be sure to leave plenty of space for children's drawings around the chart. Display the chart in the Science Center.

Animals That Swim in Water	Animals That Don't Swim in Water
alligators	goats
sea lions	tigers
penguins	zebras

- Review *I'm Going on a Dragon Hunt* with children. Then take them on a nature walk. Encourage them to observe the area around them much like the boy in *I'm Going on a Dragon Hunt* takes note of the area around him.

- Display the stones, scale, shoe-box lids or polystyrene meat trays, and glue on a table in the center.

Centers in Action! Invite children to participate in one or more of the following theme-related activities.

- **Chart It!** Children can add animals to each column in the chart depending on whether or not those animals swim or spend time in water. Children can also draw pictures and label their drawings in the space around the chart.

- **A Nature Walk** Children can tell about their nature walk by drawing and writing about it. How was their adventure like that of the boy in *I'm Going on a Dragon Hunt*?

- **Little, Middle-Size, or Big?** Children can use the shoe-box lids or trays to sort the stones into three categories: little, middle-size, and big, just as in "The Three Billy Goats Gruff" and "The Terrible Tragadabas." Then children can weigh the stones to see whether the big stones weigh more or less than the little stones. Encourage children to draw pictures of each of the stones and label the size of each as *little, middle-size,* or *big.*

Acknowledgments

The publisher gratefully acknowledges permission to reprint the following copyrighted material:

"Beware, My Child" by Shel Silverstein from O, WHAT NONSENSE! edited by William Cole. Copyright © 1966 by Shel Silverstein. Reprinted by permission of William Cole for the author.

"Big, Bigger, Biggest," © 1976 words and music by Ella Jenkins, Ell-Bern Publishing Company, 1844 North Mohawk, Chicago.

"Going to the Zoo" by Tom Paxton. © Copyright 1961, renewed 1989 Cherry Lane Music Publishing Company, Inc.

"Let's Pretend" by Tom Paxton. © Copyright 1963, renewed 1991 Cherry Lane Music Publishing Company, Inc.

"Make Believe" from CRICKETS AND BULLFROGS AND WHISPERS OF THUNDER Poems and Pictures by Harry Behn. Copyright © 1949, 1953, 1956, 1957, 1966, 1968 by Harry Behn. Copyright © renewed 1977 by Alice L. Behn. Copyright © renewed 1981 by Alice Behn Goebel, Pamela Behn Adam, Prescott Behn and Peter Behn. Reprinted by permission of Marian Reiner.

"On Our Way" from CATCH A LITTLE RHYME by Eve Merriam. Copyright © 1966 by Eve Merriam. Reprinted by permission of Marian Reiner.

"Sitting in the Soup," © 1988 words and music by Sarah Pirtle, A Gentle Wind, Box 3103, Albany, NY 12203.

"Time to Wake Up!" by Barbara Staton. © 1987 Rockhaven Music.

Cover and Program Design: Michaelis/Carpelis Design Associates, Inc.

Additional Design: Textart, Inc.

Production: Textart, Inc.
Michaelis/Carpelis Design Associates, Inc.

Illustration

Cover Illustration: Rebecca Grimes

Back Cover Illustration: Patrick Merrell

Four-color airbrush: Brian Dugan, Mark Kaplan, Mary Ellen Senor

Poetry airbrush backgrounds: Mark Kaplan

Learning Center Logos: Rachel Geswaldo

Lesson Opener Panels: Fanny Mellet Berry, 58, 88; Kathleen Kinkoff, 52, 82; Leo Monahan, 34, 64; Marti Shohet, 40, 70; Andrea Wisnewski, 46, 76.

Four-color illustration: Beth Roberge, 49; Pat Wong, 45, 61, 69.

Black line art: Network Graphics, 35, 37, 38, 39, 41, 44, 47, 53, 59, 65, 68, 71, 73, 77, 79, 83, 84, 89, 100, 104; Adam Weston, 56, 62, 63, 80, 86, 87.

Photography

All photographs are by Macmillan/McGraw-Hill School Division (MMSD) except as noted below.

51: Scott Harvey for MMSD. 53: Scott Harvey for MMSD. 55: Scott Harvey for MMSD. 57: Scott Harvey for MMSD. 73: Ken Karp for MMSD. 75: Ken Karp for MMSD. 77: Ken Karp for MMSD. 81: Scott Harvey for MMSD. 87: Scott Harvey for MMSD. 92, 93: Scott Harvey for MMSD. 97: Scott Harvey for MMSD. 98: Ken Karp for MMSD. 99: RMIP/Richard Haynes for MMSD. 100: Ken Karp for MMSD. 102: Ken Karp for MMSD. 103: Scott Harvey for MMSD. 104: RMIP/Richard Haynes for MMSD.

Index

A ZOO OF ZEBRAS AND Z's

Z z
<u>z</u>ebra

Write Z and z.

Z z

Say the picture word on each zebra.
Color the zebra if the picture word begins like <u>zebra</u>.

QUILT OF Q's FOR QUAILS

Q q
quail

Write Q and q.

Look at the quilt.
Say each picture name in each of the patches.
Color the picture and the patch
if the picture name begins like quilt.

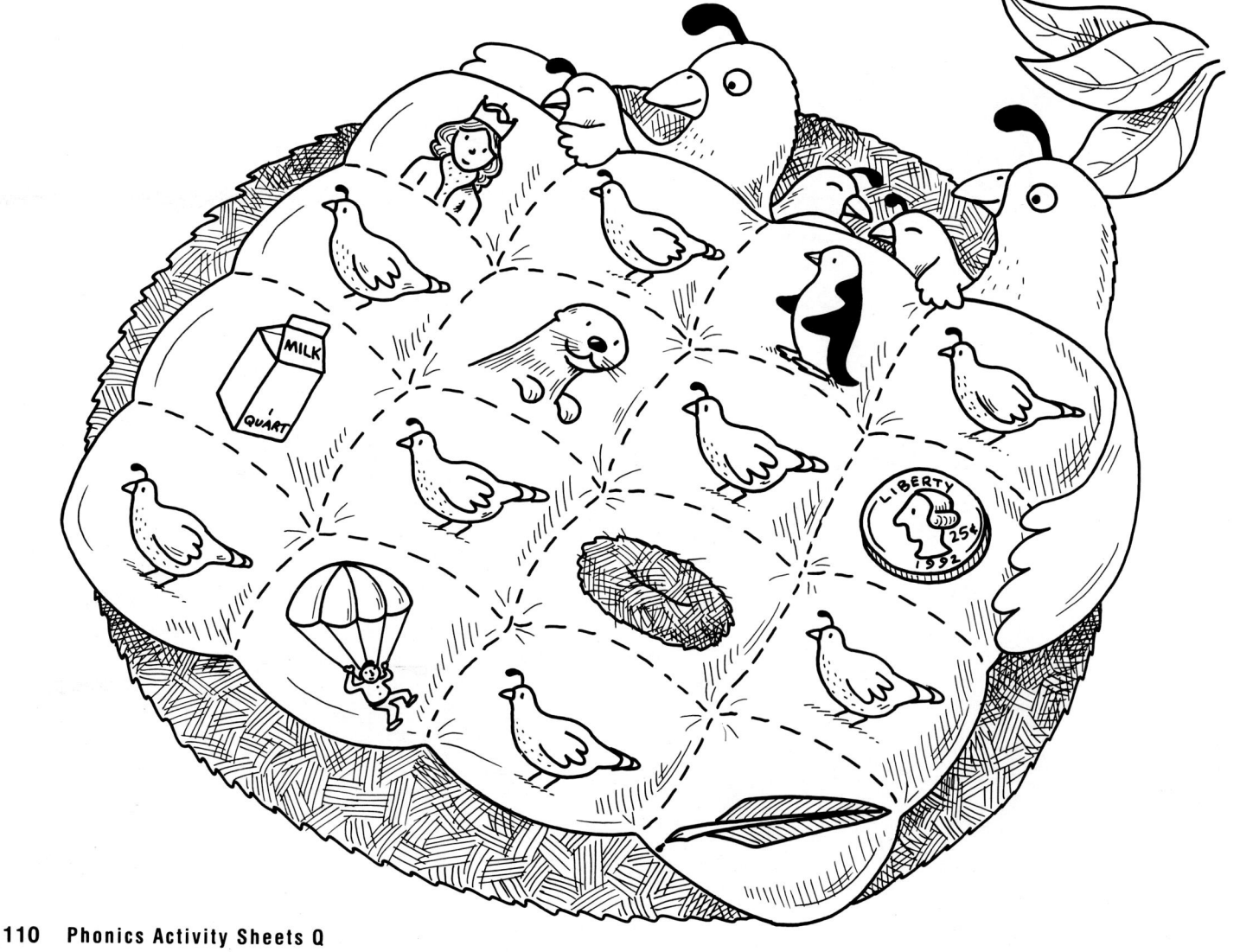

Macmillan/McGraw-Hill

THEME 12

Wonder About It!

TRADE BOOK LITERATURE

EARLY READERS

OTHER RESOURCES

- Big Book of Songs:
  pp. 38–39
- Big Book of Poems:
  pp. 34–35
- Big Book of Alphabet Rhymes
  and Chimes: pp. 16, 33
- Read Aloud Anthology:
  pp. 90–92, 93–97

- Songs and Stories
  Audiocassettes
    Story Songs: Tape 3, Side 2
    Storytellings: Tape 3, Side 2
- Sing a Sound
  Audiocassettes: Tape 2,
  Side 3; Tape 3, Side 6
- Listening Library
  Audiocassettes:
  Tape 5, Side 10

THEME OBJECTIVES

READING/WRITING LISTENING/SPEAKING

- shares ideas about the earth, sky, sun, clouds, and moon
- participates in creating and presenting a Works of Wonder display
- participates in listening, speaking, and viewing activities
- cooperates with others
- reads, writes, and draws pictures about natural phenomena
- appreciates and values diverse points of view
- develops an awareness of the classroom as a community of learners
- recognizes cultural attitudes and customs
- retells stories
- participates in a variety of activities in response to literature

PHONICS AND DECODING

- discriminates the sound of letters: /i/*Ii*, /ks/*Xx*
- identifies upper and lowercase letters: *Ii, Xx*
- recognizes sound/letter relationships: /i/*Ii*, /ks/*Xx*
- writes upper and lowercase letters: *Ii, Xx*

CONCEPTS OF PRINT

- understands book concepts: cover, title, author, illustrator
- demonstrates awareness of directionality, letters, words, sentences, punctuation

Tell a Story / Sing a Song

AUTHORS

Elaine Mei Aoki

•

Virginia A. Arnold

•

James Flood

•

James V. Hoffman

•

Diane Lapp

•

Miriam Martinez

•

Annemarie Sullivan
Palincsar

•

Michael Priestley

•

Carl B. Smith

•

William H. Teale

•

Josefina Villamil
Tinajero

•

Arnold W. Webb

•

Karen D. Wood

Macmillan
McGraw-Hill

New York   Farmington

Authors, Consultants

Multicultural and Educational Consultants

Yvonne Beamer, Joyce Buckner, Alma Flor Ada, Helen Gillotte,
Cheryl Hudson, Narcita Medina, Lorraine Monroe, James R. Murphy,
Sylvia Peña, Joseph B. Rubin, Ramon Santiago, Cliff Trafzer,
Hai Tran, Esther Lee Yao

Literature Consultants

Ashley Bryan, Joan I. Glazer, Paul Janeczko, Margaret H. Lippert

International Consultants

Edward B. Adams, Barbara Johnson, Raymond L. Marshall

Music and Audio Consultants

John Farrell, Marilyn C. Davidson, Vincent Lawrence,
Sarah Pirtle, Susan R. Snyder,
Rick and Deborah Witkowski

Macmillan/McGraw-Hill

A Division of The McGraw·Hill Companies

Copyright © 1997 Macmillan/McGraw-Hill, a Division of the Educational and
Professional Publishing Group of The McGraw-Hill Companies, Inc.

Macmillan/McGraw-Hill
1221 Avenue of the Americas
New York, New York 10020

Printed in the United States of America

ISBN 0-02-181371-X / K, U.12

2 3 4 5 6 7 8 9 BCM 02 01 00 99 98 97

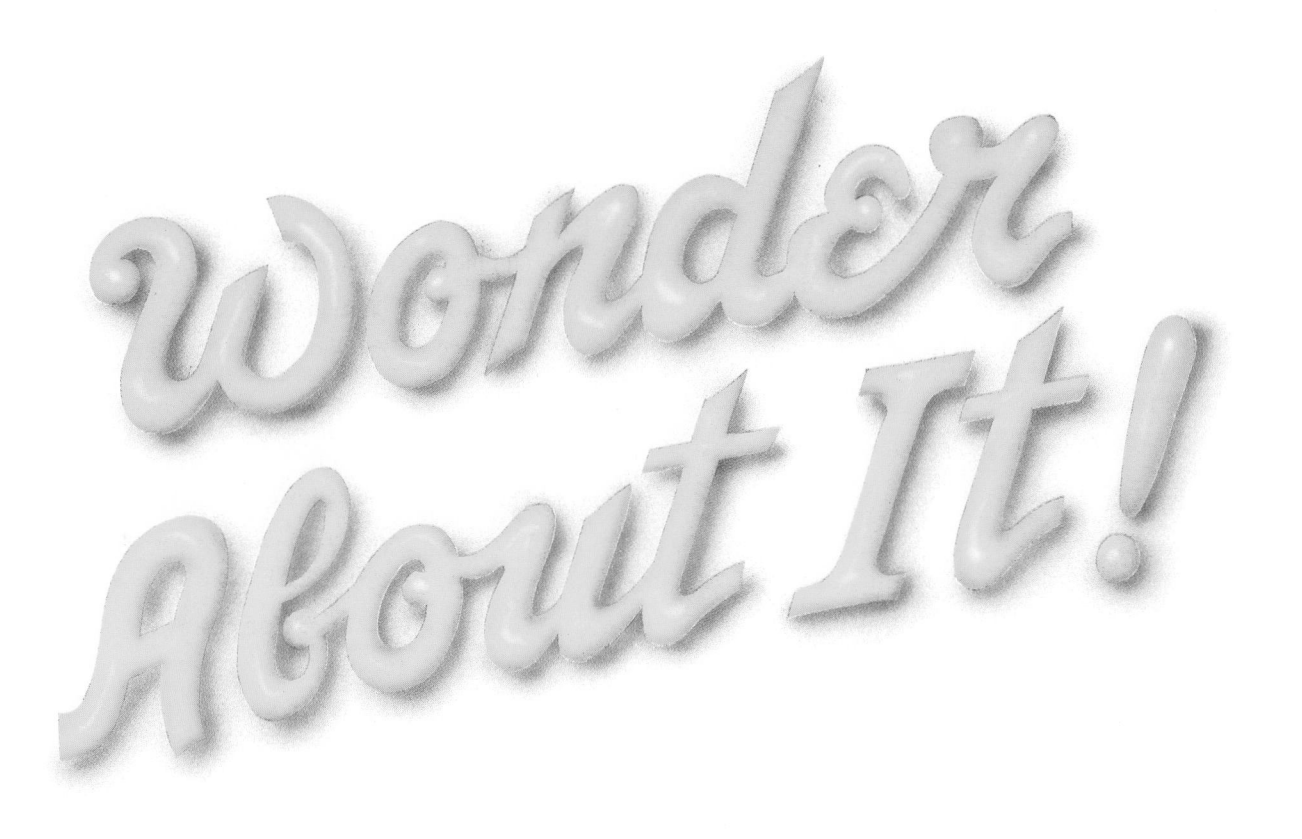

Wonder About It!

*To my husband, Roberto,
to my children, Gloria, Ana, Bert, and Pat,
for their love
and support of everything that I do and
to my former kindergarten bilingual students
for having been my best teachers.*
—Josie Tinajero

Contents

PRESENTING WONDER ABOUT IT!

1 INTRODUCING THE THEME

Wonder About It!
An exploration of thoughts and wonders!
Theme Word: THINKER
Theme Poem: "I Arise"
 an Eskimo Song
Theme Song: "Twinkle, Twinkle, Little Star"
 a traditional song

Contents

/NTRODUCING TELL A STORY/SING A SONG

A New View of Kindergarten!

Welcome children to a print-rich, activity-based environment that nurtures emergent literacy!

19 BIG BOOKS!

48 TRADE BOOKS!

16 THEMES!

PROGRAM RESOURCES

Big Book of Songs
Theme Songs!

Big Book of Poems
Theme Poems!

The more we get together,
Together, together,
The more we get together,
The happier we'll be.

For your friends are my friends,
And my friends are your friends,
The more we get together,
The happier we'll be.

Traditional

THE MORE WE GET TOGETHER

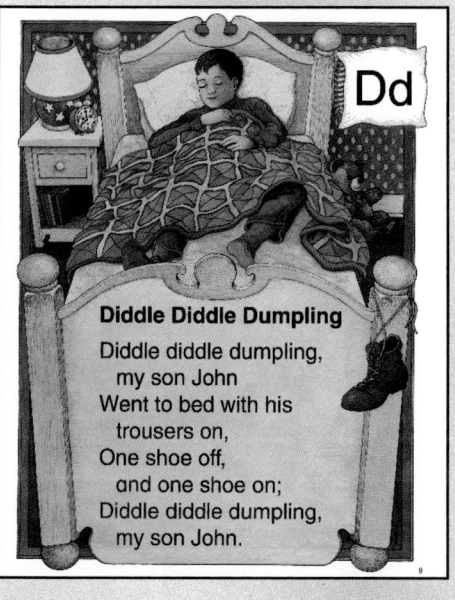

Cat's in the Cupboard

Great A, Little a,
Bouncing B!
The cat's in the cupboard
And can't see me.

Diddle Diddle Dumpling

Diddle diddle dumpling,
my son John
Went to bed with his
trousers on,
One shoe off,
and one shoe on;
Diddle diddle dumpling,
my son John.

Big Book of Alphabet Rhymes and Chimes
Verses for teaching the alphabet and concepts of print!
Plus the "Alphabet Song"!

Rhyme and Chime Strips
Each Rhyme and Chime
on illustrated strips to use in
pocket charts for
Hands On! Language
experiences!

| Cat's in the Cupboard |
| Great A, Little a, |
| Bouncing B! |
| The cat's in the cupboard |
| And can't see me. |

A a a a

B b B b

C c C c

**Teacher's Read Aloud
Anthology**
32 Read Aloud selections
from cultures around
the world!

7

16 LITERATURE THEME PACKS

including 3 Trade Books (1 with a companion Big Book) and a Teacher's Planning Guide!

"Slither," said the snake in the cool morning air.

"Twitter," said the sparrows.
"Trot," said the mare.

"Paddle," Said the Swan

Written and illustrated by Gloria Kamen

IN THE PARK
An Excursion in Four Languages
by ESTHER HAUTZIG
Pictures by EZRA JACK KEATS

Big Talk
By Miriam Schlein
Pictures by Joan Auclair

Big Book of "Paddle," Said the Swan

Also Available—

LISTENING LIBRARY AUDIOCASSETTES for Big Books!

SONGS AND STORIES AUDIOCASSETTES with Theme Songs, sound effects, and storytellings!

SING A SOUND AUDIOCASSETTES with songs to encourage language play and to develop phonemic awareness!

TEACHER'S PLANNING GUIDE

SPEAK OUT!
MACMILLAN/McGRAW-HILL

Teacher's Planning Guide for Speak Out! Your resource for organizing activities—

- Sharing Time
- Reading and Writing
- Exploring Print
- Into the Learning Centers

ANCILLARIES

ABC Cards
Textured letter forms for tactile learning!

Alphabet Posters
26 full-color posters!

Sing & Read Books and Audiocassettes
16 little books, one for each theme song, with audiocassettes of children singing and then reading the selection!

Literature Activity Book with
- Activities for introducing each theme
- Tell-a-Tale Take-Home Books
- Responding to Literature pages
- Exploring Print activities
- Just for Fun pages, too!

Also Available—

HomeWords:
Newsletters and more to send home each month!

Sights & Sounds:
Interactive software for children to use in their exploration of the sounds of language and the letters that represent them!

Tell a Story/Sing a Song

PROGRAM THEMES	TRADE BOOKS	READ ALOUDS
1 GETTING TOGETHER	**BIG BOOK: *Getting Together*** by George Ancona ***What Will Mommy Do When I'm at School?*** by Dolores Johnson ***I'm Busy, Too*** by Norma Simon, illustrated by Dora Leder	**The Great Big Enormous Turnip** a Russian tale by Alexei Tolstoi **The Rabbit and the Elephant** a folk tale from Ghana retold by Ruthilde Kronberg and Patricia C. McKissack
2 SHARING WITH FRIENDS	**BIG BOOK: *Frog in the Middle*** by Susanna Gretz ***Will I Have a Friend?*** by Miriam Cohen, illustrated by Lillian Hoban ***Friends*** by Helme Heine	**The Lion and the Mouse** a fable by Aesop **The Three Friends** a folk tale from India retold by Isabel Wyatt
3 SPEAK OUT!	**BIG BOOK: *"Paddle," Said the Swan*** by Gloria Kamen ***In the Park*** by Esther Hautzig, illustrated by Ezra Jack Keats ***Big Talk*** by Miriam Schlein, illustrated by Joan Auclair	**The Long One** a Masai tale from East Africa by Verna Aardema **The Boy Who Cried Wolf** a fable by Aesop retold by Anne Terry White
4 LISTEN FOR SOUNDS!	**BIG BOOK: *Rain Talk*** by Mary Serfozo, illustrated by Keiko Narahashi ***Country Crossing*** by Jim Aylesworth, illustrated by Ted Rand ***Apt. 3*** by Ezra Jack Keats	**The Bremen Town Musicians** a German folk tale retold by Anne Rockwell **The Race Between Toad and Donkey** a Jamaican folk tale edited by Roger D. Abrahams

Theme Words	Theme Songs	Theme Poems	Exploring Print Lessons
HELPER	**The More We Get Together** a traditional song	**Together** by Paul Engle	Games and activities related to children's names
FRIEND	**Be a Friend** a traditional song	**Making Friends** by Eloise Greenfield	Games and activities related to friends and their names, and days of the week
SPEAKER	**The Buenas Song** a Hispanic song by Aaron Schroeder and David Grover	**Good Morning** by Muriel Sipe	Rhyme Time: Games, songs, and activities for rhyming
LISTENER	**The Little Red Caboose** Bernice Johnson Reagon's version of the traditional song	**Ears Hear** by Lucia and James L. Hymes, Jr.	*Big Book of Alphabet Rhymes and Chimes:* **Cc** Cat's in the Cupboard **Pp** Pease Porridge Hot

Tell a Story / Sing a Song

Program Themes	Trade Books	Read Alouds
5 SING AND DANCE AWAY!	**BIG BOOK: *Oh, A-Hunting We Will Go*** by John Langstaff, illustrated by Nancy Winslow Parker ***Max*** by Rachel Isadora ***The Little Band*** by James Sage, illustrated by Keiko Narahashi	**The Twelve Dancing Princesses** a German fairy tale by the Brothers Grimm **The Clever Turtle** a Hispanic folk tale retold by Margaret H. Lippert
6 PAINT IT UP!	**BIG BOOK: *Who Said Red?*** by Mary Serfozo, illustrated by Keiko Narahashi ***The little Bear Book*** by Anthony Browne ***circles, triangles and squares*** by Tana Hoban	**The Black Cat** an American folk tale retold by Margaret H. Lippert **Ma Lien and the Magic Brush** a tale from China by Hisako Kimishima retold by Alvin Tresselt
7 EAT IT UP!	**BIG BOOK: *Bread, Bread, Bread*** by Ann Morris, photographs by Ken Heyman ***Gregory, the Terrible Eater*** by Mitchell Sharmat, illustrated by Jose Aruego and Ariane Dewey ***What's on My Plate?*** by Ruth Belov Gross, illustrated by Isadore Seltzer	**The Woman Who Flummoxed the Fairies** a Scottish folk tale retold by Sorche Nic Leodhas **Señor Billy Goat** a Hispanic folk tale retold by Pura Belpré
8 BUILD IT UP!	**BIG BOOK: *Changes, Changes*** by Pat Hutchins ***I Read Signs*** by Tana Hoban ***Round Trip*** by Ann Jonas	**The Three Little Pigs** an English fairy tale retold by Flora Annie Steel **Why the Moon Is in the Sky** an Ashanti folk tale from West Africa retold by Margaret H. Lippert

Theme Words	Theme Songs	Theme Poems	Exploring Print Lessons
INGER ANCER	**You'll Sing a Song and I'll Sing a Song** by Ella Jenkins	**Singing-Time** by Rose Fyleman	*Big Book of Alphabet Rhymes and Chimes:* **Hh** Hippity Hop to Bed **Mm** Miss Mary Mack
RTIST	**I Know the Colors in the Rainbow** by Ella Jenkins	**Paints** by Ilo Orleans	*Big Book of Alphabet Rhymes and Chimes:* **Ss** Sing a Song of Sixpence **Bb** Bounce High, Bounce Low
OOK	**Short'ning Bread** a traditional Southern song	**Through the Teeth** a folk rhyme	*Big Book of Alphabet Rhymes and Chimes:* **Gg** Gobble, Gobble **Aa** Eat an Apple
UILDER	**Johnny Builds with One Hammer** a traditional song	**Buildings** by Myra Cohn Livingston	*Big Book of Alphabet Rhymes and Chimes:* **Rr** R Is for Ribbon **Ee** Engine, Engine, Number Nine

PROGRAM THEMES	TRADE BOOKS	READ ALOUDS
9 MEET PAT HUTCHINS	**BIG BOOK:** *Titch* by Pat Hutchins *Rosie's Walk* by Pat Hutchins *Good-Night, Owl!* by Pat Hutchins	**It Could Always Be Worse** a Yiddish folk tale retold by Margot Zemach **Rainbow Crow** a Lenape tale retold by Nancy Van Laan
10 SHARE A STORY!	**BIG BOOK:** *I Had a Cat* by Mona Rabun Reeves, illustrated by Julie Downing *Little Red Hen* by Janina Domanska *Nessa's Fish* by Nancy Luenn, illustrated by Neil Waldman	**The Storytelling Stone** a Seneca tale retold by Joseph Bruchac **The Three Bears** an English folk tale retold by Margaret H. Lippert
11 ACT IT OUT!	**BIG BOOK:** *Handtalk Zoo* by George Ancona and Mary Beth *Stone Soup* by Marcia Brown *I'm Going on a Dragon Hunt* by Maurice Jones, illustrated by Charlotte Firmin	**The Three Billy Goats Gruff** a Norwegian folk tale retold by Margaret H. Lippert **The Terrible Tragadabas** a tale from Spanish New Mexico by Joe Hayes
12 WONDER ABOUT IT!	**BIG BOOK:** *White Is the Moon* by Valerie Greeley *Half a Moon and One Whole Star* by Crescent Dragonwagon, illustrated by Jerry Pinkney *The Park Bench* by Fumiko Takeshita, illustrated by Mamoru Suzuki	**The Spider Weaver** a folk tale from Japan retold by Florence Sakada **The One You Don't See Coming** a folk tale from Liberia retold by Harold Courlander and George Herzog

THEME WORDS	THEME SONGS	THEME POEMS	EXPLORING PRINT LESSONS
WRITER	**Read a Book** by Marcy Marxer	**Surprise** by Beverly McLoughland	*Big Book of Alphabet Rhymes and Chimes:* **Tt** Toaster Time **Kk** A Kettle's for the Kitchen
STORYTELLER	**How About You?** by John Farrell	**Worlds I Know** by Myra Cohn Livingston	*Big Book of Alphabet Rhymes and Chimes:* **Ff** Five Little Fishies **Yy** The Yak
ACTOR	**Eency, Weency Spider** a traditional song	**On Our Way** by Eve Merriam	*Big Book of Alphabet Rhymes and Chimes:* **Qq** Quack, Quack, Quack **Zz** Zippety! Zippety! Zim, zim, zim!
THINKER	**Twinkle, Twinkle, Little Star** a traditional song	**I Arise** an Eskimo song	*Big Book of Alphabet Rhymes and Chimes:* **Ii** If All the World Was Apple Pie **Xx** What Words Begin with X?

Program Themes	Trade Books	Read Alouds
13 FIND IT OUT!	**BIG BOOK: *What Do You See?*** by Janina Domanska ***Farm Animals*** photographs by Philip Dowell and Michael Dunning ***Changes*** by Marjorie N. Allen and Shelley Rotner, photographs by Shelley Rotner	**Why Bears Have Short Tails** a Navajo legend from Arizona retold by Sandra Begay **The Plumage of the Owl/ El Plumaje del Mucaro** a Puerto Rican folk tale retold by Ricardo E. Alegría
14 MEET EZRA JACK KEATS	**BIG BOOK: *Hi, Cat!*** by Ezra Jack Keats ***Kitten for a Day*** by Ezra Jack Keats ***Pet Show!*** by Ezra Jack Keats	**Belling the Cat** a fable by Aesop retold by Joseph Jacobs **The Cat's Purr** a West Indian tale by Ashley Bryan
15 THINKING ABOUT ME	**BIG BOOK: *All I Am*** by Eileen Roe, illustrated by Helen Cogancherry ***The Train to Lulu's*** by Elizabeth Fitzgerald Howard, illustrated by Robert Casilla ***Con Mi Hermano/With My Brother*** by Eileen Roe, illustrated by Robert Casilla	**The Knee-High Man** an American black folk tale retold by Julius Lester **Anansi's Rescue from the River** a folk tale from West Africa retold by Harold Courlander
16 SETTING OUT!	**BIG BOOK: *As the Crow Flies: A First Book of Maps*** by Gail Hartman, illustrated by Harvey Stevenson ***Look Out, Patrick!*** by Paul Geraghty ***Builder of the Moon*** by Tim Wynne-Jones, illustrated by Ian Wallace	**Timimoto** a folk tale from Japan retold by Margaret H. Lippert **Jack and the Beanstalk** an English fairy tale retold by Virginia Haviland

Theme Words	Theme Songs	Theme Poems	Exploring Print Lessons
RESEARCHER	**Who Fed the Chickens?** by Ella Jenkins	**Who?** by Lilian Moore	*Big Book of Alphabet Rhymes and Chimes:* **Dd** Diddle Diddle Dumpling **Ww** Wee Willie Winkie
ILLUSTRATOR	**Library Song** by Michael Mark and Tom Chapin	**Picture People** by Myra Cohn Livingston	*Big Book of Alphabet Rhymes and Chimes:* **Ll** Lily's a Lady **Jj** Jack Be Nimble
CHILD	**I Am a Person** by Sarah Pirtle	**By Myself** by Eloise Greenfield	*Big Book of Alphabet Rhymes and Chimes:* **Nn** Nicholas Ned **Uu** Umbrellas
EXPLORER	**The Bear Went Over the Mountain** a traditional song	**Come Out** by Karla Kuskin	*Big Book of Alphabet Rhymes and Chimes:* **Oo** Polly, Put the Kettle On **Vv** Very Nice

EMERGENT WRITING

MIRIAM MARTINEZ AND WILLIAM TEALE

The emergent literacy perspective is a powerful one because it lays the foundation for promoting children's literacy development through rich, exciting, and purposeful writing opportunities in the classroom.

1. **Drawing**

2. **Scribble**

Children's Writing Strategies

In their early explorations of the writing system, young children typically do not write in conventional ways. Careful observations of children's emergent writing have revealed a general, but rather complicated, developmental pathway. As children move along this pathway, they typically use some or all of the following strategies:

1. **Drawing**

2. **Scribbling**

3. **Randomly Chosen Letters:** The child uses letters, but there is not a relationship between the letters chosen and the sounds in the words that are written.

4. **Words Copied from Environmental Print**

5. **Developmental Spelling:** There is a relationship between the letters used and the sounds in the words that are written, but only one or two of the sounds heard in words are represented. This behavior later develops to the point at which children are able to use a letter to represent every (or almost every) sound in the words that are written.

6. **Transitional Spelling:** Features of conventional spelling, like silent letters or doubling of consonants, begin to appear.

7. **Conventional Spelling**

*R*ich, Purposeful Writing Experiences

Young writers, like all writers, are most successful when they have interesting experiences to feed their writing. These include "hands on" activities, creative dramatics and art activities, content area experiences, explorations beyond the classroom, and opportunities to write about personal experiences beyond school.

Central to these efforts to ignite children's writing are rich literature experiences. One form that writing in response to literature takes is the journal. The journal is a place where children can record their thoughts, feelings, and reactions to a story they have just listened to or read.

Literature also nurtures children's own original story writing. Sometimes a story-line or story theme will serve as an invitation for the child to write about a similar experience. At other times, after reading a story with a distinctive predictable pattern, children may choose to use the same story pattern to organize their own writing.

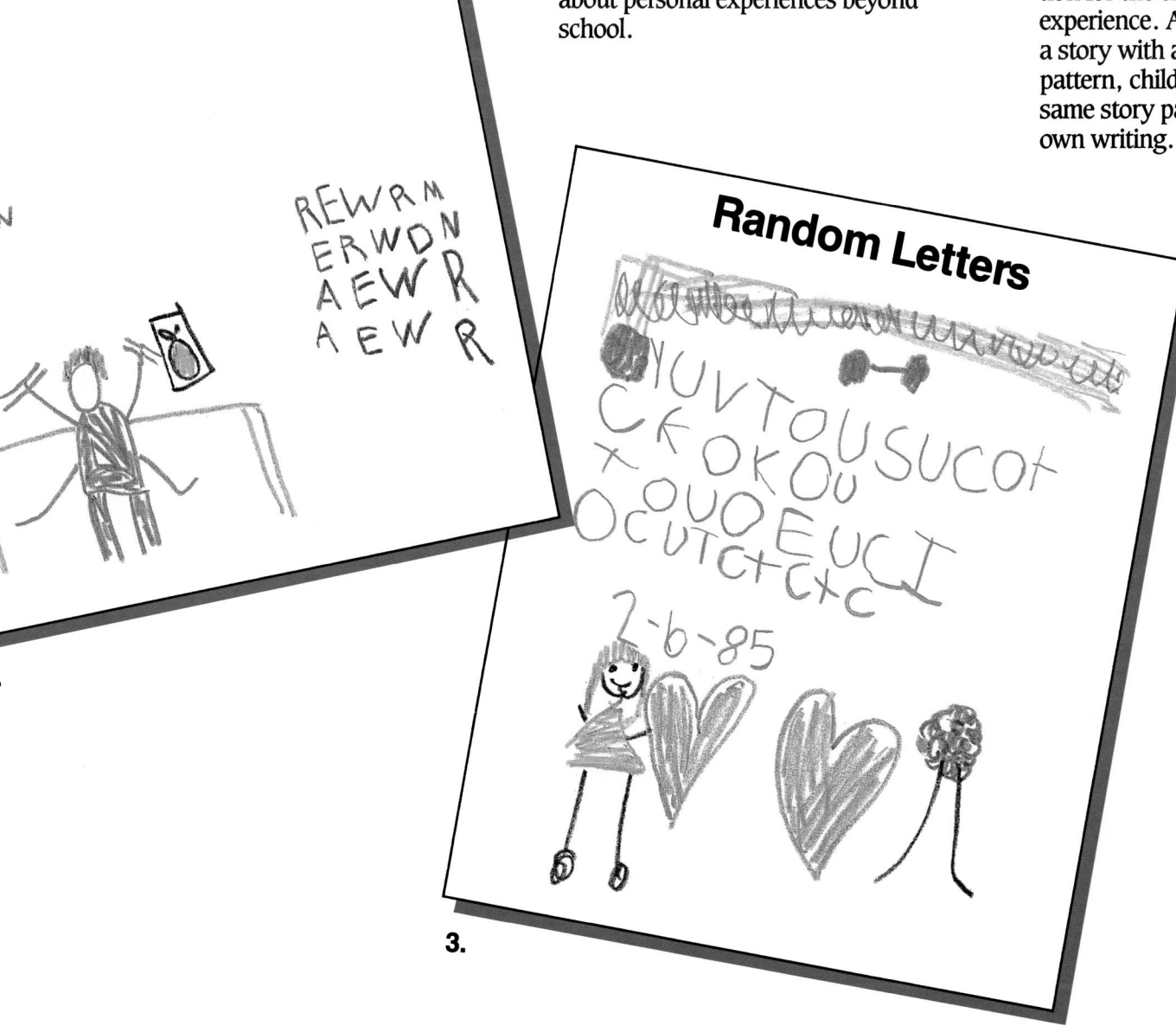

Random Letters

3.

Random Letters

3.

Emergent Writing

Children's Growth as Writers

Three dimensions signal growth in children's writing. First is evidence that the child is using increasingly more sophisticated writing strategies (drawing, scribbling, developmental spellings, and so on.). However, as we observe children's movement along this developmental pathway, it's important to remember that not every child uses all strategies, nor will a child necessarily, as he or she begins to use a more sophisticated strategy, leave less sophisticated ones behind. If anything, many children tend to expand their repertoire of strategies, using different ones for different tasks.

The second dimension of children's growth as writers is what they say. It is particularly important to look for evidence that children are learning to organize their writing better, to develop their ideas more fully, and to use features that are associated with written language rather than oral language (Once upon a time...).

However, a word of warning is in order. As children begin to use more sophisticated writing strategies (in particular, as they concentrate on developmental spellings), the content and organization of their stories and journal entries may appear to become less sophisticated for a period of time. Rather than being taken as a cause for alarm, this state of affairs should be viewed as more of a natural trade-off. When children do get more control over sound-symbol relationships, they will again be able to attend more closely to what it is they want to say and to whom they want to say it.

4.

Copying Environmental Print

OCtOb2r 18
reM
ArT
MATh
BIOC

5.

Early Developmental Spelling

imT DPMREWR
RTDPR
PiMD RCQ
QRPRCQ
RPUQRPQRPROZO

Finally, it is important to remember that children's reading and writing development are integrally related, and this reading/writing connection must be taken into account in evaluating their growth as writers.

In particular, as a child reads what he or she has written, it is important to ask questions such as these:

- Does the child attend to the picture or the print in reading what she or he has written?

- Are the child's attempts to track the print successful?

- Does the child conventionally read what he or she has written?

- Does the child's intonation sound more like oral or written language?

As children move along the developmental pathway, their rereadings of their own writing become more print-based and sound increasingly like written language rather than oral language.

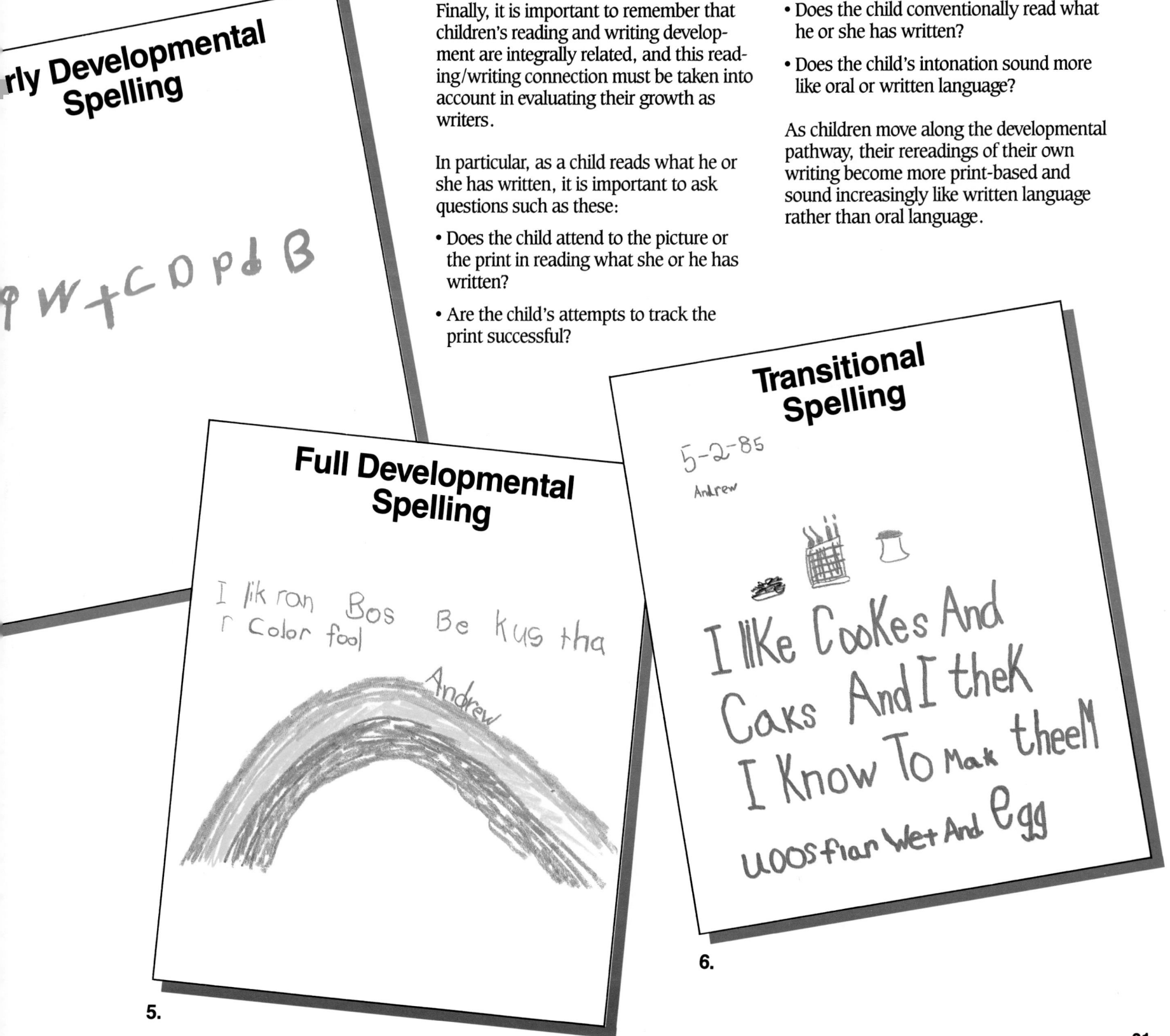

rly Developmental Spelling

φ W ┼ C O p d B

Full Developmental Spelling

I lik ron Bos Be kus tha
r color fool

Andrew

5.

Transitional Spelling

5-2-85

Andrew

I lIke CooKes And
Caks And I theK
I Know To Mak theeM

uoosfiar Wet And egg

6.

Students Acquiring English

Emergent Literacy in the Second Language

BY Josefina Villamil Tinajero

The early childhood years are a remarkably active period for acquiring language and for learning about its written form. Classroom environments have a significant effect on children's language and literacy development. This is especially true for emergent readers and writers who are also acquiring English as a second language. The physical and social environment of the classroom, teacher beliefs and attitudes about language acquisition and emergent literacy, the types of activities planned, and the strategies and techniques used by teachers all affect the opportunities children have to emerge as readers and writers and to acquire a new language.

Supporting Kindergartners' Language Acquisition

It is our position that children *acquire* rather than *learn* a language in a natural progression of stages. As language is acquired, literacy in the new language develops. That is, current research suggests that the second language is acquired in the same manner as the first and that it is acquired most effectively in a highly interactive, total communication environment.

Children acquire language when they understand what people say to them or what is read. They acquire language by understanding messages and by responding to those messages in meaningful ways. Language must make sense to young children, and somehow it must be important for them to acquire it. Some of the best ways to encourage language development are to provide children with many opportunities to interact with other children, to encourage child's play, and to engage them in natural language activities. Songs, poems, stories, games, role-play, story theater, and dramatizations are especially effective because they allow students to hear natural English while providing a meaningful, motivating, and enjoyable context for learning.

Young SAEs need a favorable environment for language acquisition, an environment that is as natural and as language-rich as that within which they learned their first language. Kindergartners acquiring English, in particular, need many opportunities to hear and use English, to experiment with it, to take risks and try out their knowledge of the language. They need to be encouraged to express their ideas and feelings as they move along the pathway toward nativelike fluency.

When students offer responses, for example, their pronunciation may be poor and their grammatical construction may include elements from their first language. When this happens, teachers need to accept their responses, model the "correct" form in a tactful and unexaggerated way, and praise them for their contributions. Praising builds confidence and helps children feel valued as members of the class. They will also be much more motivated to "experiment" with the language and to take risks—that is, express their thoughts and ideas even if they are not yet fully fluent in the language.

Teachers can integrate the following techniques with activities planned for other children in the class.

Heterogeneous Grouping. One way to provide SAEs with opportunities to practice their English is to increase the frequency and variety of interactions among students. Pairing them with proficient English speakers for activities such as partner "reading" of Big Books and partner story retellings is one way

of increasing interaction. Grouping them with students of varying proficiencies for activities such as illustrating a new ending to a story or illustrating a character map is another. At other times, however, SAEs may be grouped together for activities such as listening to a story in their native language, working on a special project, or doing partner reading with other SAEs.

Cooperative Learning. Cooperative learning also increases the frequency and variety of second language practice through different types of interactions. It provides students with many opportunities to utilize newly acquired language and to "read and write" (scribbling and drawing are considered writing at this age) in English in a "safe" social situation where they don't feel threatened by error correction. Cooperative learning also provides students with opportunities to act as resources for each other and thus assume a more active role in learning.

When working with kindergartners acquiring English, it is also important to keep in mind that, as individuals, they are at different levels of English proficiency. Thus, when planning activities for them, teachers must be aware of the level of receptive and productive language they bring to the learning task. There may be some children who may not be ready to begin producing oral English. Some may be experiencing what is often referred to as the *"silent period" of language learning*. That is, second language learners go through a period of time during which they prefer to listen rather than to produce language. As with most second language learners, children's receptive

language skills develop earlier than their productive ones (Rice, 1989).

It is important, however, to keep in mind that language learning is taking place during this time (Evans, 1990). Children don't always need to respond in order to learn new language skills. They can benefit greatly from the opportunity to absorb the conversations of others (Rice, 1989).

$\mathcal{U}$sing Literature to Nurture Children's Language Development

The best language lessons are good books and interesting discussions in which children are absorbed in the meaning of what is said to them or what is read.

For SAEs, literature cultivates language, provides language models, and facilitates language acquisition. As children listen to rhymes, poems, and patterned/predictable stories in English, they learn new language patterns and idiomatic usages, which are assimilated as children apply them to express their own thoughts and ideas during meaningful, well-planned lessons. Children with limited vocabulary can latch on to the "new" language they have heard, suddenly discovering that their former limited vocabulary takes on new dimensions.

$\mathcal{S}$torytelling with SAEs

Because storytelling encourages physical, visual, and aural/oral participation of students, it is an excellent context for teaching language and concepts to SAEs.

Listening and speaking skills, for example, are enriched through the use of puppetry, tapes, dramatic presentations, and the teacher's systematic reading to children. Children will also enjoy retelling stories they have been told or sharing stories from their own cultures, stories they may have learned at home or in their neighborhoods. Children's own creativity and ingenuity can also be encouraged and supported by allowing children to create, tell, and retell their own stories.

Following are some suggestions to take full advantage of storytelling activities to enhance language development for SAEs.

Oral Previewing. This technique adjusts the teacher's language input to children's language proficiency and comprehension level during storytelling. For SAEs, oral previewing takes the form of paraphrasing or telling the story "in your own words," both to make the story as comprehensible as possible and to facilitate language development. When using this technique, follow these guidelines.

First, screen the story, taking into account the language and experiential knowledge of students. Select areas of difficulty such as idiomatic language and difficult vocabulary. Become familiar with the story so that the retelling is as natural as possible, and so that you can be cognizant of facial expressions that might indicate whether or not SAEs are understanding the story.

Then hold up a copy of the book as you lead the children orally through the story, establishing plot and setting. Use gestures, body language, and facial expressions to help convey ideas and

concepts. Use simple, well-formed sentences; limit sentence length and complexity while maintaining appropriate grammar and intonation.

Clarify the meaning of words, phrases, and idiomatic expressions using context clues, such as pointing to the illustrations or drawing simple pictures. Make frequent repetitions of key words and ideas. At times, incorporate role play to help children understand concepts and learn language through physical activity.

As you continue to go through the story, ask questions that require yes/no responses, a nod of the head, pointing to an illustration, or one- or two-word responses to check understanding. Also ask questions to relate the story situation to children's experiences. Remember that SAEs understand more than they can verbalize. As children respond using one or two words, repeat their utterances, use their words in an expanded comment. That is, use the *semantic expansion* technique, in which you as the teacher start with something the child said and elaborate to clarify or add to the response. Also, use structural expansion in which you as the teacher repeat an incorrect utterance correctly to model for the children. Finally, have children make predictions along the way to encourage language use and development of critical thinking skills. Remember to praise children for their contributions.

These types of teacher-child interactions with storybooks create a context for comprehending meaning, for making meaning. They help SAEs get past some of the difficult language so they can concentrate on the story line. Children also internalize new language related to the story they are about to hear.

The following storytelling variations help SAEs acquire language and make stories more comprehensible. Use them as often as possible. They are good for all children.

Puppetry. Puppets make stories come alive for children, and the actions associated with using them to tell or retell stories make language more comprehensible. Most important, however, SAEs are less reluctant to talk "when they take on other identities to perform. It is somehow less threatening to make a mistake as someone else; it becomes their mistake, not that of the student" (Evans, 1990).

Participation Stories. Certain stories invite children to participate actively as they respond to certain words that act as cues for actions like clapping or stamping their feet or shaking their heads. Before reading the story, the teacher introduces the cues. The children then act out the story as the teacher reads. These types of stories develop listening skills and facilitate language acquisition (Evans, 1990).

Pantomime. Through pantomime children use their whole bodies for making meaning as they participate in storytelling activities. Text becomes more comprehensible as characters come alive.

Story Retelling. Working with a partner, children retell stories to one another. Story retelling provides a great opportunity for children to use the language they have heard in the stories to express their own thoughts and ideas.

Tape Recordings. Tape recordings of stories are an excellent way to expose students to good literature that may be beyond their reading abilities but within their listening abilities. Children will also enjoy making their own recordings of

stories. These recordings also serve as good diagnostic tools.

Choral Reading. Choral readings of stories, with a mix of SAEs and proficient English speakers, give shy learners a safe way to practice formal speaking. Remember, the desire of SAEs to produce language varies greatly—allow them to join in when they're ready.

Shared Reading and SAEs

Another excellent way to provide SAEs with rich literature experiences is to conduct shared reading with books that contain repetitive language and/or predictable outcomes. The repetitive characteristics of the texts facilitate the natural acquisition of vocabulary, pronunciation, and language structures. Big Books are particularly effective for group study and for exposing children to print.

The repeated readings help children to read more efficiently, gain confidence, practice using their reading skills, and increase their sight vocabulary. And since the illustrations in the books are closely tied to the text, children get visual support for the rapid development of a wide range of vocabulary. The reading and rereading of stories also allow SAEs to hear and practice, in an informal setting, the rhythm and structure of English.

As children recite and participate in shared reading activities using rhymes, poems, songs, and pattern stories, they learn new language patterns. They internalize these patterns and then use them to express their own thoughts and ideas. Furthermore, through shared reading, children are exposed to the written and oral forms of language and are offered

numerous opportunities to develop listening, speaking, reading, and writing skills at the "teachable moment."

Shared reading activities also establish the kind of low-anxiety environment essential to language acquisition and provide SAEs at varying/lower levels of English proficiency with the opportunity to participate with the rest of the class. It is also a pleasurable experience that helps SAEs develop a positive attitude toward acquiring English and learning to read in a second language.

In selecting materials to use with SAEs, select those with texts containing features such as rhyme, rhythmic language, predictable or repetitive plots and language patterns, or illustrations that closely parallel the text. Screen materials carefully for overload of idiomatic language and situations that are culturally unfamiliar. Finally, select materials at the appropriate instructional level that foster students' appreciation of reading and develop positive attitudes toward learning to read in English.

Language Experience Activities

The language experience approach is particularly suitable for use with SAEs because the children's language proficiency, no matter how limited, is valued and used as a starting point for further development. And because SAEs' proficiency in English often varies significantly, language experience activities help build a common knowledge and language base for them. The approach also integrates children's ideas, interests, experiences, and natural language, using them to motivate students to read.

Through language experience, SAEs are also able to acquire the basic skills of reading and writing with familiar material—their own. Thus, the text is rich in comprehensible content that further develops children's language proficiency.

Establishing Partnerships with Parents

A primary way in which we can provide more supportive learning environments for all children is to involve their parents, working with them as colleagues, inviting them to participate as valuable resources of information and perspectives, and sharing with them ways in which parents enhance education at home.

Parents can assist teachers in creating more supportive and nurturing learning environments that offer the security needed for SAEs to participate in a culturally different setting. Parents can be invited to the classroom to tell stories from the oral tradition, to read stories, read or recite poetry, share "how to" information, and present topics that have inspired and informed their lives.

Parents often think that they cannot help their children at home if they do not speak English. Teachers need to make an effort to assure them that working with their children in their native language is of benefit because concepts learned in the native language will transfer to English.

The Challenge

Kindergarten is a critical point for students acquiring English. Beyond their needs for skills in academic growth, SAEs also have motivational and emotional needs that must be met. These needs are often magnified in importance where there are cultural and linguistic differences between the school and the home. They include children's need to feel a sense of identity, to belong, to be understood by and communicate with significant others, and to succeed in environments in which they are accepted and respected. Kindergarten teachers can make a difference in the lives of these children. By simply applying some of the basic principles discussed here, teachers can provide a nurturing and intellectually stimulating environment where students acquiring English can succeed and thrive.

References

Auerbach, E. (1989). Toward a social-contextual approach to family literacy. Harvard Educational Review, 59, No. 2, pp. 165–181.

Early, M. (1991). Using wordless picture books to promote second language learning. ELT Journal. Volume 45/3. July. pp. 245–250.

Evans, L. S. (1990). Storytelling and oral language development in ESL classrooms. TESOL Newsletter. October. pp. 3, 16, 18, 30.

Flood, J.; Lapp, D.; Tinajero, J.; and Nagel, G. Parents and teachers: Partners in developing literacy for multicultural students. (unpublished manuscript).

Nurss, J. R. and Hough, R. A. (1985). Story reading: Language arts for limited English speakers. TESOL Newsletter. Vol. 8, No. 1. pp. 1–2.

Rice, M. (1989). Children's language acquisition. American Psychologist. Volume 4. February. pp. 149–156.

*I*NTRODUCING WONDER ABOUT IT!

Invite children to explore their thoughts and wonderings through trade books, read aloud selections, poetry, and songs!

TRADE BOOKS

BIG BOOK

White Is the Moon
by Valerie Greeley
Graceful verse and beautiful scenes from nature are linked by the themes of color and passing time.
Available as a Big Book and little book, and included on the
LISTENING LIBRARY AUDIOCASSETTE

The Park Bench
by Fumiko Takeshita, illustrated by Mamoru Suzuki
In the course of a day, dog walkers, park workers, young mothers, old people, children, and others all come by a white bench beneath a tree in a city park. A bilingual edition, originally from Japan.

Half a Moon and One Whole Star
by Crescent Dragonwagon, illustrated by Jerry Pinkney
This poem celebrates a summer night and the people and creatures who inhabit it while a little girl named Susan sleeps.

READ ALOUDS

TEACHER'S READ ALOUD ANTHOLOGY

The Spider Weaver
a Japanese folk tale retold by Florence Sakada
A "why" tale that explains, through the rescue of a spider from a snake, why clouds are white and cotton-soft.

The One You Don't See Coming
a folk tale from Liberia retold by Harold Courlander and George Herzog
Three hunters who want to catch Sleep soon find that "You can't see the coming of Sleep."

BIG BOOK OF POEMS
I Arise
an Eskimo song

BIG BOOK OF SONGS
Twinkle, Twinkle, Little Star
a traditional song

Also Available—

SING & READ BOOKS AND AUDIOCASSETTES
Twinkle, Twinkle, Little Star

SONGS AND STORIES AUDIOCASSETTES
Story Songs—including the
Theme Song—and Storytellings!

EXPLORING PRINT

**BIG BOOK OF ALPHABET RHYMES AND CHIMES
PLUS RHYME AND CHIME STRIPS**

- **Ii** If All the World Was Apple Pie

- **Xx** What Words Begin with X?

Also Available—

SING A SOUND AUDIOCASSETTES
Songs for language play and for
developing phonemic awareness!

THEME 12: WONDER ABOUT IT!

Overview for Week 1

BIG BOOK

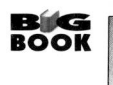

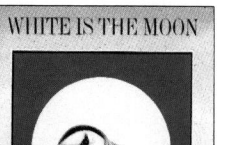

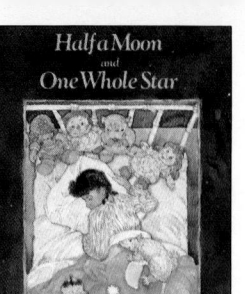

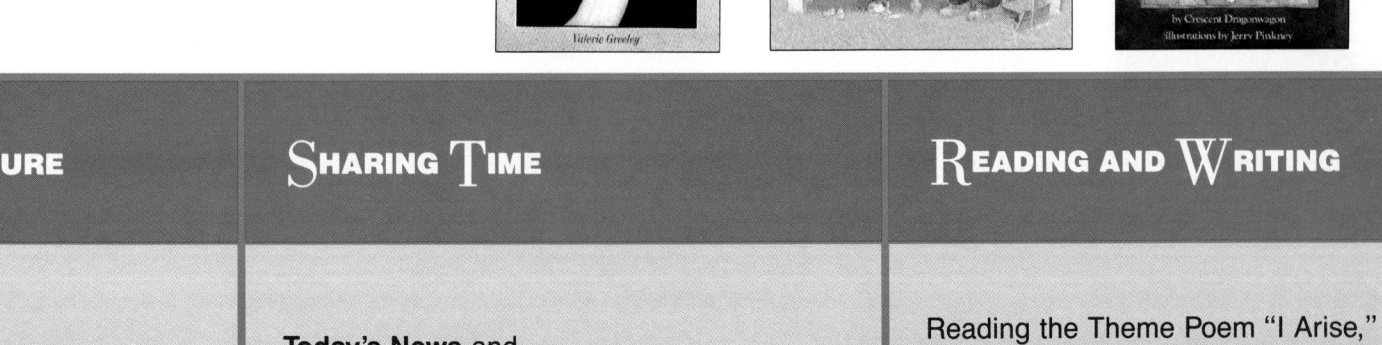

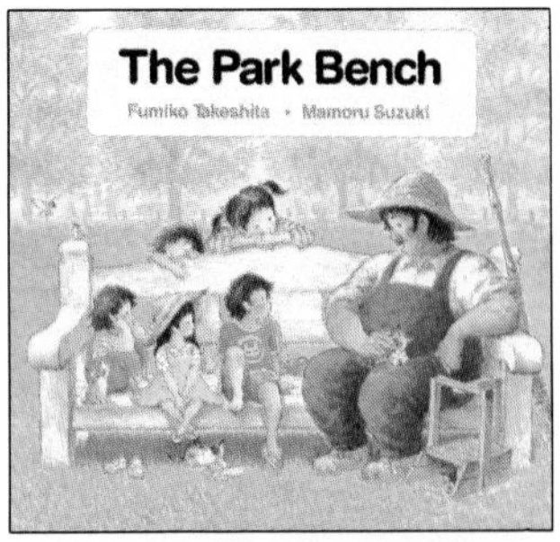

Literature	Sharing Time	Reading and Writing
1 THEME POEM "I Arise"	**Today's News** and becoming thinkers p. 35	Reading the Theme Poem "I Arise," and Responding through **Poem Talk**, Journal Writing, and Comparing Literatu pp. 36-37
2 *WHITE IS THE MOON*	**Today's News** and reading the poem "What Is Pink?" p. 43	Reading *White Is the Moon* and Responding through **Book Talk**, Journal Writing, and Creating Book Variations pp. 44-45
3 *WHITE IS THE MOON*	**Today's News** and listening to the poem "Moon-Come-Out" p. 49	Rereading *White Is the Moon* and Responding through **Book Talk**, Story Theater, and Looking at the Day-Night Cycle pp. 50-51
4 READ ALOUD "The Spider Weaver"	**Today's News** and reading the poem "I Don't Know Why" p. 55	Reading "The Spider Weaver" and Responding through **Book Talk**, Journal Writing, Cloud Pictures, and Creating "Why" Tales pp. 56-57
5 *THE PARK BENCH*	**Today's News** and reading the poem "Snowy Benches" p. 61	Reading *The Park Bench* and Responding through **Book Talk**, Journal Writing, and Creating Day-Night Books pp. 62-63

ch theme helps children see themselves from a different
rspective. This theme helps children see themselves as
inkers.

EXPLORING PRINT

ecoding and Phonics
tters *l, i*
und/Letter Relationships /i/ *l, i*
ONG: "If You're Happy and You Know It"
. 46-47

ecoding and Phonics
tters *l, i*
und/Letter Relationships /i/ *l, i*
G BOOK OF ALPHABET RHYMES AND CHIMES:
All the World Was Apple Pie"
. 52-53

oncepts of Print
rectionality, Words
HYME AND CHIME STRIPS:
All the World Was Apple Pie"
. 58-59

ecoding and Phonics
tters *l, i*
und/Letter Relationships /i/ *l, i*
oncepts of Print
rectionality, Words, Letters
HYME AND CHIME STRIPS:
All the World Was Apple Pie"
. 64-65

THEME GOALS AND OUTCOMES

The literature and activities in this theme were
carefully selected and reviewed by the program
authors and by the multicultural, literature, and
educational consultants who worked together to
develop the program goals and outcomes.

MULTICULTURAL PERSPECTIVES

Appreciate and value diverse points of view

Become aware of cultural backgrounds,
experiences, emotions, and ideas of self and
others through literature

Appreciate the literary expression of our
contemporary multicultural society and
multicultural heritage

Appreciate the universality of literary themes in
many cultures and in many different times

Appreciate the significance of traditional
literature within a culture

Recognize cultural attitudes and customs in
literary selections

PERSONAL INTERESTS AND ATTITUDES

Develop an awareness of the classroom as a
community of learners that values cooperation,
fair play, and respect for others and for oneself

Select stories and books for personal interests

Develop personal reading and writing interests

Make connections between one's personal life
and literature

Choose to read and write for a variety of
purposes

Share, review, and recommend books to others

Participate in reading, writing, listening, and
viewing activities

Appreciate the artistic interpretation of literature
through film, illustration, photography, dance,
oral presentations, and other forms of expression

LITERATURE	SHARING TIME	READING AND WRITING
6 *THE PARK BENCH*	**Today's News** and llistening to "Star Medley" p. 67	Rereading *The Park Bench* and Responding through **Book Talk** and Playing *Kagome,* a Japanese Game pp. 68-69
7 *HALF A MOON AND ONE WHOLE STAR*	**Today's News** and reading the poem "Silverly" p. 73	Reading *Half a Moon and One Whole St* and Responding through **Book Talk** and Journal Writing pp. 74-75
8 *HALF A MOON AND ONE WHOLE STAR*	**Today's News** and reading the poem "Lullaby" p. 79	Rereading *Half a Moon and One Whole* and Responding through **Book Talk**, Nighttime Compositions, and Making Night Sounds pp. 80-81
9 READ ALOUD "The One You Don't See Coming"	**Today's News** and reading the poem "The Night" p. 85	Reading "The One You Don't See Comi and Responding through **Book Talk**, Story Theater, and Sleep Drawings pp. 86-87
10 *WHITE IS THE MOON THE PARK BENCH HALF A MOON AND ONE WHOLE STAR*	**Today's News** and singing the Theme Song "Twinkle, Twinkle, Little Star" and rereading the Theme Poem "I Arise" p. 91	Reviewing the trade books in the theme and Responding through **Book Talk** and Journal Writing pp. 92-93

MORE BOOKS TO SHARE

The books on these pages can be shared with children throughout the theme. The books can also be put into the Reading Center so children can read and enjoy them.

MORE BOOKS ABOUT WONDERING

■ **ANIMALS OF THE NIGHT**
by Merry Banks, illus. by Ronald Himler (Scribners, 1990). When sleepy children go to bed, a world filled with nocturnal animals begins to stir. Beautifully illustrated, this book will intrigue young readers with the fascinating facts it provides.

■ **WHAT AM I? VERY FIRST RIDDLES**
by Stephanie Calmenson, illus. by Karen Gundersheimer (Harper Trophy, 1989). Simple riddles in verse appear on each right-hand page. When the page is turned, the answer—an everyday object—is revealed.

■ **WHY THE SUN AND THE MOON LIVE IN THE SKY: AN AFRICAN FOLKTALE**
by Elphinstone Dayrell, illus. by Blair Lent (Houghton Mifflin, 1968). Based on a Nigerian folk tale, this Caldecott Honor book explains how the sun and the moon moved into the sky as their home on earth was filled by the visiting water god.

■ **THE COLOR BOX**
by Dayle Ann Dodds, illus. by Giles Laroche (Little, Brown, 1992). A curious monkey explores the world of color in this book, superbly illustrated with three-dimensional cut-paper collages. A cut-out shape on each page reveals the next color in the series.

■ **SUN UP, SUN DOWN**
by Gail Gibbons (HBJ, 1983). Large brightly-colored illustrations highlight the simple text that skillfully incorporates just the right amount of information about the sun for a kindergartner.

■ **WHERE DOES THE SUN GO AT NIGHT?**
by Mirra Ginsburg, illus. by Jose Aruego and Ariane Dewey (Mulberry, 1981). Using a question-and-answer format, Ginsburg has created a clever adaptation of an old Armenian song. The rollicking illustrations add greatly to the fun.

■ **THE MOON IS FOLLOWING ME**
by Philip Heckman, illus. by Mary O'Keefe Young (Atheneum, 1990). Riding home in the car from her grandparents' house, a young girl notices that the moon is traveling along the same route. Sometimes it takes a shortcut or hides behind a cloud, but both moon and child arrive at her destination together.

■ **HOW MANY STARS IN THE SKY?**
by Lenny Hort, illus. by James E. Ransome (Tambourine, 1991). A warm story of a nighttime journey undertaken by a young boy, anxious to count the stars, and his father, who is determined to aid him in his efforts.

■ **WHEN SHEEP CANNOT SLEEP: THE COUNTING BOOK**
by Satoshi Kitamura (Farrar, Straus & Giroux, 1986). What do sheep do when they cannot sleep? When insomnia strikes Woolly, he takes a walk, finding interesting objects in increasing numbers. Finally Woolly falls asleep, thinking of sheep!

■ GOODNIGHT TO ANNIE: AN ALPHABET LULLABY

by Eve Merriam, illus. by Carol Schwartz (Hyperion, 1992). The well-known poet Eve Merriam has created a text filled with evocative images and alliterative language. Schwartz's magnificent illustrations set exactly the right tone for this book that is certain to become a classroom favorite.

■ A PROMISE TO THE SUN: AN AFRICAN STORY

by Tololwa M. Mollel, illus. by Beatriz Vidal (Little, Brown, 1992.) Masai author Mollel brings us an explanation of how the bat became a nocturnal animal. Vidal's delicate watercolors add yet another dimension to this charming tale.

■ HILDILID'S NIGHT

by Cheli Durán Ryan, illus. by Arnold Lobel (Macmillan, 1986). Hildilid hated the night. She tried every trick she could think of to banish it from her home. Finally, exhausted and determined to ignore her adversary, she falls into bed just as the sun rises anew. This 1972 Caldecott Honor book will speak to those children who, like Hildilid, would like to chase away the night.

■ NIGHT IN THE COUNTRY

by Cynthia Rylant, illus. by Mary Szilagyi (Bradbury, 1986). Night in the country is dark and still, but if you listen carefully, you can hear the soft *puump* of an apple falling from a tree or the patter of a rabbit moving about in the garden. Szilagyi's drawings convey to the reader that mysterious quality found in a country night.

■ ALWAYS WONDERING: SOME FAVORITE POEMS OF AILEEN FISHER

drawings by Joan Sandin (A Charlotte Zolotow Book, 1991). "'Think . . .' said the robin,/'Think . . .' said the jay," begins this collection of poems that encourages children to think and to wonder about the world around them. A marvelous resource for any classroom.

■ IT LOOKED LIKE SPILT MILK

by Charles G. Shaw (Harper Trophy, 1988, originally published in 1947). The simple pictures and text of this classic challenge the reader to solve the riddle of this ever-changing object—a cloud.

■ DAWN

by Uri Shulevitz (Farrar, Straus & Giroux, 1974). Inspired by an ancient Chinese poem, Shulevitz, winner of the 1969 Caldecott Medal, has created an exquisite portrait of the dawn. An old man and his grandson sleep by a lake until the faint rays of the sun awaken them to begin a day of fishing. As they sleep, the colors of the sky and the lake change from deep blue to radiant yellow and green.

■ OWLY

by Mike Thaler, illus. by David Wiesner (Harper & Row, 1982). A young owl begins to wonder about the world around him. He flies high above the clouds but cannot discover where the sky ends. He journeys to the shore to count the endless waves. He need not wonder, however, about his mother's love; it is as boundless as the sky, the ocean, and the stars in the sky.

MORE BOOKS BY THEME AUTHORS AND ILLUSTRATORS

■ THIS IS THE BREAD I BAKED FOR NED

by Crescent Dragonwagon, illus. by Isadore Seltzer (Macmillan, 1989). Glenda spends the day preparing a lovely dinner for Ned, who, arriving in the evening, brings with him several unanticipated guests. Can dinner for two serve a crowd? In her delightful cumulative verse, Dragonwagon provides the answer.

■ WHERE'S MY SHARE?

by Valerie Greeley (Macmillan, 1989). Sparked by an old nursery rhyme, Greeley has written and illustrated a simple circular story. "Where's my share?" wonders the robin as he catches sight of a loaf of bread. The answer takes him through the forest to a wheat field, a mill, and then back again to the loaf of bread.

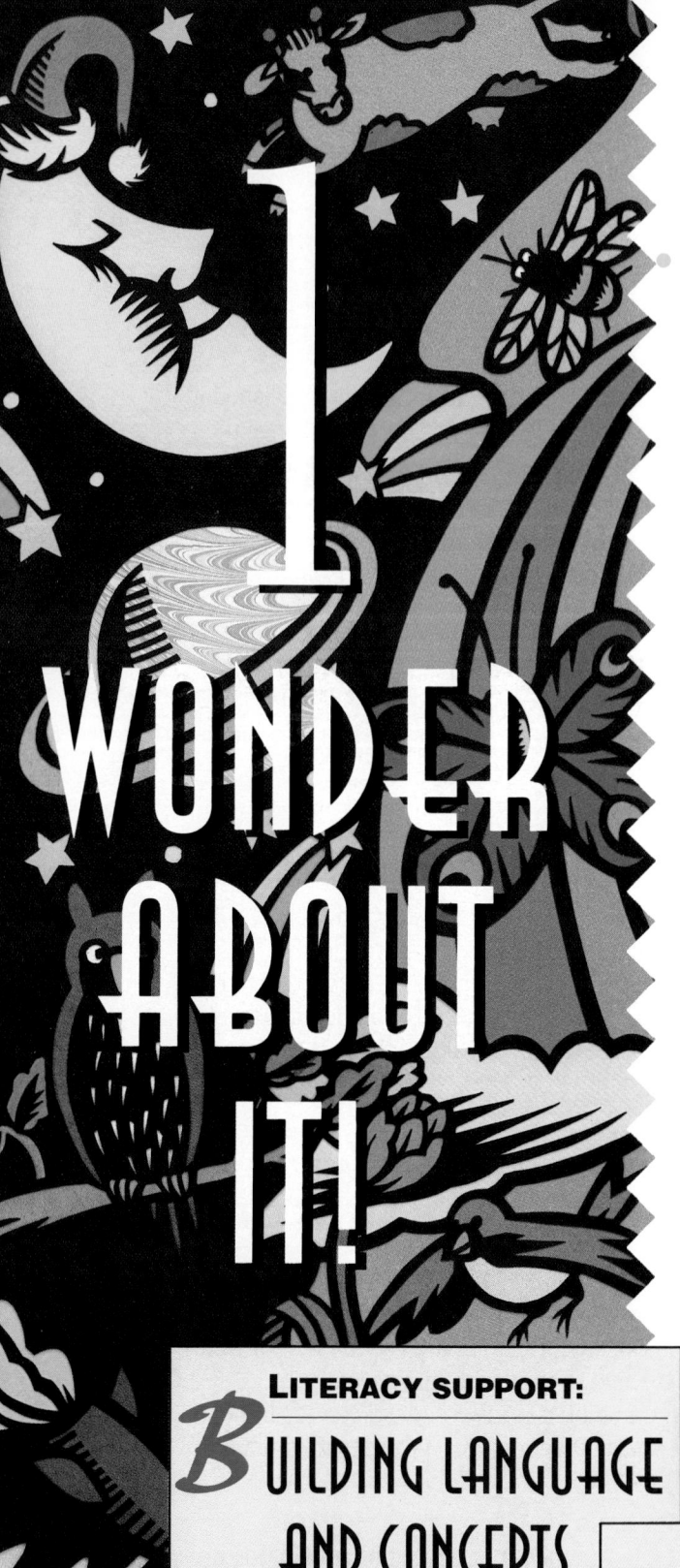

1

WONDER ABOUT IT!

LITERACY SUPPORT:
Building Language and Concepts

For children acquiring English and/or needing more intensive support, you may wish to incorporate the following suggestions into the basic lesson plan.

LITERATURE

Big Book of Poems: I Arise
an Eskimo song

Big Book of Songs:
Twinkle, Twinkle, Little Star
Traditional

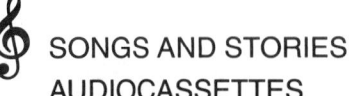 SONGS AND STORIES
AUDIOCASSETTES
STORY SONGS:
Twinkle, Twinkle, Little Star

 SING & READ BOOKS AND
AUDIOCASSETTES
Twinkle, Twinkle, Little Star

Literature Activity Book: pp. 98–99
Wonder About It!

STAFF DEVELOPMENT A to EZ Handbook

- Journals: p. 264

- Zone of Proximal
  Development: p. 303

Performance Assessment Handbook

HomeWords: Home-School Resources

To introduce this theme, take children on a "wondering" walk around the school. Begin by modeling the pattern "I wonder...," such as "I wonder how old this tree is." Then encourage children to use the same pattern to ask questions about their environment.

OTHER RESOURCES

- FLASHLIGHT
- BIG BOOK STAND
- BIG BOOK POINTER
- CHART PAPER
- MARKERS
- TO MAKE JOURNALS:
  STAPLER
  UNLINED PAPER
  CONSTRUCTION
  PAPER

SHARING TIME

TODAY'S NEWS

Write and read Today's News, tracking the words as you read. Point out the words *thinker* and *think*. Underline the *-er* ending in *thinker*. Explain to children that the word *thinker* refers to someone who thinks. Invite children to discuss the things they think about when they are alone, with friends, or with their family.

We are all thinkers. What things do you like to think about?

CREATING INTEREST AND BUILDING BACKGROUND

Because motivation matters!

Introduce the theme WONDER ABOUT IT! by explaining that thinkers wonder about many things. Write the Theme Word *thinker* on the chalkboard. Recall some of the ideas that children suggested when they talked about Today's News. Point out any responses that indicate what the children may wonder about.

Let children know that throughout this theme they will act as thinkers as they wonder about the cycle of day and night. To get started, invite children to share what they wonder about the objects they see in the sky, such as the moon, sun, stars, and clouds. Encourage them to use the language pattern, *I wonder . . .* as they state their wonderings. Record children's thoughts on chart paper and keep the chart on display throughout the theme to add other ideas children may suggest. Read the chart together each time new ideas are added.

Wonderings

I wonder where the sun is at night.   Jamara
I wonder why the moon changes shape.   Kirtan
I wonder what the stars are made of.   Bonnie
I wonder if I could fly to the moon.   Alice

READING AND WRITING

SHARING LITERATURE
"I Arise"

LISTEN TO THE SOUNDS OF POETRY   Set the mood for the Theme Poem "I Arise" by darkening the room. Invite children to share their understandings of the word *dawn;* then encourage them to pretend it is just before dawn and they are sleeping. As you read the poem, use a flashlight to shine a beam of light into the darkness.

Share that the Eskimos, or Inuits, who composed this poem lived where winter nights last for a very long time.

The sun's rising was therefore very important to them. Read the poem again, encouraging children to form pictures in their minds of what it describes.

SEE THE POEM IN PRINT   Display the Theme Poem in the *Big Book of Poems* on pages 34–35. Explain that the poem shown in the Big Book is the poem you just read.

Read the poem again, tracking the print with the Big Book pointer or your finger. Encourage children to join in with you.

I Arise

I arise to meet the day,
My face is turned from
the dark of night
To gaze at the new dawn
whitening the sky.

Eskimo Song

35

Big Book of Poems, pages 34–35

RESPONDING TO LITERATURE

POEM TALK   Encourage children to share any comments or questions they might have about the poem. You might begin by sharing your own response to provide a model for personal involvement with literature.

Build on this sharing of personal responses with a discussion of the poem itself. You may want to use some of the following questions to get the discussion started.

- *This poem reminded me of one morning when I was up at dawn. Have any of you ever been up at sunrise? What was it like?*

- *What do you remember about first waking up in the morning?*

- *How did the poem make you feel about the coming of a new day?*

JOURNAL WRITING   Provide journals for children to use throughout the theme by stapling sheets of paper together.

Invite children to share their images of and feelings about the poem in their journals. Provide a model for written response by recording your own response in your journal. Conclude by inviting volunteers to share their entries.

COMPARING LITERATURE   Share the two Tohono O'odham Indian songs. Invite children to think and talk about the similarities between the two songs and the Inuit poem. Help children discover that people from different cultures created such similar verses because the coming of day is an experience shared by all people.

Tohono O'odham Songs

Come all! Stand up!
Just over there the dawn is coming.
Now I hear
Soft laughter.

At the edge of the world
It is growing light.
The trees stand shining.
I like it.
It is growing light.

TEAM WORK/THEME WORK   WORKS OF WONDER!

Introducing the Project: An Exploration!
Share with children that throughout the theme WONDER ABOUT IT! they will be thinking about our world, the sky above it, and the objects we see in the sky! The theme gives special attention to the changes from daytime to nighttime. Children will have the opportunity to explore the things they wonder about as they create poems, songs, drawings, and three-dimensional figures and configurations. Children will be able to share their finished pieces in a classroom display entitled "Works of Wonder!"

Write the Theme Word *thinker* on the chalkboard or on chart paper. Encourage children to brainstorm about what a thinker is and to name people they know who are thinkers. Then emphasize to children that they themselves are all thinkers! For example, have they ever wondered where the sun and the moon come from, why there is daytime and nighttime, or what happens at night when they are asleep? Remind children that they think every day, such as when they decide what game to play during recess or when they learn to count "how many"!

Brainstorming and Sharing Ideas
Generate excitement about the Works of Wonder! exhibit by having children brainstorm more ideas of what they wonder about the earth, the sky, the sun, the clouds, and the moon. Make a list of wonderings and possible depictions children might like to create for the Works of Wonder! exhibit. Read the list together with children.

Things I Wonder About	Works of Wonder! project	Thinker
Is the moon near the sun? Are we?	sun-moon-earth mobile	Jason
Why does the moon look lumpy?	model of the moon's surface made out of papier-mâché	Michelle and Nilda
Why do stars twinkle?	"why" tale	LaTisha
Where does the sun come from?	poster with a poem	Minh
Which is biggest—the sun, the moon, or the earth?	clay sculptures	Susan

Sing Out!
Play the Theme Song "Twinkle, Twinkle, Little Star" on the STORY SONGS AUDIOCASSETTE. Invite children to listen to the song several times until they feel comfortable joining in.

Display the words to the song on pages 38–39 in the *Big Book of Songs*. Use the Big Book pointer to help children follow along with the words as you all sing. Invite children to find all the repetitions of the word *twinkle* and to identify the words that rhyme.

You may want to share with children that the sun is a star. All the other stars in the sky are so far away that they look like little twinkling lights.

SONGS AND STORIES AUDIOCASSETTES
STORY SONGS: Twinkle, Twinkle, Little Star

Twinkle,
Twinkle,
Little Star

Twinkle, twinkle, little star,
How I wonder what you are.
Up above the world so high,
Like a diamond in the sky.
Twinkle, twinkle, little star,
How I wonder what you are!

Traditional

Big Book of Songs, pages 38–39

TEAM WORK/THEME WORK WORKS OF WONDER!

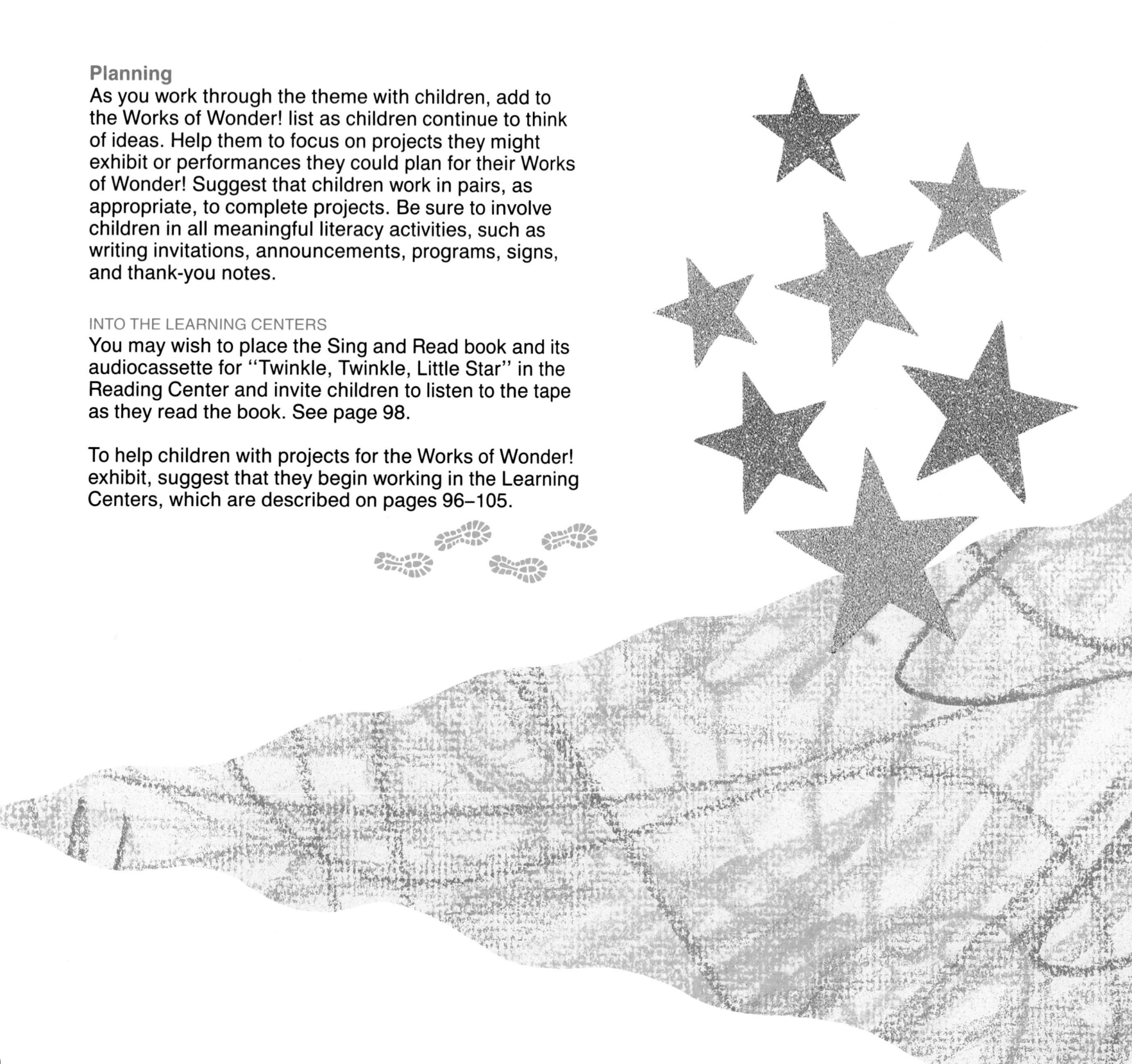

Planning

As you work through the theme with children, add to the Works of Wonder! list as children continue to think of ideas. Help them to focus on projects they might exhibit or performances they could plan for their Works of Wonder! Suggest that children work in pairs, as appropriate, to complete projects. Be sure to involve children in all meaningful literacy activities, such as writing invitations, announcements, programs, signs, and thank-you notes.

INTO THE LEARNING CENTERS

You may wish to place the Sing and Read book and its audiocassette for "Twinkle, Twinkle, Little Star" in the Reading Center and invite children to listen to the tape as they read the book. See page 98.

To help children with projects for the Works of Wonder! exhibit, suggest that they begin working in the Learning Centers, which are described on pages 96–105.

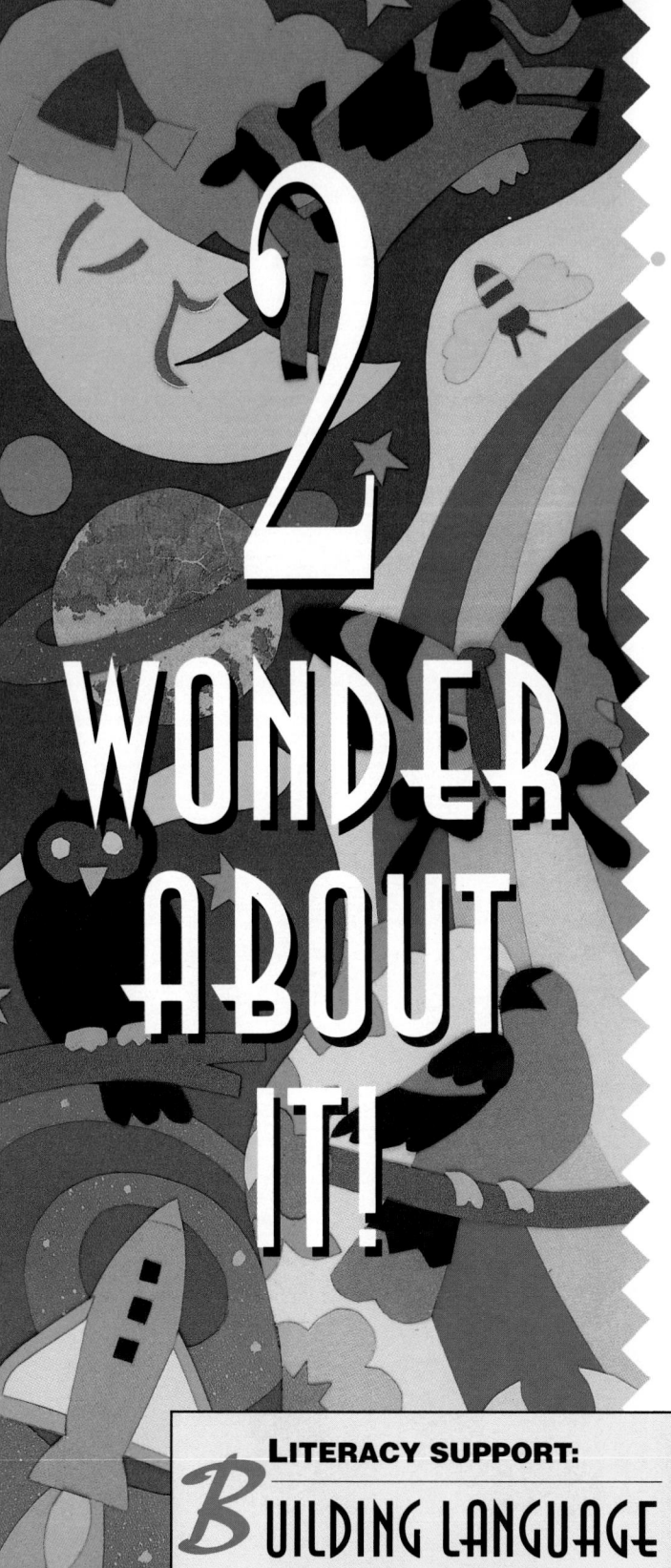

2 WONDER ABOUT IT!

LITERATURE

White Is the Moon
by Valerie Greeley

LISTENING LIBRARY
AUDIOCASSETTES
White Is the Moon

SING & READ BOOKS AND
AUDIOCASSETTES
Twinkle, Twinkle, Little Star

EXPLORING PRINT

SING A SOUND AUDIOCASSETTES
If You're Happy and You Know It

Learning the Code: I, i

Practice Book: p. 59

BRWL: Letterbook I(8)

STAFF DEVELOPMENT A to EZ Handbook
  • Big Books: p. 246
  • Shared Reading: p. 299

Performance Assessment Handbook

Valerie Greeley

OTHER RESOURCES

• BIG BOOK STAND
• BIG BOOK POINTER
• CHART PAPER
• MARKERS
• WORD MASK

LITERACY SUPPORT:

BUILDING LANGUAGE AND CONCEPTS

For children acquiring English and/or needing more intensive support, you may wish to incorporate the following suggestions into the basic lesson plan.

Build vocabulary by having children find and name all the objects of the colors discussed in the text. Also explain or demonstrate the difficult adjectives such as "steely stare" and "sly and fast." After reading, form heterogeneous groups of three or four children for a language development game. As you ask "What is (white)?" invite children to take turns naming things that are the same color.

SHARING TIME

TODAY'S NEWS

Write Today's News. Then track the print as you read it. Encourage children to think about the different colors that they notice in the sky, on the ground, and around the school. Make a list of the colors and objects that children mention. Read the list together when it is complete.

Let's think about the colors in our world.

CREATING INTEREST AND BUILDING BACKGROUND

Because motivation matters!

Introduce Christina Rossetti's poem "What Is Pink?" Encourage children to picture in their minds what the poem describes.

What Is Pink?

What is pink? A rose is pink
By the fountain's brink.
What is red? A poppy's red
In its barley bed.
What is blue? The sky is blue
Where the clouds float through.
What is white? A swan is white
Sailing in the light.
What is yellow? Pears are yellow,
Rich and ripe and mellow.
What is green? The grass is green,
With small flowers between.
What is violet? Clouds are violet
In the summer twilight.
What is orange? Why, an orange,
Just an orange!

—Christina Rossetti

After reading the poem, you may want to help children create a word web listing several colors and objects associated with each color. Then tell children that the book you are going to share today gives examples of many of the colors seen in our world. As you read the book, add new colors or related objects to your web.

READING AND WRITING

SHARING LITERATURE
White Is the Moon

BIG BOOK

LOOK IT OVER   Display the Big Book for *White Is the Moon.* Tell children that this Big Book will help them all see the words as you read. Place a little book version in the Reading Center so they can look at the words on their own.

Use the Big Book pointer or your finger to track the first three words in the title: *White Is the _____*. Invite children to use the cover illustration to predict the final word: *Moon.* Then read the author's name, Valerie Greeley. Open the book to display both front and back covers simultaneously. Invite children to talk about what appears on the covers and to name the colors that are shown.

SHARE THE STORY   Help children recognize the pattern of the story by inviting them to chime in on the first line of each left-hand page. Asking *What color is the _____?* as you turn each page may help children respond in the appropriate language pattern. You may also want to draw attention to the box outlining the text on each page so that children notice that it varies according to the color mentioned.

About the Author/Illustrator

Valerie Greeley, an artist/writer who lives in London, England, has had her artwork exhibited at the Design Center and the Royal Academy. Her first effort at illustrating children's literature was a series of wordless board books about animals. She subsequently began to write her own text, producing the books *Where's My Share?* and *White Is the Moon.*

Red is the fox
Sly and fast
Sees a frog
Hopping past

8

9

RESPONDING TO LITERATURE

BOOK TALK   Invite children to share any personal comments or questions about the book. You may want to share your own reactions to the story as a way of modeling how readers actively respond to literature. Prompts such as the following might also be used.

- *I liked the description and pictures for the color green. Which was your favorite part?*

- *If you had written the book, what objects might you have used as examples of the colors?*

- *Did you like the rhyme in the book? Did you like anything else about the book?*

JOURNAL WRITING   Encourage children to draw and write about their favorite color examples from the book in their journals. Using the language pattern of the book, _____ *is the* _____, in your own journal may prompt children to do the same. Some children might want to simply draw and label a favorite animal or object from the book.

WONDERINGS: A COLOR BOOK   Invite children to wonder about the colors in our world as they create their own variations of the book. Children might want to compose pages for colors not included in *White Is the Moon,* such as purple, silver, or gold. Examining the names of the colors in a large box of crayons would provide a wellspring of ideas. They might also choose to depict other examples for any of the given colors.

TEAM WORK/THEME WORK
How do children want to display their wonderings about colors in their theme finale Works of Wonder? See pages 38–41 and 94–95.

INTO THE LEARNING CENTERS
Invite children into the Art Center to make images of the sun, moon, and stars. See page 103.

O.J. announced he couldn't write. However, with adult encouragement he produced a string of randomly chosen letters to accompany his picture of "penguins" (puffins) and the sun.

O.J. read his message like this: "Special."

EXPLORING PRINT — LEARNING THE CODE

In the Exploring Print lessons for this theme, children will focus on the letters I, i and X, x and the sounds they represent. Take advantage of opportunities to point out these letters and the sounds they represent as you share Today's News, as you talk with children about their writing, and as you reread the theme-related literature.

DECODING AND PHONICS

LETTERS: *I, i*
SOUND/LETTER RELATIONSHIPS: /i/I, i

Developing Phonemic Awareness
Discuss with children that throughout this year they have been (or will be) wondering about and listening for different sounds in our language. Today they will focus on the sound heard at the beginning of the word *It* in the theme title WONDER ABOUT IT!

Sing or play "If You're Happy and You Know It" on the SING A SOUND AUDIOCASSETTE and encourage children to join in.

If You're Happy and You Know It

If you're happy and you know it, clap your
   hands. (*Clap, clap*)
If you're happy and you know it, clap your
   hands. (*Clap, clap*)
If you're happy and you know it, then your
   face will surely show it.
If you're happy and you know it, clap your
   hands. (*Clap, clap*)

♪ SING A SOUND AUDIOCASSETTES
   If You're Happy and You Know It

Sing the song again, and then point out that *If* and *it* begin with the same sound. Say these words again, emphasizing the beginning sound.

Invite children to create other verses telling what they might do if they're happy and they know it, such as shout "hurrah," jump around, or nod their heads.

Developing Print Awareness
Write the title and first line of "If You're Happy and You Know It" on the chalkboard or on chart paper. Encourage children to say the words with you as you point to each one.

If You're Happy and You Know It

If you're happy and you know it, clap your hands.

Use a word mask to frame a capital and lowercase *i* in these lines.

- *Let's look at some i's together. Here is a capital, or uppercase, I in the word If in the title. Say If with me. What other word can you find in the title that begins with capital I?*

- *Here is a lowercase i in the word it. Say the word it with me.*

Encourage children to trace over the uppercase and lowercase *i*'s with their fingers.

Explain that the letter *i* stands for the sound heard at the beginning of *if* and *it*. Have children name the word that begins with that sound in the title *White Is the Moon*. Encourage children to name other words that begin with that sound.

Then invite children to play "Inspector Izzy" with you. Explain that you will complete the following phrase: "Inspector Izzy inspects _____." If the word you use to complete the phrase begins with the same sound as *inspector* and *Izzy* (/i/), children should form lowercase *i*'s by pointing their index fingers straight up. If the word does not begin with /i/, children should point their fingers down. Have children imagine that their fingernails represent the dots over the *i*'s. Some words to use are *igloos, infants, and insects.*

To round off the above activity, you may wish to create a bulletin board titled "Inspector Izzy inspects _____." Invite children to draw and label pictures that begin with the same sound as *Izzy* and *inspects.*

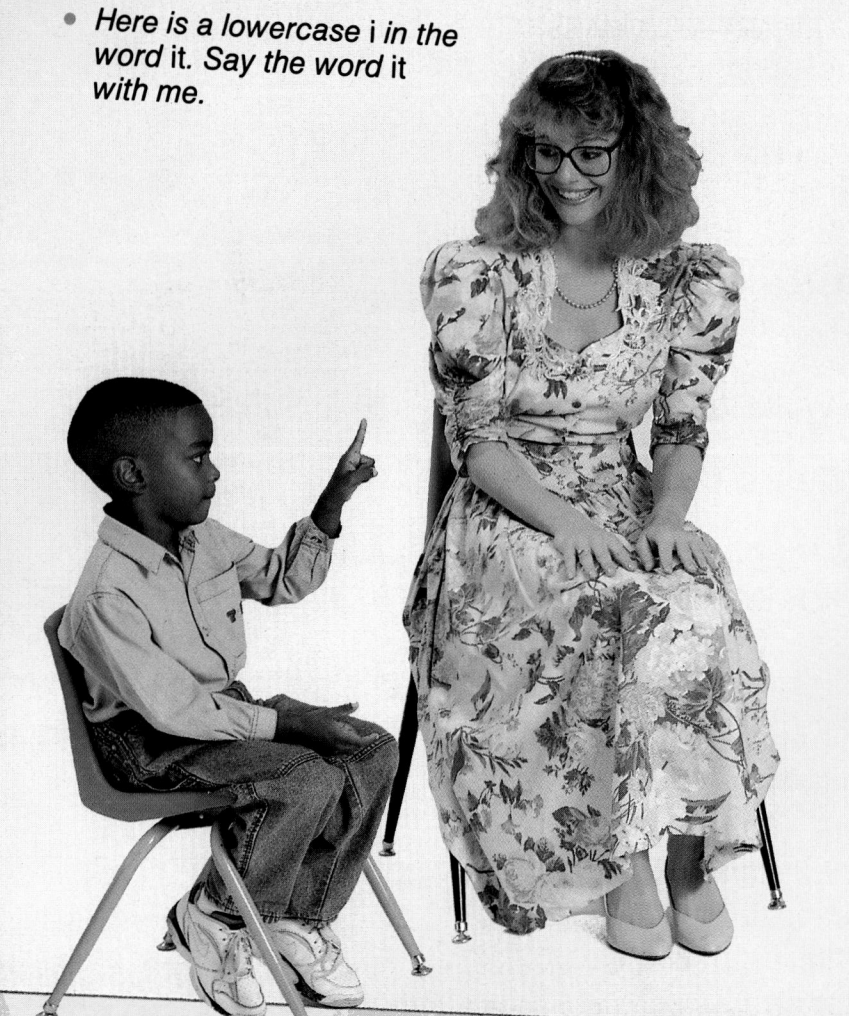

3 WONDER ABOUT IT!

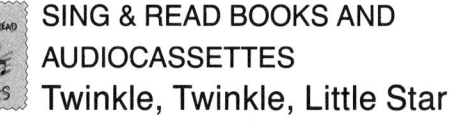

LITERATURE

White Is the Moon
by Valerie Greeley

Big Book of Poems: I Arise
An Eskimo Song

Big Book of Songs:
Twinkle, Twinkle, Little Star
Traditional

 SING & READ BOOKS AND AUDIOCASSETTES
Twinkle, Twinkle, Little Star

LISTENING LIBRARY AUDIOCASSETTES
White Is the Moon

Literature Activity Book: p. 102
Just for Fun

EXPLORING PRINT

Big Book of Alphabet Rhymes and Chimes:
If All the World Was Apple Pie

Alphabet Poster for Ii

ABC cards

Literature Activity Book: p. 100
Learning the Code: I, i

Practice Book: p. 60

BRWL: Letterbook I(8)

 A to EZ Handbook
- Dramatization: p. 252
- Phonics: p. 283

Performance Assessment Handbook

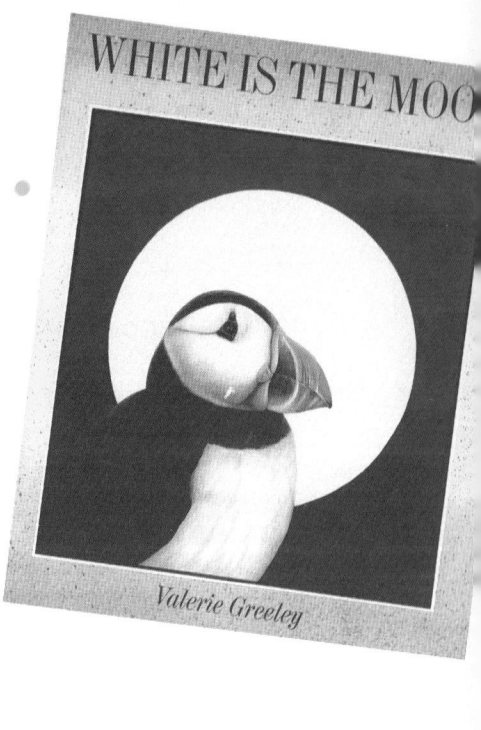

WHITE IS THE MOON

Valerie Greeley

OTHER RESOURCES

- BIG BOOK STAND
- BIG BOOK POINTER
- CHART PAPER
- MARKERS
- INDEX CARDS
- OAKTAG
- FLASHLIGHT
- GLOBE
- TAPE OR SMALL FIGURE
- WORD MASK

SHARING TIME

TODAY'S NEWS

After you write and read Today's News, encourage children to talk about their observations and wonderings about daytime and nighttime.

Day and night.
Day and night.
Do you ever wonder about day and night?

CREATING INTEREST AND BUILDING BACKGROUND

Because motivation matters!

Read the poem "Moon-Come-Out" and invite children to decide whether each verse is describing day or night. Children might also enjoy reciting the Theme Poem "I Arise" in the Big Book of Poems on pages 34–35 and singing the Theme Song "Twinkle, Twinkle, Little Star" in the Big Book of Songs on pages 38–39 again. Ask children which verse or part of "Moon-Come-Out" talks about the same thing as each of these.

Moon-Come-Out

Moon-Come-Out
And Sun-Go-In,
Here's a soft blanket
To cuddle your chin.

Moon-Go-In
And Sun-Come-Out,
Throw off the blanket
And bustle about.

—Eleanor Farjeon

As you reread the poem, invite children to join in on any parts they remember. You might want to have children improvise the actions in the poem.

READING AND WRITING

SHARING LITERATURE
White Is the Moon

BIG BOOK

REREAD THE STORY   As you read the story again, use the top panel of each left-hand page to focus on the progression from night to day and back to night. Encourage children to describe what is occurring in these panels.

As children become familiar with the structure of the story, you might pause each time the phrase *Sees a(n)/the* _____ is repeated and encourage children to predict what will be seen next based on the illustration.

PHONEMIC AWARENESS
. . . .

Initial Sounds: /i/i
- Read the title of the book and invite children to identify the word that has the same beginning sound as *if.* Then read page 22 and have children name the two words that begin with *i.*

Alliteration
- Reread the phrase *Sees a(n)/the* _____ on each page. Invite children to determine whether the object named begins with the same sound as *sees.* Record their responses.

PRINT AWARENESS
. . . .

Alliteration
- Invite children to look at the words in the two categories they created in Phonemic Awareness. Have children name the initial letters and their sounds and help them to see that those words that begin with the same sound also begin with the same letter.

Color Words
- Then write each of the color words from the book *(White, Brown, Red, Green, Yellow, Black, Pink, Grey, Orange, Blue)* on an index card. As you reread *White Is the Moon,* have volunteers match the first word on each page to one of the cards.

SEES	
Same Sound	Different Sound
sun	owl
seal	fox
sky	frog
	bird
	crab
	moon

RESPONDING TO LITERATURE

BOOK TALK   Invite children to share any comments or questions they may have had about *White Is the Moon*. Then use questions such as the following to focus on the progression from night to day and back to night.

- *How did the time of day change throughout the book? Let's look back at the pictures at the top of each left-hand page to help us remember.*

- *When you draw a circle, you begin at one spot, draw the circle, and end up at the same spot where you started. This story begins and ends with night. How is the story like drawing a circle?*

- *Did you see any pattern in the book? Does what is on one page have anything to do with what's on the next page? In what way?*

STORY THEATER   Have children form ten groups and invite each group to draw on oaktag one of the animals or objects described and pictured in the book. After coloring their drawings, they can cut them out. Then children can come forward in sequence and hold up their cut-outs, as you reread the story.

LET THE SUN SHINE   To help children visualize how the cycle of day and night is caused by the earth's rotation, invite them to think of a flashlight as the sun and a globe as the earth. Mark your location on the globe with a piece of tape or a small figure. Then darken the room and shine the flashlight on the globe. Have one of the children slowly rotate the globe to demonstrate how we move from dark to light each day.

Exploring Print LEARNING THE CODE

DECODING AND PHONICS

LETTERS: *I, i*
SOUND/LETTER RELATIONSHIPS: /i//I, i

If all the world was apple pie
And all the sea was ink,
And all the trees
   were bread and cheese,
What would we have
   to drink?

Big Book of Alphabet Rhymes and Chimes,
page 16

Developing Phonemic Awareness

Remind children that they are learning about the sounds of language and the letters that stand for those sounds. Remind them of the song "If You're Happy and You Know It." Explain that the sound they focused on in that song will be highlighted again today in a rhyme.

Invite children to listen as you read "If All the World Was Apple Pie." As you come to words that begin with *i*, slightly emphasize the initial sound. Repeat the rhyme a few times, encouraging children to chime in.

- *Listen to the sound you hear at the beginning of* if *and* ink. *What other words do you know that begin with that sound?*

Developing Print Awareness

Display "If All the World Was Apple Pie" on page 16 in the *Big Book of Alphabet Rhymes and Chimes* and repeat the rhyme with children. Use the Big Book pointer or a word mask to highlight words that begin with uppercase and lowercase *i*. Explain that the letter *i* stands for the beginning sound, /i/, in the words *If* and *ink*.

Reread the poem and encourage children to form a picture in their minds of what the poem is describing. Invite children to share these visual images.

Then display the Alphabet Poster and ABC cards for Ii, or write the letters on the chalkboard and on cards of your own.

Invite pairs of children to go on a Word Hunt to find words on charts, signs, and in books that begin with the same sound and letter as *if* and *ink*. Have children copy any words they find on cards. You may wish to point out the words *is* and *In* on the first and last pages of *White Is the Moon*. Display the words on a Word Wall or bulletin board entitled "Imagine It!"

INTO THE LEARNING CENTERS
Encourage children to visit the Hands On! Language Center for more activities with sounds and letters. See page 100.

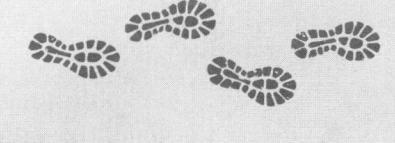

Have children compare the *i*'s on the Big Book page with the letters on the poster. Encourage children to talk about the iguana pictured on the poster.

■ **Literature Activity Book:** page 100

53

4
WONDER ABOUT IT!

LITERATURE
Read Aloud Anthology
  "The Spider Weaver"
  a Japanese folk tale
  retold by Florence Sakada

SONGS AND STORIES
AUDIOCASSETTES
STORYTELLINGS:
The Spider Weaver

Literature Activity Book: pp. 103–104
  Tell a Tale

SING & READ BOOKS AND
AUDIOCASSETTES
Twinkle, Twinkle, Little Star

EXPLORING PRINT
*Big Book of Alphabet Rhymes
and Chimes:*
  If All the World Was Apple Pie

Rhyme and Chime Strips:
  If All the World Was Apple Pie

Learning the Code: I, i

BRWL: Letterbook I(8)

STAFF DEVELOPMENT A to EZ Handbook
  • Emergent Literature: p. 253
  • Pocket Chart: p. 285

Performance Assessment Handbook

OTHER RESOURCES

- MAP OR GLOBE
- TO MAKE CLOUD
    PICTURES:
      PAPER
      CRAYONS
      COTTON
      GLUE
- BIG BOOK STAND
- BIG BOOK POINTER
- WORD MASK
- POCKET CHART AND
    STAND

Sharing Time

TODAY'S NEWS

Write and read Today's News. Invite children to look out a window at clouds or picture clouds in their minds. Encourage children to think about any questions they may have about clouds.

Fluffy, white clouds. What do you wonder about clouds?

CREATING INTEREST AND BUILDING BACKGROUND

Because motivation matters!

Use the poem "I Don't Know Why" to introduce some common wonderings about the world. Then invite children to compare the poet's wonderings with their own. Children may want to add to the brainstorming chart started during Team Work/Theme Work on pages 38–41.

You may wish to reread the "cloud" stanza of the poem for extra emphasis and connection to today's tale "The Spider Weaver." Encourage children to wonder what the explanation for white clouds might be.

I Don't Know Why

I don't know why
   the sky is blue
   or why the raindrops
   splatter through

   or why the grass
   is wet with dew . . . do you?

I don't know why
   the sun is round
   or why a seed grows
   in the ground

   or why the thunder
   makes a sound . . . do you?

I don't know why
   the clouds are white
   or why the moon
   shines very bright

   or why the air
   turns black at night . . . do you?

   —Myra Cohn Livingston

Reading and Writing

Sharing Literature
"The Spider Weaver"

SHARE THE STORY Discuss with children that people all over the world often wonder about some of the same things. Just as the American poet Myra Cohn Livingston wondered why clouds are white, so did the Japanese people who first told the tale "The Spider Weaver."

Invite children to listen as you read the story or play the STORYTELLINGS AUDIOCASSETTE of "The Spider Weaver." Before you begin, use the story title to introduce the concept of spiders as weavers. Explain that spiders have silk glands in their abdomens that produce a liquid silk. This liquid silk flows from the spider's abdomen to the tip of the *spinnerets,* the spider's small, fingerlike organs that spin the silk.

♪ SONGS AND STORIES AUDIOCASSETTES
STORYTELLINGS: The Spider Weaver

■ **Read Aloud Anthology:** pages 90–92

About the Story — Developing Multicultural Awareness

This version of "The Spider Weaver" was taken from *Japanese Children's Favorite Stories,* compiled by Florence Sakada. Her first collection, *Japanese Children's Stories,* was so popular that the printing plates wore out. Florence Sakada felt the popularity of those stories clearly proved her belief that "the stories that please children of one land are likely to please children of other lands."

RESPONDING TO LITERATURE

BOOK TALK   Invite children to share their personal reactions to the story. You might begin the discussion by sharing any of your personal reactions.

- *Do you think this story offers a good explanation for why clouds look white and cotton-soft? What did you guess the explanation would be?*

- *I liked this story because the characters were helpful and thoughtful. Who was helpful in the story? What do you think this story shows about helping others?*

JOURNAL WRITING   Because this story contains several different scenes, children may enjoy drawing and writing about their favorite part of the story in their journals.

CLOUD PICTURES   Invite children to draw scenes with a large expanse of sky and then to glue on cotton to create fleecy clouds. You might then take children outside to watch clouds and to look for images that the "spider weaver" has woven into the cloud formations.

WONDERINGS: "WHY" TALES   Share with children that people all over the world often told tales to explain things in nature. These stories are known as "why" tales, or *pourquoi* tales. Invite children to create their own "why" tales to explain things in nature or other wonderings.

TEAM WORK/THEME WORK
Encourage children to work on their "why" tales throughout the theme and to display their completed tales in the theme project Works of Wonder! See pages 38–41 and 94–95.

INTO THE LEARNING CENTERS
Children might work together in the Writing Center to create a Big Book of "The Spider Weaver" showing all of the story episodes. See page 101.

Exploring Print   Developing Concepts of Print

Using the Rhyme and Chime Strips gives children a Hands On! Language experience that allows them to explore important concepts of print.

Concepts of Print
Directionality, Words

Ii

If all the world was apple pie
And all the sea was ink,
And all the trees
     were bread and cheese,
What would we have
     to drink?

16

Big Book of Alphabet Rhymes and Chimes, page 16

Developing Print Awareness
Display page 16 in the *Big Book of Alphabet Rhymes and Chimes* and encourage children to recite the rhyme with you as you use the Big Book pointer to point to each word.

Use a word mask to frame each word in the first line. Point out the spaces between the words. Explain that the spaces help readers see where one word ends and another begins.

Then use the Rhyme and Chime Strips for "If All the World Was Apple Pie" to build the rhyme in the pocket chart as shown. Encourage children to recite the rhyme with you.

If all the world was apple pie
And all the sea was ink,
And all the trees
were bread and cheese,
What would we have
to drink?

Encourage children to notice what is the same about the first word in the first line and the last word in the second line. Invite them to say the words with you as you emphasize the initial sound.

Cut out the word cards for *If* and *ink* in the second set of Rhyme and Chime Strips. Invite children to place these cards over the matching words in the pocket chart.

Then use the picture cards to have children match the pictures of pie, ink, trees, bread, cheese, and child with empty glass to the appropriate phrases.

INTO THE LEARNING CENTERS
Allow children to use the *Big Book of Alphabet Rhymes and Chimes*, the Rhyme and Chime Strips, and the word and picture cards to build the rhyme "If All the World Was Apple Pie" in the pocket chart in the Hands On! Language Center. See page 100.

5

WONDER ABOUT IT!

LITERATURE

The Park Bench
   by Fumiko Takeshita,
   illustrated by Mamoru Suzuki

SING & READ BOOKS
AND AUDIOCASSETTES
Twinkle, Twinkle, Little Star

EXPLORING PRINT

Rhyme and Chime Strips:
If All the World Was Apple Pie

Alphabet Poster for Ii

Learning the Code: I, i

BRWL: Letterbook I(8)

STAFF DEVELOPMENT A to EZ Handbook
   • Invented Spelling: p. 260
   • Language Experience Writing: p. 268

Performance Assessment Handbook

OTHER RESOURCES

• CHART PAPER
• MARKERS
• BIG BOOK POINTER
• POCKET CHART AND
  STAND

LITERACY SUPPORT:

BUILDING LANGUAGE AND CONCEPTS

For children acquiring English and/or needing more intensive support, you may wish to incorporate the following suggestions into the basic lesson plan.

Before reading, have children focus on the setting and the details on the book's front cover by asking questions such as "Where do you think these people are?" "Who do you think this man is?" and "Why do you think parks have benches?"

Aid comprehension during reading by inviting children to find the illustrations that match the descriptions found in the text.

SHARING TIME

TODAY'S NEWS

Write and read Today's News, tracking each word as you read. Then invite children to share their ideas about what happens in a park during the day, when there are many people, and at nighttime, when people have gone home.

Today we'll spend a day and a night at a park.

CREATING INTEREST AND BUILDING BACKGROUND

Because motivation matters!

Encourage children to think about whether there are as many people in a park on a rainy day as on a sunny day, on a winter day as on a summer day. Then share the poem "Snowy Benches" by Aileen Fisher.

> ### Snowy Benches
>
> Do parks get lonely
> in winter, perhaps,
> when benches have only
> snow on their laps?
>
> —Aileen Fisher

Read the poem again and encourage children to close their eyes and to see in their minds what the poem is describing. Then invite them to think about whether or not a bench could really feel lonely.

Tell children that the next story is about a park bench that doesn't have much of a chance to feel lonely because lots of people sit on its lap!

READING AND WRITING

SHARING LITERATURE
The Park Bench

LOOK IT OVER Read the book title while tracking the print with your finger. Then read the names of the author, Fumiko Takeshita, and the illustrator, Mamoru Suzuki. Explain that this book was originally written in Japanese and published in Japan, and later translated into English. Turn to the title page and show the title written in Japanese. The same pictures were used in both books. Invite children to share what they notice in the illustrations on the front and back cover.

SHARE THE STORY As you read, give children time to explore the subtle details of the illustrations. On the pages that involve multiple panels, you may want to indicate the order of the panels to help children follow the proper sequence.

Developing Multicultural Awareness

About the Author and Illustrator

Fumiko Takeshita lives in Japan. She originally wrote the text for this book in 1985. It was published under the title *Benchi ga Hitotsu*. Ruth A. Kanagy translated the text for the American edition, which was published in 1988.

Mamoru Suzuki is a well-known children's book illustrator who also lives in Japan. He was born in Tokyo, but now lives in Shimoda. He graduated from Tokyo Art University and has received many awards for his illustrations.

こうえんに　いちばんのりは、はやおきの　ひと。　たいそうを　する　ひと。いぬを　つれた　ひと。
しろい　ベンチも　めを　さます。　あ、いつもの　おじさんが、ちいさな　くるまで　やって　きた。

The early risers are the first to arrive.　Some do exercises. Others walk their dogs.
The white bench is just now waking up.　Look, here comes the park worker in his little motor cart.

9

RESPONDING TO LITERATURE

BOOK TALK Invite children to share their personal reactions to the book. You may model such response to literature by sharing any of your own reactions or by using prompts such as the following.

- *This park reminded me of a park I used to play in because it had a duck pond. Did it remind you of any parks you know? What part of this park would you like to visit?*

- *Did you notice the pictures on the back cover? Do you remember some of these characters from inside the book? Tell us what you remember about them.*

- *Show me how you think the park bench felt when people sat on it. Show me how it felt when no one was sitting on it.*

JOURNAL WRITING Invite children to draw and write about the story in their journals, perhaps about their favorite part of the story. As children write, model writing in your own journal. Ask children if they would like to share what they wrote with the group.

WONDERINGS: A DAY-NIGHT BOOK Children can create a variation on *The Park Bench* by choosing a favorite spot and depicting it at daybreak, noon, twilight, and nightfall.

TEAM WORK/THEME WORK
Invite children to include their Day-Night Books in the theme project, Works of Wonder! See pages 38–41 and 94–95.

INTO THE LEARNING CENTERS
Children might enjoy acting out the visitors to the park bench in the Dramatic Play Center. See page 99.

The TWOZNic

Book

MelanieLuna

After drawing the book and park bench, Melanie wrote the word *book*. However, she expressed reluctance to write anything about the book because she was unable to write the words conventionally. Only with adult encouragement to "say the words and listen for the sounds in them" did she write her message.

Melanie read her message like this: "That was nice of him to give back the book."

DECODING AND PHONICS

LETTERS: *l, i*
SOUND/LETTER RELATIONSHIPS: /i/*l, i*

CONCEPTS OF PRINT
Directionality, Words, Letters

Developing Phonemic Awareness
Remind children that they have been learning about the sounds heard at the beginning of words like *is, in, it, it's, if,* and *ink* (words found in *White Is the Moon* and *The Park Bench* as well as "If All the World Was Apple Pie"). Ask children to suggest other words that have the same beginning sound.

Developing Print Awareness
Display the Alphabet Poster for Ii and point to the word *iguana.* Frame the letter *i* in the word. Remind children that the letter *i* stands for the sound heard at the beginning of the word *iguana.*

Use the strips and word cards from the Rhyme and Chime Strips for "If All the World Was Apple Pie" to build the rhyme as shown.

If	all	the	world	was	apple	pie
And	all	the	sea	was	ink,	
And	all	the	trees			
were	bread	and	cheese,			
What	would	we	have			
to	drink?					

Encourage children to say the rhyme with you as you point to each word with the Big Book pointer. Have children clap each time they hear a word that begins with the same sound as *iguana.*

Next, ask a volunteer to track the print on a line with the Big Book pointer as you say the rhyme with children. Point out that the print is read from left to right.

After children have read and clapped a third time, invite them to remove any card from the chart which does not begin with the letter *i* and for which they did not clap.

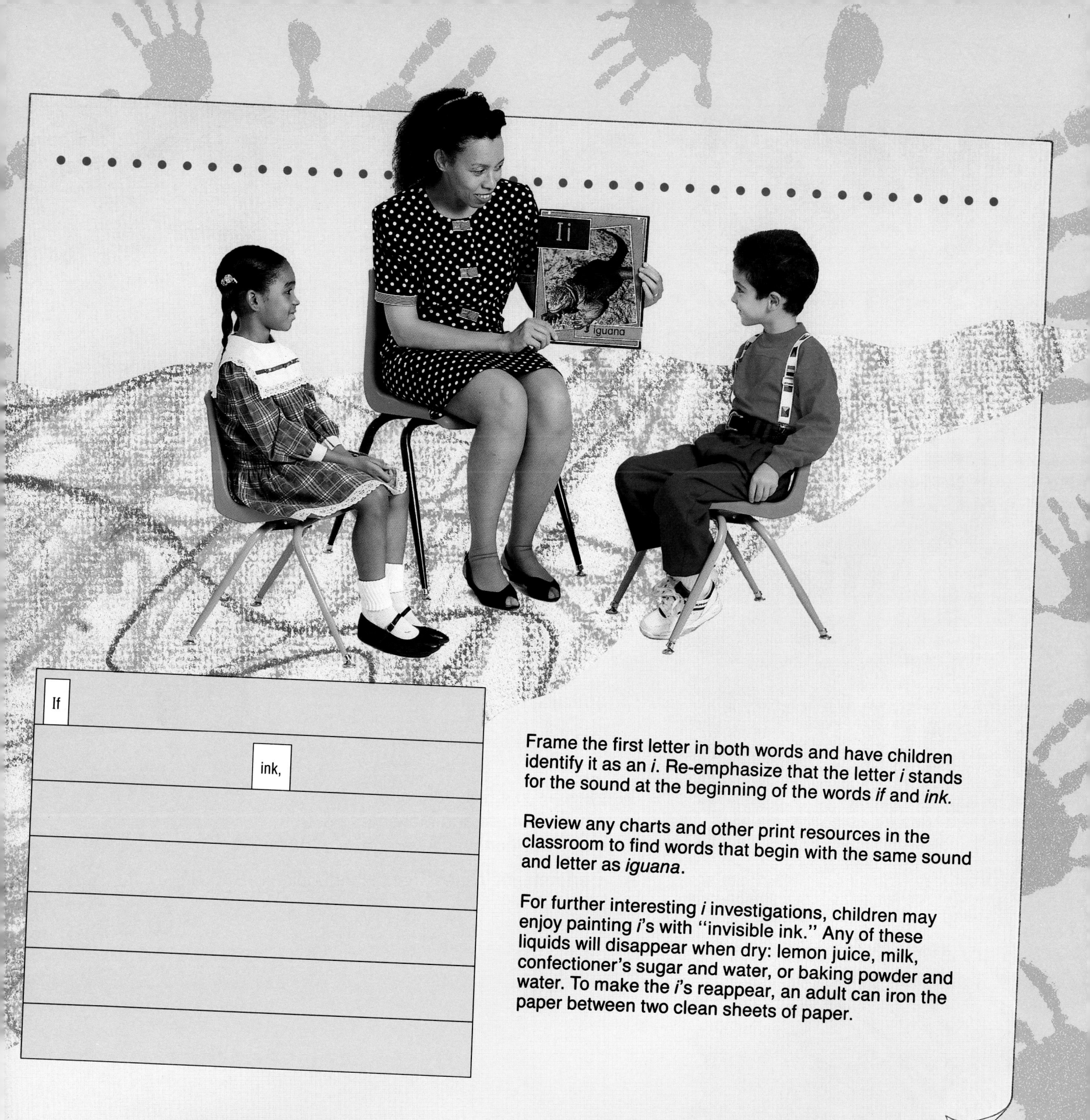

Frame the first letter in both words and have children identify it as an *i*. Re-emphasize that the letter *i* stands for the sound at the beginning of the words *if* and *ink*.

Review any charts and other print resources in the classroom to find words that begin with the same sound and letter as *iguana*.

For further interesting *i* investigations, children may enjoy painting *i*'s with "invisible ink." Any of these liquids will disappear when dry: lemon juice, milk, confectioner's sugar and water, or baking powder and water. To make the *i*'s reappear, an adult can iron the paper between two clean sheets of paper.

6
WONDER ABOUT IT!

The Park Bench
Fumiko Takeshita • Mamoru Suzuki

LITERATURE
The Park Bench
 by Fumiko Takeshita,
 illustrated by Mamoru Suzuki

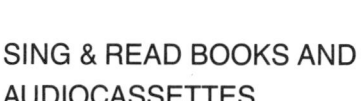 SONGS AND STORIES
AUDIOCASSETTES
STORY SONGS: Star Medley
STORY SONGS: Kagome

 SING & READ BOOKS AND
AUDIOCASSETTES
Twinkle, Twinkle, Little Star

EXPLORING PRINT
Learning the Code: X, x

SING A SOUND AUDIOCASSETTES
Oh, A-Hunting We Will Go

Practice Book: p. 61

BRWL: Letterbook X(23)

STAFF DEVELOPMENT  A to EZ Handbook
 • Music and Movement: p. 279
 • Phonemic Awareness: p. 281

Performance Assessment Handbook

OTHER RESOURCES
• CHART PAPER
• MARKERS
• WORD MASK

SHARING TIME

TODAY'S NEWS

After you write Today's News and read it with children, invite children to talk about the different activities they do when they visit a park. Help children realize that children in Japan do many of the same things when they go to parks.

Let's visit the park again!

I wish it was sunny

I wisd I hada pet

CREATING INTEREST AND BUILDING BACKGROUND

Because motivation matters!

Point out that children all over the world think about many of the same things. To reinforce this idea, compare the Japanese song "Star Wishes" with the English song "Star Light, Star Bright." Children will be interested in knowing that "Star Wishes" is sung at the Star Festival celebrated each summer in Japan. Children write wishes, tie them to trees, and wish on the stars.

After comparing the words to both songs, play "Star Medley" on the SONGS AND STORIES AUDIOCASSETTES, which includes "Star Wishes" and "Star Light, Star Bright." As the songs are replayed, invite children to chime in.

Star Wishes

Star, oh, star
So brightly shining
Give my wish to me—
As we hang our wishing cards—
On the wishing tree.

—Yutaka Suzuki and Tadamasa Yamamoto

Star Light, Star Bright

Star light, star bright,
First star I see tonight,
I wish I may, I wish I might,
Have the wish I wish tonight.

♪ SONGS AND STORIES AUDIOCASSETTES
STORY SONGS: Star Medley

Developing Multicultural Awareness

READING AND WRITING

SHARING LITERATURE
The Park Bench

REREAD THE STORY   As you reread, encourage children to point out examples of things both the children in a Japanese park and the children in a park in the United States do.

PHONEMIC AWARENESS

Initial Sounds: Review /p/p
- Invite children to listen for words that begin with the same sound as *park* in the following sentence on page 13: *"The perfect bench in just the right place," he thinks.*

Initial Sounds: Review /b/b
- Encourage children to listen for words that begin with the same sound as *big* in the following sentence on page 21: *A gentle breeze is blowing, and the park bench begins to feel drowsy, too.*

PRINT AWARENESS

Comparison
- Ask children to differentiate between the print using our alphabet and the print using Japanese characters. Encourage them to talk about how they were able to tell the difference between the two.

Repetition
- Demonstrate the regularity of print by inviting children to compare the word *white* as it appears on the first page of *White Is the Moon* to its two uses on page 6 of *The Park Bench*.

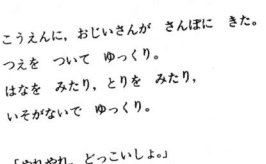

こうえんに、おじいさんが さんぽに きた。
つえを ついて ゆっくり。
はなを みたり、とりを みたり、
いそがないで ゆっくり。

「やれやれ、どっこいしょ。」
しろい ベンチで ひとやすみ。
「ちょうど いい ところに、
ちょうど いい ベンチが あるね。」

Here comes an old man taking his walk.
He moves very slowly, leaning on his cane.
He stops to smell the flowers and then to feed the birds.
He's not in any hurry.

"Now it's time for a rest," says the old man.
He sits on the white bench.
"The perfect bench in just the right place," he thinks.

12

13

RESPONDING TO LITERATURE

BOOK TALK   Invite children to share any new ideas or observations about *The Park Bench.* After sharing any comments or questions of your own, focus on the cultural similarities and differences. The following prompts might get the discussion started.

- *In what ways was this Japanese park similar to a park in the United States? Different from a park in the United States?*

- *Look at pages 26 and 27. If you were at this park, what would you be doing?*

Developing Multicultural Awareness

***KAGOME*, A JAPANESE GAME**   Point out the children in the center of page 27 who are circling around the girl who has her eyes covered. Explain that they are probably playing the Japanese game *kagome* (kä gō mā), which means "bird in a cage." Form groups of seven or eight and play the song "Kagome" on the STORY SONGS AUDIOCASSETTE as children play the game.

- Children hold hands and form a circle around one child; that child keeps his or her eyes covered.

- Children sing the song "Kagome" as they circle.

- When the song ends, children stop. The center child has three chances to guess who is behind him or her.

- If a guess is correct, that child moves to the center; three incorrect guesses means the center child stays.

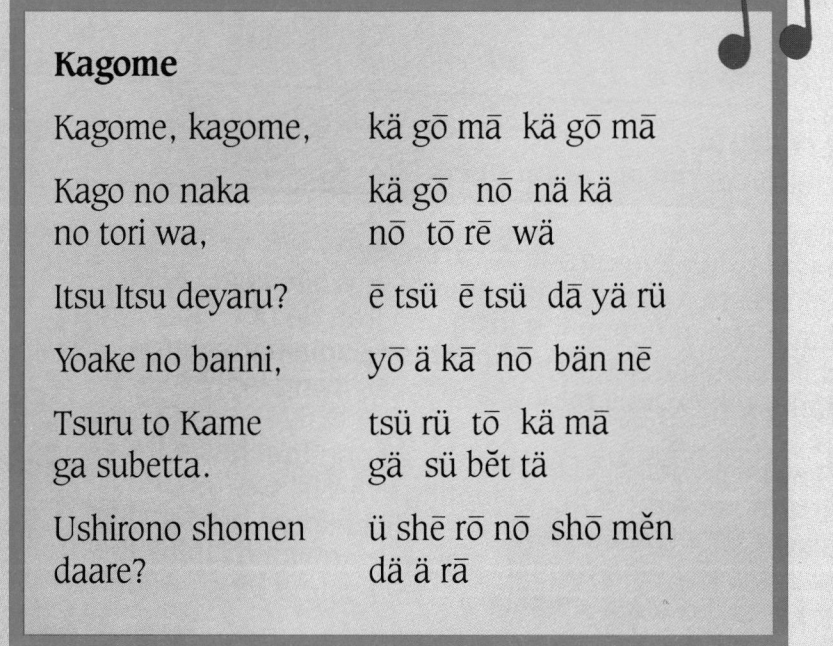

Kagome

Kagome, kagome,	kä gō mā kä gō mā
Kago no naka no tori wa,	kä gō nō nä kä nō tō rē wä
Itsu Itsu deyaru?	ē tsü ē tsü dā yä rü
Yoake no banni,	yō ä kā nō bän nē
Tsuru to Kame ga subetta.	tsü rü tō kä mā gä sü bĕt tä
Ushirono shomen daare?	ü shē rō nō shō mĕn dä ä rā

♪ SONGS AND STORIES AUDIOCASSETTES
STORY SONGS: Kagome

INTO THE LEARNING CENTERS
Children can make their own star wishes in the Writing Center. See page 101.

Exploring Print — LEARNING THE CODE

In the Exploring Print lessons for this theme, children will learn about the letters I, i and X, x and the sounds they represent. Take advantage of opportunities to point out these letters and the sounds they represent as you share Today's News, as you talk with children about their writing, and as you reread the theme-related literature.

DECODING AND PHONICS

LETTERS: X, x
SOUND/LETTER RELATIONSHIPS: /x/X, x

Developing Phonemic Awareness

Ask children to name the animal in *White Is the Moon* that is red; mention the fox if children do not. Do children think foxes live in parks? Explain that large parks with woods might have foxes living in them.

Now invite children to listen to a song that has a fox in it. Sing or play "Oh, A-Hunting We Will Go" on the SING A SOUND AUDIOCASSETTE until children are familiar with the rhyming format. Ask children if they think the fox and the other animals in *White Is the Moon* would like the song.

Oh, A-Hunting We Will Go

Oh, a-hunting we will go,
A-hunting we will go;
We'll catch a fox and put him in a box,
And then we'll let him go!

♪ SING A SOUND AUDIOCASSETTES
Oh, A-Hunting We Will Go

Sing the song again and have children clap when they hear the words *fox* and *box*. Point out that the words *fox* and *box* end with the same sound. Explain to children that /x/ is never heard at the beginning of words, but is sometimes heard at the end of words.

Developing Print Awareness

Write a capital x on the chalkboard or on chart paper; below it write the third line of the song, "Oh, A-Hunting We Will Go." Encourage children to say the letter and words with you as you point to them.

> X
>
> We'll catch a fox and put him in a box,

Use the word mask to frame a capital and lowercase x.

- Let's look at some x's together. Here is a capital, or uppercase, X. It is not in a word because x is rarely used at the beginning of words. You won't often see a capital, or uppercase, x.

- Here is a lowercase x in the word fox. Say the word fox with me. What other word can you find that ends with a lowercase x?

Encourage children to trace over with their fingers uppercase and lowercase x's on the chalkboard or chart paper.

Explain that the letter x stands for the sound heard at the end of fox and box. Have children say other words that end with this sound. If children suggest words such as rocks or tricks, confirm their answers and explain that the same sound is heard in words that end with the letters cks.

Then invite children to illustrate the verse of "Oh, A-Hunting We Will Go" in which a fox is caught in a box and then freed. Encourage them to label their drawings.

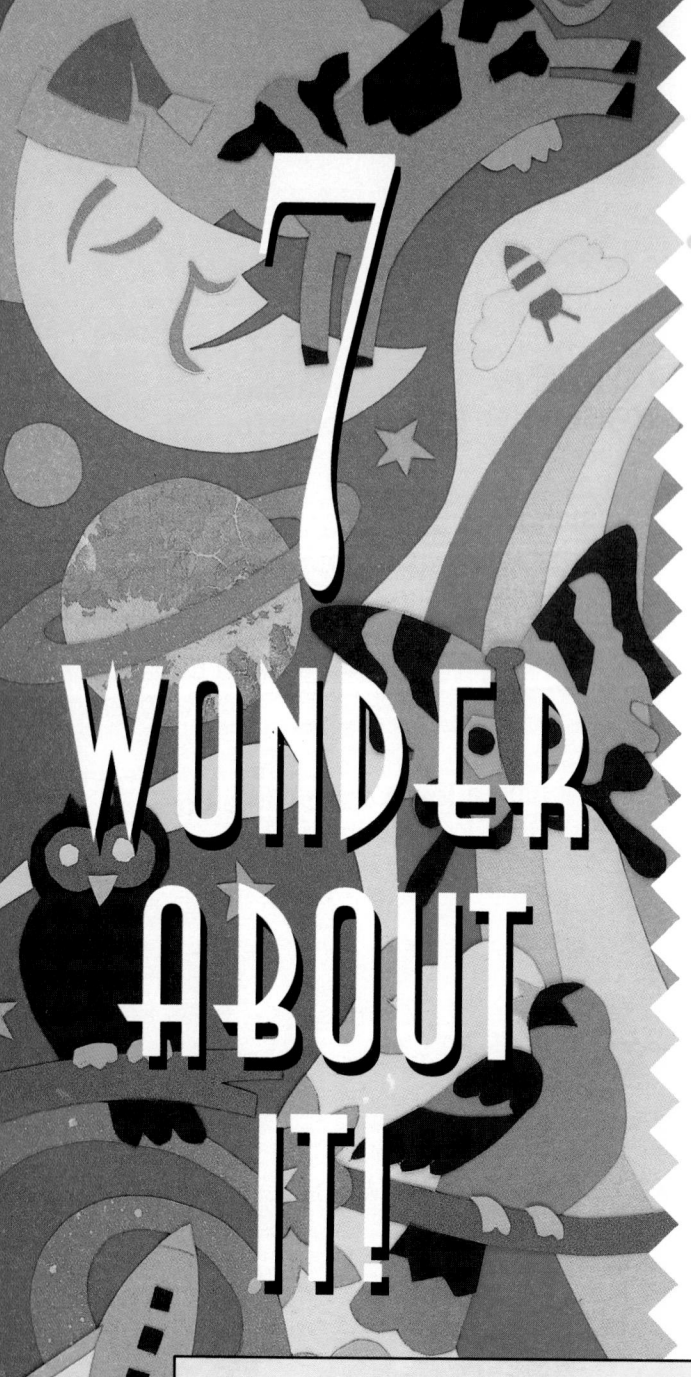

7

WONDER ABOUT IT!

LITERATURE

Half a Moon and One Whole Star
by Crescent Dragonwagon,
illustrated by Jerry Pinkney

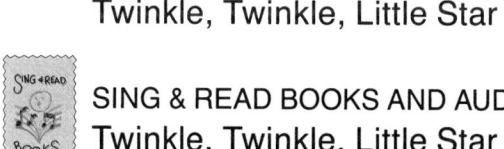

SONGS AND STORIES
AUDIOCASSETTES
STORY SONGS:
Twinkle, Twinkle, Little Star

SING & READ BOOKS AND AUDIOCASSETTES
Twinkle, Twinkle, Little Star

EXPLORING PRINT

Big Book of Alphabet Rhymes and Chimes:
What Words Begin with X?

Alphabet Poster for Xx; ABC cards

Literature Activity Book: p. 101
Learning the Code: X, x

Practice Book: p. 62

BRWL: Letterbook X(23)

STAFF DEVELOPMENT A to EZ Handbook
  • Environmental Print: p. 255
  • Pointing: p. 287

Performance Assessment Handbook

OTHER RESOURCES

• BIG BOOK STAND
• BIG BOOK POINTER
• WORD MASK

LITERACY SUPPORT:
Building Language and Concepts

For children acquiring English and/or needing more intensive support, you may wish to incorporate the following suggestions into the basic lesson plan.

Before reading, explain the concepts "half" and "whole." Give each child a different pre-cut construction-paper shape and have them say, "I have a whole (circle)." Then allow them to cut their shapes in half and say, "I have half a (circle)." Invite children to describe a full moon and a crescent moon.

Sharing Time

TODAY'S NEWS

Write and then read Today's News. As you read, slightly emphasize the beginning sounds of the words *imagine, it,* and *is.* Ask children to identify the words that have the same beginning sounds and name the letter that each word begins with.

♪ SONGS AND STORIES AUDIOCASSETTES
STORY SONGS: Twinkle, Twinkle, Little Star

> Close your eyes and imagine it is nighttime.

CREATING INTEREST AND BUILDING BACKGROUND

Because motivation matters!

Invite children to imagine it is nighttime. Ask them to describe what they see and hear. You may wish to play the Theme Song, "Twinkle, Twinkle, Little Star" on the SONGS AND STORIES AUDIOCASSETTES to set the mood. Then, read the poem "Silverly." Encourage children to talk about the images they pictured in their minds as they listened to the poem.

Silverly

Silverly,
   Silverly,
Over the
   Trees
The moon drifts
   By on a
Runaway
   Breeze.

Dozily,
   Dozily,
Deep in her
   Bed,
A little girl
   Dreams with the
Moon in her
   Head.

—Dennis Lee

73

READING AND WRITING

Half a Moon and One Whole Star

LOOK IT OVER   Read the title and names of the author and the illustrator while tracking the print.

Display the front and back covers. Invite children to point out "half a moon" and "one whole star" on the back cover, along with the planet Earth.

SHARE THE STORY   Reading the text as a lullaby may enhance its soothing, rhythmic quality. As you read, pause after each unanswered question to invite children to consider a response, in order to increase their involvement with the text.

About the Author and Illustrator

Crescent Dragonwagon is the daughter of children's book editor and writer Charlotte Zolotow. Originally named Ellen Zolotow, she chose her new name when she was sixteen years old. Her diverse writings include picture books, novels for young adults, poetry for adults, and cookbooks.

Jerry Pinkney has won numerous awards for his illustrations, including the Coretta Scott King Award for *Half a Moon and One Whole Star, The Patchwork Quilt,* and *Mirandy and Brother Wind.* The latter book was a Caldecott Honor book. Jerry Pinkney lives in Croton-on-Hudson, New York.

Will morning glories, closed up tight,
Conceal their blueness through the night?
Yes, yes, yes, they will, sleep, Susan, sleep.

RESPONDING TO LITERATURE

BOOK TALK   Invite children to share their personal reactions to the book. Sharing your own response will help get the discussion started. Questions such as the following might also be included.

- *This book reminded me of times I slept over at my grandmother's when I was young. Did any of the things in the poem remind you of what it's like to fall asleep?*

- *I liked the way the illustrator Jerry Pinkney decorated Susan's bedroom with things from the night. What night things do you see on pages 10–11?*

- *I wondered why the picture on page 29 shows Susan under the table. Do you have any idea why? Was there anything in the illustrations that you wondered about?*

JOURNAL WRITING   Invite children to share their impressions of nighttime in their journals. They might want to focus on what they like or don't like about the night. Encourage volunteers to share their entries with the group.

INTO THE LEARNING CENTERS
Children can learn to recite bedtime rhymes in the Listening Center. See page 104. They can write story extensions describing Susan's activities from morning to night in the Writing Center. See page 101. Today would also be a good day for children to prepare announcements for their Works of Wonder! project.

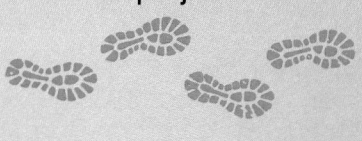

Shyra initially drew a bird and a butterfly. Only after an opportunity to talk about the story did she draw the moon and add the letters at the top of the page.

Shyra read her message like this: "Stars."

DECODING AND PHONICS

LETTERS: *X, x*
SOUND/LETTER RELATIONSHIPS: /x/X, *x*

What words begin with X?
Very few.
X-ray and xylophone
Will do.

Margaret and John Travers Moore

Xx

***Big Book of Alphabet Rhymes and Chimes,
page 33***

■ **Literature Activity Book:** page 101

Developing Phonemic Awareness
Invite children to listen as you read "What Words Begin with X?" Repeat the rhyme a few times, encouraging children to chime in.

- *There are not many words that begin with X. In some words the letter* x *sounds like the name for the letter* x, *and in others, the letter* x *sounds like* /z/.

Developing Print Awareness
Display "What Words Begin with X?" in the *Big Book of Alphabet Rhymes and Chimes* on page 33 and repeat the rhyme with children. Use the Big Book pointer or a word mask to highlight the words that begin with uppercase and lowercase *x*.

Reread the poem and encourage children to share what they know about X-rays and xylophones.

Then display the Alphabet Poster and the ABC cards for Xx, or write the letters on the chalkboard and on cards of your own.

Have children compare the *x*'s on the Big Book page with the letters on the poster and cards. Encourage children to talk about the fox pictured on the poster.

fox

Invite pairs of children to go on a Word Hunt to find words on charts, signs, and in books that end with the same sound and letter as *fox* and *box.* You may wish to point out the word *fox* on pages 6 and 8 of *White Is the Moon* and *relax* on page 21 of *The Park Bench.* Words ending in *x* will be hard for children to find, but you might create a bulletin board entitled *Six X Words,* with such words cards as *fox, box, fix, mix, wax,* and *relax.*

INTO THE LEARNING CENTERS

Encourage children to visit the Hands On! Language Center for more activities with sounds and letters. See page 100.

8

WONDER ABOUT IT!

LITERATURE
Half a Moon and One Whole Star
by Crescent Dragonwagon,
illustrated by Jerry Pinkney

 SING & READ BOOKS AND
AUDIOCASSETTES
Twinkle, Twinkle, Little Star

EXPLORING PRINT
*Big Book of Alphabet Rhymes
and Chimes:*
   What Words Begin with X?

Rhyme and Chime Strips:
   What Words Begin with X?

Learning the Code: X, x

BRWL: Letterbook X(23)

STAFF DEVELOPMENT A to EZ Handbook
   • Hands On! p. 258
   • Masking: p. 273

Performance Assessment Handbook

OTHER RESOURCES

• CHART PAPER
• MARKERS
• BIG BOOK STAND
• BIG BOOK POINTER
• POCKET CHART AND
  STAND
• WORD MASK

SHARING TIME

TODAY'S NEWS

Write and read Today's News, tracking each word as you read. Invite children to describe the last sounds they hear before they fall asleep at night.

Whir. Whir. Whir. What sounds do you hear at night?

CREATING INTEREST AND BUILDING BACKGROUND

Because motivation matters!

Read the poem "Lullaby." Encourage children to form pictures in their minds of what the poem describes.

Lullaby

Near and far, near and far,
Over the hill there hangs a star.
Over the star is a slice of moon,
And a cloud will cover them very soon.
Far and near, far and near,
My teddy and I are dreaming here
And over us both my mother is bending,
Crooning a tune without any ending,
Near and far, near and far,
Over the hill there hangs a star.

—Margaret Hillert

Help children understand that the mother in the poem is singing a lullaby to her child, a comforting song sung to put the child to sleep. The lullaby will be among the last sounds the child will hear this night.

Invite children to describe ways in which the poem is similar to *Half a Moon and One Whole Star*. You might then display the first page of the book and read that text, before reading the poem again for comparison.

READING AND WRITING

SHARING LITERATURE
Half a Moon and One Whole Star

REREAD THE STORY Before you begin to reread the story, ask children to note all the sounds Susan hears before she falls asleep.

PHONEMIC AWARENESS

Alliteration
Point out the alliterative phrases on page 17 and invite children to repeat them.

> He'll play it black and blue and right
> And at the club they'll dance tonight
> He'll play while bakers bake their bread
> While Susan turns and dreams in bed.

PRINT AWARENESS

Repetition
- Invite children to find and count the repetitions of the word *yes* and the phrase *sleep, Susan, sleep* on pages 11, 15, 18, 22, 27, 30, and 32.

Print in Artwork
- Help children recognize the print included within the illustration on pages 12–13. Encourage them to include print within their own artwork.

Outside her window, summer night
And summer scents and summer's right
For honeysuckle, green-cut lawns
Susan breathes green smells and yawns
Susan hears the crickets whir
Susan sees the curtains stir
Sees them stir through half-closed eyes
Hears the Steinkamps call good-byes
Half-closed eyes are drooping low
She hears laughter down below
On the porch her parents talk

RESPONDING TO LITERATURE

BOOK TALK   Invite children to share any thoughts or questions they may have had about the story since the previous reading. Share any new thoughts of your own.

Then use questions such as the following to focus on the sights and sounds of night as presented in the book.

- *What are some of the things Susan heard as she was falling asleep? What sounds do you think Susan might hear if she lived in a big city?*

- *Pictures can set a mood, or feeling, for a story. On pages 4 and 5, I could imagine the stillness of the night. Which pictures helped you to imagine the night sounds?*

WONDERINGS: A NIGHTTIME COMPOSITION   Invite children to wonder about the night and to create a poem, song, or book to communicate their feelings. To get started, work as a group to create a list of night sights, jobs, and other activities. When the list is complete, read it together.

Things to do at Night
- sleep
- dream
- bake bread
- play jazz
- talk on the phone

THE SOUNDS OF NIGHT   Invite children to create the sounds of night! Children can imitate night sounds, either from the book or their own imaginations.

INTO THE LEARNING CENTERS
Children can make star gazers in the Science Center and a "night sounds" tape in the Listening Center. See pages 102 and 104.

TEAM WORK/THEME WORK
Have children think about how they want to present their nighttime compositions in the theme project Works of Wonder! See pages 38–41 and 94–95.

Exploring Print DEVELOPING CONCEPTS OF PRINT

Using the Rhyme and Chime Strips gives children a Hands On! Language experience that allows them to explore important concepts of print.

CONCEPTS OF PRINT
Directionality, Words

What words begin with X?
Very few.
X-ray and xylophone
Will do.

Margaret and John Travers Moore

Xx

Big Book of Alphabet Rhymes and Chimes, page 33

Developing Print Awareness
Display page 33 in the *Big Book of Alphabet Rhymes and Chimes* and encourage children to recite the rhyme with you as you use the Big Book pointer to point to each word.

Read the rhyme again using the Big Book pointer. This time, emphasize the return sweep as you finish one line and go to the next.

Now use a word mask to frame each word in the first line. Point out the spaces between the words. Explain that the spaces help readers see where one word ends and another begins.

Then use the Rhyme and Chime Strips for "What Words Begin with X?" to build the rhyme in the pocket chart as shown, and encourage children to recite it with you.

| What words begin with X? |
| Very few. |
| X-ray and xylophone |
| Will do. |

Ask children to look at the words *X-ray* and *xylophone* in the third line. Children should note that the two words begin with the same letter but they don't begin with the same sound. Then use the picture cards to have children match the pictures of X-ray and xylophone to those words.

Encourage children to identify the word that has the most letters. Invite a volunteer to count the letters in *xylophone*.

INTO THE LEARNING CENTERS

Allow the children to use the *Big Book of Alphabet Rhymes and Chimes*, the Rhyme and Chime Strips, and the word and picture cards to build the rhyme "What Words Begin with X?" in the pocket chart in the Hands On! Language Center. See page 100.

9 WONDER ABOUT IT!

LITERATURE
Read Aloud Anthology
"The One You Don't
See Coming"
a folk tale from Liberia
retold by Harold Courlander
and George Herzog

SING & READ BOOKS AND AUDIOCASSETTES
Twinkle, Twinkle, Little Star

EXPLORING PRINT
Rhyme and Chime Strips:
What Words Begin with X?

Alphabet Poster for Xx

Learning the Code: X, x

BRWL: Letterbook X(23)

STAFF DEVELOPMENT A to EZ Handbook
- Concepts of Print: p. 248
- Retelling: p. 295

Performance Assessment Handbook

OTHER RESOURCES

- WORLD MAP OR GLOBE
- WORD MASK
- POCKET CHART AND STAND

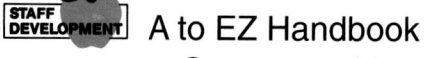
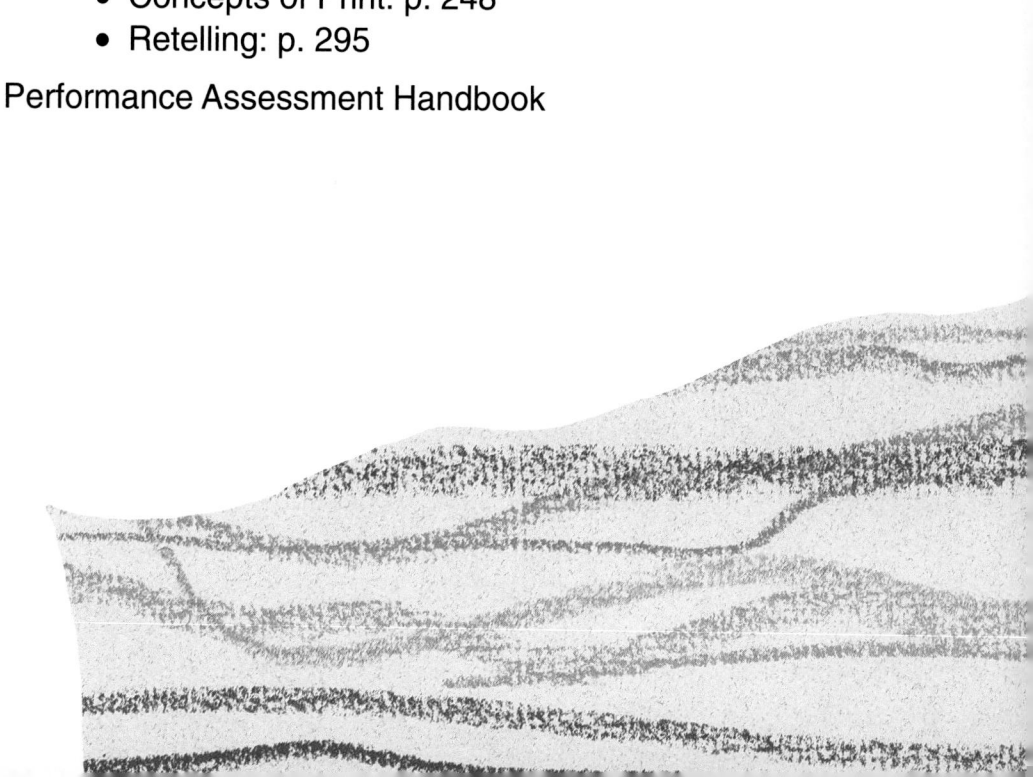

SHARING TIME

TODAY'S NEWS

Before you read Today's News, point out to children that it is a riddle. As children try to answer the riddle, encourage them to think about things that happen to them at night. Write children's suggested answers. Then let them know that they will find out the answer as they listen to the story "The One You Don't See Coming."

Think. What comes every night but is never seen?

CREATING INTEREST AND BUILDING BACKGROUND

Because motivation matters!

Explain that today's story tells about something that happens at night. Before reading the story, share the poem "The Night."

The Night

The night
  creeps in
  around my head
  and snuggles down
  upon the bed
  and makes lace pictures
  on the wall
  but doesn't say a word at all.

—Myra Cohn Livingston

Then focus on the poem's personification of night to help prepare children for the personification of sleep in "The One You Don't See Coming."

- *Listen as I read the poem again. What things does the poet say night does? Can night really creep in or snuggle down on the bed? Why or why not?*

- *Why do you think the poet describes night as if it were alive and could do things?*

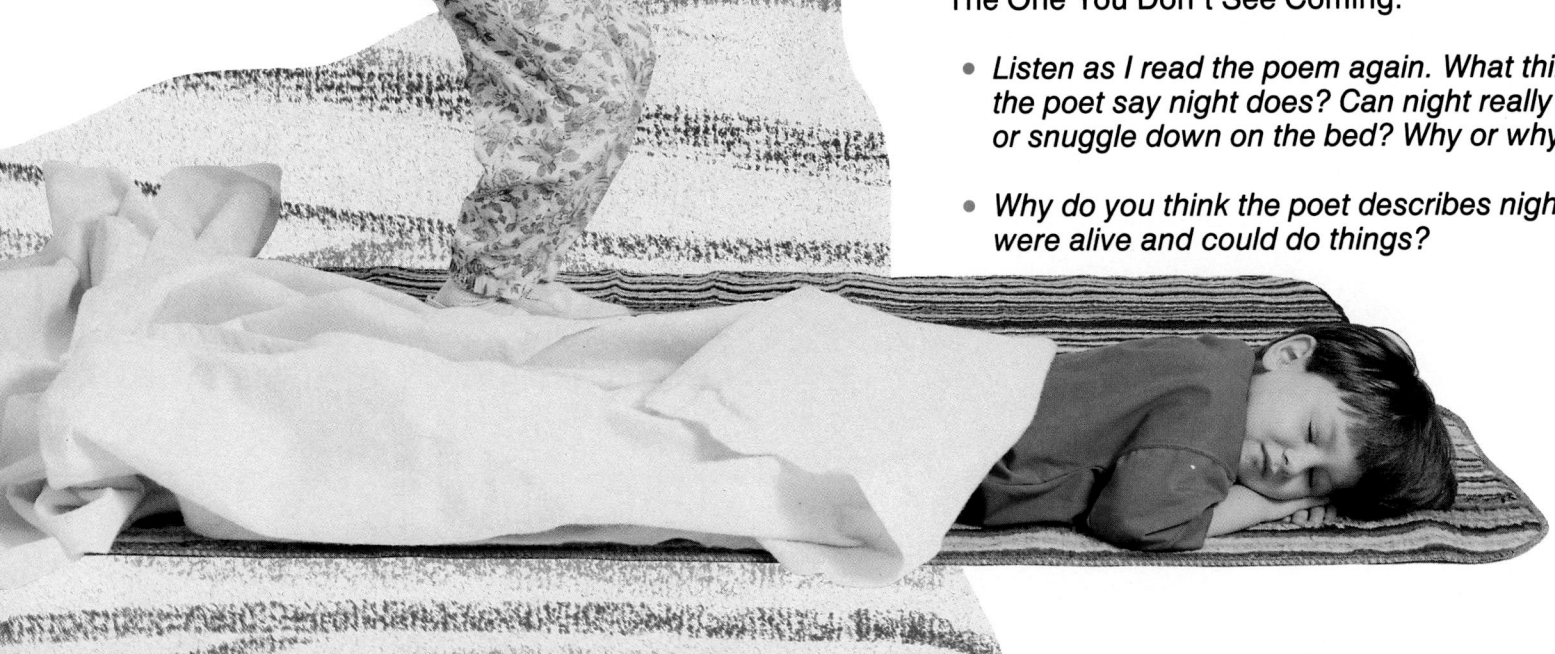

85

READING AND WRITING

SHARING LITERATURE
"The One You Don't See Coming"

SHARE THE STORY Explain to children that stories they listen to without looking at pictures or words are special because listeners get to make their own pictures in their minds. Invite children to form pictures of the hunters in their minds as they listen to the story.

As you tell the story, slow down during the passages that describe Biafu drifting off to sleep. Then pick up the pace abruptly each time he is jolted awake.

■ **Read Aloud Anthology:**
 pages 93–97

About the Story
Developing Multicultural Awareness

Point out the continent of Africa and the country of Liberia on a map or globe. Share that "The One You Don't See Coming" was originally told in that country. The Cavally River mentioned in the story forms the border between Liberia and the Ivory Coast.

Liberia was founded in 1822 to provide a home to freed Africans who were formerly enslaved in the United States. Today, about 5 percent of Liberia's population are descendants of those African Americans; the rest are primarily descendants of Africans who settled the area in the 1400s.

This version of "The One You Don't See Coming" was collected by George Herzog and included in the Newbery Honor book *The Cow-Tail Switch and Other West African Stories*, which he co-authored with noted folk-tale researcher Harold Courlander.

RESPONDING TO LITERATURE

BOOK TALK Invite children to share any personal reactions to the story. You might begin the discussion by sharing any of your own reactions or by using questions such as the following.

- *This story reminded me of times I have tried to stay awake but couldn't. Have you ever tried to stay awake? What was it like?*

- *Why did Biafu, Deeba, and Gunde want to catch Sleep? What do you think would have happened if they had caught Sleep?*

- *How would you try to catch Sleep?*

WONDERINGS: SLEEP DRAWINGS Remind children that no one has ever seen Sleep. Invite them to create and label their own images of Sleep using either paints or crayons. Children can then share their images.

STORY THEATER Help children visualize the story action by inviting three young hunters to dramatize the actions as you read the story. Create the setting by inviting children to use objects and areas in the classroom to serve as the tree, the bush, and the river.

TEAM WORK/THEME WORK
Is everybody ready for the Works of Wonder! exhibit? Allow children time to add finishing touches to their projects. See pages 38–41 and 94–95.

INTO THE LEARNING CENTERS
Children might enjoy creating Reward Notices in the Writing Center to encourage the capture of Sleep. See page 101.

DECODING AND PHONICS

LETTERS: *X, x*
SOUND/LETTER RELATIONSHIPS: /x/*X, x*

CONCEPTS OF PRINT
Directionality, Words, Letters

Developing Phonemic Awareness
Remind children that they have been learning about the sound heard at the end of words like *fox, box,* and *relax* (words found in *White Is the Moon* and *The Park Bench* as well as in "Oh, A-Hunting We Will Go"). Ask children to suggest other words that have the same ending sound. Review with children that very few words actually begin with the letter *x.*

Developing Print Awareness
Display the Alphabet Poster for Xx and point to the word *fox.* Frame the letter *x* in the word. Remind children that the letter *x* stands for the sound heard at the end of the word *fox.*

Use the strips and word cards from the Rhyme and Chime Strips for "What Words Begin with X?" to build the rhyme as shown.

What	words	begin	with	X?

Very	few.

X-ray	and	xylophone

Will	do.

Encourage children to say the rhyme with you as you point to each word with the Big Book pointer. Then invite children to point to any capital or lowercase *x*'s.

Again, frame the letter *x* in the word *fox* on the Alphabet Poster, and then frame the *x* in *xylophone* in the Rhyme and Chime Strips. Discuss with children that the beginning sound in the word *xylophone* is not the same as the ending sound in the word *fox,* even though they are both written with the letter *x.* Emphasize again that very few words begin with the letter *x,* but some frequently used words, like *fox* and *box,* end with *x.*

Finally, review any charts and other print resources in the classroom that children found with words that end with the same sound and letter as *fox.*

INTO THE LEARNING CENTERS
Encourage print exploration! Send children to the Hands On! Language Center to work with letter stamps, sponge letters, and magnetic letters. See page 100.

89

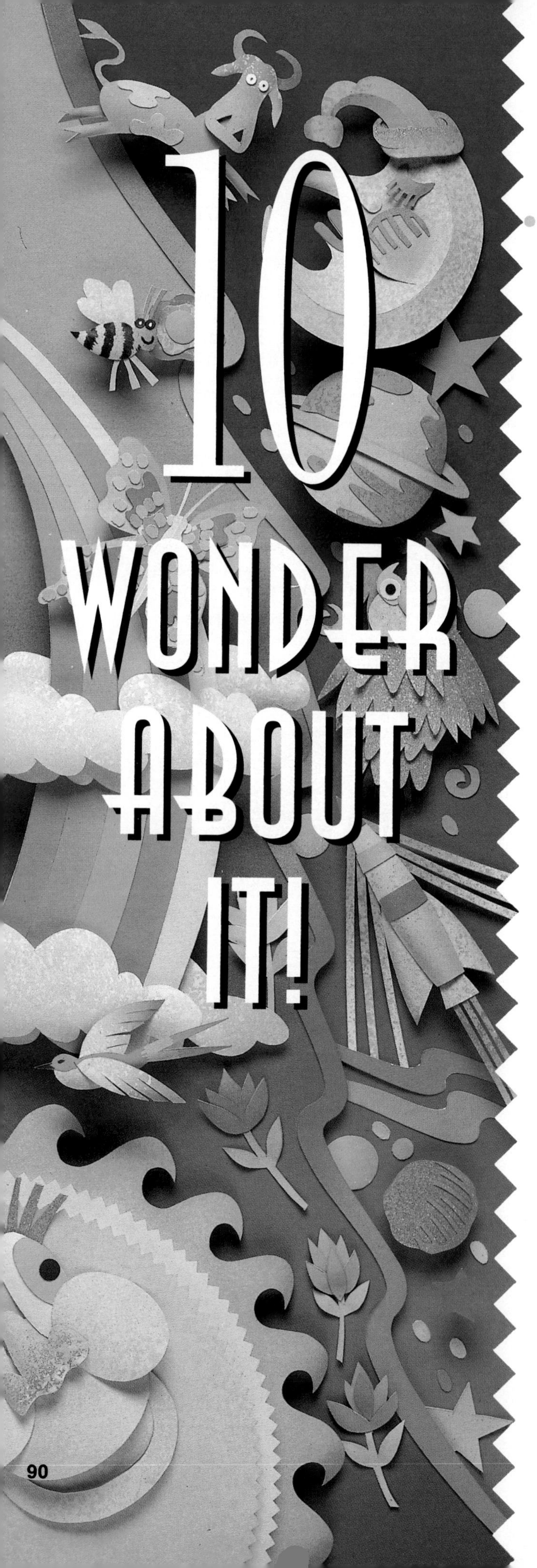

10
WONDER ABOUT IT!

LITERATURE

White Is the Moon
by Valerie Greeley

The Park Bench
by Fumiko Takeshita,
illustrated by Mamoru Suzuki

Half a Moon and One Whole Star
by Crescent Dragonwagon,
illustrated by Jerry Pinkney

Big Book of Poems: I Arise
an Eskimo song

Big Book of Songs:
Twinkle, Twinkle, Little Star
Traditional

SONGS AND STORIES
AUDIOCASSETTES
STORY SONGS:
Twinkle, Twinkle, Little Star

SING & READ BOOKS AND
AUDIOCASSETTES
Twinkle, Twinkle, Little Star

Literature Activity Book: p. 105
Responding to Literature

 A to EZ Handbook

- Observation: p. 279

- Technology: p. 301

Performance Assessment Handbook

OTHER RESOURCES

- BIG BOOK STAND
- BIG BOOK POINTER

Sharing Time

TODAY'S NEWS

After you read Today's News, highlight the word *thinkers* and invite children to compare it to the Theme Word *thinker.* Children can then complete any tasks that need to be accomplished before presenting their Works of Wonder!

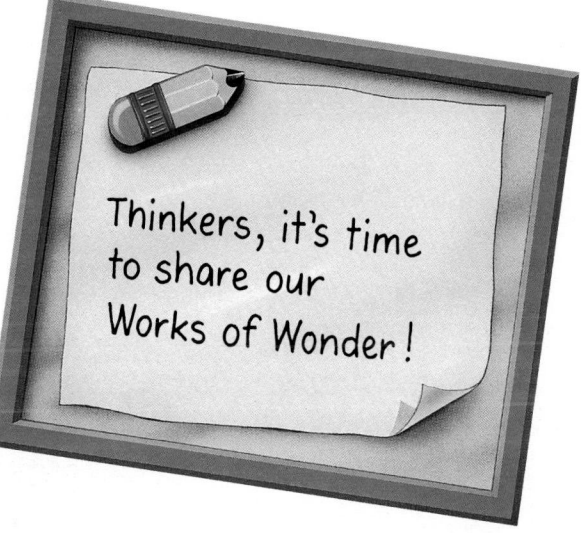

Thinkers, it's time to share our Works of Wonder!

WRAPPING IT UP

To encourage an atmosphere for wondering, reread the Theme Poem "I Arise" and sing the Theme Song "Twinkle, Twinkle, Little Star." Children can follow along as you track the print with the Big Book pointer in the *Big Book of Poems,* pages 34–35, and the *Big Book of Songs,* pages 38–39. Reintroduce the Theme Word *thinker* by asking children to think about all the things they learned this week.

I Arise

I arise to meet the day,
My face is turned from
the dark of night
To gaze at the new dawn
whitening the sky.

Eskimo Song

35

Big Book of Poems, pages 34–35

♪ SONGS AND STORIES AUDIOCASSETTES
STORY SONGS: Twinkle, Twinkle, Little Star

Reading and writing

Sharing Literature

LOOK IT OVER   Display all the theme books (*White Is the Moon, The Park Bench,* and *Half a Moon and One Whole Star*) and read the titles. Invite volunteers to share what they remember about each book. Ask the class to choose one book for you to reread.

REREAD THE STORY   Reread the chosen selection. Invite children to think about what time of day is being described.

Review the letters children learned about by asking children to listen for and name words that begin with *i* and that end with *x*. To give children additional practice, you may wish to use the Phonics Activity Sheets on pages 109–110.

RESPONDING TO LITERATURE

BOOK TALK   Invite children to share their personal opinions of the three books. Be sure to express your thoughts as well.

Encourage children to talk about how the books are similar and how they are different. The following questions might be used to initiate this comparative discussion.

- *In which two books was the moon important? Can you find the word* moon *in the title of those books?*

- *Think about the stories* White Is the Moon *and* The Park Bench. *How do these stories tell about day turning into night?*

- *If Susan in* Half a Moon and One Whole Star *and the park worker in* The Park Bench *could talk to each other, what things might they both wonder about day and night?*

JOURNAL WRITING   Point to the Theme Word *thinker* where you wrote it at the beginning of the theme or rewrite it on the chalkboard. Talk with children about their experiences as thinkers who wondered about our world.

Provide a sense of closure by inviting children to record in their journals the questions that they wondered about as *thinkers.* Provide a model for journal writing by writing in your own journal. Conclude by inviting volunteers to share their entries with the class.

INTO THE LEARNING CENTERS
Invite children into the Reading Center where they may enjoy reading the theme books. See page 98.

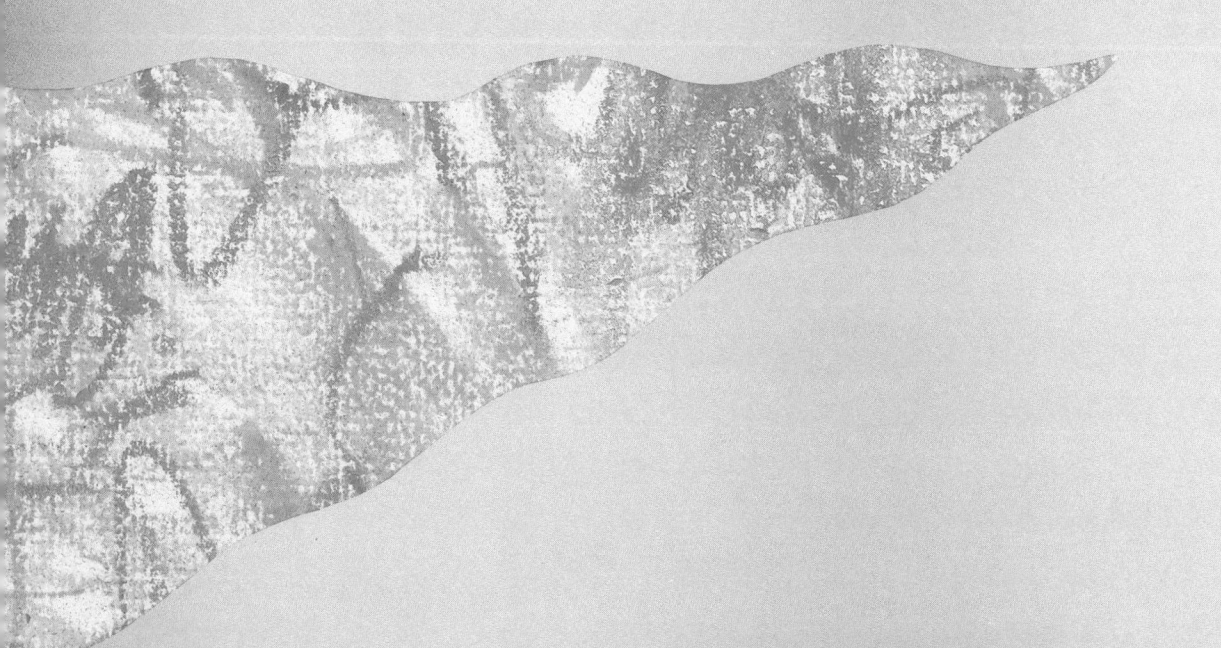

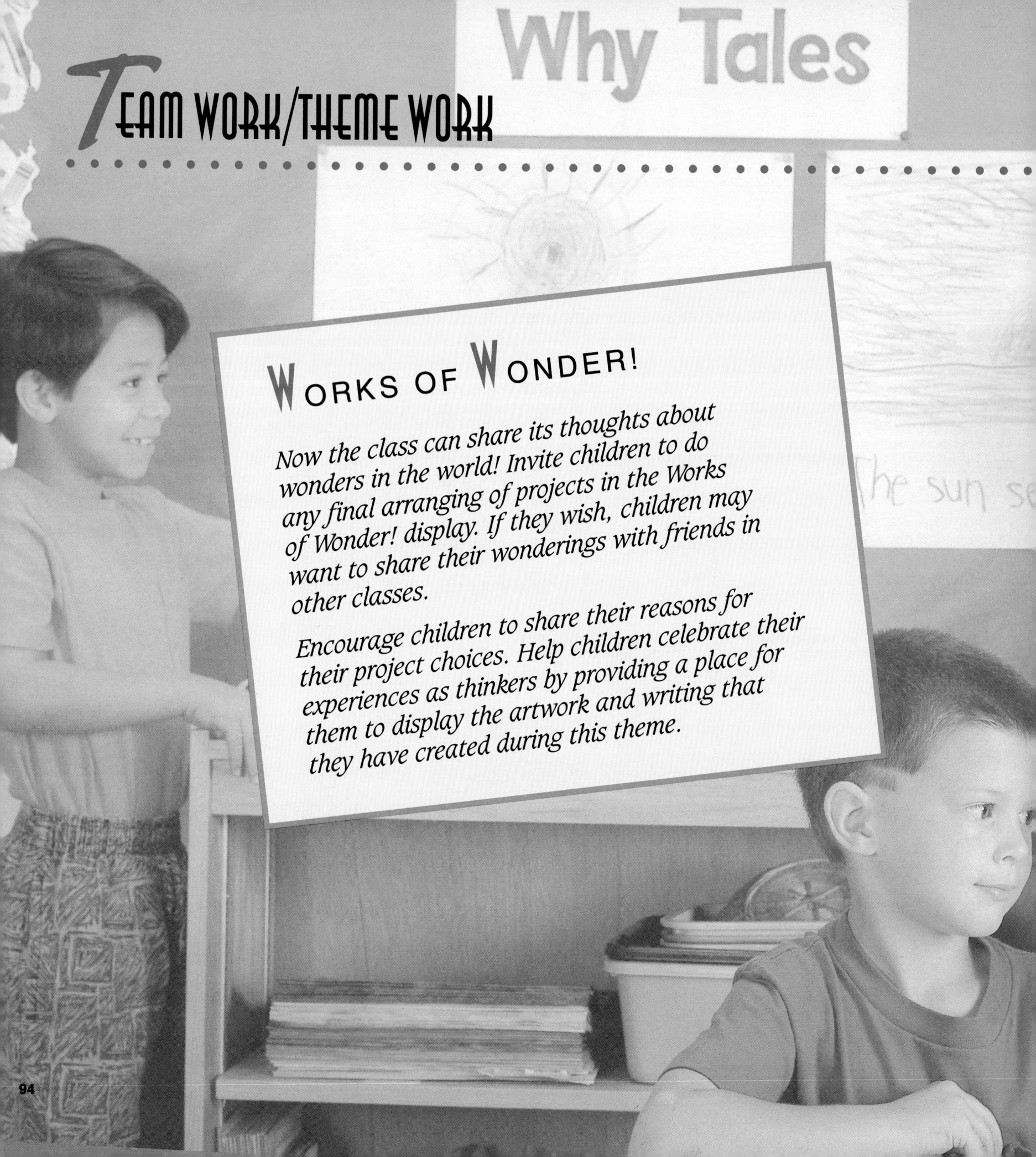

WORKS OF WONDER!

Now the class can share its thoughts about wonders in the world! Invite children to do any final arranging of projects in the Works of Wonder! display. If they wish, children may want to share their wonderings with friends in other classes.

Encourage children to share their reasons for their project choices. Help children celebrate their experiences as thinkers by providing a place for them to display the artwork and writing that they have created during this theme.

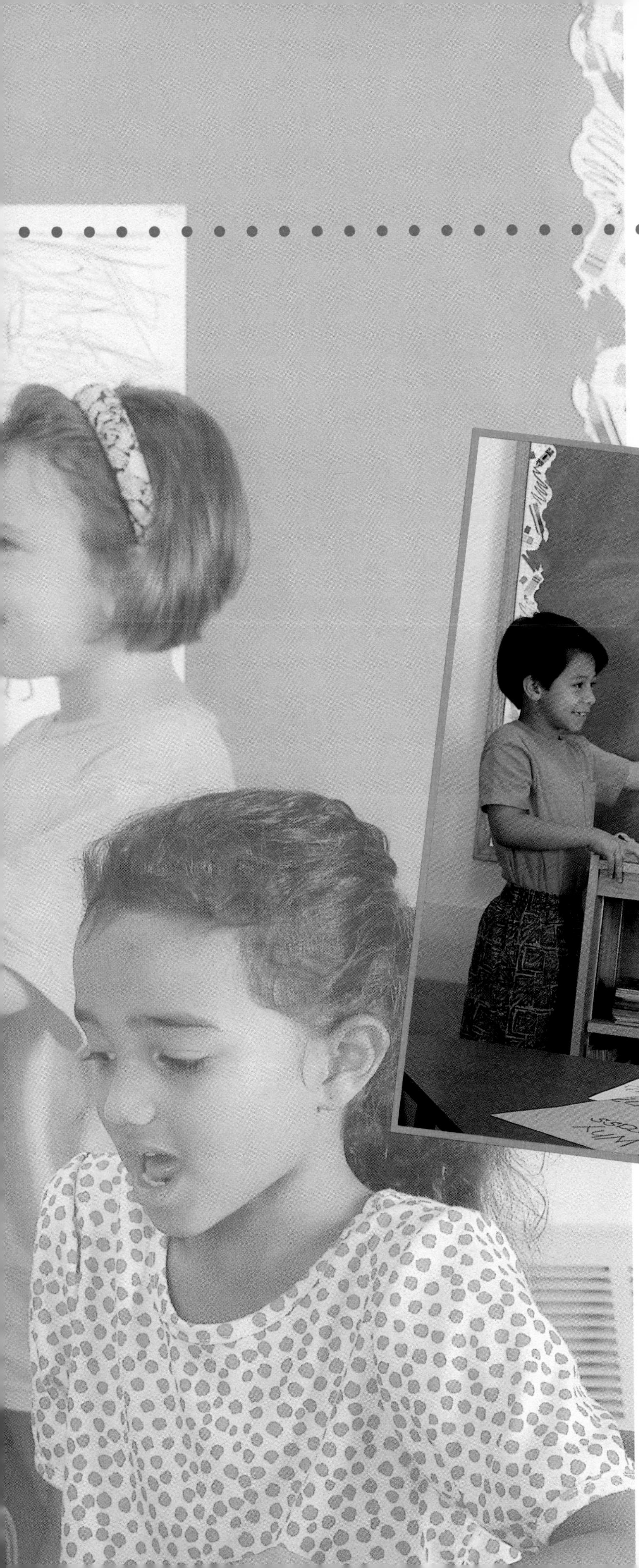

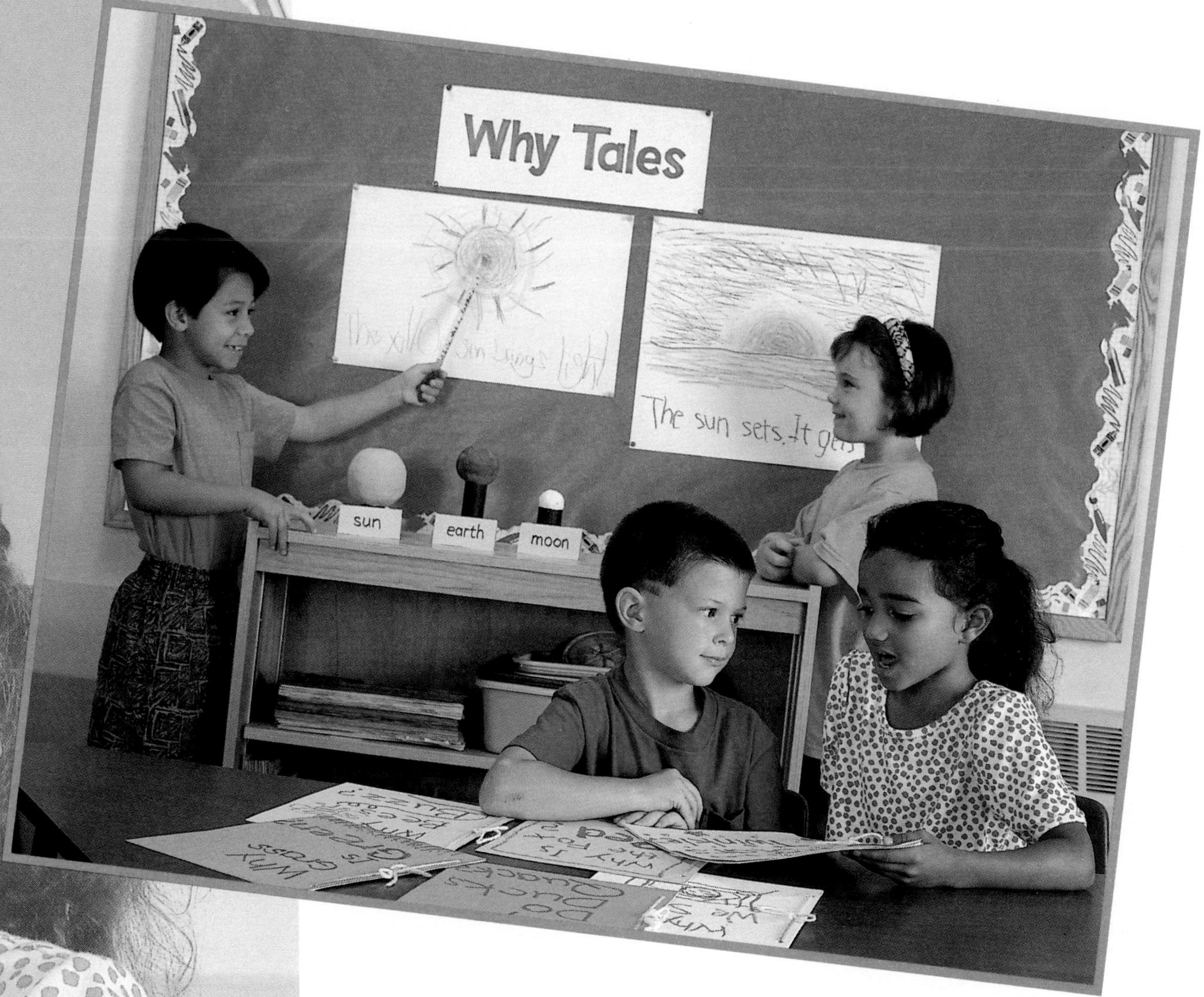

INTO THE LEARNING CENTERS!

▼

Learning Centers can be places where children learn independently, from one another, and from you! Engaging activities can motivate children to become literacy explorers!

STAFF DEVELOPMENT **A to EZ Handbook**
• Learning Centers: page 270

READING CENTER

—*Wonder About Books!* *page 98*

DRAMATIC PLAY CENTER

—*Act It Out! page 99*

HANDS ON! LANGUAGE CENTER

—*Explore Language through Manipulatives! page 100*

WRITING CENTER

—*Promote Emergent Writing! page 101*

SCIENCE CENTER

—*Make Discoveries About Day and Night! page 102*

ART CENTER

—*Explore Space! page 103*

LISTENING CENTER

—*Listen to Nursery Rhymes! page 104*

GAME CENTER

—*Play with Sounds! page 105*

Reading Center

Resources *White Is the Moon * The Park Bench * Half a Moon and One Whole Star * Big Book of White Is the Moon * Big Book stand * Big Book pointer * Big Book of Poems * Big Book of Songs * Sing & Read Books and Audiocassettes * Listening Library Audiocassettes * Songs and Stories Audiocassettes * * theme-related books (See MORE BOOKS TO SHARE! pages 32–33) * tape recorder * index cards * markers

Setting Up! Display books for shared and emergent readings. To encourage small groups of children to explore and talk about the books and materials together, create a "reading circle" in the center. Arrange several chairs, floor mats, or cushions in a semicircle.

- Place the Sing & Read Book and Audiocassette for "Twinkle, Twinkle, Little Star" by the tape recorder.

- Place the little book for *White Is the Moon* and the Listening Library Audiocassette for it nearby.

You might promote a questioning atmosphere by providing index cards with large question marks on them as children explore the books. When children wonder about something they see or read in a book, they can write their names on one of the question cards and then use the card to mark the page.

Theme books give children many things to wonder about!

Centers in Action! Invite children to explore the books and materials in the center. Periodically check the books for children's question cards and invite children to share their wonderings.

Continue to add books to the center throughout the theme and encourage children to do the same. Note which books are frequently visited and reread those books to small groups or to the whole class.

Dramatic Play Center

ACT IT OUT!

Resources a bench or four chairs *
The Park Bench * signs (with yarn
attached, to be worn around child's
neck) to identify visitors to the park
bench, such as park worker, old man,
mother (two signs), baby, young man,
child * markers * dolls * cardboard
rake and other tools, cardboard cane,
a shopping bag for the knitting bag,
Big Book pointers for knitting
needles, a book and other props as
desired

Setting Up! Use a bench or position
about four chairs to serve as the park
bench from the story *The Park Bench.*
Place the signs and markers on a
nearby table. On one sign, make a
simple drawing of the park worker to
encourage children to illustrate the
signs. Have *The Park Bench* opened to
page 30 and the sign for the park
worker positioned by it to encourage
children to match the sign to the text.

Centers in Action! Invite children to
illustrate the signs with the story
characters from *The Park Bench.*
Children can take turns acting out the
visitors to the park bench.

Invite children to think about what the
characters were saying to each other
as they sat on or near the park bench.
For example, children can think about
and discuss what the two mothers
were whispering about and laughing
about. Children may enjoy acting out
what the park bench became to the
children in the park. Was it, like the
book said, a house, a castle, an island,
a boat, or was it something else?

Children may add new characters by
examining the illustrations in the book
or deciding on characters of their own.

*Children will enjoy
acting out what they
think story characters
were talking about!*

99

HANDS ON! LANGUAGE CENTER

EXPLORE LANGUAGE THROUGH MANIPULATIVES!

Resources *Rhyme and Chime Strips* ("If All the World Was Apple Pie" for Week One and "What Words Begin with X?" for Week Two) * *pocket chart and stand* * *Alphabet Posters for Ii and Xx* * *ABC cards* * *slate board* * chalk * *sponge letters* * mixture of paint in water * *letter stamps* * letter blocks * *magnetic letters* * magnetic board * posters * large sheets of white paper * paper * pads * pencils * crayons * *theme books—Half a Moon and One Whole Star, White Is the Moon, The Park Bench*

Setting Up! You may want to set up this center near the Word Walls suggested in the Exploring Print lessons. Initially provide only some of the materials and add others throughout the theme. Encourage children to explore language independently and periodically suggest any of the theme-related activities listed in Centers in Action!

Centers in Action!

- Children can create letter posters of things that begin with *I, i* or end with the letter *x.* Tell children that they may include the word *sax*, a shortened form of the word *saxophone*. They can print or use sponge letters dipped in paint or letter stamps to print the words and then illustrate them.

Theme books are excellent resources for exploring language!

- Children can use magnetic letters or sponge letters to spell the name of each animal in *Half a Moon and One Whole Star* and *White Is the Moon*.

- Children can make a big book of their favorite characters from *The Park Bench* by completing the following sentence frame and illustrating it:

    See the ＿＿ sit on the bench!

- Children can make a big book of animals from *Half a Moon and One Whole Star* and *White Is the Moon*. They can complete the following sentence frame with a word that names a color and then a word that names an animal:

    ＿＿(Red)＿＿ is the ＿＿(fox)＿＿.

Children will enjoy illustrating their sentences.

WRITING CENTER

PROMOTE EMERGENT WRITING!

Resources plain white construction paper * yarn * crayons * pencils * markers * unlined index cards * ribbons * hole punch * poster board or papier-mâché model of tree * ***Story Songs Audiocassette—"Star Medley"* * *Read Aloud Anthology* * *Half a Moon and One Whole Star***

Setting Up! As children work in the Writing Center, encourage them to choose their own topics to write about. Invite children to collaborate with partners and in small groups as well.

Centers in Action!

Story Big Book Children can work together to determine the major story events to depict in a Big Book of "The Spider Weaver." Children can then illustrate and label each scene, and bind the pages together in sequence.

Star Wishes Children can record their wishes on cards. These wishes can then be tied with ribbons to a poster-board or papier-mâché tree, as described in the Japanese Star Festival on page 67. Children can play the "Star Medley" on the Story Songs Audiocassette and sing along.

Story Extension Little Book Invite children to extend *Half a Moon and One Whole Star* to show Susan's activities from morning to night. Such an extension would mirror the pattern of day to night in the other two books in the theme. Children might choose to create little books with their story that could be placed with *Half a Moon and One Whole Star* in the Reading Center.

Reward Notices Children might enjoy creating reward notices to post around the classroom to help catch "the one you don't see coming" from the story on pages 93–97 in the *Read Aloud Anthology*.

Invitations and Announcements Provide time for children to create the invitations and announcements for the theme finale Works of Wonder! on pages 94–95.

Illustrating story events gives children something to write about!

SCIENCE CENTER

MAKE DISCOVERIES ABOUT DAY AND NIGHT!

Resources refrigerator box or a darkened area * small table * globe * flashlight * paper cups * sharp pencils * drawing of the star formation of the Big Dipper * *White Is the Moon* * crayons * books about nocturnal animals, such as *Half a Moon and One Whole Star* and *Animals of the Night*

Setting Up! On a table, arrange materials for making the star gazers. On another table, arrange the materials for the nocturnal animals activity. Using a refrigerator box or a darkened area, create a door (that can be closed) and a sign that reads: Daytime/Nighttime Room. Attach a piece of masking tape to the globe to indicate the location of the children's community. Inside of the Daytime/Nighttime Room, place the table with the globe and flashlight on it.

Theme science activities help develop children's awarenesses of the world around them!

Centers in Action!

Star Gazing! Children will enjoy making star gazers to view the "Big Dipper." They can look at a drawing of the Big Dipper and use a pencil to punch the pattern into the bottom of a paper cup. Holding their star gazers up to the light, they can view the constellation. If they wish, they can decorate their star gazers with star and moon shapes.

Daytime/Nighttime Room In a darkened room, shine a flashlight on the globe and then rotate the globe to see how daytime turns into nighttime where children live.

Animals Who Stir at Night On a table, display books about nocturnal animals. Children can draw pictures of their favorite nocturnal animals and label the pictures. They might also write what they wonder about that animal and its life awake at night.

Art Center

Art Center

Resources colored chalk * a mixture of water and sugar (3 tablespoons sugar per $\frac{1}{2}$ cup water) * crayons * blue, gray, and white tempera paint * paintbrushes * paper clips * masking tape * glitter * glue * mural paper * wire hangers * strips of yarn * hole punch * child-safe scissors * construction paper * large white circles cut from construction paper * markers * newspaper * white glue * balloons * clay * oaktag strips

Setting Up! On three tables, arrange the materials for making the sun, moon, and star shapes; the papier-mâché moons; and the clay sculptures. Display the Big Book *White Is the Moon* on the Big Book stand.

Centers in Action! Children will enjoy making mobiles, murals, and models of the sun, moon, stars, and earth.

Sun Shapes
- Dip colored chalk (yellow, red, orange tones) in the sugar/water mixture and make sun shapes on white paper. The colors will sparkle with the crystallized sugar.

- Color an entire sheet of paper with yellow crayon and paint over the crayon with blue paint. When dry, use paper clips to scratch a circle with outwardly radiating spokes.

Theme books inspire children to create!

Star Shapes
- Tape strips of masking tape on a sheet of paper, crossing at a central point. Paint over the entire sheet with dark blue or black paint. When dry, slowly remove the masking tape to reveal a white starlike image. Apply glue to this area and sprinkle on glitter.

Moon Shapes
- Cut white circle shapes into half-moon and crescent-moon shapes. Children may enjoy making faces on their full moons.

Children may position their sun, star, and moon images across a mural to show the passing of time, much like the top panels in *White Is the Moon.* Or, they may enjoy using their shapes to make mobiles by attaching them to wire hangers.

Papier-Mâché Moons
- Tear newspaper into small pieces and coat the pieces with the white glue. Glue them onto balloons to make papier-mâché moons. After the glue dries, paint the moons.

Clay Sculptures of the Sun, Moon, and Earth
- Make clay sculptures of the sun, moon, and earth and label them *big, bigger,* and *biggest*.

LISTENING CENTER

Resources blank audiocassette *
tape recorder

Setting Up! Provide an opportunity
for children to listen to nursery
rhymes, a part of oral heritage, by
making a recording of bedtime nursery
rhymes. Place your recording along
with a tape recorder in the Listening
Center.

Bedtime

The Man in the Moon
     looked out of the moon,
Looked out of the moon
     and said,
" 'Tis time for all children
     on the earth
To think about getting
     to bed!"

Wee Willie Winkie

Wee Willie Winkie
     runs through the town,
Upstairs and downstairs,
     in his nightgown;
Rapping at the window,
     crying through the lock,
"Are the children in their beds?
     Now it's eight o'clock."

Star Light, Star Bright

Star light, star bright,
First star I see tonight,
I wish I may, I wish I might,
Have the wish I wish tonight.

Centers in Action! Children will
enjoy listening to the tape of rhymes.
Invite them to record their favorite
bedtime rhymes, adding them to the
tape. Encourage each child to learn a
rhyme to share with his or her family at
bedtime. To help children remember
the rhyme, they may write and draw
pictures.

*Listening to and reciting
rhymes gives children
opportunities to
appreciate the sounds
of language!*

Listening Center

Games Center

Play with Sounds!

Resources tape recorder * blank tape * copies of ***Half a Moon and One Whole Star*** * paper horns made from paper rolled in cone shapes

Setting Up! Place the tape recorder, blank tape, and copies of the book *Half a Moon and One Whole Star* on a table.

Centers in Action! Invite children to look through the book *Half a Moon and One Whole Star* and create a list of words or pictures of things that make sounds. For example, they can use words or pictures to represent owls, crickets, and a saxophone.

When the list is finished, ask children to make recordings of the sounds of each entry on the list. Children can then write each word or draw each picture from the list on separate sheets of paper.

Children will enjoy taking turns playing the tape and selecting the paper that names the person, animal, or thing that makes each sound.

A theme book comes alive as children create sounds from it!

ACKNOWLEDGMENTS

The publisher gratefully acknowledges permission to reprint the following copyrighted material:

"At the edge of the world" and "Come all! Stand up!" from SINGING FOR POWER: THE SONG MAGIC OF THE PAPAGO INDIANS OF SOUTHERN ARIZONA by Ruth Murray Underhill. Copyright 1938, 1966 by Ruth Murray Underhill. Reprinted by permission of the Regents of the University of California and the University of California Press.

"Hoshimatsuri" ("Star Wishes") by Yutaka Suzuki, Tadamasa Yamamoto. Used by permission of JASRAC. License #9293014-201.

"I Arise...." from KA-HA-SI AND THE LOON An Eskimo Legend by Terri Cohlene. Copyright © 1990 The Rourke Corporation, Inc. Copyright © 1990 Terri Cowman. Reprinted by permission of the publisher.

"I Don't Know Why" from A SONG I SANG TO YOU by Myra Cohn Livingston. Copyright © 1984, 1969, 1967, 1965, 1959, 1958 by Myra Cohn Livingston. Reprinted by permission of Marian Reiner for the author.

"Lullaby" by Margaret Hillert. Used by permission of the author who controls all rights.

"Moon-Come-Out" from ELEANOR FARJEON'S POEMS FOR CHILDREN by Eleanor Farjeon. "Moon-Come-Out" originally appeared in OVER THE GARDEN WALL by Eleanor Farjeon. Copyright 1933, renewed 1961 by Eleanor Farjeon. Reprinted by permission of HarperCollins Publishers.

"The Night" from A SONG I SANG TO YOU by Myra Cohn Livingston. Copyright © 1984, 1969, 1967, 1965, 1959, 1958 by Myra Cohn Livingston. Reprinted by permission of Marian Reiner for the author.

"Silverly" from JELLY BELLY by Dennis Lee. Copyright © 1983 by Dennis Lee. Reprinted by permission of MGA Agency Inc.

"Snowy Benches" from OUT IN THE DARK AND DAYLIGHT by Aileen Fisher. Copyright © 1980 by Aileen Fisher. Reprinted by permission of the author.

Cover and Program Design: Michaelis/Carpelis Design Associates, Inc.

Additional Design: Textart, Inc.

Production: Textart, Inc.
Michaelis/Carpelis Design Associates, Inc.

Illustration

Cover Illustration: Leo Monohan

Back Cover Illustration: Patrick Merrell

Four-color airbrush: Brian Dugan, Mark Kaplan, Mary Ellen Senor

Poetry airbrush backgrounds: Mark Kaplan

Learning Center Logos: Rachel Geswaldo

Lesson Opener Panels: Kathleen Kinkoff, 48, 78; Leo Monahan, 60, 90; Nicolai Punim, 54, 84; Marti Shohet, 42, 72; Andrea Wisnewski, 34, 66.

Four-color illustration: Pat Wong, 53, 71.

Black line art: Network Graphics, 35, 38, 43, 49, 50, 55, 61, 67, 73, 79, 81, 85, 91; Adam Weston, 58, 64, 65, 83, 89.

Photography

All photographs are by Macmillan/McGraw-Hill School Division (MMSD) except as noted below.

37: RMIP/Richard Haynes for MMSD. 40, 41: Scott Harvey for MMSD. 43: Ken Karp for MMSD. 51: Scott Harvey for MMSD. 57: Scott Harvey for MMSD. 61: Scott Harvey for MMSD. 67: Bob Krist for MMSD. 79: RMIP/Richard Haynes for MMSD. 86: Ken Karp for MMSD. 87: Scott Harvey for MMSD. 92, 94, 95: RMIP/Richard Haynes for MMSD. 96: Bruce Berman for MMSD. 98, 99: Bob Krist for MMSD. 100: RMIP/Richard Haynes for MMSD. 101: Scott Harvey for MMSD. 103: RMIP/Richard Haynes for MMSD. 104, 105: Scott Harvey for MMSD.

INDEX

• •

AN IGUANA OF I's

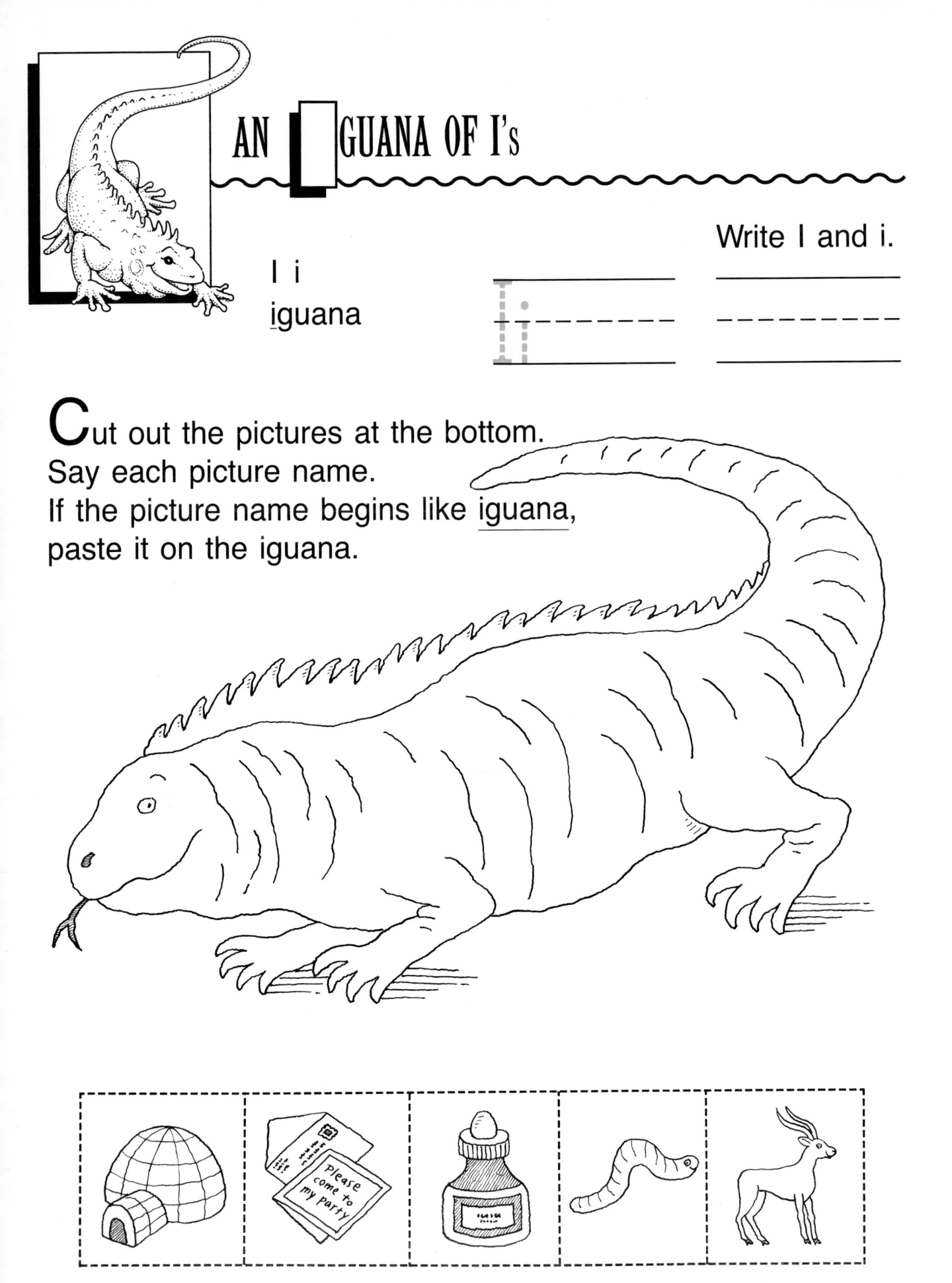

I i
iguana

Write I and i.

Cut out the pictures at the bottom.
Say each picture name.
If the picture name begins like iguana,
paste it on the iguana.

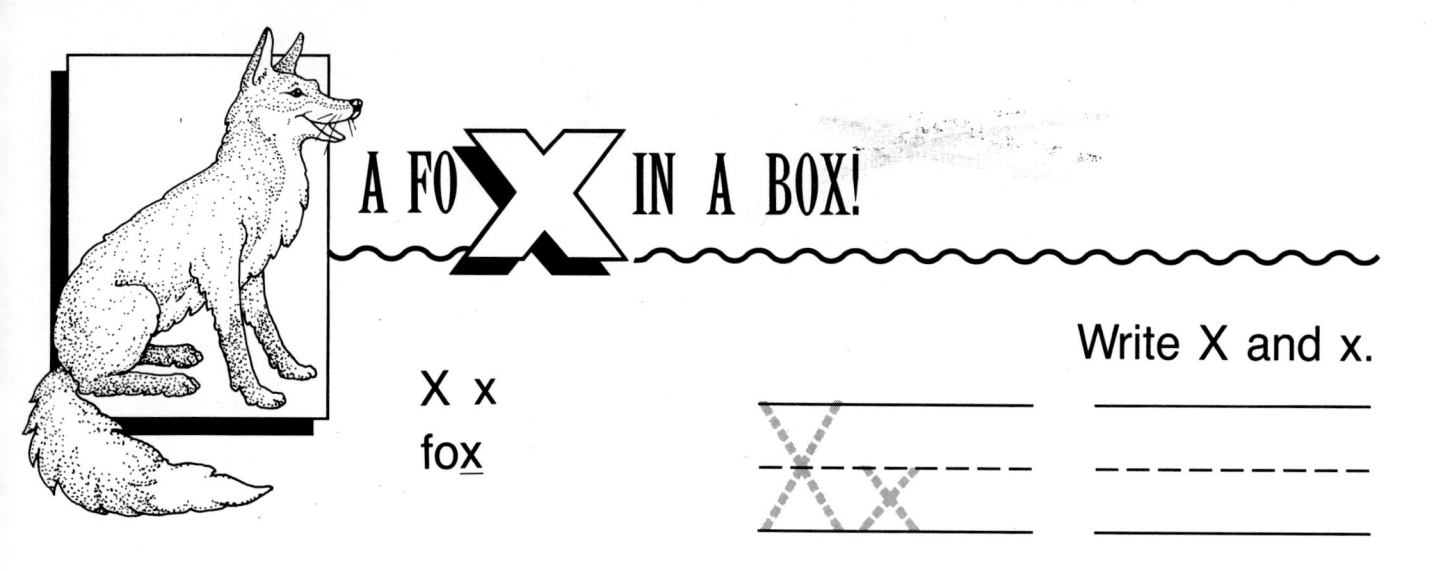

A FO**X** IN A BOX!

X x

fo<u>x</u>

Write X and x.

Look at the fox in each box.
Then look at the pictures on each of the boxes.
Write the letter that ends each word.
Color the picture if it ends like <u>fox</u> and <u>box</u>.